zechariah

GOD REMEMBERS

Designed by WeKREATIVE Co.

Limited Commemorative Paperback Edition
ISBN-13: 978-0-9969176-8-1

Printed in the United States of America

THE MASTER'S PRESS

Los Angeles, California
www.tms.edu

THE MACARTHUR OLD TESTAMENT
COMMENTARY ON THE BOOK OF

ZECHARIAH

EDITED BY

JOHN MACARTHUR

LOS ANGELES, CALIFORNIA

THE MASTER'S PRESS

CONTENTS

Preface

Psalm 1:1–3
How blessed is the man
Who does not walk in the counsel of the wicked,
Nor stand in the way of sinners,
Nor sit in the seat of scoffers!
But his delight is in the law of Yahweh,
And in His law he meditates day and night.
And he will be like a tree *firmly* planted by streams of water,
Which yields its fruit in its season
And its leaf does not wither;
And in whatever he does, he prospers.

Jeremiah 15:16
Your words were found, and I ate them,
And Your words became for me joy and gladness in my heart,
For I have been called by Your name,
O Yahweh God of hosts.

Both preaching through every verse of the New Testament and writing the *MacArthur New Testament Commentary* series over the past half century have been an incomparable gift of divine grace that has allowed me to live in the blessedness of Psalm 1:1–3 and the joy of Jeremiah 15:16. As I thought about continuing the commentary series into the Old Testament, I knew I wanted to begin with the book of Zechariah. Written to comfort Israel after the remnant's return from captivity in Babylon, Zechariah's message intended to assure the post-exilic Israelites that though the remnant nation was small and weak, the Lord had neither abandoned His people nor changed His promises. He was actively advancing His plan to fulfill all the promises He had made to Israel, and He revealed His intentions for Israel's history and future to the prophet.

More than five centuries before Jesus was born, Zechariah predicted the coming of Alexander the Great (Zech 9:1–7), the Roman destruction of Jerusalem (11:1–9), and the future tyranny of the Antichrist (11:15–17). The prophet also detailed the battle of Armageddon (12:1–9; 14:1–5), the cleansing of Israel (12:10; 13:1–9), and the millennial reign of Christ (Zech 13–14). Filled with visions, prophecies, signs, and vivid imagery, this prophetic revelation traces the flow of history to its climax when Christ will reign over the earth from His throne in Jerusalem. The name "Zechariah" means "Yahweh remembers," and through the revelation given to this prophet, God confirmed for Israel that He would keep His Word and never forget His promises.

Necessarily, to highlight the focus of God's plan in redemptive history, Zechariah is replete with prophecies about the Messiah. The Messiah, the Lord Jesus Christ, is the primary figure in Zechariah's revelation. When Zechariah received his first vision, the Angel of Yahweh—the pre-incarnate Christ who is the second Person of the Trinity—unveiled God's plan for Israel (1:8–11). Later, Zechariah was given a vision of the Angel of Yahweh removing the iniquity of Joshua the High Priest (3:4). Zechariah revealed Christ in His first coming, predicting His entry into Jerusalem on a donkey (9:9), His betrayal for thirty pieces of silver (11:12), and ultimately His sacrificial death (12:10). Zechariah revealed Christ in His second coming, portraying the Lord's return to the Mount of Olives (14:4) and the establishment of His kingdom over the earth (14:9). At that future time, Israel will turn to God (12:10–14). The Lord will say, "They are My people," and Israel will respond, "Yahweh is my God" (13:9). Then the words of Paul will be fulfilled: "All Israel will be saved" (Rom 11:26).

No eschatology is complete or true which does not embrace the prophecy of Zechariah. It was that requirement that motivated me to preach through this book over forty years ago and to provide an accurate interpretation and exposition of the divine revelation in this remarkable book. I am delighted to partner with Abner Chou, Iosif Zhakevich, and

Nathan Busenitz to produce a commentary covering the text word by word, being true to the approach of expository preaching—unleashing God's truth one verse at a time. We are all grateful for the assistance of Stephanie Blood, Marco Bartholomae, Karl Walker, and Anastasia Prinzing on this project.

While the commentary is presented plainly, it is based on thorough exegesis of the text in the original Hebrew. The intent is to understand the meaning and theology of the text with accuracy, precision, and clarity. While each section is arranged and titled to aid the preacher, the commentary is designed to be read and applied by every believer for personal blessing and joy. Zechariah is considered to be among the most difficult Old Testament books to interpret. Recognizing this, we approach the task of this study with prayerfulness and humility.

The goal is singular—to magnify our Lord Jesus Christ and exalt His name above all names.

Soli Deo gloria!

Introduction

Zechariah, along with his contemporary Haggai, preached to the Israelites who had returned from Babylon to Judah to build the house of God and restore proper worship in Jerusalem. As the people began to rebuild the city and the temple, they were confronted with formidable difficulties. The people who returned to Judah were few in number (Ezra 2:64–65), and the city of Jerusalem had been utterly destroyed (Ezra 4:12–16; Hag 1:4; Neh 1:3; 2:5). Not only did the city and the temple lie in ruins (Ezra 3:8–13; 5; Hag 1:4), but enemy opposition was strong (Ezra 4:1–24). These overwhelming obstacles tempted the people of Israel to question God's devotion to the nation and the integrity of the promises He had made repeatedly to their forefathers. They pondered how to gain the Lord's favor (Zech 7:3, 5; 8:19) and wondered if building God's house was even worthwhile, especially since their efforts seemed so meager and inferior to the beauty of the first temple (Hag 2:3–4; Zech 8:9). All these questions disheartened the people to the point that they became distracted and apathetic. Disillusioned, they turned from building the house of God to building their own houses (Hag 1:4).

Because the discouraged people abandoned their responsibility to participate in God's plan, the Lord raised up Haggai and Zechariah to confront the nation and charge them to reengage in building the temple. Haggai directly rebuked Israel for having faulty priorities (Hag 1:1–15), reminding them that God would be faithful to use their efforts for His glory (2:1–23). Zechariah continued this same exhortation, directing the people to recognize what the Lord was planning to do for Israel both in their time and in the future. These divine revelations were intended to motivate Israel to renew the effort to rebuild the temple and restore worship. As to the heart of that duty, the Lord called His people to repent (Zech 1:1–3), walk in holiness (2:6–7), flee from ritualism (7:5), and obey with courage (8:9–22), while placing their hope solely in the coming Messiah (10:1–12).

Though Zechariah spoke to a particular audience in his day, he revealed truths relevant for all of God's people through history. His prophecies foretold events fulfilled in his own day (6th century BC) and in the subsequent centuries up to Christ's first coming (1st century AD). Zechariah also predicted what will take place in the future at Christ's second advent. The prophet's ultimate aim was to direct the attention of all peoples—Jews and Gentiles—to the Messiah through whom God will finally and fully deliver His people (Zech 12:10; Rev 1:7). Armed with that hope, the faithful remnant of Zechariah's day found the strength to persevere. That same hope has continued to strengthen all the saints through the ages.

TITLE

The title "Zechariah," which is also the name of the prophet, means "Yahweh remembers," and this is the undergirding reality of the book, both to the generation of Zechariah's time and to the people of God beyond. Yahweh, as the covenant God of Israel, remembers all His promises and will fulfill each of them through His Son, the Messiah.

AUTHOR

According to both Jewish and Christian tradition, the author is the one named as such, the prophet Zechariah. In Zechariah 1:1, the prophet introduces himself as "the son of Berechiah, the son of Iddo." Born in Babylon, Zechariah returned with the Jews from exile to Judah under the leadership of Zerubbabel the governor and Joshua the High Priest (Neh 12:1, 16). Zechariah was closely associated with his grandfather Iddo, the head of a priestly line (12:1, 4), being called his son (Ezra 5:1; 6:14; Neh 12:16) and evidently returning with him from Babylon to Judah (Neh 12:1, 4, 16). For this reason, it is plausible that Zechariah's father Berechiah had died early (cf. Matt 23:35).

Because Zechariah was referred to as a "young man" (Zech 2:4), he was conspicuously youthful when he began his ministry. In addition to being a prophet, he was also a priest (Neh 12:1, 12–16). His priestly lineage adds to his interest in the building of the temple (Zech 1:16; 4:1–10; 6:9–15) and his excitement in the vision of the High Priest Joshua (3:5). Zechariah's life ended when he was murdered between the altar and the sanctuary in the temple (Matt 23:35), similar to an earlier Zechariah (cf. 2 Chr 24:20, 21).

DATE

The time stamp for the book is 520 BC, in the eighth month of the second year of Darius I (Zech 1:1). Zechariah received additional revelation approximately two years later in 518 BC ("in the fourth year of King Darius...on the fourth day of the ninth month, which is Chislev"; 7:1). However, Zechariah's ministry continued much longer, as reflected in chapters 9–14, which seem to represent a later time period in his ministry. Two reasons suggest a later date for chapters 9–14: first, the style of writing is different from the earlier chapters (e.g., 1:1, 7 and 7:1 have "the word of Yahweh came to Zechariah"; but 9:1 and 12:1 have "the oracle of the word of Yahweh"); second, references to Greece (9:13) presuppose a date ranging from 480 BC to 470 BC. While the exact duration of Zechariah's ministry is unknown, it appears that he prophesied across two major junctures of history spanning a period of about fifty years.

HISTORICAL CONTEXT

That Zechariah began to prophesy in 520 BC indicates that it was after the Judaean exiles had returned to the land of Judah and had been commanded by God to rebuild Jerusalem and the temple. But the historical setting in the book references the time when the Israelites were still in exile (cf. Zech 7:2–5; 8:19) and even before the nation went into captivity (cf. 1:1–6; 8:14). In three different military campaigns—605 BC, 597 BC, and 586 BC—Nebuchadnezzar took the people of Judah captive to Babylon, which culminated with the destruction of Jerusalem in 586 BC (cf. 2 Kgs 20:16–19; 24–25; 2 Chr 36:6–21; Jer 25:1–11; Dan 1:1–2). For seven decades, the Judaeans were in exile, living outside their land and away from the house of God (cf. Jer 25:11–12; 29:10; Dan 9:1–2). These seventy years of captivity fulfilled the Lord's promise to punish the Israelites for their disobedience and violation of the covenant (Deut 28:15–68; Lev

27:14–46). To mark God's displeasure, His glory departed from the temple and from Jerusalem shortly before the exile of Judah (Ezek 10:4–5, 18–19).

In 539 BC, the Persian Empire conquered Babylon and gained political dominance in the ancient Near East under the rule of Cyrus the Great (Isa 44:28; 45:1). Cyrus issued an edict allowing the Jewish exiles to return to Judah and rebuild Jerusalem and the temple (Ezra 1:1–4; 2 Chr 36:22–23; cf. Isa 44:28; 45:13; Ezra 6:1–5). In 538 BC, the first group of about fifty thousand Jews returned to Judah under the leadership of Zerubbabel the governor and Joshua the High Priest. This group included Haggai and Zechariah (Ezra 1:1–4, 9–11; 2; Neh 12:1, 16). A short time later (ca. 536 BC), the Jewish returnees restored the Levitical sacrifices (Ezra 3:1–6), laid the foundation of the temple (3:8–13; 5:16), and began to rebuild (3:1–4:5). Soon they faced challenges and obstacles that brought their reconstruction efforts to a halt. Continued threats and hostilities from neighboring enemies intimidated the people (4:1–7), discouraging them from persevering in the hard work (Hag 1:2–4). Added to that, the people realized that the temple they were building would be smaller and far less impressive than Solomon's (Hag 2:3; cf. Ezra 3:12–13). As a result of these issues, work on the temple stopped, and it remained incomplete for sixteen years (Hag 1–2; Ezra 4:24).

To restart the work, God sent the prophet Haggai in 520 BC (in the second year of Darius) to call the people to finish building the temple (Ezra 5:1–2; 6:14; Hag 1:1). Two months after Haggai delivered his message from the Lord, Zechariah was sent to reiterate that same call (Ezra 5:1–2; 6:14; Zech 1:1). Zechariah encouraged the people by revealing to them that their work on the temple was a crucial feature in God's plan, culminating in the ultimate reign of the Messiah in the millennial kingdom. The people responded to the divine message proclaimed by both Haggai and Zechariah, with the result that they completed the temple in 516 BC, four years after the rebuilding effort had resumed (Ezra 6:15).

THEMES

Zechariah's prophecy is marked by some central features, including the following:

Yahweh

Appearing 133 times in Zechariah's prophecy—alone or within titles—the name "Yahweh" dominates God's self-expression in this book. Yahweh, God's covenant and personal name, conveys His loyalty, love, and relationship with His people (Exod 3:14–16). Because of His enduring covenant love, God desires for Israel to repent and be reconciled to Him (Zech 1:3, 16; 8:3; 10:6; 13:9; 14:9). He is presented as a jealous protector of Israel (1:14; 2:8, 9). The name Yahweh ("I am") expresses the Lord's ever-present faithfulness to Israel until the day He permanently inhabits Jerusalem (1:16; 2:5, 10) and says of Israel, "They are My people," and Israel says, "Yahweh is my God" (13:9). God's covenant name is employed to showcase the Lord's persistent fidelity, that He remembers His promises and will fulfill them according to His sovereign purposes to the end of history.

The title "Yahweh of hosts," Zechariah's favorite appellation for God, occurs 53 times throughout the book. While the title appears elsewhere (cf. 2 Sam 6:18; Ps 84:12; Isa 39:5; Hag 1:7), in Zechariah this title emphatically depicts Yahweh's supernatural activity in commanding the angelic hosts to accomplish His plan (Zech 1:7–16; 6:1–9). The Lord's faithfulness utilizes all of heaven to carry out His good will and purpose. Yahweh's promises are therefore backed by the full force and sovereign authority of the Commander of heaven's angelic armies. Hence, Zechariah's prophecy frequently repeats the exclamation, "Thus says Yahweh of hosts" (e.g., 8:2, 3, 4, 6, 7, 9, 14, 19, 20, 23).

"The Angel of Yahweh," appearing six times in Zechariah, is identified as God Himself (12:8), and He is none other than the second Person of the Trinity (cf. 3:4, where the Angel of Yahweh removes Joshua's iniquities), reflecting God's Triunity.

References to Yahweh culminate in the final chapter where the prophet reveals that, one day, "Yahweh will be *the only* one, and His name one" (14:9b). This was God's intent from the beginning, as Moses declared in the *Shema*. "Hear, O Israel! Yahweh is our God, Yahweh is one!" (Deut 6:4). Ultimately, the world will acknowledge that God is one and that He shares His glory with no other (Isa 42:8). When Christ returns to judge the wicked, redeem Israel and His elect, and establish

His earthly kingdom, the world will be brought into full conformity with His nature, and all will profess that Yahweh alone is God (cf. Phil 2:9–11). All that the name of Yahweh represents will be put on full display, and all the redeemed will worship Him (Zech 14:11–21).

Remembrance

A resounding theme throughout the book is accentuated in the meaning of Zechariah's name, "Yahweh remembers." The Lord not only does not forget what He has declared, but He will fulfill every promise He has made (Deut 4:31). He will refine Israel, restore Jerusalem, rebuild the temple, and reveal His glory to the world (Zech 2:1–13; 5:1–4). Nor will He fail to keep His promises regarding the nations (1:18–21; 5:5–11).

God also remembers His plans for His Son (9:8), the Messiah (3:1–4:14; 6:9–15). Though the Messiah will initially be betrayed (11:12; 13:7), He will ultimately be embraced by a future generation of Jews so that they will be saved (12:10–13:1). The Lord will establish the Messiah's earthly kingdom, one in which death will be curtailed (8:4), peace secured (8:5), earth transformed (14:6–8), Jerusalem exalted (14:10), the nations subdued (14:17–18), the temple rebuilt (14:20), and holiness ordained to prevail (14:21). As Zechariah's prophecy demonstrates, Yahweh is not slow about His guarantees but is always active in their fulfillment (1:7–17; 6:1–8). With the glorious refrain that "Yahweh remembers," the prophet calls the reader to rest in the Lord and look for hope only in Him. He is the One who remembers His promises so that His people will remember Him (10:9).

Repentance

Zechariah opens with a call to repentance (Zech 1:1–6, 16), and that theme is sustained throughout the entire book (1:1–6, 16; 8:3; 9:12; 10:6, 10). From the start, the end is in view, when Israel returns to God and the Lord returns His glorious presence and blessings to Israel (1:3). For Israel, repentance included not only the physical return and national restoration to the Promised Land, but also the spiritual return to the Lord (1:1–6; 2:6–7). The people of Israel were called to embrace the

Messiah, the Angel of Yahweh sent by God (4:9). They were not to look to any substitute for this Good Shepherd (10:1–4). Instead of depending on their ritualistic works (7:5), they were called to delight in God's promises (8:1–8) as they cast off fear and apathy and began rebuilding the temple in obedience (1:16; 4:9; 8:9). In calling the people to repentance, Zechariah revealed and anticipated a future day when "all Israel" would turn to God and be saved (12:10–13:1; Rom 11:26).

Temple (House of Yahweh)

The historic and immediate reason for Zechariah's prophecy was to call Israel to persevere in rebuilding the temple in Jerusalem, showing that Yahweh remembered the place of the temple in His plan. In the future kingdom, Jerusalem will also be the location of the millennial temple (cf. Ezek 40–48) to which God's glory will return and in which the Lord Himself will dwell with His redeemed people (Zech 1:16; 2:5). That eschatological temple will be the epicenter of the world, the earthly pinnacle reflecting the presence and worship of Yahweh (2:7; 14:10, 16; cf. Isa 2:2–4). God will tear down all competing houses of sinful worship (Zech 5:4) and false religion (5:11), so that His house and glory will be the only one. From that future temple, the Messiah will reign (6:12–13).

So Zechariah revealed to the Israelites of his day that the humble temple they were building anticipated that future glorious temple (4:4–14; cf. Hag 2:9). Though another temple would be destroyed in AD 70 (Zech 11:1–3), and the millennial temple would not be built until Christ's return and reign because of Israel's rejection of the Messiah (11:4–15; cf. Matt 24:2), Zechariah encouraged the people that God wanted His house built in His city as a part of His plan. In much the same way that the Lord is building His visible church, and, imperfect as it is, still employing it as a testimony of His kingdom to the world—until one day in the future when it is perfected in its glory—so also the temple had a testimonial place to God's rule in the world.

Messiah

The book of Zechariah reverberates with the presence of the Messiah. The prophet discussed the pre-incarnate work of Christ to advance God's plan for Israel (Zech 1:8) and to intercede for the nation (1:12; 3:2). Zechariah foretold Christ's first coming in humility (9:9), His rejection and betrayal for thirty pieces of silver (11:12–13), and His ultimate crucifixion and death for the sins of His people (12:10; 13:7). Zechariah also prophesied of Christ's second coming as the glorious King (9:10), who will gather His people (10:1–12), conquer Israel's foes (10:4–7), cleanse His elect (12:10–13:6), build the temple (6:12), stand victorious on the Mount of Olives (14:1–3), reign supreme (14:9), and receive worship from all of earth's inhabitants (14:16).

Zechariah also revealed the Messiah as the true and Good Shepherd in contrast to Israel's corrupt leaders, the false shepherds. While the true Shepherd cares for His own (11:4, 7, 9; 13:7), the false shepherds devour and betray their nation (10:2–3; 11:3, 5, 8, 15–17). In His first coming, the Good Shepherd would rebuke and destroy these false shepherds, namely the priests, elders, and scribes of Israel (11:8). Because Israel rejected the true Shepherd (11:12–13), the nation will one day fall prey to the ultimate false shepherd, the Antichrist (11:15–16). But the Messiah will return to overcome and destroy him (11:17), saving His flock physically and spiritually (9:16), so that they become beautiful in the land as a testament to His love as the Good Shepherd (9:16–17).

Another messianic role Zechariah emphasized was that of the Priest-King. Though no Israelite could assume these two offices (2 Chr 26:16–21), the Old Testament anticipated the coming of One in the order of Melchizedek, the Priest-King (Gen 14; Ps 110). God revealed that His Son would merge these two offices into one in Himself (Zech 3:5; 4:11–14; 6:11–13), redeeming His people as their Priest and reigning over them as their King. As Priest-King, Christ will achieve what no merely human king or priest could achieve. He will bring reconciliation between God and man and establish perfect peace and righteousness on earth (6:13).

Millennial Kingdom

Because Zechariah was tasked by heaven with showing that Israel's work was never in vain, he prophesied all the way to the culmination of God's plan in the millennial kingdom. He revealed that this kingdom will be earthly and climactic (Zech 1:18–21). Jerusalem and the temple will be rebuilt (1:16), God's glory will return to dwell in the midst of the city (2:5), and God will be a wall of fire around it (2:5a). When the Messiah establishes this earthly kingdom, Jerusalem will be known as the City of Truth (8:3).

At that time, the Messiah will cleanse His people (3:1–5; 13:1–5), and the Lord will call Israel "My people," and Israel will exclaim, "Yahweh is my God" (13:9; cf. 8:8). Populated initially only with redeemed Israelites, this kingdom will be governed by competent leaders (10:4–6) and priests who will lead God's people in true worship (3:7). Along with righteous Israel, regenerate Gentiles will also enter the kingdom and worship Yahweh (8:20–23). Specifically, they will gather in Israel at least once a year to celebrate the Feast of Booths (14:16). The Messiah's reign will command world peace (14:11) as Jews and Gentiles join together to worship Yahweh (8:23; cf. Matt 25:31–46).

The millennial kingdom will be part of the renewed creation, in which there will be new light (Zech 14:6–7) and new topography (14:8). The Lord will introduce Edenic rest (3:10), so that both death and the curse on creation are severely curtailed (8:4). Jerusalem will be filled with people—old and young—living in peace and security (8:4–5; cf. Isa 65:20). Things that currently seem mundane or even unclean will become holy to Yahweh (Zech 14:20–21).

At the center of the millennial kingdom will be the ultimate King: the Lord Jesus Christ. The kingdom will begin with His inauguration as the world celebrates His accomplishments throughout redemptive history (6:9–15). He will be the only King over the whole earth (14:9), and all peoples will bring Him worship (14:17).

PURPOSE

God sent Zechariah to proclaim that Yahweh remembered His covenant to Israel and would fulfill it through the Messiah; therefore, the Judaeans were to be faithful to God by continuing to rebuild the temple as a part of His testimony in the world. Instead of succumbing to their doubts and fears, they were to look to the Lord and cling to His promises as they worshiped Him with singular purity and responded to His commands with bold obedience, looking to the arrival of the Messiah and His kingdom of salvation.

OUTLINE

Repentance: The Prerequisite for Blessing

1

Zechariah 1:1–6

In the eighth month of the second year of Darius, the word of Yahweh came to Zechariah the prophet, the son of Berechiah, the son of Iddo, saying, "Yahweh was very wrathful against your fathers. Therefore say to them, 'Thus says Yahweh of hosts, "Return to Me," declares Yahweh of hosts, "that I may return to you," says Yahweh of hosts. "Do not be like your fathers, to whom the former prophets called out, saying, 'Thus says Yahweh of hosts, "Return now from your evil ways and from your evil deeds."' But they did not listen or give heed to Me," declares Yahweh. "Your fathers, where are they? And the prophets, do they live forever? But did not My words and My statutes, which I commanded My slaves the prophets, overtake your fathers? Then they returned and said, 'As Yahweh of hosts purposed to do to us in accordance with our ways and our deeds, so He has done with us.'"'"

Though often neglected by New Testament believers, Zechariah is a marvelous book that should not be overlooked. Its rich content warrants careful study, thorough contemplation, and bold proclamation. Like an intricate diamond, the glory of its truth shines from many angles. Those who ignore the beauty and power of this treasure trove of Old Testament theology do so to their own great loss.

In approaching this profound prophecy, several key facets should be noted. First, it is a book about the Lord Jesus Christ. With the mention of the Angel of Yahweh (cf. Zech 1:11–12), the Priest-King Messiah (3:3–4; 4:11–14; 6:12–13), the anointed King (6:9–15), as well as the prophecies of His riding into Jerusalem on a donkey (9:6), being betrayed for thirty pieces of silver (11:12), being pierced for His people (12:10), cleansing Israel by His death and resurrection (13:1–2), and delivering His own upon His return (14:1–3), the Lord Jesus appears on almost every page of this book. This prophecy, with revelation that described Christ before His first coming and all the way to His second, is one of the most extensive explorations into the glories of the Messiah.

Second, the book of Zechariah features a vast number of eschatological prophecies, in addition to predictions about the Messiah's return and reign. These include the rise of the Antichrist (11:15–17); the martyrdom of God's people in the Great Tribulation (11:16–17; 13:7); the battle of Armageddon (12:1–9; 14:1–3); the judgment of the nations (12:1–9; 14:12–15); the salvation of Israel (12:10; 13:1–9); the ultimate salvation of the nations (14:16); and the blessings experienced during the Millennium (8:4). Moreover, Zechariah's astounding imagery ranges from visions of horses (1:7–17) to a flying scroll (5:1–4), a lampstand with two olive trees beside it (4:1–14), and a woman sitting in an ephah (5:5–11). Though these promises are couched in an element of mystery, they anticipate prophetic truths found in the New Testament.

Third, in revealing truth about the future, Zechariah is also a book about divine comfort (1:13). To demonstrate His divine care, the Lord repeatedly assured His people that He would one day restore Israel (1:14; 2:11–13) and judge the nations (1:15; 9:1–8). All of Zechariah's content—including visions, prophecies, signs, celestial visitors, direct words from God, and the outline of redemptive history, sweeping from Zechariah's day to Messiah's reign on earth—is meant to assure God's people that Yahweh remembers. Indeed, the name "Zechariah" means "Yahweh remembers." This book demonstrates that God remembers all His promises, both to Israel and the world.

Fourth, in keeping with the theme of divine comfort, the book of Zechariah also emphasizes the conditions required for it. God's prerequisite for receiving all these promises is repentance. The Lord will not bless those who are disobedient. He made that clear to Israel from the beginning. In Deuteronomy, God established the condition for blessing, stating, "All these blessings will come upon you and overtake you if you listen to the voice of Yahweh your God" (Deut 28:2). But "it will be, if you do not listen to the voice of Yahweh your God, to keep *and* to do all His commandments and His statutes with which I am commanding you today, that all these curses will come upon you and overtake you" (28:15). The Lord made it plain that He fully blesses only an obedient people. He is a righteous, perfect, and holy God, who necessarily punishes wickedness and rewards righteousness (cf. Exod 20:5–6).

As the nation engaged in an entire history of disobedience, God sent prophet after prophet to urge Israel to repent. In Isaiah 55:6–7, Isaiah said to the people, "Seek Yahweh while He may be found; call upon Him while He is near. Let the wicked forsake his way and the unrighteous man his thoughts; and let him return to Yahweh, and He will have compassion on him, and to our God, for He will abundantly pardon." There is mercy and pardon for the one who turns to God and turns away from sin. The words of Jeremiah 3:12–13 emphasized this truth: "'Return, faithless Israel,' declares Yahweh; 'I will not look upon you in anger. For I am One of lovingkindness,' declares Yahweh; 'I will not be angry forever. Only acknowledge your iniquity, that you have transgressed against Yahweh your God.'" In Ezekiel 18:30–31, Ezekiel delivered the same message, saying, "Turn back and turn away from all your transgressions, so that iniquity may not become a stumbling block to you. Cast away from yourselves all your transgressions which you have committed and make yourselves a new heart and a new spirit!" Every call for repentance was a reminder that God is merciful. With such admonitions and appeals, the prophets reminded the nation that if they repented, God would take them back and bless them as He had promised (Isa 55:1–4; Jer 31; Ezek 36).

Despite the promised blessing, Israel did not heed the prophets. As the report of 2 Kings 17:13–14 makes clear:

> Yet Yahweh warned Israel and Judah by the hand of all His prophets *and* every seer, saying, "Turn from your evil ways and

keep My commandments, My statutes according to all the law which I commanded your fathers, and which I sent to you by the hand of My slaves the prophets." However, they did not listen, but stiffened their neck like their fathers, who did not believe in Yahweh their God.

The price of impenitence was that Israel was exiled to a pagan land. Nevertheless, God did not remove His pledge or change His promise. He never abandoned His loyalty to His people. He brought them back to the Promised Land (Ezra 1:1–2), and in this book, He again reaffirmed His faithfulness to His people. Zechariah opens with God's demand that His people repent. He will be merciful, but He cannot compromise His holy standard.

For Zechariah's original audience, the message of this book encouraged their hearts with the hope of God's good promises. But it also reminded them that the path to divine blessing begins at the gateway of repentance (cf. Luke 24:47; Acts 20:21; 26:20). Genuine repentance, consisting of a radical change of heart and mind, is a gift of God's mercy and grace (2 Tim 2:25; cf. Eph 2:8–10). It includes an immediate change of affection, causing the heart to turn away from sin and idolatry and to turn toward the living and true God (1 Thess 1:9). The results of that internal heart change are attitudes of worship and acts of obedience. This "fruit in keeping with repentance" (Matt 3:8) provides evidence that repentance is genuine (cf. 2 Cor 7:10). The call to repent is a call for sinners to turn from their idolatry and iniquity and instead to love and worship the true God and walk in His ways. The right response of the sinner to such a call is to cry out to the Lord for mercy (Luke 18:13–14), asking Him to receive the change of heart that only He can provide (2 Cor 5:17). The Lord delights in answering that prayer (cf. Luke 15:7; John 6:37), transforming sinners from the inside out, so that they become people who worship and obey Him from the heart (cf. Mark 12:30–31).

The book of Zechariah begins with a call for Israel to repent and return to the Lord. The people were not to be like their ancestors, who hardened their hearts and rebelled against God. Instead, the Lord Himself called His people to return to Him in repentance, so that He might return to them in blessing (Zech 1:1–3). But the Lord warned the Israelites about the consequences of resisting His Word and rebelling against Him (1:4–6). If they did not repent, they would be punished like their wicked fathers before them.

THE CALL TO REPENTANCE

In the eighth month of the second year of Darius, the word of Yahweh came to Zechariah the prophet, the son of Berechiah, the son of Iddo, saying, "Yahweh was very wrathful against your fathers. Therefore say to them, 'Thus says Yahweh of hosts, "Return to Me," declares Yahweh of hosts, "that I may return to you," says Yahweh of hosts.'" (1:1–3)

Unlike other prophetic books, in which the author began by noting the duration of his ministry (Isa 1:1) or the year he started his work (Jer 1:1), Zechariah introduced his prophecy with a very specific date: **the eighth month of the second year of Darius**. This important detail links Zechariah's prophecy with events in Israel's history following the Babylonian exile, and specifically places Zechariah's ministry alongside that of the prophet Haggai.

Zechariah ministered to Israel shortly after the people had returned to the land from the Babylonian captivity. That remnant was initially enthusiastic to repopulate Jerusalem and to rebuild the temple. They constructed the sacred altar and began to restore the prescribed sacrifices within seven months, seeking to return to the worship that God had commanded (Ezra 3). Not long after the start of the second year, they began to rebuild the temple itself in the face of strong opposition from the neighboring peoples. The mention of the **second year of Darius** was a reminder that Israel was still under pagan rule, under the jurisdiction of Medo-Persia and its monarch, Darius the Great. Without a king of their own, and in the face of rising antagonism, the Israelites grew fearful and discouraged. As a result, they ceased their efforts to complete the temple.

But God required His house to be rebuilt because it was essential to His plan. For Israel, it signified that God dwelt with His people and was the center of worship, where His people corporately declared His praise and obediently offered sacrifices to Him. It also served a prophetic role, illustrating that just as God filled the temple in Jerusalem, so He would one day fill the earth with His glory (1 Kgs 8:10; Isa 6:3). More than 500 years later, this rebuilt temple would also play a significant part in the earthly ministry of the Lord Jesus, as many events during His first advent took place within the temple complex (Matt 21:14–15; Luke 2:46; 22:53; John 7:28; 8:2, 20). Since God designed the temple to serve His purposes in Israel's history, He commanded it to be rebuilt. This call came first through the prophet Haggai.

Haggai gave four short messages that challenged, exhorted, and encouraged the people to act on God's will. Within this, he showed them their hypocrisy in building their own homes before completing the temple (Hag 1:4). He also declared that God would use their obedience, even if meager, for His glory (2:1–9). Haggai wanted the Israelites to know that their obedient actions would be part of God's much grander plan.

Haggai gave this encouragement on the "twenty-first of the seventh month" (2:1), pointing the people to the final majestic reality:

> For thus says Yahweh of hosts, "Once more—in a little while—I am going to shake the heavens and the earth, the sea also and the dry land. And I will shake all the nations; and they will come with the desirable things of all nations, and I will fill this house with glory," says Yahweh of hosts. "The silver is Mine, and the gold is Mine," declares Yahweh of hosts. "The latter glory of this house will be greater than the former," says Yahweh of hosts, "and in this place I will give peace," declares Yahweh of hosts. (Hag 2:6–9)

Haggai thus revealed that ultimately, God will do a worldwide work—a cosmic work—and a glory-filled temple will be built that will be far greater than any previous temple. Haggai made clear that the restored temple in his day was a step toward millennial glory.

People might have yearned for more details about this prophecy, yet Haggai's prediction was brief. While his message started the Israelites in their obedience, they needed another prophet to keep them going. So God raised up Zechariah **on the eighth month**, sending him to address the people essentially a week after Haggai's prophecy. Zechariah's message was timed specifically to expound on the revelation God had given through Haggai. To that end, **the word of Yahweh came** to Zechariah. A true prophet spoke only what the Lord revealed (Deut 18:20). Like other prophets before him (Hos 1:1; Joel 1:1; Jonah 1:1; Mic 1:1; Zeph 1:1), Zechariah was commissioned to speak the very words of God.

Theologically, it should be noted that the **word of Yahweh** referred not just to a message, but also to a messenger. Starting from creation, God's Word creates (Gen 1:3), directs history (1 Kgs 13:26; Ps 33:6–12), and speaks (Gen 15:1, 4). Moreover, that the Word is sent by God indicates that this Word is not the Father but the second Person of the Triune Godhead, the Son (Ps 147:18; John 5:30; 6:38). This book carries divine authority because it is a revelation directly from the Messiah about the Messiah (cf. Zech 3:5; 4:14; 6:9–15; 9:6; 11:12; 12:10; 14:1–5). He is the Word of God who speaks the word of God (John 1:1–3).

The message came to **Zechariah the prophet, the son of Berechiah, the son of Iddo.** These names provide another reminder of God's character and the purpose of this prophecy. **Berechiah** means "Yahweh blesses," foreshadowing a key theme in this book: the ultimate blessing of God for Israel in the future. Zechariah's grandfather was **Iddo,** meaning "in its time." This name anticipates another key theme—namely, that God will accomplish His promises according to His perfect timetable. The name **Zechariah** means "Yahweh remembers," which sums up the entire message of the book. Zechariah's mission as a **prophet,** one who proclaims God's Word, was to declare that the Lord remembers. Yahweh will work everything out so that "the latter glory of this house will be greater than the former...and in this place I will give peace" (Hag 2:9).

Though it was a message of hope and encouragement, Zechariah's prophecy began with a sobering reminder for the Israelites, especially given their recent return from exile. He declared, **"Yahweh was very wrathful against your fathers." Wrath** expresses the notion of extreme annoyance, contempt, and vehement displeasure, almost to the extent of abhorrence and hatred. Though God is love (cf. 1 John 4:16), He is also holy and furious against sin, such that Hebrews 12:29 describes God as "a consuming fire." The Lord is angry with the wicked every day (Ps 7:11), including those who forsake Him (Ezra 8:22), abandon the truth (Heb 10:26–27), or lead others into falsehood (1 Thess 2:16). In His wrath, God promised to curse idolaters and eject them out of the land of Israel (Deut 29:27). In Zechariah 1:2, the prophet used the same word for wrath found in Deuteronomy 29:27. Both passages emphasized that the reason for Israel's exile was the wrath of God kindled against the wickedness of the people.

Though Yahweh **was very wrathful against your fathers**, a reference to past generations of Israelites before the exile, that did not have to be the case for the people in Zechariah's day. Unlike their ancestors, they could experience God's blessing rather than His judgment. The prophet Haggai, just a short time earlier, revealed that God was with His people (Hag 1:13). In fact, the Lord had been at work the entire time as He stirred up the hearts of the rulers of Medo-Persia to allow Israel to come home (Ezra 1:1). Thus, while saying that God was wrathful with past generations, Zechariah simultaneously offered hope to the people of his day.

Therefore, in light of this, Zechariah was instructed to **say to them** what God expected of His people, so that they might enjoy His blessing instead of experiencing His displeasure, as prior generations had done. The Lord's call to repent and return was clear: **Thus says Yahweh of hosts, "Return to Me."** The One speaking was **Yahweh of hosts**, a title used three times in this verse. The repetition emphasized that this command was backed by the sovereign authority and supreme majesty of the King of the universe, who rules over all the hosts of heaven. The imperative to **return** underscored the heart of repentance. To repent is to return, to turn away from sin and turn back to the Lord. As noted above, the repentance God requires is not merely an external change of behavior, but an internal change of heart. Israel was not merely to return to a certain way of life, they were to return **to Me**, namely to Yahweh Himself. Those who returned to the Lord in love (Deut 6:4–5) would demonstrate that reality through their worship and obedience. This was the kind of repentance the Lord would bless.

This call to repentance was evidence of Yahweh's goodness and remembrance toward His people, indicating His gracious desire to save and bless them. Throughout Scripture, God promised that a day will come when His people will repent because of His transforming work within their hearts (cf. Deut 30:1–6; 1 Kgs 8:48–50; Ezek 36:26–31). The prophets viewed Israel's repentance as an event God would use to change their humiliation into exaltation (Deut 30:1–10; Joel 2:12–32). In all times, repentance functions as the gateway to blessing. By issuing this command, God demonstrated that He had not forgotten His people or His promises to them. Divine condemnation was not the end of the story for the nation of Israel. God promised grace and hope for the penitent.

Accordingly, the Lord assured His people that if they would return to Him, He would **return to you**, namely to His people Israel. The repetition of the word "return" tightly ties Israel's repentance together with God's restoration of the nation. One will not happen without the other. As dramatic as Israel's turn from sin to God would be, so God's turn from wrath to blessing would be equally spectacular. By returning to the Lord in love and walking in obedience to Him, Israel's relationship with God would be restored, and they would experience His goodness.

The Lord's promise to return to His people had clear implications for Zechariah's original audience, prompting them to turn to Him in obedient expectation, resting in the assurance of His abiding presence and abundant blessing. But the full realization of this divine promise is still future. Yahweh's promise to return anticipates His final and glorious return to the final temple at the end of the age. As the prophet Haggai had already predicted:

> For thus says Yahweh of hosts, "Once more—in a little while—I am going to shake the heavens and the earth, the sea also and the dry land. And I will shake all the nations; and they will come with the desirable things of all nations, and I will fill this house with glory," says Yahweh of hosts. "The silver is Mine, and the gold is Mine," declares Yahweh of hosts. "The latter glory of this house will be greater than the former," says Yahweh of hosts, "and in this place I will give peace," declares Yahweh of hosts. (Hag 2:6–9)

There is no Scripture to indicate that God's glory ever returned to

Zerubbabel's temple in the same way the first temple was filled with the Shekinah glory (cf. 1 Kgs 8:10, 11; 2 Chr 5:13, 14). This glory also cannot refer to Jesus Christ's physical presence in Herod's temple, because the other events mentioned in Haggai 2:6–9 have not yet occurred. Haggai spoke of God shaking the nations, instituting worldwide peace, and filling Jerusalem with silver and gold. None of that happened during Christ's first advent. The promise of Yahweh's glorious return to His temple, foretold by both Haggai and Zechariah, has no historical fulfillment. It remains to be realized in the future, as the prophet Ezekiel predicted (Ezek 43:5). There will be a day when Israel returns to the Lord (Rom 11:26) and the Lord will return to His people and dwell with them fully, intimately, and majestically (Isa 4:2–6; 6:1–3; Ezek 40–48). That this was declared by **Yahweh of hosts** reinforced its certainty, since He possesses all the authority and power to accomplish His plan as promised.

In a dark time for the nation, Zechariah's opening verses reminded the people that Yahweh had not forgotten them. The Lord called Israel to repent and return. That message appeared at the outset of the book because it introduced what God's people needed to know as a baseline for this entire prophecy. As the prophet unfolded the amazing blessings of grace God has in store for Israel—both historically and eschatologically—they needed to know how to respond rightly. The Lord revealed the answer at the very beginning of the book: Israel needed to repent and return to Him.

THE CONSEQUENCES OF REBELLION

""""Do not be like your fathers, to whom the former prophets called out, saying, 'Thus says Yahweh of hosts, "Return now from your evil ways and from your evil deeds."' But they did not listen or give heed to Me," declares Yahweh. "Your fathers, where are they? And the prophets, do they live forever? But did not My words and My statutes, which I commanded My slaves the prophets, overtake your fathers? Then they returned and said, 'As Yahweh of hosts purposed to do to us in accordance with our ways and our deeds, so He has done with us.'"""" (1:4–6)

God continued His exhortation to repentance by relating not only what it is but also what it is not. Yahweh warned them: **"Do not be like your fathers."** The **fathers** represented the past generations that were under God's wrath (cf. Zech 1:2). Zechariah pointed out that the present generation was in a parallel peril to that of their forefathers, in that **the former prophets**—namely all the prophets before the exile, including Isaiah, Jeremiah, Hosea, Joel, Amos, Micah, Habakkuk, and Zephaniah—had also **called out** to the prior generations of Israelites. These prophets faithfully exhorted past generations with some form of this divine warning: **Thus says Yahweh of hosts, "Return now from your evil ways and from your evil deeds"** (cf. 1:3). While Zechariah urged Israel to return to God, the former prophets urged them to return **from your evil ways and from your evil deeds**. Turning to God and turning away from evil are two sides of the same coin of repentance. The condemnation of Israel's ancestors for both their general conduct **(from your evil ways)** and their particular actions **(from your evil deeds)** provides an important reminder: true repentance is thorough. It marks a change of one's entire lifestyle and also puts to death specific sins (cf. Rom 8:13). Both are components of genuine, God-honoring repentance.

Former generations were warned by God with the same truth. The problem of those earlier generations was their response: **they did not listen.** Listening refers to hearing with a readiness to respond, whether that be accepting a request (Gen 17:20) or obeying a command (Exod 24:7). Israel's forefathers did not obey God's call to repent. Yahweh also stated that their forefathers did not **give heed to Me,** showing that they did not even pay attention to the prophets' message. Zechariah warned his hearers not to be like the stubborn and recalcitrant generations before them. Their response needed to be different.

The Lord impressed upon Israel the full weightiness and urgency of their response. Since sinful people tend to live in denial, ignoring the warnings from God as if they were meaningless artifacts of ancient history, the Lord showed by history that the consequences of disobedience to His Word are serious, real, and inescapable. To make that clear, the Lord again pointed back to Israel's past, asking: **"Your fathers, where are they?"** The answer was obvious, especially for those who had just returned from captivity in Babylon. The Israelites understood the historic consequences of the wickedness of their people. They knew their fathers had either been slaughtered by Nebuchadnezzar's armies or forced into exile. As Ezra 9:7 recorded, "Since the days of our fathers to this day we *have been* in great guilt, and on account of our iniquities we, our kings *and* our priests have been given into the hand of the kings of the lands, to the sword, to captivity and to plunder and to open shame, as *it is* this day." The people of Israel knew well that past generations had been killed in judgment (2 Chr 29:8). Zechariah reminded his audience that, if they were unwilling to repent and return to God, they would be no better than their unfaithful forefathers. If they were not penitent, they would also face God's judgment.

God further asked, **"And the prophets, do they live forever?"** Unlike Israel's fathers, the prophets were God's servants in a right relationship with Him. The point of this rhetorical question is not to emphasize God's judgment but rather to demonstrate both human frailty and the absolute authority of God's Word. Even though the prophets faithfully delivered God's message, as sinners they too faded away and died physically (Ezek 18:20). They will not **live forever** in this world. If even the servants of God die, surely no person has the ability to overcome the effect of divine revelation. No one is above God's Word, not even the prophets who proclaimed it. Moses provides an obvious example of this. Though used by God to receive the first five books of the Bible, when he sinned, God punished him without partiality (cf. Num 20:9–13, 24; 27:13; Deut 1:37; 3:26–27). Since no one can defy God's Word, its warnings are true and unavoidable, and Israel needed to take it seriously.

In contrast **(but)** with man's fallenness and frailty, God reminded His people about the nature of His Word. The statement **"My words and My statutes which I commanded My slaves the prophets"** describes the authoritative nature of Scripture. The phrase **My words** emphasizes that God is the author and authority of Scripture (cf. Ps 147:19; Zech 1:1; 2 Tim 3:16). The meaning of **My statutes** carries the notion of a boundary, as God's law sets the line between good and evil, defining the very standard to which God holds someone accountable. God's Word is not only divine but definitive, and to show how sovereign it is, Zechariah reminded

the people that God's Word is that **which** God **commanded My slaves
the prophets** to deliver. No one has leverage over God's Word, not even
the prophets who declared it. They were not peers or co-counselors
with God; they were, rather, **commanded** by Him and were His **slaves**.
Because it comes with the power and prerogative of its divine Author,
Scripture dominates all.

Given Scripture's absolute authority, it is no surprise that its
warnings **overtook your fathers.** The phrase fundamentally describes
how a person is suddenly overtaken from behind (Gen 3:25; Deut 28:45;
Josh 2:5; 1 Sam 30:8). Sinners might assume, at first, that the consequences
laid out in God's Word are far behind and will never catch up to them. But
the Word of God is always fully operative and triumphant. The judgment
on Israel's **fathers** provides historic proof of this. The Babylonian exile
stands as irrefutable evidence that God's judgment will fall on sinners
just as He has declared in His Word. Divine wrath overtook the sinful,
impenitent Israelites and it will ultimately overtake any sinner (cf. Lam
2:17; Ezra 7:6ff). As Moses warned, "Be sure your sin will find you out"
(Num 32:23).

Any survivor of that historic judgment would have acknowledged
this truth. As verse 6 explains, **then they returned and said, "As Yahweh
of hosts purposed to do to us in accordance with our ways and our
deeds, so He has done with us."** Those who remained confessed the
sovereignty of God as they referred to **Yahweh of hosts**, whose powers
and resources are unlimited. The word **purposed** denotes God's
predetermined and decretive plan that cannot change and always comes
to pass (Jer 4:28; 51:12; Lam 2:17). Specifically, the survivors acknowledged
that what Yahweh foreordained and set out **to do to us** is exactly what
He has done with us. The symmetry of the wording shows that God
executed exactly what He intended. Moreover, God's judgment was
perfectly appropriate, as it was **in accordance with our ways and our
deeds.** This admission showed not only that God's punishment was just
but that it was exact. It precisely fulfilled what the earlier prophets had
predicted would happen if the people refused to turn from their evil **ways**
and **deeds** (cf. Zech 1:4). No Israelite could say he was not duly warned.

One final observation should be made regarding verse 6. The

survivors of the exile **returned and said**. Some translations render this phrase as "repented and said." However, the sense of the word in Hebrew in this context is "return," and it is the same word that appeared in the opening verses of the passage, calling Israel to return to God even as He would return to them (cf. 1:3, 4). By using the word **return** here, Zechariah continued the wordplay he had been making throughout this section. The prophet was calling upon all those who had returned from the land of Babylon to return also to God. Israel's physical return to the land needed to include their spiritual return to love and obey the Lord, so that He would return to them. But within this, the wordplay equally carried a warning. If they failed to return to the Lord in repentance, they could only **return** to their land in shame, as mere survivors lamenting the reality that God had judged them just as He did their fathers. Because God's Word is always effective, the call to repentance is a call either to blessing or to judgment. Those who turn away from sin and turn to the Lord, embracing Him in faith and love, will experience His blessing. But those who reject His invitation, walking in rebellion against Him, will inevitably face His wrath and judgment.

Practical Insight for the Present

2

Zechariah 1:7

On the twenty-fourth day of the eleventh month, which is the month Shebat, in the second year of Darius, the word of Yahweh came to Zechariah the prophet, the son of Berechiah, the son of Iddo, saying...

In a single night, Zechariah received eight visions depicting details of God's sovereign power to accomplish His will for the future. These visions will be recounted over the next six chapters of Zechariah's prophecy. They are arranged in a chiasm, where the first vision and the last vision are paralleled, the second and the seventh visions are paralleled, and so on. In such a structure, the center provides the main emphasis. In this case, the center consists of prophecies about the Messiah (cf. Zech 4–5) who is central to everything in God's plan. In character, the visions themselves are extraordinary. They include descriptions of horses (1:7–17), horns (1:18–21), a man with a measuring cord (2:1–13), the High Priest (3:1–10), a lampstand (4:1–14), a flying scroll (5:1–4), a woman in a basket (5:5–11), and four chariots (6:1–8). These scenes are spectacular in their symbolism and profound in the theological truth they reveal. For Zechariah to have received them all in a single night must have been an intense experience.

Regarding these visions, two preliminary questions arise. First, is there a practical purpose for these visions? Readers might be caught up in the wonder of the drama that plays out in front of Zechariah's eyes, but what implications do these visions have for God's people? This leads to the second and related question. All eight visions commence with Zechariah 1:7, which sets the date, indeed the very night, that Zechariah beheld them all. Is there any point to knowing the date, or is it an inconsequential detail? Since the Bible is God-breathed and entirely profitable (2 Tim 3:16), no detail of Scripture is inconsequential, and the date of Zechariah's visions is no exception to this rule. In fact, understanding the timing and setting of his visions demonstrates how relevant they truly are. With matters like persistence in God's work (Zech 1:7a), perseverance in trial (1:7b), and perspective that God remembers (1:7c), Zechariah's visions are indeed applicable to God's people in every age.

PERSISTENCE IN GOD'S WORK

On the twenty-fourth day of the eleventh month... (1:7a)

By design, Zechariah's visions occurred **on the twenty-fourth day of the eleventh month**. Several important events had happened on the twenty-fourth day of earlier months. For instance, on the twenty-fourth day of the sixth month the work on the temple recommenced (Hag 1:15). Since rebuilding God's house was a primary focus for Israel at this point in history (see notes on Zech 1:1), this date was a major moment in God's plan. Exactly three months later—on the twenty-fourth day of the ninth month—God commissioned Haggai to encourage Israel to persevere in their obedience. He revealed that the Lord would bless them and their work of rebuilding the temple (Hag 2:10). When God again spoke on the **twenty-fourth day**, the people would have known He was revealing yet another message related to the construction of the temple. God was further strengthening His people in persisting in the effort because building the temple was not easy. There was opposition and danger from those on the outside (Ezra 4:1–7), to the point that the project had stalled for years (4:24). Equally, those within Israel were also tempted to distraction and apathy (Hag 1:2–4). Beyond that, the people were disappointed that the temple was smaller than Solomon's (2:3). Many might have wondered if all the work, labor, risk, and even spiritual struggle was worth it for a structure seemingly so insignificant. Others might have wondered if they would even finish. So, five months into the restarted project **(eleventh month)**, the people needed to be fortified with confidence that God would honor their obedience and strengthen them in all their efforts. That is why Zechariah's vision happened at this time. Zechariah's visions showcased God's promises and plans to assure His people that what they were doing was necessary and meaningful no matter how hard it was.

Though the church is never called to build a physical temple, the content of Zechariah's visions is a reminder that the future drives believers to persist in whatever work the Lord has for them in the present. In 1 Corinthians 15, Paul, similar to Zechariah, revealed God's plan for the future—the resurrection of the saints in glory. The apostle's conclusion to knowing the future was: "Therefore, my beloved brothers, be steadfast, immovable, always abounding in the work of the Lord, knowing that your labor is not *in* vain in the Lord" (15:58). Knowing the certainty of the divine design for the future produces confidence that present obedience matters. Zechariah's visions provide an elaborate picture of the truth that God remembers His promises and the glorious plans He has in store for His people. Seeing this is an admonition to believers in any age that God will honor obedience. In the Lord, their labor is never in vain.

PERSEVERANCE IN TRIAL

...which is the month Shebat, in the second year of Darius... (1:7b)

Zechariah's visions gave hope to the Israelites in their state of struggle. These visions occurred in **the month Shebat**, the Babylonian name for the eleventh month. That Zechariah used the calendar of Babylon was a reminder that their subjection to pagan rulers continued even in their homeland.

Identifying the year as **the second year of Darius**, the ruler of the Medo-Persian empire which had political control over the Promised Land at that time, was also a reminder that Israel was not free from bondage. The times of the Gentiles (cf. Zech 9:1; Luke 21:24) had already begun, and Israel was living in them. God had promised to Abraham that Israel would be a great nation, having dominion over land that stretched from Egypt to the Euphrates (cf. Gen 15:18). Through the prophets, God assured His people that these promises were still true. In the end, they would not only be a free nation, but every nation would support them as they would return to Jerusalem to learn and worship (cf. Isa 2:2). At that time, God's glory would emanate from Jerusalem throughout the whole world (Isa 60:19–22; Ezek 40–48). However, in Zechariah's time, only a remnant of Israelites had returned to their land, and Israel had not experienced the fulfillment of these promises. Other nations fought against them and overpowered them. Israel was anything but free and fulfilled. In Nehemiah 9:36, the people acknowledged that reality: "Behold, we are slaves today, and as to the land which You gave to our fathers to eat of its fruit and its goodness, behold, we are slaves in it." Though they were in the Promised Land, the people felt more like slaves in Egypt than citizens of a restored nation in their own land. Like their ancestors in Egypt, they were awaiting another Exodus to truly deliver them (cf. Isa 43:1–7, 18–19; Hos 11:1–10; Zech 10:6–12). The situation was arduous, frustrating, and discouraging.

So, Zechariah's visions came at an opportune time when things were hard and there was widespread disappointment. These visions essentially bombarded God's people with promises of divine blessing. They explained to Israel that the way things were at that time would not always remain the same. They imparted hope so that Israel could be comforted and strengthened to persevere in confidence of the coming day of blessing. Yet there is an important sense in which Israel's exile continues to this very day. Even now, Israel does not enjoy all that God promised. The nation does not dwell in peace, the people have not repented, and they do not know their Messiah (cf. Zech 12:10; John 1:11; Matt 23:37–39).

Similarly, Peter reminded New Testament believers that they are sojourners and exiles in this world because Christ has not yet returned and fulfilled all His promises (cf. 1 Pet 1:1–2). All believers acutely feel the reality that everything has not been made right, that full justice is unresolved. They need to be reminded that God's covenants and promises will be fully realized, just as He promised (cf. 2 Pet 3:1–13). Zechariah's visions sustain that hope. While the promises in these visions pertained directly to historic Israel, they unveiled the outcome of a greater plan, one which relates to the church. Zechariah's visions provided hope in God's power and purposes for troubled times. In that way, they are immensely pertinent to believers of every age, since all the saints will be included in the final glory of God's plan.

PERSPECTIVE THAT GOD REMEMBERS

...the word of Yahweh came to Zechariah the prophet, the son of Berechiah, the son of Iddo, saying... (1:7c)

In days of testing and waiting, people do not need opinions or speculations. They need divine revelation, and that is exactly what God provided. **The word of Yahweh came** not merely bringing information but coming as a person, the Son of God (see discussion on Zech 1:1). At a time when Israel was exhausted and disheartened, the pre-incarnate Christ took action for them. He was working on their behalf even though they as a nation did not know Him. The Lord Jesus sent a message through a **prophet** whose name and heritage related to God's faithful remembrance **(Zechariah)**, gracious blessing **(Berechiah)**, and sovereign timing **(Iddo)**. For those wondering if their work was in vain, they needed reassurance that God remembered His promises of blessing. For those wondering if Israel's bondage would ever end, they needed to know that God had not forgotten, but had ordained the right timing. These themes of God's remembrance, blessing, and timing are vital truths for His people to recount in seasons of suffering.

Since this seventh verse is the heading for all eight visions, it is appropriate to see how these far-reaching themes run throughout the revelations Zechariah saw on the night of the twenty-fourth day of the eleventh month. What did God reveal about what He remembers? He remembered the state of His plan (1:7–17; 6:1–8), as the first vision declared that He had not forgotten His promises (1:7–17), and the eighth and parallel vision showed that He would implement them (6:1–8). God also remembered His promises about the nations (1:18–21; 5:5–11). The second vision showed the broad sweep of His plan for the nations (1:18–21), while the seventh demonstrated that He had a specific plan regarding their wickedness (5:5–11). In addition, the Lord recalled His guarantees about Israel (2:1–13; 5:1–4). The third (2:1–13) and sixth (5:1–4) visions, respectively, showed the promise of restoration for God's people and the judgment needed to obtain it. Above all, God most centrally remembered His prophecies about the coming Messiah and His work (3:1–10; 4:1–14). The fourth (3:1–10) and fifth (4:1–14) visions—those at the heart of Zechariah's eight night visions—centered on the supremacy of the Messiah. They portrayed Him as Priest-King, who will intercede for and cleanse His people (3:1–10), and as King-Priest, who will mediate the glory of God through Israel to the world (4:1–14). By revealing visions that pertain to the present and the future, to Jews and Gentiles, to a nation and its true King, and to the Messiah Himself, God showed He remembers every aspect, detail, and component of His promises. He remembers everything. In effect, Zechariah's visions show that not one good word of all the words God has spoken will fail (cf. Josh 23:14; Isa 55:11). The Lord's meticulous faithfulness to His promised plan should drive His people to persist in the work of obedience and persevere in times of trouble.

The First Night Vision, Part I: God Is Active

3

Zechariah 1:8–13

I saw at night, and behold, a man was riding on a red horse, and he was standing among the myrtle trees which were in the ravine, with red, sorrel, and white horses behind him. Then I said, "My lord, what are these?" And the angel who was speaking with me said to me, "I will show you what these are." And the man who was standing among the myrtle trees answered and said, "These are those whom Yahweh has sent to patrol the earth." So they answered the angel of Yahweh who was standing among the myrtle trees and said, "We have patrolled the earth, and behold, all the earth is sitting *still* and quiet." Then the angel of Yahweh answered and said, "O Yahweh of hosts, how long will You have no compassion for Jerusalem and the cities of Judah, with which You have been indignant these seventy years?" Yahweh answered the angel who was speaking with me with good words, comforting words.

As Hebrews 1:1 explains, in the past God spoke "Long ago to the fathers in the prophets in many portions and in many ways." One of those ways was by visions. When Yahweh, in anger, confronted Aaron and Miriam for speaking against their brother Moses, He revealed three ways in which He spoke through His servants, the prophets.

He said, "Hear now My words: If there is a prophet among you, I, Yahweh, shall make Myself known to him in a vision. I shall speak with him in a dream. Not so, with My servant Moses, He is faithful in all My household; with him I speak mouth to mouth, indeed clearly, and not in riddles, and he beholds the form of Yahweh. (Num 12:6–8a)

To Moses God spoke directly and clearly, but to many of the prophets He spoke in visions and dreams, which required careful interpretation. As the Lord declared in Psalm 78, "I will open my mouth in a parable; I will pour forth dark sayings of old, which we have heard and known, and our fathers have recounted to us" (78:2–3). "Dark sayings" included enigmatic visions which, unlike dreams, were revelatory scenes given to the prophet while he was awake. Even so, they were not tangible, physical realities, but realities that were spiritually perceived. Paul's testimony to the character of a vision in 2 Corinthians 12:1–4 shows that sometimes even the recipient was not certain of the nature of a vision.

It is necessary to boast, though it is not profitable, but I will go on to visions and revelations of the Lord. I know a man in Christ who fourteen years ago—whether in the body I do not know, or out of the body I do not know, God knows—such a man was caught up to the third heaven. And I know how such a man—whether in the body or apart from the body I do not know, God knows—was caught up into Paradise and heard inexpressible words, which a man is not permitted to speak. (2 Cor 12:1–4)

Visions, then, were one of the means through which God revealed His message to His spokesmen. As Amos explained, "Surely Lord Yahweh does nothing unless He reveals His secret counsel to His slaves the prophets" (Amos 3:7). In apocalyptic literature, where God revealed truth about His plan for the end of the age, visions formed an integral part (e.g., Ezekiel, Daniel, Zechariah, and Revelation). The prophet, to whom visions were given, observed scenes that portrayed future events, and he was usually guided by an angelic interpreter. Zechariah had eight such visions depicting details of God's unfolding purposes for the future.

The beginning of Zechariah's first vision disclosed that, though Israel could not see the visible hand of God at work, the Lord was aware of their circumstances and was actively advancing His plan. God is always active, and that truth is encouraging for believers in every age, as they cry out for His intervention in times of trial. As the psalmist asked, "How long, O God, will the adversary reproach? Will the enemy spurn Your name forever?" (Ps 74:10). The answer to such questions does not lead to doubting but to greater confidence in the Lord. Believers can rest in knowing that God does everything both for His glory (Rom 11:36) and for the good of His people (8:28). His sovereign providence reigns over every detail, even turning evil intentions into good results (Gen 50:20). God rules over all things (Ps 115:3), and He is moving within the natural and spiritual realms to ensure His predetermined plan will be accomplished.

In Zechariah's day, the Israelites were facing formidable challenges from unfriendly nations as they attempted to rebuild the temple (see discussion on Zech 1:7). Though a remnant of the people had returned, they were still under the threat of foreign powers. All they could see were obstacles and opposition. To encourage and strengthen them, God gave Zechariah a series of visions to show him what Israel could not see. Centuries earlier, the Lord gave a similar vision to the prophet Elisha and his attendant:

> Then the attendant of the man of God arose early and went out, and behold, a military force with horses and chariots was all around the city. And his young man said to [Elisha], "Alas, my master! What shall we do?" So he said, "Do not fear, for those who are with us are more than those who are with them." Then Elisha prayed and said, "O Yahweh, I pray, open his eyes that he may see." And Yahweh opened the eyes of the young man and he saw; and behold, the mountain was full of horses and chariots of fire all around Elisha. (2 Kgs 6:15–17)

Like He had done for Elisha, the Lord gave Zechariah a supernatural glimpse of His sovereign authority and supreme power. The things Zechariah saw reassured him, and by extension the Israelites, that God was at work on behalf of His people.

In the opening half of Zechariah's first night vision (Zech 1:8–13), the Lord revealed that He was presently active (1:8), precisely aware (1:9–11), and personally advocating (1:12–13) on behalf of His people. Though it was not obvious to the Israelites at that time, the Lord demonstrated to Zechariah that He is always advancing His plan. His people could therefore trust Him to accomplish His perfect purposes.

THE LORD IS PRESENTLY ACTIVE

I saw at night, and behold, a man was riding on a red horse, and he was standing among the myrtle trees which were in the ravine, with red, sorrel, and white horses behind him. (1:8)

Zechariah began recounting his visions by saying, **"I saw at night."** God granted the prophet spiritual sight into realities beyond what anyone could naturally observe. Zechariah was about to see images that would reveal to him the purposes of God, unfolding both in his time and at the end of history.

The timing, **at night**, was similar to Daniel's night vision (Dan 7:13). This was no coincidence since Zechariah's visions recalled elements similar to what Daniel had seen. Daniel's night vision was positioned at the center of his prophecy (cf. Dan 7), and for good reason. It encompassed God's plan for the future, from Daniel's day forward, recounting the progression of major nations throughout world history (7:1–8). Daniel's vision showed that although history is filled with trials and struggles for the saints, they will ultimately overcome because of the Messiah (7:21–22). It further revealed that all kings and kingdoms will fall, and only one King, the Christ, will reign in the end (7:9–14). It also called the Messiah the "Son of Man" (7:13), for He is the final Adam who will rule over the entire cosmos. Daniel's vision provided the background for Jesus to claim the title "Son of Man" throughout the Gospels (Matt 8:20; Mark 2:28; Luke 21:27; John 3:13). By revealing similar truths to Zechariah through his night visions, the Lord reiterated His commitment to fulfill the things He had shown to Daniel. Zechariah's visions also demonstrated that God had not forgotten His people or His promises.

As the first vision began, Zechariah's attention was immediately directed to a man at the center of the scene. The prophet's exclamation, **and behold, a man,** with no other description, initially leaves the man's identity a mystery. Since he appears in a vision, there is a sense that the man is supernatural (cf. Gen 32:24–32; Hos 12:3–4). This is later confirmed when the man is identified with the Angel of Yahweh (Zech 1:11), who is none other than the pre-incarnate Christ, the second Person of the Trinity. In Genesis 16:11–13, the Angel of Yahweh appeared to Hagar and interacted with her. She then said of Him, "You are a God who sees" (Gen 16:13). Hagar, realizing the Angel who spoke with her was in fact Yahweh, rightly called Him God. Likewise, Exodus says that the Angel of Yahweh who spoke from the burning bush was God Himself (Exod 3:2–4; cf. Acts 7:30). In such cases, the Angel of Yahweh is Yahweh, sent by God to deliver His own message.

That the Angel of Yahweh, God Himself, was described as a **man** is not surprising given the background of the book of Daniel (see discussion on Zech 1:8). Daniel described the Messiah this way, calling Him "one like a Son of Man" (Dan 7:13), because He is the final Adam. In fact, Daniel's night vision deliberately mirrored creation (Dan 7:2, 4–8; cf. Gen 1:1–13, 24–25) to cast the Messiah as the one who fulfills Adam's role. The Lord Jesus employed the title "Son of Man" to that effect. He declared that the Son of Man will come on the clouds to have dominion over the whole earth (Luke 21:27). The Apostle Paul also spoke of Christ in a similar manner, describing Him as the Adam to come (Rom 5:14) and the last Adam (1 Cor 15:45). So, when the Lord showed Zechariah a **man** in his vision, He did so to reiterate what He had previously revealed to Daniel, that the Son of Man is the final Adam.

That the Angel of Yahweh, the second Person of the Godhead, was not only present but advancing is revealed by the fact He **was riding on a red horse.** Historically, **horses** were crucial for battle (cf. Deut 20:1). Zechariah himself wrote about horses in such a context (Zech 9:10; 10:3, 5). The image of the Messiah charging on a red horse represents His triumphant fight against all the threats confronting His people. He will charge into battle, and He will win. The color of the horse is **red** because red is often associated with blood, judgment, and vengeance.

When God judged Edom, His garments were red (Isa 63:2). Also, in John's vision in Revelation, the apostle saw a red horse depicting violence and bloodshed (Rev 6:4). Zechariah received something of a preview of what was revealed in the book of Revelation. The Messiah was riding on the red horse to demonstrate His active engagement in advancing God's purposes against all adversaries, from the time of Zechariah to history's culmination at the end of the age.

Having ridden onto the scene, the man in the vision dismounted his horse and began **standing among the myrtle trees which were in the ravine.** His posture, in standing, showed that although he was ready for battle, he had not yet ridden into war. The image pictured the coming Messiah, who was prepared for battle, yet who was awaiting the proper time to engage. He was not standing passively but ready to receive a report in order to spring into action (cf. Zech 1:11).

The vision revealed the Messiah standing **among the myrtle trees,** shrubs commonly found in Israel. Their ordinariness, fragrance, and abundance could easily represent the people of Israel. The Israelites were humiliated, yet they flourished, and in the Messiah's kingdom they will be incomparably enriched. Myrtle trees were used to make booths for the Feast of Booths (Neh 8:15), a feast that celebrated God's deliverance of Israel from their time of wilderness wandering (Lev 23:42–44). This feast received attention from both Haggai (Hag 2:21) and Zechariah (Zech 14:16). In the millennial kingdom, the whole world will celebrate the Feast of Booths to commemorate God's faithfulness, not only in bringing Israel home from their wilderness wanderings, but also in bringing God's people back from their dispersion among the nations (Zech 14:16; cf. 1 Pet 1:2). During the thousand-year reign of Christ (Rev 20:1–6), God will make myrtle trees plentiful even in the wastelands to facilitate that celebration (Isa 41:19; 55:13). The presence of the myrtle tree in this vision symbolized God's faithfulness, Messiah's victory, and Israel's ultimate restoration.

The trees **were** located **in the ravine.** The term **ravine** can refer to the depths of the sea (Exod 15:5; Jonah 2:3). But in this context, it describes a deep place on land, most likely the lowest point of the Kidron Valley outside of Jerusalem. The myrtle trees would grow in this area because, as the low point of the region, it was where water would drain. Earlier in Israel's history, a garden was present in that location, which was also the place to which Israel's army fled from the Babylonian invaders (2 Kgs 25:4). So, a man on a red horse, the Messiah, was standing ready at the location of Israel's humiliation, waiting to save His people, restore Jerusalem, and bring the promised blessings of His kingdom to fruition.

Accompanying the man in the vision were **red, sorrel, and white horses. Sorrel** probably refers to a speckled horse or a mixture of a color that was red and white. The horses were red, white, and a combination of the two colors. As discussed, **red** is the color of bloodshed and judgment. **White** is associated with purity and holiness, and in Daniel's night vision, it was also a sign of triumph (Dan 7:9). The book of Revelation confirmed this as John beheld a rider on the white horse going out to conquer (Rev 6:2). Moreover, Christ's return will also be on a white horse (Rev 19:11). Hence, the colors of the horses evidenced that their riders will be messengers of violence and victory in the advancement of God's plan. This vast host rode at the command of the Messiah, the Lord of hosts. Of course, the Messiah Himself will conquer all (Zech 14:3; Rev 19:11–14), but His angelic armies will be **behind Him**, following His direction and executing His will, as He engages in certain and overwhelming victory (Matt 24:29–31; 25:31).

For any Israelite wondering if God was dormant at this time, the opening scene of Zechariah's first vision provided a clear answer to the contrary. Not only was God's plan active, but the main Person in the plan—the coming Messiah, the last Adam, the supreme Ruler over all creation—was poised at the ready. Accompanied by an innumerable army of angels, His final victory is assured and will unfold exactly as God has sovereignly ordained. This glorious truth should instill confidence in the hearts of all believers—whether living in ancient Israel or during the church age.

THE LORD IS PRECISELY AWARE

Then I said, "My lord, what are these?" And the angel who was speaking with me said to me, "I will show you what these are." And the man who was

standing among the myrtle trees answered and said, "These are those whom Yahweh has sent to patrol the earth." So they answered the angel of Yahweh who was standing among the myrtle trees and said, "We have patrolled the earth, and behold, all the earth is sitting *still* and quiet." (1:9–11)

Having beheld in his vision the Messiah and His angelic host, Zechariah asked, "**My lord, what are these?**" The word **lord** refers to the angel who spoke to him and is not the title for God (*Adonai*), but a related word (*adon*) often used to address someone respectfully (Gen 31:35; 32:36; 1 Kgs 1:17; 2 Kgs 8:12). Zechariah's request was simple: "**What are these?**" The prophet's question was not about the identity of the objects in front of him. He knew he was seeing different colored horses, myrtle trees, and a man riding and then standing. Rather, his question inquired into the significance of those things. What purpose did God have in revealing these elements of the vision?

The angel who was speaking with Zechariah here was different than the man among the myrtle trees mentioned in verse 8. Therefore, he was not the Angel of Yahweh. Instead, he was an interpreting angel sent to give the prophet understanding into the meaning of the vision. Such an angel had also appeared in earlier prophetic books (Ezek 40:3; Dan 7:16), and he will appear throughout Zechariah's prophecy a total of eleven times (cf. Zech 1:9, 13, 14, 19; 2:3; 4:1, 4, 5; 5:5, 10; 6:4).

The interpreting angel responded immediately to Zechariah's question: "**I will show you what these are.**" The exchange illustrates both the necessity and graciousness of divine revelation. In Zechariah's case, revelation was necessary because the prophet could not grasp the meaning of the vision. God had to reveal its meaning through His angelic messenger. In asking politely (**my lord**), Zechariah did not demand an explanation. Rather, he believed that since God had allowed him to see the vision (Zech 1:8), He would also grant him an explanation of it.

Surprisingly, though the question was directed to the angel, **the man who was standing among the myrtle trees answered.** As explained above, this **man** represented the Messiah. He was among the **myrtle trees,** anticipating Israel's construction of booths from such trees to celebrate God's faithfulness in the millennial kingdom (cf. Neh 8:15;

Isa 41:19; 55:13; Zech 14:16). While that will be the future outcome, in the vision the man was **standing** and had not yet engaged in action. But He was the One who answered Zechariah: **"These are those whom Yahweh has sent to patrol the earth."** The horses Zechariah saw were on a reconnaissance mission. The Hebrew word for **patrol** has the notion of going to and fro. The same language is used of Satan in Job 1:7 as he roams the world seeking to challenge God. Unlike the devil, the Lord's holy hosts patrol the earth to do His will, serve His people, and assess the enemy. **Yahweh** Himself **has sent** forth these angels for this purpose.

The statement **so they answered** shows that the angelic horsemen brought their report to **the angel of Yahweh who was standing among the myrtle trees.** The description of the **angel of Yahweh** here in verse 11 matches exactly the description of the man in verse 10. That both were standing among the myrtle trees indicates that they are one and the same. The last time the Angel of Yahweh appeared was in the days of Hezekiah, roughly two centuries earlier, when He struck down 185,000 Assyrians to deliver Judah (2 Kgs 19:35). Just as He had come to accomplish a massive deliverance for His people in Hezekiah's time, so He appeared in the vision of Zechariah ready to act on their behalf. The Angel of Yahweh was standing by the **myrtle trees**, symbols of Israel's triumph, previewing the victory to come (see discussion above).

Given the Messiah's readiness for battle (Zech 1:8), the report of the angels who patrolled the earth was unexpected. They said, **"We have patrolled the earth, and behold, all the earth is sitting *still* and quiet."** Despite the anticipation to see God's eschatological plans fulfilled (cf. Rev. 6:10), the condition of the earth was not yet ready. The words **and behold** expressed the angels' surprise that **all the earth is sitting *still* and quiet.** While a restful state is usually good, in this case it was troubling because the prophets had predicted that before God establishes His kingdom on earth, there would not be rest but immense turmoil and upheaval. There would be a massive battle (Ezek 38–39; Joel 3:9–21) along with the judgment of the nations (Zeph 2:4–9), as the Messiah would go to war and win the victory for His people (Isa 63:1–2; Hab 3:2–15; Obad 17–21). That is anything but peaceful. So, when the angels said that **all the earth** was **sitting *still* and quiet**, the implication was that the world was restful in all the wrong ways. The earth was **sitting** *still* as opposed to being shaken by God. While the word **quiet** denotes a relaxed and tranquil state (cf. Judg 18:7), such quiet can be used to describe a smug sense of self-security (cf. Jer 48:11, Ezek 16:49). In their arrogance, the pagan nations assumed the serenity they enjoyed would continue indefinitely (cf. 2 Pet 3:3–7). The promised upheaval signaling the culmination of history had not yet begun.

So far, Zechariah's first vision revealed that God had a marvelous plan for His people and that He was actively advancing that plan. Here, however, it also showed that the timing of that plan, in terms of its fulfillment, was yet a long way off. Like the angels in verse 11, the Israelites would have perceived this reality as well. They knew the nations around them were quiet and tranquil, while the people of God were distressed and disturbed in their efforts to rebuild the temple. Undoubtedly, they wondered if God was aware of their circumstances. Zechariah's first night vision declared to troubled Israel that God knew precisely what they were facing. The Lord had thoroughly and supernaturally surveyed the scene, both in Israel and throughout the entire world. This provided assurance to the people that their current experience was within God's plan for the nation, perfectly progressing toward their deliverance and triumph through the Messiah.

THE LORD IS PERSONALLY ADVOCATING

Then the angel of Yahweh answered and said, "O Yahweh of hosts, how long will You have no compassion for Jerusalem and the cities of Judah, with which You have been indignant these seventy years?" Yahweh answered the angel who was speaking with me with good words, comforting words. (1:12–13)

While the earth was sitting still and all was at rest, many in Israel, including Zechariah, may have wondered if God was doing anything on their behalf. In response, a marvelous act commenced in Zechariah's vision. **Then the angel of Yahweh** took up their cause and **answered and said.** The second Person of the Trinity, the pre-incarnate Christ, the Messiah who is the Advocate (cf. 1 John 2:1), took His place as the intercessor. While the world seemed at a standstill, the Son of God advanced redemptive history by interceding for His people. We may be familiar with Christ pleading for His people after the cross (cf. Rom 8:34; 1 John 2:1). But the Lord's intercessory work has been ongoing from ancient times (cf. Job 16:19), into the time of Zechariah, and continuing to the present moment of history. Christ has always been pleading for the wellbeing of His own. At a time when Israel might have been tempted to wonder if God had abandoned them, the Lord revealed that their cause was still championed not only by the most able Advocate, but by the most glorious and honored representative ever.

The Son, the Angel of Yahweh, said to the Father, **"O Yahweh of hosts, how long will You have no compassion for Jerusalem and the cities of Judah?"** This passage reveals the nature of the Lord's intercession as He prayed to His Father to show compassion toward His people. First, He appealed on account of the character and nature of God—noting both His might and resources as the Commander of heaven's armies **(hosts)**, and His Person and promises as the covenant God of Israel **(Yahweh)**. Since God had committed His name—Yahweh of hosts—to restore His people (cf. Zech 1:3), the Angel of Yahweh appealed to God the Father to act on what He had pledged Himself to do. This is a repeated theme throughout Zechariah's prophecy, since God is referred to by the name "Yahweh of hosts" fifty-three times.

Second, He appealed on account of God's love for His people. The Son called on His Father to consider the length of Israel's suffering, saying, **"How long will You have no compassion?"** This rhetorical question expressed the Lord's sympathy for His people even as it assumed **God's compassion for Jerusalem and the cities of Judah.** **Compassion** relates to the intensity a mother feels toward her newborn child. This describes deep and tender affection, connection, and care. Such compassion is empathetic and proactive to defend and comfort. The prophets proclaimed that God would demonstrate compassion on Jerusalem and Israel eschatologically (Ps 102:14; Isa 54:8; Ezek 39:25, Lam 3:32; Hos 2:25; Mic 7:19). They prophesied that one day He would see Jerusalem in great distress and, motivated by love, take action to defend the city and deliver the people. With divine knowledge of the profound love the Father has for His own, the Son cried out, **"How long?"** As their Advocate, the Son interceded for Israel, asking the Father to save and bless His people.

Third, the Son's intercession was based upon the will of the Godhead. His plea **how long** was particularly appropriate given the circumstances Israel faced in Zechariah's day. As the Son acknowledged, God had **been indignant these seventy years**, referring to the Babylonian captivity. **Indignant** is a strong word reflecting the wrath that precedes judgment. God carried out such indignation against His people during their time in exile. But even before Israel went into exile, Jeremiah predicted that the Jews would be brought back to the land after seventy years (Jer 29:10). Now that **seventy years** had passed, the divine Advocate was appealing to His Father because the time for indignation had been completed. The time had come for God to renew His compassion toward His people. The Son's plea was grounded in and based upon the singular will of the Godhead revealed in Scripture. Though the world was still, God's Son was personally interceding for Israel even the way that He intercedes for His beloved Church today (cf. John 17:6–26; Heb 7:25–28).

Not only did God's Son plead for His people, but **Yahweh answered** the Son's plea. The Son's perfect intercession is always effective. Thus, in response to the Son, the Father spoke with **the angel who was speaking with** Zechariah. God spoke to this angel because he was the one tasked with explaining the vision to the prophet (cf. Zech 1:9). God's answer consisted of **good words, comforting words. Good words** reveal that God was giving a positive answer in response to His Son's petition. They are equally **comforting words**, a heavenly message that provided solace to those experiencing anguish and despair.

Previous revelation fills in the content of these good and comforting words. The word "comfort" began the latter half of Isaiah's prophecy. Isaiah famously proclaimed, "Comfort, O comfort My people" (Isa 40:1). According to Isaiah, the Lord will provide comfort to Israel by saving them through the atoning work of His Servant (52:13–53:12), bringing His people home (60:4–14), providing peace across the world (60:10–14), and filling the earth with His glory (60:18–22). When the Father spoke words of comfort to the angel here in Zechariah, He was not speaking something unfamiliar, but that which had already been revealed, perhaps even by the angel himself (cf. Dan 7:16–28). God promised comfort to His people—comfort that would heal the wounds of exile, ensure a glorious future for the nation, and ultimately be secured by the saving work of the Son. In speaking **good** and **comforting words** to the angel, God relayed to Zechariah that His plan for His people had not changed.

The Lord revealed to His prophet that though all appeared to be quiet and still, God was advancing His purposes. The Lord was presently active, even if the people could not see all He was doing behind the scenes. He was precisely aware of the circumstances, both the current situation faced by Israel and the timing of events in keeping with His plan for world history. Moreover, the Son was personally advocating on behalf of His people, interceding for them before the Father. In response to the Son's appeal, the Father affirmed that He would bring comfort to His people even as He had promised in times past. For these reasons, the people of Israel could take courage, confident that Yahweh had not forgotten or abandoned them. He was at work on their behalf, even if they could not see it visibly. As the Apostle Peter reminded his readers, the Lord is never slow in keeping His promises, but always has a purpose for what He does and when He does it (2 Pet 3:9). That truth, reflected in Zechariah's vision, would have been a great encouragement to the Israelites as they turned to the Lord and trusted in Him (cf. Zech 1:3). For believers in any age, that truth brings the comfort and courage needed to live by faith and walk in obedience.

The First Night Vision, Part 2: God Is Faithful

Zechariah 1:14–17

So the angel who was speaking with me said to me, "Call out, saying, 'Thus says Yahweh of hosts, "I am exceedingly jealous for Jerusalem and Zion. But I am very wrathful with the nations who are at ease; for I was only a little wrathful, but they helped *increase* the calamity." Therefore thus says Yahweh, "I will return to Jerusalem with compassion; My house will be built in it," declares Yahweh of hosts, "and a measuring line will be stretched over Jerusalem."' Again, call out, saying, 'Thus says Yahweh of hosts, "My cities will again overflow with good, and Yahweh will again comfort Zion and again choose Jerusalem."'"

Before Israel entered the Promised Land, Moses warned the people against becoming proud and forgetting the One who brought them out of Egypt (Deut 4:9; 6:12; 8:11, 14, 19). The psalmist also called on Israel not to forget any of God's benefits (Ps 103:2). Despite reminders like these, the Israelites failed to remember the Lord. Judges 3:7 chronicled how the people "forgot Yahweh their God and served the Baals and the Asheroth," beginning a downward spiral of spiritual amnesia through Israel's history. Jeremiah recorded the words of God Himself in response to Israel's unfaithfulness:

For My people have forgotten Me; they burn incense to worthless gods, and they have stumbled from their ways, from the ancient paths, to walk in bypaths, not on a highway, to make their land an object of horror, *an object* of perpetual hissing; everyone who passes by it will be horrified and shake his head. Like an east wind I will scatter them before the enemy; I will show them My back and not My face in the day of their disaster. (Jer 18:15–17)

Forgetting the Lord led Israel into idolatry and consequently into judgment and captivity.

God, on the other hand, does not forget (Deut 4:31). He always remembers. That is the theme of Zechariah, a book that repeatedly reveals how perfectly the Lord remembers. Throughout redemption history, God has made multiple and specific promises, beginning with His very first promise of blessing concerning the Messiah (Gen 3:15). He also promised never again to destroy the world in a flood (9:13–15). He promised to provide His chosen people with land, seed, and blessing (12:1–3; 15:1–5, 22:17–18). He made assurances concerning other nations, including that the older Esau and his offspring would serve the younger Jacob and his descendants (25:23), that the Amalekites would be wiped out (Exod 17:16), and that other nations like Babylon (Isa 13:1–22) and Edom (Obad 1–21) would suffer terrible judgment for their mistreatment of Israel. In the New Testament, the Lord promised never to leave His people (Heb 13:5) but rather to sustain believers through the indwelling Spirit (Eph 5:18). He promised that His Father will keep those whom He has chosen to the last day (John 5:21–23; 18:9), and that those who know Him savingly will never be cast out (6:37) but will dwell in the heavenly place He has prepared for them (14:2–3). He guaranteed that they will overcome death, for they are united with Him (Rev 3:10–11), and He promised that they will enjoy a new heaven and earth forever (21:1). This is but a sampling of the plethora of divine promises revealed to believers on the pages of Scripture.

The astonishing character and number of such promises provide clear testimony to God's benevolent grace which He showers on those who are utterly undeserving. God's people are called to remember these promises and to be encouraged because the Lord will fulfill every one of them. God never forgets! As He declared to the Israelites, "Remember these things, O Jacob, and Israel, for you are My servant; I have formed you, you are My servant; O Israel, you will not be forgotten by Me" (Isa 44:21). Elsewhere, He emphasized that forgetfulness is contrary to His nature: "But Zion said, 'Yahweh has forsaken me, and the Lord has forgotten me.' Can a woman forget her infant and have no compassion on the son of her womb? Even these may forget, but I will not forget you. Behold, I have inscribed you on the palms *of My hands*; Your walls are continually before Me" (Isa 49:14–16).

The people of Zechariah's day may have wondered if God remembers. They were experiencing trouble and it seemed like God was slow in keeping His promises (cf. Zech 1:11). However, the conclusion of Zechariah's first night vision showed Israel that, although God's timing may be different than His people prefer, He had certainly not forgotten His Word. He remembered everything. Therefore, Zechariah was to proclaim boldly that God remembered His promises for His people.

The promises in this passage—including divine pronouncements regarding the nations, Jerusalem, and future blessing for Israel—demonstrate the nature of God's faithfulness. He is faithful in His commitment to His people (1:14), in the condemnation of the wicked (1:15), in His compassion towards Jerusalem (1:16), and in the completion of all He has said He will do (1:17). His promises are certain, concrete, and precise. God knows the breadth and depth of those promises, and He will uphold them all in every detail.

FAITHFUL IN COMMITMENT

So the angel who was speaking with me said to me, "Call out, saying, 'Thus says Yahweh of hosts, "I am exceedingly jealous for Jerusalem and Zion."'" (1:14)

God had just spoken comforting words (in v. 13), which were so encouraging and hope-filled that **the angel who was speaking with me said to me, "Call out."** That command **(call out)** employs a standard word for proclamation often used with the prophets (Isa 40:6; Jer 3:12; Joel 3:9; Jonah 1:2). It denotes a bold declaration. Throughout Scripture, God called on His people to recall His benefits (cf. Ps 103:2), confront doubts with confidence in God (42:5), and remember God's final victory in Christ (2 Tim 4:16–18). For those who thought God was taking too long to fulfill His promises, the Lord commanded Zechariah to **call out** and shatter their doubts with a forceful proclamation of divine faithfulness.

First, Zechariah was to declare to his hearers that God remembered His zeal for His people. **Thus says Yahweh of hosts, "I am exceedingly jealous for Jerusalem and Zion."** Again, the name **Yahweh of hosts** conveyed how Yahweh commands the entire angelic host to serve His purposes and support His people (cf. Zech 1:3, 8). God has not abandoned His own but is powerfully committed to fulfilling His promises on their behalf.

Yahweh conveyed the intensity of His commitment by saying He was **exceedingly jealous for Jerusalem and Zion**. Long before, God revealed Himself to be characterized by a holy jealousy for His people (Exod 20:5). As a truly loving husband cannot be indifferent if his wife acts unfaithfully, so Yahweh, as a jealous God, refused to ignore the waywardness of His chosen nation. With an entire history of chastisement for spiritual adultery, Israel was intimately familiar with God's jealous love (Ezek 23:19–24). But here God assured His people that as zealous as He had been to punish them, He will be equally zealous to restore **Jerusalem and Zion** (cf. 2 Chr 6:6; Isa 31:5; Zech 8:14–15). **Jerusalem** was the capital of the nation, and **Zion** was the name of the hill in Jerusalem that David conquered and on which the temple was built (2 Sam 5:7). In the coming kingdom, **Zion** will be the dominant city of the whole world (cf. Pss 69:35; 128:5; Isa 2:3; Jer 31:12; 50:5) and the very location of the Messiah's throne (Ps 2:6). In His opening declaration to Israel, God announced His jealous commitment to fulfill His intentions for His people. As Paul said, "The gifts and calling of God are irrevocable" (Rom 11:29).

FAITHFUL IN CONDEMNATION

""But I am very wrathful with the nations who are at ease; for I was only a little wrathful, but they helped *increase* **the calamity.""** (1:15)

Second, Zechariah was to declare that God not only remembered His commitment to Israel, but that He was **very wrathful with the nations who are at ease.** The word **wrathful** denotes extreme contempt and readiness to lash out in condemnation and judgment (cf. Zech 1:2). This is God's disposition toward the wicked **nations who are at ease.** Earlier the angels reported to the Messiah that the entire world was sitting still and quiet (cf. 1:11), and that these countries were at ease in their arrogant self-confidence (2 Kgs 19:28) and flagrant sin (Isa 32:9). For God's plan to be fulfilled, the nations would need to be overturned, and God revealed to His people that He was not merely wrathful but **very wrathful.** He stood ready to retaliate against the Gentiles in His full fury to complete all He had promised.

The Lord explained that the nations were particularly ripe for judgment because He **was only a little wrathful, but they helped increase the calamity.** Anthropomorphically speaking, God was at first **only a little wrathful** toward Israel for their sins, as Zechariah himself had noted in his opening (see Zech 1:2). Because of this anger, the Lord sent other nations, like Edom, Assyria, and Babylon, to punish and discipline His chosen people. Those wicked nations, though accomplishing God's discipline, actually **helped increase** their own **calamity.** They reveled in Israel's suffering and afflicted them with cruelty far beyond what was just. God was fully aware of the atrocities committed by these nations. Consequently, what began as a **little wrath** against His people, resulted in Him becoming **very wrathful** against the nations. God was determined to shift His fury away from Israel and multiply it against Israel's oppressors. As Obadiah prophesied against those pagan peoples, "As you have done, it will be done to you" (Obad 15). The world scene may have seemed quiet at that specific time, but God's wrath had been kindled to shake heaven and earth (cf. Hag 2:21) for His people and against their enemies.

FAITHFUL IN COMPASSION

"'Therefore thus says Yahweh, "I will return to Jerusalem with compassion;
My house will be built in it," declares Yahweh of hosts, "and a measuring
line will be stretched over Jerusalem."'" (1:16)

Third, Zechariah was to declare that God remembered His
compassion for Jerusalem and its inhabitants. **Therefore thus says
Yahweh, "I will return to Jerusalem with compassion."** The word
therefore is a reminder that God never acts arbitrarily (Num 23:19) but
always in accordance with His character. In this case, God's zealous
love for His people (Zech 1:14) and His wrath against the nations (1:15)
compelled Him to take decisive action. Because of His commitments,
God irrevocably resolved to **return to Jerusalem**. The word **return**
appears throughout this chapter and richly conveys the way God will
restore Israel at the end of the age. He will return to them (1:3) when they
sincerely return to Him (1:3, 4, 6). This return will include His physical
presence returning **to Jerusalem**. Before Israel's exile, God's presence
departed from Jerusalem (Ezek 10:9–22), abandoning it to devastation.
But Zechariah affirmed Ezekiel's prophecy that God's glory will return
to the city (Ezek 43:1–5), reversing His earlier judgment and bringing
unparalleled blessing. So, God will return to Zion **with compassion**.
Earlier in this vision, the Angel of Yahweh cried out, "How long will
You have no compassion for Jerusalem and the cities of Judah?" (Zech
1:12). The Father here answered the Son's intercession, confirming His
compassion toward Israel and reiterating that one day He will commune
with His people with the tenderness of a mother loving her child.

As He will return to Jerusalem with such lavish affection, God
revealed that one of the benefits will be that **"My house will be built in
it."** Four years after this prophecy, the post-captivity temple was finished
(Ezra 6:15), but that did not fulfill Zechariah's prophecy. The completion
of the temple in Zechariah's day evidenced and advanced God's plan
toward the fulfillment of these words in the millennial kingdom. At
that time, God will build the magnificent temple that will demonstrate
that His glory has filled the world (Isa 6:3; Ezek 43:2), that His Spirit

has indwelt the hearts of His people (Ezek 36:26–27), and that He has returned to commune with His saints (40–48). Thus, Zechariah did not call the building a "temple" but a **house** (cf. Ezek 40:5, 45, 47, 48; 41:7), in which God will dwell. God even called it **My** house because of the personal fellowship Yahweh will have with His people.

Additionally, **a measuring line will be stretched over Jerusalem**. Eighty years after Zechariah's prophecy, Nehemiah finished the wall of Jerusalem (Neh 6:15). However, that project, like the temple of Zechariah's time, merely previewed and pointed to the city and temple to be completed in the millennial kingdom. The reference to a **measuring line** is similar to Ezekiel's vision of an interpreting angel who held a measuring rod (Ezek 40:3) to measure the millennial temple and a measuring line to measure the river running through restored Jerusalem (47:3). God remembered what He had promised through Ezekiel. As He had previously stretched a line out to destroy Jerusalem (2 Kgs 21:13), so He will one day extend a line over Jerusalem to ensure it is gloriously reconstructed. To those in Zechariah's day who were laboring to rebuild Israel's temple and capital city, God confirmed that He was still compassionately committed to all His promises related to Jerusalem and her citizens.

FAITHFUL IN COMPLETION

"Again, call out, saying, 'Thus says Yahweh of hosts, "My cities will again overflow with good, and Yahweh will again comfort Zion and again choose Jerusalem."'" (1:17)

Fourth, Zechariah was called to proclaim that God remembered the outcome of His promises. Having already summoned His prophet to call out (Zech 1:14), the Lord exhorted him **again** to **call out**. The word **again** is repeated four times in this verse, reiterating the certainty of Israel's future restoration. Because the nation will **again** have what they had in the past, and indeed far more, the angel commanded Zechariah to declare this message **again** and again. The message was to be communicated repeatedly to convey its comforting content.

Yahweh declared that **"My cities will again overflow with good,"** signifying the physical blessings God will lavish upon restored and united Israel. The word **overflow** can have the idea of "scattered," and was elsewhere used to refer to Israel's dispersion all over the world in judgment (Deut 4:27; Jer 9:16; 13:24; 23:1; Ezek 11:16). But in the future, the Lord will reverse this. God's people will not be spread around the world, but rather, their wealth and prosperity will spread out from their cities. Haggai, Zechariah's contemporary, declared that this reality will be fulfilled in the Millennium:

> "And I will shake all the nations; and they will come with the desirable things of all nations, and I will fill this house with glory," says Yahweh of hosts. "The silver is Mine, and the gold is Mine," declares Yahweh of hosts. (Hag 2:7–8)

Joel similarly spoke of Israel's prosperity during that future age:

> And it will be in that day,
> *That* the mountains will drip with sweet wine,
> And the hills will flow with milk,
> And all the brooks of Judah will flow with water;
> And a spring will go out from the house of Yahweh
> To water the valley of Shittim. (Joel 3:18)

Isaiah predicted the complete transformation of the nation from waste to wealth:

> Then they will rebuild the ancient waste places;
> They will raise up the former desolations;
> And they will make new the ruined cities,
> The desolations from generation to generation.
> Strangers will stand and pasture your flocks,
> And foreigners will be your farmers and your vinedressers.
> But you will be called the priests of Yahweh;
> You will be spoken of *as* ministers of our God.
> You will eat the wealth of nations,
> And in their glories you will boast. (Isa 61:4–6)

Zechariah's description of Israel's future wealth was not hyperbole. He reiterated the consistent testimony of the prophets who came before him.

The economic prosperity of Israel will reflect the spiritual and relational restoration between God and His chosen people. The Lord will call the towns of Israel **My cities**. Just as the prophets predicted Israel's physical return, they also prophesied Israel's spiritual salvation, accomplished by the Suffering Servant's work of atonement for His own (Isa 52:13–53:12). His substitutionary sacrifice provides His people with justification (53:10–11), regeneration (Ezek 36:26), the gift of the indwelling Holy Spirit (36:27), true repentance (cf. Joel 2:13), and the ability to obey God's Word from the heart (Jer 31:31–33). The comprehensive salvation accomplished by the Servant of Yahweh will reconcile the nation to God and bring His people into full fellowship with Him (cf. Ezek 36:28). At that time, God will truly call the cities of Israel, **My cities**.

With such physical and spiritual transformation, **Yahweh will again comfort Zion and again choose Jerusalem**. In verse 13, God spoke comforting words, which encompassed His plans for Israel's future (see discussion on Zech 1:13; cf. Isa 40:1). So, only after God has completed all that has been promised in this passage—His wrath poured out against Israel's enemies (Zech 1:15; cf. Matt 25:30), His return to Jerusalem (Zech 1:16a; cf. Ezek 48:35), the rebuilding of His house (Zech 1:16b; cf. Ezek 40–48), the reconstruction of Jerusalem (Zech 1:16c; Jer 31:38–40), the reinstatement of the nation (Zech 1:17a; Isa 60:4–9), and the renewal of His covenant relationship with Israel (Zech 1:17b; cf. 9:17)—could it be said that Yahweh has provided full and final comfort to His own (cf. Isa 14:1; 40:1). Only then will the city of Jerusalem be **Zion**, the capital of the world under the reign of the Messiah King (cf. Pss 102:13; 110:2; 146:10; Isa 2:3; 4:5; 24:23; Jer 31:6). Only then will Yahweh **again choose Jerusalem**. Throughout Israel's history, God repeatedly declared that He had chosen Jerusalem (cf. Deut 12:5; 1 Kgs 11:13, 32; 2 Kgs 21:7). But only when His people and their capital city are fully restored will the Lord ultimately fulfill that declaration, since the city will be everything God desires it to be (cf. Pss 48:1–2; 68:15–16). The declaration that God will comfort Zion means that He will exhaustively complete all He said He would do.

God showed His people that though things may have seemed quiet at that moment, He had not forgotten any of His promises. To the returning Jews who lost sight of their priorities (cf. Hag 1:1–12), God's message in this scene was that He had not forgotten them. Even when the Israelites were faithless, the Lord remained faithful to His promises, His plan, and His people. His zealous commitment to them was unwavering. Though He would judge the wicked nations with wrath and condemnation, He looked upon Jerusalem with great compassion and favor. Out of that love, He assured His people that what He promised He would one day complete. For that reason, they could find comfort in Him, knowing that those who hope in the Lord will not be disappointed.

The Second Night Vision: God Remembers the Nations

5

Zechariah 1:18–21

Then I lifted up my eyes and saw, and behold, *there* were four horns. So I said to the angel who was speaking with me, "What are these?" And he said to me, "These are the horns which have scattered Judah, Israel, and Jerusalem." Then Yahweh showed me four craftsmen. And I said, "What are these coming to do?" And he said, "These are the horns which have scattered Judah so that no man lifts up his head; but these *craftsmen* have come to cause them to tremble, to throw down the horns of the nations who have lifted up *their* horns against the land of Judah in order to scatter it."

Psalm 2:1–3 declares:

Why do the nations rage
And the peoples meditate on a vain thing?
The kings of the earth take their stand
And the rulers take counsel together
Against Yahweh and against His Anointed, *saying*,
"Let us tear their fetters apart
And cast away their cords from us!"

The psalmist's opening question, regarding the nations' hostility toward God and His people, would have been particularly pressing for Zechariah's audience. By the time he prophesied, Israel had already suffered severely at the hands of the Gentiles (cf. Deut 28:49–68). Psalm 44:22 said, "But for Your sake we are killed all day long; we are counted as sheep for the slaughter." Throughout their history, the Israelites faced opposition, subjugation, and death from foreign invaders. For those returning to Jerusalem after the Babylonian captivity, this was neither abstract theory nor ancient history. They had experienced such oppression firsthand. Given Israel's past, filled with seasons of suffering and abuse, the people needed reassurance that God remembered His promise to judge the nations. In the first vision, the Lord revealed that He was zealous for His people. In this second vision, He offered Israel the confidence that He remained absolutely sovereign over the nations and that He had a plan to punish Israel's enemies.

The doctrine of divine sovereignty provides consolation and comfort, not only for ancient Israel, but for all of God's people. In every age, the saints face enmity from the world. The early church was persecuted by both Jews (Acts 4:13–31) and Gentiles (14:1–28). Paul recounted to the Thessalonians, "For you, brothers, became imitators of the churches of God in Christ Jesus that are in Judea, for you also suffered the same things at the hands of your own countrymen, even as they *did* from the Jews" (1 Thess 2:14). The apostle later said, "I fill up what is lacking of Christ's afflictions in my flesh, on behalf of His body, which is the church" (Col 1:24). The idea there is that Paul participated in Christ's afflictions because the persecution against Paul was really aimed at the Lord Jesus. Paul's own former participation in the persecution of believers illustrates this truth. On the road to Damascus, headed to antagonize Christians, Paul was blinded, and the Lord declared to him, "Saul, Saul, why are you persecuting Me?" (Acts 9:4; cf. 5:38–39). To persecute the church was to persecute the Lord of the church. From God's perspective, to assault His people is to attack Him.

Thus, in their hatred toward God's people, the nations have in fact been raging and railing against God. It was true of Israel in the past; it is true of the church in the present; and it will be true of Israel again in the future. Addressing this mistreatment of God's people, Zechariah's second night vision unveiled God's plan to conquer and punish the nations. This vision revealed that God's plan is so comprehensive that it not only answered the concern of the people in Zechariah's day, but it also provides encouragement for believers throughout all time. With a vision of horns (Zech 1:18–19) and craftsmen (1:20–21), God showed that what He had already revealed (cf. Dan 7) is exactly what will happen in history's glorious conclusion: the nations will ultimately bow to one ruler, the Lord Jesus Christ. That promise is the hope for God's people in a world that fumes against God and His Anointed One.

THE HORNS

Then I lifted up my eyes and saw, and behold, *there were* four horns. So I said to the angel who was speaking with me, "What are these?" And he said to me, "These are the horns which have scattered Judah, Israel, and Jerusalem." (1:18–19)

The statement that the prophet **then lifted up** his **eyes**, an expression that often begins a new vision (cf. Zech 2:1; 5:1, 5; 6:1), describes heightened attention and alertness to something new. Abraham lifted up his eyes to see a ram caught in the thicket (Gen 22:13). Jacob lifted up his eyes to see Esau coming (33:1). Joshua lifted up his eyes to see the captain of God's army (Josh 5:13). Zechariah lifting up his eyes indicates that a new revelation had captured his attention, and he **saw** that new vision carefully, as it provided more spiritual insight into the heavenly perspective.

In this second vision, Zechariah's attention was immediately and intently drawn **(and behold)** to a new scene. In place of the Angel of Yahweh and a group of battle-ready horses, **there were four horns.** **Horns** refers to the antlers of an animal (Gen 22:13), often signifying power or might. David called God the horn of his salvation (2 Sam 22:3). Hannah spoke of the horn of God's Anointed One, or the Messiah (1 Sam 2:10). These images all depict effectual power, symbolic of a strength that overcomes and prevails against its foe.

Though Zechariah would have understood the symbolism of the horns, he sought clarity on their meaning in his vision. **So I said to the angel who was speaking with me, "What are these?"** The prophet wanted to know the interpretation of the imagery. He certainly asked this question of the right person because the angel speaking with Zechariah was also the angel who had explained the significance of the previous vision (cf. Zech 1:9, 13, 14). This angel may have been the interpreting angel in other prophets' visions as well (Ezek 40:3; Dan 7:16). His task was to provide Zechariah with illumination.

The angel replied, **"These are the horns which have scattered Judah, Israel, and Jerusalem."** In the Old Testament prophets, only one other book focuses on the imagery of **horns**: Daniel. There are many ties between Zechariah's visions and the visions of Daniel. Zechariah had his visions at night (Zech 1:8), as did Daniel. Both involved interpreting angels (cf. Dan 7:16–28), perhaps even the same angel. Daniel's vision in chapter 7 described horns associated with four different animals (7:1–9; cf. 8:1–27); Zechariah in this second vision saw four horns (Zech 1:18–21). The interpreting angel's explanation pointed Zechariah to Daniel's vision to help the prophet understand what he was seeing.

This allusion reveals what these horns represent. In the book of Daniel, the animals with their horns represented four nations: Babylon, Medo-Persia, Greece, and Rome (with a modified Roman empire). These nations were superpowers in world history, all of which oppressed Israel. Similarly, the four horns in Zechariah also represented these four nations. This is evident from Zechariah's description of these horns— that they **scattered Judah, Israel, and Jerusalem.** Scattering refers to casting something out and dispersing it (Exod 32:20; Num 16:37; Isa 30:22). Both Moses (Lev 26:33) and the prophets (Jer 31:10; 49:32; Ezek 5:12) used this same word to describe Israel's exile. The nations were indeed involved in the dispersion of the northern and southern kingdoms of Israel and Judah from their land, resulting in the scattering of the people from Jerusalem and the surrounding areas.

The fact that the horns in this vision represented the four Gentile powers is confirmed both by the background of Daniel and by the description of the horns in Zechariah itself. They were described as horns to show they had pierced or would pierce the nation at major points in its history. However, Yahweh had not forgotten the anguish of His people. He was not ignorant of the aggression of these nations nor of the plan He revealed through Daniel. Again, this vision demonstrated that God was still sovereign over every nation, and nothing these Gentile powers did to Israel would alter His purpose for the restoration and salvation of His chosen people.

THE CRAFTSMEN

Then Yahweh showed me four craftsmen. And I said, "What are these coming to do?" And he said, "These are the horns which have scattered Judah so that no man lifts up his head; but these *craftsmen* have come to cause them to tremble, to throw down the horns of the nations who have lifted up *their* horns against the land of Judah in order to scatter it." (1:20–21)

God did not merely remember the maltreatment of Israel by these nations but also the judgment He had planned and would execute on them. Thus, **Yahweh showed** Zechariah **four craftsmen**, meaning artisans who work with precious metals (1 Sam 13:19) or stones (Exod 28:11; Isa 41:7; 44:11). Such skill involved hammering, chiseling, smelting (Isa 41:7), engraving (Exod 28:11), or casting (Isa 40:19). A skilled worker would break things down from the raw materials to build something stronger or more beautiful. The fact that there were **four** craftsmen suggests a tight correspondence with the four horns. There was a craftsman for each horn.

Once again, Zechariah sought clarity on the elements in the vision, so he asked: **"What are these coming to do?"** He knew they had arrived to build, but what exactly? The angel answered him, **"These are the horns which have scattered Judah...."** By referring again to **the horns**, the angel explained that the craftsmen entered onto the scene because the four horns, or nations, all deserved judgment. These nations had been used by God as instruments of divine discipline in that they **scattered Judah**. But they also went too far, such that **no man lifts up his head**. To lift up one's head was an act of triumph and victory (cf. Ps 110:7).

Conversely, not to lift up one's head denoted shame, humiliation, and defeat. The four nations referred to in Daniel pummeled God's people, leaving them weak, crushed, and despondent. As noted above (cf. Zech 1:15), God was only a little angry with Israel when He sent these nations to discipline His people. But they went too far and increased the calamity. They acted with severe cruelty, committing barbarous acts against Israel with violent hubris.

As a result, these nations would be judged. The Lord introduced **these *craftsmen*** into the vision **to cause** the horns **to tremble.** Trembling can denote physical shaking, often brought on by extreme fear and worry (cf. Exod 19:16, 18; 1 Sam 13:7; 1 Kgs 1:49). This description is frequently used of people who experience complete and catastrophic loss in the face of an enemy (Judg 8:12; 2 Sam 17:2; Ezek 30:9). The craftsmen had come to cause each horn or nation to be overwhelmed in utter defeat. The angel stated that the craftsmen would **throw down the horns of the nations who have lifted up *their* horns in order to scatter it.** These nations had the audacity to **lift up** their own horn, or might, against God's chosen nation. Such language makes a wordplay on what was just said above. The nations sought to "lift up" their own power and pride, to the point that the people of Israel could not even "lift up" their own heads (cf. Isa 10:5–14). Instead of strictly carrying out God's righteous judgment, these nations flaunted their power and might. In so doing, they went overboard in **scattering** Israel into exile. God responded in judgment, sending the four craftsmen to **throw down** those nations who were lifted up, a direct punishment on them for their arrogance. Divine judgment would crush these superpowers who had violently **scattered** Israel into exile. The Lord would execute vengeance for His own.

One more feature remains in order to grasp the fullness of this revelation––the identity of the craftsmen. Who are they? Once again, the vision of Daniel 7 becomes crucial for answering this question. In Zechariah's vision, each horn had a craftsman who destroyed it. In Daniel's vision, each nation was destroyed by a succeeding nation. Thus, the craftsmen in Zechariah's vision appear to be the very nations that destroyed and succeeded their predecessor. Babylon (the first horn) was conquered by Medo-Persia (the first craftsman). Then, Medo-Persia (the second horn) was replaced by Greece (the second craftsman). Afterwards, Greece (the third horn) was destroyed by Rome (the third craftsman). With that, God assured His people that He would deal with the cruel and godless Gentiles. He would not allow them to go unpunished for their injustice against His people. His plan was advancing the way He had revealed it to Daniel.

However, Zechariah's message does not stop here, because only three horns and three craftsmen have been identified. Who is the fourth horn and the fourth craftsman? Per Daniel's vision, the final major nation is Rome (the fourth horn), and it will be overthrown by a stone not made with hands, who is the Lord Jesus Christ. His kingdom will be a great mountain that will fill the earth (Dan 7:9–14; cf. 2:34–35). The fourth and final craftsman is the Messiah, the Son of God, and His kingdom will never be defeated.

Historically, parts of Daniel's and Zechariah's visions have already taken place. Babylon was conquered by the Medo-Persians (539 BC). Medo-Persia was defeated by Greece (333 BC). Greece was overpowered by the Romans (in the first or second century BC). Ultimately, some semblance of the Roman Empire will be revived and then destroyed by the Messiah (cf. Dan. 2:34, 35, 45). As Daniel and Zechariah revealed, there are no other craftsmen after the Messiah, for His kingdom will never be overthrown. In summary, in this second vision of the horns and the craftsmen, God revealed that He not only remembered the nations, their wrongdoing, and their judgment, but that He will also cause all godless nations to be ultimately subjugated by the One who can never be defeated—the Lord Jesus Christ. His plan has not changed but rather continues to determine the climax of world history. For those in every age who witness the chaos of the evil nations, such a message gives immense hope and enduring comfort.

The Third Night Vision, Part I: God Remembers Israel

Zechariah 2:1–5

Then I lifted up my eyes and saw, and behold, *there* was a man with a measuring cord in his hand. So I said, "Where are you going?" And he said to me, "To measure Jerusalem, to see how wide it is and how long it is." And behold, the angel who was speaking with me was going out, and another angel was coming out to meet him and said to him, "Run, speak to that young man, saying, 'Jerusalem will be inhabited without walls because of the multitude of men and cattle within it. Indeed I,' declares Yahweh, 'will be a wall of fire around her, and I will be the glory in her midst.'"

When the Lord elected Israel to be His chosen nation, He did so purely out of His own sovereign love. In Deuteronomy 7:7–8, Moses said to the Israelites, "Yahweh did not set His affection on you nor choose you because you were more in number than any of the peoples, for you were the fewest of all peoples, but because Yahweh loved you and kept the oath which He swore to your fathers, Yahweh brought you out with a strong hand and redeemed you from the house of slavery, from the hand of Pharaoh king of Egypt." As the nation graciously chosen by God, Israel was commissioned to shine as a light to the world. The Lord called His people to do this in a number of ways. First, Israel was to proclaim the existence and excellencies of the true God. In Isaiah 43:21, the Lord said, "The people whom I formed for Myself will recount My praise." That public declaration of praise began with personal devotion to the Lord. God directed His people accordingly in Deuteronomy 6:6–9: "These words, which I am commanding you today, shall be on your heart. You shall teach them diligently to your sons and shall speak of them when you sit in your house and when you walk by the way and when you lie down and when you rise up. You shall bind them as a sign on your hand, and they shall be as phylacteries between your eyes. You shall write them on the doorposts of your house and on your gates." Having internalized God's Word, the Israelites were uniquely positioned to declare the truth about Him to the world.

Second, God chose Israel to be the nation through which He would reveal the Messiah. In Genesis 12:3, the Lord said to Abraham, "In you all the families of the earth will be blessed." God accomplished this by sending the Messiah through the line of Abraham. As Jesus explained in John 4:22, "Salvation is from the Jews," meaning that the Savior came through the seed of Israel. Paul also declared this in Galatians 3:16, when he said: "Now the promises were spoken to Abraham and to his seed. He does not say, 'And to seeds,' as *referring* to many, but *rather* to one, 'And TO YOUR SEED,' that is, Christ." God determined that the Messiah would come through Israel, and that Israel would point the world to the Messiah.

Third, God's chosen nation was to represent Him as a kingdom of priests (Exod 19:5–6). A priest is one who mediates between God and men, and who intercedes for sinners. The Lord chose Israel to be this intermediary—providing a sacrificial system and priestly ordinances by which sinners could approach God in worship. Those sacrifices and ordinances, of course, pointed to the perfect Lamb of God and the Great High Priest, the Lord Jesus Christ (cf. John 1:29; Heb 4:14–16). Though Old Testament Israel often failed in this regard, Zechariah 8:23 states that in the Millennium, the Israelites will again serve in this way, by bringing the Gentiles to Yahweh: "In those days ten men from every tongue of the nations will take hold of the garment of a Jew, saying, 'Let us go with you, for we have heard that God is with you.'"

Fourth, God chose Israel to be a nation that would preserve and transmit Scripture. The nation was entrusted with divine truth revealed through the prophets (cf. Rom 3:1–2; Heb 1:1). In response, the people were to esteem, obey, guard, and preserve the Word of God. They were also to proclaim it, both to their children and to the world. Thus, the Lord commanded Israel's king in Deuteronomy 17:18: "Now it will be when he sits on the throne of his kingdom, that he shall write for himself a copy of this law on a scroll in the presence of the Levitical priests." Regarding His commandments, God said to all Israel in Deuteronomy 4:6: "You shall keep and do *them*, for that is your wisdom and your understanding in the sight of the peoples who will hear all these statutes and say, 'Surely this great nation is a wise and understanding people.'" The Lord chose Israel to be the nation that stewarded His Word and showcased it to the world.

Fifth, God chose Israel to be the nation that would demonstrate His faithfulness. Through His irrevocable loyalty to His people, the Lord proved the nature of His enduring love. In Romans 11:26–29, Paul reiterated that, although temporarily blinded by unbelief, one day all Israel will be saved in keeping with God's promises. As Paul explained, "From the standpoint of *God's* choice they are beloved for the sake of the fathers; for the gifts and the calling of God are irrevocable" (vv. 28–29). What God promised to Abraham and his descendants, He will surely do. Despite Israel's repeated unfaithfulness, the Lord remains unwaveringly faithful. One need only look at Israel's history to see the proof of God's loyal love.

Sixth, it was through Israel that God showed His grace toward those who repented from sin. In Exodus 34:6–7, the Lord declared of Himself: "Yahweh, Yahweh God, compassionate and gracious, slow to anger, and abounding in lovingkindness and truth; who keeps lovingkindness for thousands, who forgives iniquity, transgression, and sin; yet He will by no means leave *the guilty* unpunished, visiting the iniquity of fathers on the children and on the grandchildren to the third and fourth generations." Remarkably, this divine declaration came immediately after the Israelites sinned greatly by worshiping the golden calf. Throughout Israel's history, no matter how grievous their transgression, the Lord was willing to forgive those who acknowledged their sin and turned away from it (cf. Ps 32:5). Indeed, the system of Levitical sacrifices revealed the Lord's mercy and grace, while simultaneously acknowledging His righteousness and justice. As the prophet Micah exclaimed, "Who is a God like You, who forgives iniquity?" (Mic 7:18).

Seventh, God also intended Israel to be the nation through which He manifested His justice and righteous anger toward those who refused to repent. Just as Israel provided a living illustration of God's grace, the people also put divine wrath on display when they hardened their hearts and persisted in sin. Exodus 34:7 reminded Israel that God "will by no means leave *the guilty* unpunished, visiting the iniquity of fathers on the children and on the grandchildren to the third and fourth generations." When Israel continued in patterns of wickedness, the Lord responded with various forms of divine judgment, including drought, famine, plague, pestilence, invasion, and exile.

As these purposes illustrate, God raised up the nation of Israel to be a platform from which He would magnify His character, reveal His Word, and introduce His Messiah, the Lord Jesus Christ. Within these purposes, God not only has a specific function for the nation, but also for its capital city: Jerusalem. Located fourteen miles west of the Dead Sea and 33 miles east of the Mediterranean, Jerusalem sits atop a rocky plateau about 2,500 feet above sea level. But its physical features are not what make the city unique. Like the nation surrounding it, Jerusalem enjoys special status because the Lord sovereignly set His love upon it (cf. Isa 62:1–4). As a result, the whole of redemptive history from Genesis to Revelation features Jerusalem.

Of all the cities on earth, Jerusalem (also called Zion) is uniquely special to God. As Psalm 132:13 exclaimed, "For Yahweh has chosen Zion; He has desired it for His habitation" (cf. Pss 48:2–3; 102:13–14; 122:6). This city was known not only among the Israelites but across the ancient world. In extrabiblical records, Jerusalem is mentioned in Egyptian Execration Texts (likely as early as the 19th century BC); later it appears in diplomatic documents in the Amarna letters (around the 14th century BC); and even later in Assyrian texts, such as in the records of Sennacherib's siege of Jerusalem, when Assyria was dominating the ancient Near East (in the early 700s BC).

In Scripture, more importantly, the city first appears in Genesis as the city of Salem, ruled by Melchizedek. In Genesis 14:18, Melchizedek was called the king of Salem. The name "Salem" is associated with Jerusalem (cf. Ps 76:2) and is believed to be related to the Hebrew word "shalom," meaning peace. After Genesis 14, Jerusalem next appears in reference to Joshua, during Israel's entry into the Promised Land (Josh 10). Joshua said this city and the territory around it belonged to the tribe of Judah (Josh 15). However, it was not until several centuries later, in 1003 BC, that David finally conquered Jerusalem from the Jebusites. According to 2 Samuel 5:7, after David's conquest, the city became known as the City of David. Under Solomon, Jerusalem reached its golden age as the wall around the city was extended (1 Kgs 3:1) and a palace was built within it (1 Kgs 7). The crowning jewel was the construction of Solomon's temple, a marvelous wonder of the ancient world (1 Kgs 6–8). But after Solomon, Israel neglected the temple and God Himself (2 Kgs 22–23). As a result, the presence of the Lord departed from the temple (Ezek 10), and then Jerusalem, along with the temple, was destroyed by Nebuchadnezzar in 586 BC.

Nonetheless, God never forgot His promises about His city or His people. Seventy years after Israel's deportation, a remnant of Israelites returned to Jerusalem to rebuild the temple. Zechariah ministered to these returning exiles, calling the people to rebuild the temple and restore the worship that took place there. About a hundred years later, Nehemiah returned to Judah and rebuilt the city walls. Even so, Jerusalem remained rather insignificant in terms of political and economic power. Finally, in AD 70, after the earthly ministry of Jesus Christ, the city was attacked and the temple destroyed by the Romans.

For nearly two millennia after that, Jerusalem was controlled by various world powers—including the Romans, the Muslims, and even the Crusaders for a short period. But in 1948, the state of Israel was reborn, and Jerusalem was once again controlled by the Jewish people. Thus, from the time of Melchizedek in Genesis 14, for thousands of years thereafter, and all the way to today, the story of Jerusalem testifies to God's faithfulness. Against all odds, the Lord has preserved His chosen people and restored them to His chosen city. Other cities come and go;

they flourish and disappear; but not Jerusalem. The city of Melchizedek, the city of David, and the city of the early church is now the capital city of a reconstituted nation. One day, Jerusalem will become the city of the Messiah, under the power and righteous reign of the Lord Jesus Christ. For centuries, the Jewish people have gone to the Wailing Wall to pray for the peace of Jerusalem, to plead with God to send the Deliverer and break the yoke of Gentile oppression. There is coming a time when God will do so according to the Scripture. One day, the world will come to Jerusalem to learn God's law and exult in Him (Isa 2:2–4; Zech 8:23). It will become the epicenter of global worship (cf. Isa 19:16–25; Zech 14:16).

The exiles who returned to Judah from Babylon found a dilapidated city and a temple in ruins. Undoubtedly, they wondered if God would continue to be faithful to Israel and particularly to Jerusalem. God revealed the answer to Zechariah in the prophet's third night vision. In verses 1–2, the Lord provided a measurable promise, affirming that Jerusalem would be rebuilt so that its dimensions could be accurately calculated. He followed that, in verses 3–5, with an immeasurable promise, noting that Jerusalem would one day overflow both with citizens and, more importantly, with divine glory. In all of this, the Lord reaffirmed His plan for Israel and even for all those who will share in their millennial blessing (Zech 1:14, 16; 8:23; Isa 56:6–7; 66:23).

A MEASURABLE PROMISE:
JERUSALEM WILL BE REBUILT

Then I lifted up my eyes and saw, and behold, there was a man with a measuring cord in his hand. So I said, "Where are you going?" And he said to me, "To measure Jerusalem, to see how wide it is and how long it is." (2:1–2)

Zechariah once again **lifted up** his **eyes and saw** a new vision, **and behold, there was a man with a measuring cord in his hand.** Previously, the Lord had declared to Zechariah that "a measuring line will be stretched over Jerusalem" (Zech 1:16). This third vision expounded upon that truth—that God would rebuild Jerusalem. It also affirmed that the

Lord remembered what He earlier revealed to Ezekiel, when He showed Ezekiel a vision of a man with "a measuring rod in his hand" (Ezek 40:3; cf. 40:3–42:20). Zechariah's vision of the **man with a measuring cord** was similar to the vision Ezekiel had received. Who was this man? In Ezekiel's vision, the prophet implied that the man was the Messiah, describing him the same way he described the Messiah in other passages (Ezek 8:2; 10:2; 40:3). Zechariah's context affirms this interpretation. Most likely, the man in Zechariah's vision was the same man he had seen in his first vision, the one who rode on the red horse (Zech 1:8). If that is the case, then this man is none other than the pre-incarnate Christ (cf. 1:11). Appropriately, He is the central figure of Zechariah's visions, a reminder that He is central to God's redemptive plan for His people.

Upon meeting this important man, Zechariah asked, **"Where are you going?"** As in Ezekiel's vision, the man with the measuring cord was on a mission. In Ezekiel, the man measured the future temple (Ezek 40–41) as well as the city of Jerusalem and the boundaries of Israel (47–48). In Zechariah's vision, the prophet wanted to know whether the man would do the same. His question implied a deeper query about whether God would change His plan or keep His promises.

The man responded by saying He was going to **measure Jerusalem, to see how wide it is and how long it is.** The man with the measuring cord in Ezekiel's vision did the same. The language of **wide** and **long** was also used there frequently (cf. Ezek 40:5, 6, 7, 20, 21; 41:1; 46:22; 48:8, 9, 10, 13, 18). The message to Zechariah was clear: the Lord had not changed anything regarding His plan. Jerusalem would be rebuilt in its fullness, so that it could be measured in keeping with the very specifications God had revealed earlier to Ezekiel. For Zechariah's immediate audience, as they struggled to rebuild the temple and the surrounding city, this truth would have been deeply encouraging.

AN IMMEASURABLE PROMISE:
JERUSALEM WILL OVERFLOW WITH GLORY

And behold, the angel who was speaking with me was going out, and another angel was coming out to meet him and said to him, "Run, speak to that young man, saying, 'Jerusalem will be inhabited without walls because of the multitude of men and cattle within it. Indeed I,' declares Yahweh, 'will be a wall of fire around her, and I will be the glory in her midst.'" (2:3–5)

Though Zechariah's vision was only beginning, **the angel who was speaking with me was going out, and another angel was coming out to meet him.** The **angel who was speaking with** Zechariah, the interpreting angel found throughout his visions (cf. Zech 4:1; 5:10; 6:4), abruptly **went out** and left, and **another angel was coming out to meet him.** God wanted to give Zechariah an additional message, so He dispatched another angel to declare it. The urgency of this message is evidenced in two ways: by the interpreting angel's abrupt departure to meet the other angel, and by the other angel's instruction to the interpreting angel to **run** back with the message. Upon returning, the interpreting angel was to **speak** this revelation to the **young man** Zechariah, who would in turn proclaim it to God's people. This new revelation was so wonderful that the Lord did not want it concealed or delayed, but rather immediately made known to the people so that their hearts would be encouraged.

This timely word was that **Jerusalem will be inhabited without walls because of the multitude of men and cattle within it.** One might have thought that since Jerusalem was to be measured, it would need to have walls, since walls set the boundary of a city. However, the Lord revealed that although Jerusalem will be reconstructed and measured, it will not have walls, but instead will overflow with an immeasurable **multitude of men and cattle within it.**

The promise that Jerusalem will one day overflow with people was not new. Isaiah 49:19 had already said, "For your devastated and desolate places and your destroyed land—surely now you will be too cramped for the inhabitants…." Jeremiah also wrote, "Thus says Yahweh, 'Behold, I will return the fortunes of the tents of Jacob, and have compassion on his dwelling places; and the city will be rebuilt on its ruin, and the palace will sit on its just place. From them will come forth thanksgiving and the voice of those who celebrate; and I will multiply them, and they will not decrease; I will also honor them, and they will not be insignificant" (Jer 30:18–19).

In addition to filling Jerusalem with people, God also prophesied that the city would abound with **cattle**. In Jeremiah 31:24, Jeremiah wrote, "Judah and all its cities will inhabit it together, the farmer and they who go about with flocks." Normally, farms would be outside the city and animals would only be brought in for commerce or sacrifice. However, because Jerusalem will one day be so prosperous, its city limits will expand to encompass all the surrounding land. Thus, Zechariah's words about a **multitude of men and cattle** corresponded to what God had already revealed.

While God had already shown earlier prophets that He would cause the city to enjoy great abundance, He had not revealed up to this point the *extent* of such restoration. In this vision, the Lord revealed that Jerusalem will be a city **without walls**. The Hebrew term for this does not merely denote a lack of physical walls, but more so speaks of a certain kind of city. In Deuteronomy 3:5, Moses used this word to describe cities which had no barriers or marked boundaries, as opposed to walled cities. There were certain cities designed to have walls separating rural areas from metropolitan areas. There were other cities that were unwalled, where the boundary between farmland and the city proper was indistinguishable. Out of necessity, Jerusalem had always been a fortified city with walls (cf. 2 Sam 5:6–9). But God declared a surprising turn, that in the end, Jerusalem will be transformed into a city without walls. Furthermore, the term **without walls** is plural in Hebrew, which usually denotes multiple open cities (Esth 9:19). But here, the plural term is applied to only one city: Jerusalem. Although Jerusalem will be a single city, it will be so expansive that it will seem like multiple unwalled towns. Around the time of Zechariah's prophecy, Jerusalem was barely populated. Only one in ten of an already small group of returnees dwelt in the city (cf. Ezra 2:64; Neh 11:1). But God revealed that one day it would **be inhabited** in a spectacular way. Though those in Zechariah's time could not see it, their work in returning home and starting to rebuild would have an outcome far beyond what they could anticipate.

The Lord's encouragement did not stop there. Another new detail emerged, one that was even more wonderful. Being familiar with the city's history of enemy attacks, the Israelites might have wondered how the city could be safe without walls. God Himself answered: "'**Indeed I,**' **declares Yahweh, 'will be a wall of fire around her.**'" While an angel could serve as a mighty guardian (cf. Gen 3:24), the words **indeed I** reinforce the fact that Yahweh Himself will be the protector of this city. He will stand guard with brilliance and magnificence as He **will be a wall of fire** around Jerusalem. Previously, God appeared in a burning bush (cf. Exod 3:2–3) and dwelt with His people in a pillar of fire (cf. 13:21–22). Here, the Lord will dwell with them in a more extensive and glorious way. His presence of fire will not only protect and secure His people but consume and destroy any enemy (Exod 24:17; Amos 1:4, 10). Such an impenetrable defense will be all **around her** (Jerusalem). A wall is secure only if it completely surrounds a city, and God's protection will do exactly that. For miles and miles, His presence will extend around Jerusalem without any breach or gap, securing the city and encircling its citizens with His glory.

But God's presence will not only be around the city, for the Lord also declared, "**And I will be the glory in her midst.**" This statement confirms that God's **glory** will return to Jerusalem (Ezek 43:1–3), and that from there His glory will fill the earth (cf. Isa 6:1–3) in an immeasurable way. His light, emanating from Jerusalem (4:4–6; 24:23), will be the only light, brighter than any other light the world has ever known (60:19–20). Such magnificent glory will dwell **in** the **midst** of Israel's capital, inhabiting a glorious temple (Ezek 37:28; 40–48). God will occupy the hearts of His people and the city to such a degree, that Jerusalem will be called "Yahweh is there" (48:35). That future reality will fulfill the words **I will be**, which is actually the same word in Hebrew as "I AM" found in Exodus 3:14. At this moment, when God's presence envelops the city of Jerusalem, His people will realize the depth and splendor of "I AM." Thus, in Christ's millennial reign, Jerusalem will not only experience God's perfect protection but also enjoy uninhibited fellowship with Him.

Fascinating implications arise from these truths. For one, in building the wall in Nehemiah's day, Israel should have recognized that this time of their history was far from the end. Since God revealed to Zechariah that the final Jerusalem will not have walls, the nation should have continued looking forward to their glorious future under the reign of the Messiah. Even Satan understands this. Ezekiel prophesied that during the reign of the Antichrist, Israel will be a land of unwalled villages, using the same term found in this passage (Ezek 38:11; cf. Dan 9:27; Rev 6:2). Through the Antichrist, Satan will falsely offer Israel the protection that God promises His people, but Satan's peace will be counterfeit (see discussion on Zech 11:15–17). What was described in Zechariah's vision will be a distinctly future and literal reality, but only through the Messiah. Only the Lord Jesus Christ, the man with the measuring cord in Zechariah's vision, can fulfill these promises for His people, doing more than anyone asks or thinks (cf. Eph 3:20).

The Third Night Vision, Part 2: Flee from the World

Zechariah 2:6–9

"Ho there! Flee from the land of the north," declares Yahweh, "for I have dispersed you as the four winds of the heavens," declares Yahweh. "Woe, Zion! Escape, you who are living with the daughter of Babylon." For thus says Yahweh of hosts, "After glory He has sent Me against the nations which have taken you as spoil, for he who touches you, touches the apple of His eye. For behold, I will wave My hand over them so that they will be spoil for their slaves. Then you will know that Yahweh of hosts has sent Me."

When the Israelites first entered the Promised Land, the Lord commanded them not to be defiled by the idolatry and immorality of Canaanite culture (Deut 20:17–18). God's people were to destroy such influences, choosing to consecrate themselves exclusively to Him (cf. Lev 20:22–26). For the Israelites to adopt the religious, ethical, or even cultural practices of their pagan neighbors would have constituted blatant unfaithfulness to Yahweh. Everything about God's chosen people, including their daily diet, was to be devoted to the Lord and distinct from the world around them (cf. Lev 11).

During the exile to Babylon, the Jewish people suddenly found themselves surrounded by a pagan culture. Though immersed in an idolatrous and immoral society, the Israelites were called to maintain their singular devotion to the Lord and His law. Daniel's example, when he refused to eat meat offered to idols, serves as a powerful example of that kind of obedience (Dan 1:8–16). When the years of exile ended, and the Israelites were permitted to return home, many of them chose not to go back. Having settled in Babylon, they were content to stay there. But doing so involved significant spiritual danger. The ungodly influence of the unbelieving world around them posed a constant threat. God Himself warned His people about this, calling them to separate themselves from the pagan culture in which they resided, and to return to Jerusalem where they could worship Him without distraction or defilement (cf. Isa 52:11–12; Ezra 6:21).

This passage (Zech 2:6–9) joins the chorus of texts in which God warns His people to avoid contamination from the world (cf. 2 Cor 6; Heb 11:15–16; Jas 4:4; 1 John 2:15–17). In verses 1–5, the Lord revealed to Zechariah that He remembered the extraordinary things He promised to His people. In verses 6–9, He continued by charging His people to respond rightly to these marvelous truths. First, God exhorted the Israelites to leave the world behind and live wholly for Him (Zech 2:6–7). Second, He explained the motivation for doing this: because His promises are far better than what the world can offer, and those promises are sure in the Messiah (2:8–9).

THE EXHORTATION

"Ho there! Flee from the land of the north," declares Yahweh, "for I have dispersed you as the four winds of the heavens," declares Yahweh. "Woe, Zion! Escape, you who are living with the daughter of Babylon." (2:6–7)

At the outset of verse 6, Yahweh interjected, **"Ho there!"** While the word can denote a strong sense of condemnation (as in the next verse; see also Amos 6:1), it is fundamentally a cry of intense urgency that can express deep grief (Amos 5:18) or passionate longing (cf. Isa 1:4). In the original, the word is repeated ("Ho! Ho!") to punctuate the profound level of God's desire for Israel to pay attention.

The urgent cry from God was both a command and a warning: **"Flee from the land of the north."** Yahweh exhorted His people to leave the land of their exile, disentangling themselves from its customs and culture. This was not the first time God addressed His people about this matter. Long before they had been taken into captivity, Isaiah proclaimed these words to Israel: "Go forth from Babylon! Flee from the Chaldeans! Declare with the sound of joyful shouting, cause this to be heard, bring it forth to the end of the earth; say, 'Yahweh has redeemed His servant Jacob'" (Isa 48:20). The prophet urged the Israelites to depart from Babylon physically and spiritually because of Yahweh's promised redemption. Two centuries later, Zechariah reiterated that same exhortation to the people of his day. To **flee** is to get away or escape from danger deliberately and as quickly as possible. When Potiphar's wife seized Joseph to seduce him, he "left his garment in her hand and fled" (Gen 39:12). The Israelites needed to respond the same way regarding Babylon, **the land of the north.** Babylon is described as **the land of the north** because Nebuchadnezzar's armies invaded Judah by coming down from the north (cf. Jer 6:22; 10:22). As a pagan nation, characterized by idolatry, violence, greed, and immorality, Babylon stood in opposition to the law of God and the purity of His people.

God's people also needed to remember that their presence in Babylon was the direct result of divine judgment. It was the Lord who **dispersed you as the four winds of the heavens.** The word **dispersed** denotes something being scattered (Ps 68:14) and spread out (Isa 1:15)—an apt description of how God distributed the Israelites in exile. The language of **the four winds of the heavens** describes how far Israel had been dispersed. The Jewish people were scattered as far as Nineveh and Media, respectively two to three hundred miles from the Promised Land (cf. 2 Kgs 17:6). Some had also taken refuge in Moab, Ammon, Edom, and Egypt. Indeed, the people were scattered from their homeland in every direction. The phrase **four winds of the heavens** also depicted the instability and violence of that time. The only other occurrences of that entire phrase are in Daniel, describing kings and kingdoms being broken up by the four winds of heaven (Dan 8:8; 11:4). The exile was a time of punishment, when God thrust Israel into the swirling chaos of a godless world. But once the time of judgment was over, why would the Israelites want to cling to any part of it? The subsiding of God's wrath was reason enough to abandon the corruption of foreign nations and return to the Promised Land.

Yahweh continued to declare, **"Woe, Zion!"** The Lord did not address His people as **Zion** because they were all living in Jerusalem. The next phrase stated that many Israelites were still residing in Babylon. Rather, the Lord called His people **Zion** because that was what they were supposed to be. The first part of Zechariah 2 already explained that Jerusalem will one day be filled with God's glory (Zech 2:4–5). As other prophets foretold, Israel's capital city will be the center of the world, the throne of the King of kings (cf. Isa 2:1–4; 60:14; Jer 31:6–12; Mic 4:1–5). God called His people Zion to remind them of their destiny, and to encourage them to return to their homeland. For those reluctant to do so, He issued a severe warning. By declaring **woe** upon them, a term of strong condemnation, the Lord rebuked them for becoming entangled with the pagan culture of their exile. He urged them to **escape** from Babylon and regather in Jerusalem.

The Lord pressed that point further in the final part of this verse: **"You who are living with the daughter of Babylon." Living** is the same Hebrew word used in verse 4 to describe Israel inhabiting Jerusalem at the end of the age. Clearly, the Israelites who remained in Babylon were living in the wrong place. The pagan culture of Babylon was antithetical to the pure worship of Zion, where the temple was being rebuilt. God called the Israelites to recognize that the two were mutually exclusive. The Apostle Paul, addressing New Testament believers, issued a similar call for the saints to separate themselves from the world:

> Do not be unequally yoked with unbelievers; for what partnership have righteousness and lawlessness, or what fellowship has light with darkness? Or what harmony has Christ with Belial, or what has a believer in common with an unbeliever? Or what agreement has a sanctuary of God with idols? For we are a sanctuary of the living God. (2 Cor 6:14–16)

In warning Israel about **the daughter of Babylon**, God not only personified the Chaldean nation but also emphasized her demise; this title is consistently used in contexts that speak about Babylon being judged (cf. Ps 137:8; Isa 47:1; Jer 50:42; 51:33). To stay in Babylon was not only foolish, but dangerous. Zion and Babylon had two dramatically different destinies—one as the ultimate object of God's blessing and the other as the object of His wrath. Israel needed to escape the place that would become the epicenter of divine judgment, and return to Jerusalem that would be the center of God's glory.

This exhortation to come out of the world and live in God's promises goes beyond Israel's past and extends to the end times. In the book of Revelation, Babylon refers to both a city in the future and to the anti-God system it perpetuates. God's people are warned against having any part in it. In Revelation 18:4, God declares, "Come out of her, my people, so that you will not participate in her sins and receive of her plagues." These words parallel the exhortations and warnings found in Zechariah. The implications for believers remain the same from past to future. God's people should always stand apart from the world and cling to His promises and purposes for them.

THE EXPLANATION

For thus says Yahweh of hosts, "After glory He has sent Me against the nations which have taken you as spoil, for he who touches you, touches the apple of His eye. For behold, I will wave My hand over them so that they will be spoil for their slaves. Then you will know that Yahweh of hosts has sent Me." (2:8—9)

The Lord continued by giving the reason why His people should respond to His call: **"For thus says Yahweh of hosts, 'After glory He has sent Me.'"** The word **glory** was used in verse 5 to refer to God's magnificent presence dwelling in the temple, filling Jerusalem (and the earth, cf. Isa 6:3), and protecting the city of Zion. The promises revealed (in vv. 1—5) coalesce around the glory of God. In going **after** this glory, Yahweh committed Himself to fulfilling everything shown to Zechariah in this third vision.

The speaker in verse 8 is identified as **Yahweh of hosts**. But to whom does that specifically refer? In the statement **"After glory He has sent Me,"** the reference to **Me** must be to Yahweh, for Yahweh was the One speaking at that point **(for thus says Yahweh of hosts)**. Likewise, the pronoun **He** must also refer to Yahweh, a point made explicit in verse 9, which says, "Yahweh of hosts has sent Me." In light of this, the Lord's statement in verse 8, **"After glory He has sent Me,"** expressed a profound truth—namely, that Yahweh has sent Yahweh. But how can Yahweh send Yahweh? This question cannot be answered apart from the doctrine of the Trinity. Clearly, the Father was sending His Son.

This is not the first time such an interaction within the Godhead was revealed in the Old Testament. Genesis 19:24 stated, "*Yahweh* rained on Sodom and Gomorrah brimstone and fire from *Yahweh* out of heaven" (emphasis added; cf. Amos 4:10–11). In addition, Isaiah 61:1, also using the language of sending, said: "The Spirit of Lord Yahweh is upon me because Yahweh has anointed me to bring good news to the afflicted; He has sent me to bind up the brokenhearted" (cf. Isa 48:16). Isaiah 61:1 not only describes each Person of the Trinity, but also uses the same language as Zechariah, that Yahweh "has sent me." Since Isaiah 61:1 was spoken by the Messiah, as the Lord Jesus confirmed (Luke 4:18), the One speaking in the parallel passage of Zechariah 2:8–9 must also be the Messiah. Thus, the phrase could rightly be rendered, "After glory the Father has sent Me, the Messiah." Because the divine Messiah promised to pursue and to fulfill God's glorious promises to Israel, the people could trust Him with steadfast confidence.

In working to restore His people, the Messiah pledged to go **against the nations which have taken you as spoil**. Though foreign invaders have historically antagonized and abused Israel (Isa 10:6; Ezek 26:12; 38:12–13), none have been able to thwart the Lord's purposes for His people. In response, God promised to send His Son, the Messiah, to strike back at Israel's adversaries. He promised to take drastic action because **he who touches you, touches the apple of His eye**. The apple of the eye is the pupil, an essential component of a critical organ that one protects instinctively. God had already declared that Israel was the apple of His eye (Ps 17:8). So, when the nations took Israel as spoil, it was as if they had poked God in the eye, provoking His vengeance. The Lord's great love for His people compelled Him to unleash His fierce wrath against Israel's captors.

Indeed, God promised that one day the Messiah will take dramatic steps **(for behold)** to deal with the nations and prepare the way for His promises to be fulfilled. He said: "**I will wave My hand over them.**" Since the **hand** is the symbol of one's power, to **wave** the hand back and forth is to enact that fierce power. God did this to hurl His plagues against Egypt (Exod 7:4–5), to strike the Nile and split it (Isa 11:15), and to cause the nations to dissolve in fear (19:16). At the end of the age, the Messiah will wave His hand against the nations to unleash such power that they **will be spoil for their slaves.** The upheaval will be massive as these nations which took spoil (see Zech 2:8) will become **spoil** (cf. Hab 2:8). These very nations, which made Israel their **slaves** (cf. Neh 9:36; 2 Chr 12:8), will now be possessed by those they had formerly enslaved. Metaphorically, with a wave of His mighty hand, the Messiah will permanently deliver Israel from their history of bondage and oppression, one that spans from Egypt to the advent of the millennial kingdom. Because He has promised to accomplish this on behalf of His people, its fulfillment is absolutely sure.

There is only one outcome to this: "**Then you will know that Yahweh of hosts has sent Me.**" The language of **sending** is very important throughout Scripture. As already discussed, it is distinct language about the messianic Servant of Yahweh, the second Person of the Trinity (cf. Isa 48:16; 61:1; Zech 2:8–9; John 3:17; 4:34; 5:23–24, 37; 6:29, 44, 57; 7:16). Sending demonstrates that the Messiah is commissioned by God (Isa 61:1), comes from heaven (John 6:38), and is Yahweh Himself (Isa 40:3; Mark 1:1–3; and see discussion above). Thus, in declaring that Israel will **know** that Yahweh has sent Him, the Messiah announced that His work for them will be so amazing that one day Israel will see it and categorically recognize that He is God's Son sent from heaven (cf. Zech 12:10).

The reality of that grand revelation should have made Israel even more eager to flee the wickedness of Babylon. The Israelites needed to remember that God had made magnificent promises to His people, promises personally secured by His Son, the Messiah. By fixing their hope in the Lord, focusing on the future glory that God guaranteed, His people would be motivated to flee the ungodliness of this world and cling to Him in love and obedience.

The Third Night Vision, Part 3: Singing and Silence

Zechariah 2:10–13

"Sing for joy and be glad, O daughter of Zion; for behold, I am coming and I will dwell in your midst," declares Yahweh. "And many nations will join themselves to Yahweh in that day and will become My people. Then I will dwell in your midst, and you will know that Yahweh of hosts has sent Me to you. Then Yahweh will inherit Judah as His portion in the holy land and will again choose Jerusalem. Be silent, all flesh, before Yahweh; for He is aroused from His holy habitation."

In the previous passage (Zech 2:6–9), the Lord exhorted the Israelites to separate themselves from the world and live solely for Him. This section (vv. 10–13), which concludes Zechariah's third night vision, specifies two additional ways God's people ought to respond to His promises: in song and in silence. These responses may seem antithetical to one another, but each has a proper place in worship. A survey of biblical examples evidences the value of both singing and silence.

Singing was a critical part of Israel's worship. After their dramatic deliverance at the Red Sea, the Hebrews sang praise to the Lord (cf. Exod 15:1–18; Judg 5:1–31). Moses later commanded the people to sing a song recounting God's faithfulness throughout their history (Deut 32:1–43).

That hymn, known as the Song of Moses, was so profound and timeless that Paul quoted from it in Romans 9–11 (cf. Rom 10:19). Centuries after Moses, David wrote dozens of hymns of praise to Yahweh, composing a significant portion of the Psalms. David's son, Solomon, commissioned singers to lead people in praise when they came to the temple (1 Chr 25:1–31). Throughout the book of Psalms, the word "new" appears more times with "song" than any other noun. Salvation brings a new song (Pss 33:3; 40:3; 96:1; 98:1; 144:9; 149:1), and the Holy Spirit's working produces a melody in the heart that expresses itself in psalms, hymns, and spiritual songs (cf. Eph 5:18–19; Col 3:16). Such praise is not limited to this life. In the future, believers will sing praise to the Lord both in heaven (Rev 5:9) and at the return of Christ (14:1–3).

Silence can also be an appropriate form of worship. The Psalms call the saints to be silent in awe of God (Ps 65:1) and when waiting for Him (cf. Ps 62:5). Isaiah commanded the world to be silent before the Lord, so as to listen to His declaration (Isa 41:1). The Apostle John even noted a period of silence in heaven after the breaking of the seventh seal of judgment (Rev 8:1). While worship is often associated with loud praise— and while remaining silent may sometimes be the wrong response (cf. Ps 30:12)—there is a time and place for solemn silence in worship.

Whether worshiping in song or in silence, genuine praise is never superficial. Both expressions flow from a heart meditating deeply on divine truth. Such rich theology forms the basis for the directives in this passage (Zech 2:10–13). Here, the Lord Himself issued the call for His people to sing (vv. 10–12), and also the command for all flesh to be silent (v. 13). The reason to sing and to be silent was the same, flowing from a right response to the promises, presence, and power of Yahweh.

THE CALL TO SING

"Sing for joy and be glad, O daughter of Zion; for behold, I am coming and I will dwell in your midst," declares Yahweh. "And many nations will join themselves to Yahweh in that day and will become My people. Then I will dwell in your midst, and you will know that Yahweh of hosts has sent Me to you. Then Yahweh will inherit Judah as His portion in the holy land and will again choose Jerusalem." (2:10–12)

Zechariah's third vision affirmed God's promises for His people and explained how they should live in light of them (see discussion in chapter 7 of this volume). In light of the wonder of those promises, the Lord commanded His people to **sing for joy**. The Hebrew word behind the phrase **sing for joy** conveys the notion of a loud cry (cf. Pss 17:1; 61:1; 88:2). It describes the vocal outburst of someone reacting to wonderful news. The singing here is exuberant, passionate, and expressive—all of it in response to the Lord's amazing promises. The companion command, to **be glad**, describes an attitude of elation and disposition of joy. The only right response to God's goodness was for Israel to engage in fervent worship and heartfelt praise.

The call to sing and be glad was addressed to **the daughter of Zion**. While the language of **daughter of Zion** personified the city in her desolation (Isa 1:8; 52:2), purity (2 Kgs 19:21), and hopeful expectation (Isa 62:11; Zech 9:9), this occurrence personified Jerusalem in her praise. The people were to sing so enthusiastically that it would be as if the city itself was singing. The phrase **daughter of Zion** also contrasts the "daughter of Babylon" (v. 7), reminding the people of Israel of the vastly different cultures and destinies that distinguished those two places. The call for the **daughter of Zion** to worship reminded God's people to separate themselves from the corruption of Babylon and return to the sanctity of Jerusalem. After all, acceptable worship requires not just passionate praise but personal purity.

A parallel call to sing is found in the earlier prophecy of Zephaniah. According to Zephaniah 3:14, a future generation of Israelites will be refined by God (cf. 3:9). With purified lips, they will burst forth in praise, and in response God Himself will rejoice over them with joyful singing (3:17). What a stunning day it will be when God joins His people in song! Zechariah's language was a reminder that God had not forgotten what He had promised through Zephaniah.

In the remainder of verses 10–12, the Lord provided Israel with four reasons they should sing and be glad. The first of these reasons focused on God's relationship with His people. Israel was called to rejoice because God promised to dwell with them. The Lord declared, **"Behold I am coming and I will dwell in your midst."** The language of **behold** with the words **I am coming** conveys the certainty and imminence of the Lord's return. There is no doubt that He will come and intervene in the affairs of this fallen world. As a result, He will **dwell in** the **midst** of Jerusalem, promising unending habitation and intimate communion with His people. Yahweh's promise recalled how He dwelt with Israel in a pillar of fire and cloud in the wilderness (cf. Exod 25:8; 29:45; 40:35). However, in the future, God will dwell with His people in a far more magnificent way. He will not merely be above them in a pillar of cloud, but He will be in their very **midst**. He will dwell in the magnificent temple prophesied by Ezekiel and Haggai, with His glory flooding Jerusalem and the entire earth (Isa 6:3; Ezek 43:2). He will be with His people personally and permanently (Ezek 43:7).

With such a marvelous promise—"**I will dwell in your midst**"—an important question arises: Who issued this promise to come and dwell in Jerusalem? The end of verse 10 explains that this statement was **declared** by **Yahweh**. To be more specific, however, the One speaking is the One sent by Yahweh (vv. 8–9), namely, the Messiah. He is the One promising to dwell in Jerusalem. Verse 11 confirms this, saying, "You will know that Yahweh of hosts has sent Me to you." Once again, Yahweh is sending Yahweh, confirming that the speaker is the second Person of the Trinity, Christ Himself (see discussion on 2:8). Therefore, Yahweh, the Messiah, declared that one day Israel will live and fellowship with Him, the One sent by the Father to give His life for His people (cf. Zech 12:10). Indeed, this is the grounds of joy and praise for all the saints: knowing that they will be with the Lord forever (cf. 1 Thess 4:17–18).

A second reason for Israel to sing is given in verse 11. God's people were to sing not only because of what the Lord will do for Israel, but also because of what He will do for the nations. The Messiah Himself declared in the vision, "**And many nations will join themselves to Yahweh in that day.**" The prophets consistently used the phrase **in that day** to denote the eschatological and climactic moment in and around the Day of Yahweh (cf. Isa 26:1; Zeph 1:7–10; Zech 12:3, 6, 8). Like everything in this context, these words referred to the future, when **many nations** beyond Israel will know God's salvation. Throughout its history, the world has opposed Christ and His people. As the Lord Jesus said, "In the world you have tribulation" (John 16:33). However, a day will come when those from every nation, tribe, and tongue will bow in adoration to the Messiah (cf. Dan 7:14).

In that day, the nations will **join themselves** to Yahweh. The Hebrew word for **join** is used to describe a husband and wife being united (Gen 29:34). It was also used of forming an alliance with and supporting the cause of another (Esth 9:27). Accordingly, when the nations join themselves to Yahweh, they will unite with Him in life, loyalty, and love. This wonderful reality had already been anticipated by earlier prophets. Jonah's story of the salvation of Nineveh demonstrated that God was willing to show mercy on those outside Israel. Isaiah frequently wrote about the nations joining themselves to Israel and being reconciled to God (Isa 14:1; 56:3, 6). By reiterating that truth here, Zechariah reinforced the fact that God will certainly remember His promises—even those promises that involve the Gentiles. Though the Messiah will judge the nations that have harmed His people (cf. Zech 2:8), He will also save many from the nations for Himself. The Hebrew word for **join** (*lavah*), moreover, is the root word for the word "Levi," the priestly tribe (Gen 29:34). Just as the tribe of Levi was set apart to join the Lord in a distinct relationship for special service, so the nations will have close and intimate fellowship with Him. God emphasized that point by using His covenant name, **Yahweh**. In the future, He will have a covenant relationship with the nations in addition to Israel.

But the nations will not merely join themselves to God; He will join Himself to them. Yahweh declared that the nations **will become My people**. While this might have been startling to Zechariah's original audience, that truth was not new. Two centuries earlier, God had said through Isaiah, "Blessed is Egypt My people, and Assyria the work of My hands, and Israel My inheritance" (Isa 19:25). Hosea had poignantly revealed that the description **My people** defined God's saving relationship with Israel (Hos 1:9; 2:23). However, in Zechariah, the Lord declared that one day He will commune with the nations with that same kind of closeness.

For the faithful remnant in Zechariah's day, such a promise would have been a joyful revelation—to know that God's salvation would ultimately reach the ends of the earth (cf. Isa 49:6). After millennia of sin, hostility, and turmoil, the nations would one day come to know the Lord and enjoy His perfect peace. Though Christ's saving work graciously extends to Gentiles in the church age (cf. Eph 2:11–12), the full realization of the promise given in Zechariah 2:11 awaits future fulfillment during the millennial kingdom. Revelation 7:9 presents a preview of that future reality. In a vision of heaven, prior to Jesus' return, John saw a "great multitude which no one could count, from every nation and *all* tribes and peoples and tongues, standing before the throne and before the Lamb."

The Lord articulated a third reason to sing in the second half of verse 11—because Israel will come to know their Savior. He declared, **"Then I will dwell in your midst, and you will know that Yahweh of hosts has sent Me to you."** The promise to **dwell in your midst** repeated God's words from the previous verse. Those words signified that one day His Shekinah glory will be with His people in an unparalleled and unmistakable way (see Zech 2:10). However, the Lord emphasized that He will not only be with His people but that **you will know that Yahweh of hosts has sent Me to you**. A similar statement appeared earlier describing the immediacy with which the people would recognize the Messiah (cf. Zech 2:9). However, the statement here in verse 11 adds two words that provide an important nuance: **to you**. Zechariah prophesied that Israel would not merely *know* that God sent the Messiah, but they would *embrace* Him and realize He had come *for their sake*. This describes not only intellectual apprehension but genuine faith. God's promise was clear: one day Israel will know the Lord Jesus in a personal, relational, and saving way just as the prophets, including Zechariah, predicted (cf. Ezek 34:23; Hos 3:5; Mic 7:14–15; Zech 12:10). In the end, the nation will finally love the One who had always loved them, which is certainly a good reason to sing out in worship.

Verse 12 provides a final reason for Israel to sing: for the honor and glory of the Messiah. The Lord stated, **"Then Yahweh will inherit Judah as His portion in the holy land and will again choose Jerusalem."** When He comes, the Messiah will be honored, beginning with the reception of His rightful inheritance. Expressing this point, verse 12 explains, **"Then**

Yahweh will inherit Judah." Believers rightly focus upon the promise of an incorruptible inheritance awaiting them in glory (cf. 1 Pet 1:4). At the same time, they are also destined to be an inheritance for Christ (cf. Titus 2:14). God the Father had always intended for His people to be a love gift, a bride, for His Son (cf. John 6:37; Eph 1:11). Though all the people of God are Christ's inheritance, **Judah**, the royal tribe, is singled out in this passage to show that all authority and nobility belong to Christ (cf. Phil 2:9–11). For His redeeming work, the Messiah will receive a people who will laud Him with all glory, honor, and power (cf. Dan 7:14; Rev 7:12). Upon seeing His redeemed bride, His soul will be satisfied (Isa 53:10–11) to the joy of His people.

In addition to His rightful inheritance, the Messiah will also receive proper recognition. Zechariah referred here to Judah as **His portion**. The word **portion** denotes what is allocated to someone, sometimes a share of the spoils of victory. The root word was used this way in Isaiah 53:12: "Therefore, I will divide for Him a portion with the many." God promised His Son a reward in honor of His atoning sacrifice. The Servant of Yahweh, the Messiah, will receive a people for His possession in distinct recognition of His incomparable work of redemption. Even the land will glorify Christ, as Judah will be His **in the holy land**. This is the only place the words **holy land** occur in the Old Testament. Jerusalem's transformation (cf. Zech 2:1–5) will spread to the entire country, as God changes it from a desolate place to one that reflects the Messiah's purity and glory.

All of this reflects the glorious truth that Yahweh **will again choose Jerusalem**. The statement was used earlier (Zech 1:17) to show that in the future, Jerusalem will be God's chosen city, unique above all others. At the same time, in choosing Jerusalem again, God will demonstrate that He finally rejoices over the city. He had loved and chosen the city before (1 Kgs 11:13, 32; 2 Chr 33:7), but it became corrupt and His glory departed from it (Ezek 10:18–22). However, this separation was not permanent. Because of the Messiah, Jerusalem will be transformed, so that God will **again** set His unique affection upon her. He will have pleasure in His people, in the land He promised to them, and in the city He has chosen for Himself. In view of such marvelous salvation, it should be the supreme joy of all the saints to sing praise to the Lord and be glad in Him.

THE COMMAND TO BE SILENT

"Be silent, all flesh, before Yahweh for He is aroused from His holy habitation." (2:13)

Surprisingly, after such a compelling call for exuberant praise, the Lord suddenly cried out with a strong imperative, **"Be silent, all flesh, before Yahweh."** The command to **be silent** reflects a fearful awe and solemn reverence for God. The prophet Zephaniah recorded people being stunned into silence as they beheld the Lord's power to judge (Zeph 1:7). Habakkuk wrote of the whole earth falling silent before God, knowing they were unable to oppose Him (Hab 2:20). So this call for such silence commanded all people to worship by surrendering to the Lord.

The Messiah (who is still speaking) demanded such silence from **all flesh**, every living person. God equated humanity with flesh when He said in Genesis 6:3, "My Spirit shall not strive with man forever because he indeed is flesh." God is spirit and perfectly holy, transcending all that He has created. Silence befits the sinner who stands defenseless and condemned **before Yahweh**. The sheer contrast between fleshly, sinful people and the eternal, holy God demands such a stunned hush (cf. Job 40:4). People perish, but the Lord endures forever (Pss 78:39; 90:2–3). All creation is dependent upon Him, but He depends on no one (cf. Exod 3:14; Ps 136:25; Acts 17:24–25). God is uncreated, infinite, independent, and immutable. Man is none of those things (Num 23:19). Describing His unparalleled greatness, Isaiah declared:

> All the nations are as nothing before Him;
> They are counted by Him as non existent and *utterly* formless.
> To whom then will you liken God?
> Or what likeness will you compare with Him? . . .
> It is He who inhabits above the circle of the earth,
> And its inhabitants are like grasshoppers.

> It is He who stretches out the heavens like a curtain
> And spreads them out like a tent to inhabit.
> It is He who reduces rulers to nothing,
> Who makes the judges of the earth *utterly* formless.
> (Isa 40:17–18, 22–23)

Given His transcendent splendor and infinite power, all humanity should obviously be silent in His glorious presence.

Though the exhortation to silence is a general call to stand in awe and worship, it goes beyond that. All are commanded to be silent because the Lord **is aroused from His holy habitation**. The term **aroused** depicts someone waking up from sleep (Judg 5:12) or being incited to action (Isa 10:26; 13:17; Jer 50:9, 41; 51:1). In the latter half of Isaiah, the prophet frequently mentioned that God was aroused to deliver His people (Isa 41:2, 25; 42:13; 45:13; 50:4; 64:7), and that is the divine work Zechariah envisioned here. Thus, a day is coming when God, from His heavenly throne room—**His holy habitation**—will be roused to redeem His people. He will come down from the heights of heaven, with infinite and incorruptible authority, to intervene in the affairs of this world (cf. Deut 26:15; Jer 25:30; Ps 68:6). This sight will be so awesome that all flesh will need to fall instantly silent. Indeed, this silence is seen in the book of Revelation. When Christ breaks the seals, and before the trumpets sound (Rev 6:1; 8:1–2), there will be silence in heaven for about half an hour (8:1). All flesh will be braced for God to take action by delivering His people and judging their enemies.

What then should be the response of God's people to His wonderful promises? This passage provided two answers to that question. On the one hand, they should sing in joyful praise for what God has said He will do—both for Israel and for the nations, and all through His Son, the Messiah. On the other hand, they should also silence their hearts in reverence before Him, knowing He will one day come to judge the world in righteousness. Whether expressed through singing or through silence, God's people must always respond to Him in worship, knowing that He will certainly accomplish all that He has promised to do.

The Fourth Night Vision, Part I: The Messiah's Priestly Work

Zechariah 3:1–5

Then he showed me Joshua the high priest standing before the angel of Yahweh, and Satan standing at his right hand to accuse him. And Yahweh said to Satan, "Yahweh rebuke you, Satan! Indeed, Yahweh who has chosen Jerusalem rebuke you! Is this not a brand delivered from the fire?" Now Joshua was clothed with filthy garments and standing before the angel. And he answered and spoke to those who were standing before him, saying, "Remove the filthy garments from him." Again he said to him, "See, I have made your iniquity pass away from you and will clothe you with festal robes." Then I said, "Let them put a clean turban on his head." So they put a clean turban on his head and clothed him with garments, while the angel of Yahweh was standing by.

In Romans 8, the Apostle Paul declared: "If God *is* for us, who *is* against us?" (Rom 8:31). In the courtroom of heaven, the saints stand justified not because of their own efforts, but because of the atoning work of God's Son. Although present suffering and sin may seem like obstacles to glory (8:18), Paul reminded believers that nothing can separate them from the love of God, which is in Christ Jesus (8:38–39). Those whom God elected He will also glorify (8:28–30). No one can bring a lasting charge against His elect, for Christ intercedes for His own (8:34). The believer's complete vindication and ultimate glorification are secured by the unstoppable work of the Lord Jesus, "since He always lives to make intercession for" His people (Heb 7:25).

Long before Romans 8 was written, a parallel scene was revealed by God to Zechariah. The prophet beheld a heavenly courtroom where Satan attempted to accuse elect Israel represented by Joshua the High Priest. In that scene, as in Romans 8, only One was able to intercede for God's people: the Lord Jesus Christ. In the opening part of the vision, Zechariah beheld that in the courtroom of heaven, Israel had only one great High Priest and Advocate: the Angel of Yahweh, God the Son. In depicting that scene, the prophet emphasized two aspects of the Messiah's priestly ministry on behalf of His people: His work of intercession (3:1–2) and His work of imputation (3:3–5).

Though Zechariah's vision was specifically for the nation of Israel, believers of all ages should deeply appreciate the truth it reveals about Christ's work of intercession and imputation. Here, the Lord provided an in-depth look at the power, effectiveness, and fervency of Christ's priestly work. As Paul reminded his readers in Romans 8, the Lord Jesus does this not only for Israel but for all of God's people. Thus, Gentile believers join with the remnant of Israel in giving thanks to the Lord that He is the great High Priest (cf. Heb 4:14–16).

THE WORK OF INTERCESSION

Then he showed me Joshua the high priest standing before the angel of Yahweh, and Satan standing at his right hand to accuse him. And Yahweh said to Satan, "Yahweh rebuke you, Satan! Indeed, Yahweh who has chosen Jerusalem rebuke you! Is this not a brand delivered from the fire?" (3:1–2)

This vision (and the next) began differently than Zechariah's other six visions. In the other visions, Zechariah typically saw (Zech 1:8) or lifted up his eyes to see what God would reveal (cf. 1:18; 2:1; 5:1, 5; 6:1). But here the text says, **"Then he showed me."** The language of **showed** has the idea of causing one to see. Zechariah was unable to perceive on his own what was happening, so God compelled the prophet to behold glorious truths beyond anything he had seen thus far.

As the fourth and fifth visions of the eight that Zechariah received, this vision and the next are central to what the Lord revealed to His prophet. Collectively, all eight visions showed that God remembered His word, including His present plan for His people, His purpose for the nations, and His promises to Israel. Specifically, the two middle visions focused on Christ, and God's promises regarding the work of the Messiah.

The first person to appear in this scene was **Joshua the high priest**. **Joshua** served as Israel's High Priest at the time of Zechariah (cf. Ezra 5:2; Hag 1:1; Zech 6:11). The role of the **high priest** in the vision is of great significance. A priest's function was to mediate the relationship between God and man. The Lord even called Israel to be a kingdom of priests as they mediated His relationship with the world (Exod 19:5–6). The priesthood within Israel led the nation in this endeavor. They mediated Israel's relationship with God as they carried out offerings of worship and made sacrifices for sin. At the center of this, the High Priest led the other priests in this sacred service. Once a year, the High Priest would both offer sacrifices for sin and sprinkle their blood on the mercy seat of the ark of the covenant in the Holy of Holies (cf. Lev 16:11–14; Heb 9:7). This would symbolically atone for sin (Lev 16:15–16) and reset the Levitical system for another year. In that elevated role, from a human perspective, the High Priest bore the greatest weight of responsibility for God's fellowship with His people. If the High Priest fulfilled his role acceptably, the Lord would continue to commune with Israel. If he failed, that relationship would rapidly deteriorate (cf. Ezek 8:10–18). So, the appearance of **Joshua the high priest** in this scene raised an important issue, especially after decades of exile: Would the Lord continue to have a positive relationship with His people?

As Joshua stood there, representing the nation, God made it clear that Israel's blessings did not depend on Joshua. Rather, they depended on the One before whom Joshua was **standing**, namely **the angel of Yahweh**. The idea of **standing before** someone denotes engaging in priestly service and intercession (cf. Deut 10:8; 18:5–7; Judg 20:28; 2 Chr

29:11; Ezek 44:15). That Joshua was serving **before** and praying to the **angel of Yahweh** is clear evidence that the Angel of Yahweh is Yahweh Himself, since only God alone can rightly receive worship (cf. Rev 19:10; 22:8–9). This is confirmed by the larger context, in which the Angel of Yahweh is repeatedly called Yahweh (cf. Zech 2:8, 10, 11).

The priestly ministry of the Angel of Yahweh was introduced earlier in Zechariah's prophecy. In the first vision, the Angel interceded on behalf of Jerusalem (cf. 1:12). In the third vision, He was the Suffering Servant who was prophesied to be the sacrifice for His people (cf. Zech 2:8; Isa 53:6; 61:1). So, by ministering **before the Angel of Yahweh**, Joshua was standing before the Lord Himself. Hence, Joshua appealed to the great High Priest (cf. Heb 7:25), the One who is both Yahweh and the divine Intercessor for His people. If Israel were to be acceptable to God, a merely human High Priest would not suffice. Only the Angel of Yahweh, the second Person of the Trinity, God the Son, could accomplish that for His people.

One more figure appeared in the dramatic heavenly courtroom. **Satan** was **standing at** Joshua's **right hand to accuse him**. In Hebrew, the word "Satan" means accuser. In fact, the Hebrew literally reads, "And Satan [was] standing at his right hand to satanize him." In keeping with his nature, Satan was hurling allegations against Joshua to condemn him and to argue that the people he represented were unworthy to receive God's promises. Satan has always accused the saints (Rev 12:10). In Job 1, he entered God's presence to accuse Job and even to indict the Lord for blessing him. Similarly, here in Zechariah 3, Satan proclaimed Joshua's guilt and unworthiness to God. The situation was critical. If Joshua were to be vindicated, that meant Israel would be accepted by God. But if Joshua were to be condemned and cast off, then Israel would stand condemned and cast off. Of course, the outcome was not dependent on Joshua. Rather, Joshua had entrusted these matters to the Angel of Yahweh. With that, the question raised by this courtroom drama became clear. Would Satan's accusations against Joshua stand, or would the Messiah intercede for His people so that Joshua and the nation could continue to enjoy God's favor and promised blessings (cf. Rev 12:1–3; 17:1–8; 22:15–18)?

In the moment that defined the destiny of Israel, the Angel of **Yahweh said to Satan, "Yahweh rebuke you, Satan!"** As in other places in Zechariah where Yahweh sent Yahweh (2:8) or Yahweh addressed Yahweh (cf. Zech 1:12), here too the second Person of the Trinity (the Angel of Yahweh) invoked the first Person of the Trinity **(Yahweh)** in order to rebuke Satan (cf. Gen 19:24). In rebuking Satan, the Angel of Yahweh countered the devil's accusations and interceded for His people as their great High Priest (cf. Heb 7:25; also John 17:9–10; Rom 8:34; 1 John 2:1). At this time of desperate need in Israel's history, the High Priest of heaven, the eternal Son, directly and decisively defended His own.

The intercession made by the Angel of Yahweh in this vision was efficacious. Several observations demonstrate this point. First, it came with God's power. The Angel of Yahweh said, **"Yahweh rebuke you, Satan!"** Christ's intercession appealed to the infinite authority of **Yahweh** Himself, as Christ asked the Father to **rebuke** Satan. In Scripture, the idea of rebuke was not merely to point out someone's wrong (cf. Gen 37:10; Jer 29:27; Ruth 2:16) but to pronounce judgment. Divine rebuke is an irresistible force. For example, God rebuked the sea, and it dried up (Ps 106:9; Nah 1:4). He rebuked the nations, and they fled (Isa 17:13). God's rebuke is not merely a warning but potent speech that conveys divine might and devastation. So, when the Angel of Yahweh appealed to Yahweh to rebuke the accuser, He called upon God to silence and negate any accusation Satan brought. The power of this specific phrase is also seen in its directness. The Angel of Yahweh confronted **Satan** directly, ready to counter and defeat every charge brought by the accuser.

Second, the Messiah's intercession was effective because it was grounded in God's promise of election. The Angel of Yahweh exclaimed, **"Indeed, Yahweh who has chosen Jerusalem rebuke you!"** The Lord reminded everyone that God will surely **rebuke** and silence Satan because He **has chosen Jerusalem.** The truth of God's election of Jerusalem was repeated not only throughout the Old Testament (cf. Deut 7:6 8; 1 Kgs 11:13, 32; 14:21; 2 Chr 12:13) but also in the immediate context of Zechariah (cf. Zech 1:17; 2:13). These verses revealed that God had already made a promise regarding Jerusalem, and Satan's accusations could not undermine what God had predetermined to do (cf. Num 23:19; 1 Sam 15:29; Rom 8:33).

Third, the Messiah's intercession was also effective because it was based on God's purpose. The Angel of Yahweh exclaimed, **"Is this not a brand delivered from the fire?"** This statement described how a log or a stick in a fire might be plucked out and preserved. Such intervention, by reaching into the flames, could be risky. However, one would take that risk if he needed to retrieve that object before it burned up. Israel found itself surrounded by flames of persecution, judgment, and exile. The story of the Old Testament could have ended with God's people being consumed among the nations. But God snatched them out of the fire of foreign conflagration, and brought them home, preserving them and promising ultimately to redeem them (Rom 11:26). Clearly, God was not done with Israel.

In pointing out that Israel **was a brand delivered from the fire**, the Messiah declared that God's purpose for this people was still in place. Satan's accusations would not incite the Lord to destroy His chosen nation. To do so would go against God's purposes and the covenants He had made with Israel. As Moses said earlier, in appealing to the Lord on Israel's behalf, "If You put this people to death as one man, then the nations who have heard of Your fame will say, 'Because Yahweh was not able to bring this people into the land which He swore to them, therefore He slaughtered them in the wilderness'" (Num 14:15–16; cf. Exod 32:11–14). If God's saving purpose were to fail, His name would be dishonored. Thus, for His own name's sake, God would not abandon His people (cf. 1 Sam 12:22).

God will not go back on His promises. Though Satan constantly accuses the elect, pointing out their failures and unworthiness, there is One who intercedes on their behalf. He is none other than the great High Priest, the Messiah. Where no sinner can stand, He will intercede before the judgment seat of God, triumphing over the accuser so that His people are pardoned and declared righteous. In the courtroom of heaven, the Father remembers the mediatorial work of His Son, by which the redeemed of all ages are justified (cf. Rom 8:34).

THE WORK OF IMPUTATION

Now Joshua was clothed with filthy garments and standing before the angel. And he answered and spoke to those who were standing before him, saying, "Remove the filthy garments from him." Again he said to him, "See, I have made your iniquity pass away from you and will clothe you with festal robes." Then I said, "Let them put a clean turban on his head." So they put a clean turban on his head and clothed him with garments, while the angel of Yahweh was standing by. (3:3–5)

To sin is to transgress God's law and to miss the mark of His righteous standard. Sin stains people and renders them guilty before God. Even from the start of human history, the Lord made it clear that covering sinners required death. That fact was symbolized by God killing an animal and using its skin to cover the nakedness of sinful Adam and Eve (cf. Gen 3:21). The sacrificial system which God ordained continued to illustrate both the necessity and the nature of the work God must do to deal with sin. Animals were slaughtered to show that death is required to satisfy God's justice and wrath (cf. Lev 4:4; 17:11). Sin offerings demonstrated the price of forgiveness and the need for a substitute (cf. 1:4; 16:21–22). Furthermore, the sacrificial system illustrated that any hint of sin rendered a person guilty and unacceptable in God's sight (cf. 14:10–20). These theological truths are illustrated in this part of Zechariah's fourth night vision, including the need for positional righteousness (Zech 3:3), the imputation of that righteousness (3:4), and the resulting change in the sinner's status before God (3:5).

The reason Joshua depended entirely on the Angel of Yahweh for His intercession (3:1–2) was that **Joshua was clothed with filthy garments**. The garments of the priest needed to be in a state of purity for him to act as an intercessor (cf. Exod 28:1–43). Immaculate attire was required because it symbolized his representative role for God before the people. However, Joshua **was clothed** in **garments** that were anything but clean. The term **filthy** comes from a root denoting dung or excrement (cf. Deut 23:13; Ezek 4:12). This would not only be repugnant but especially problematic for a priest. Priests were forbidden to come into contact with anything unclean. To serve as the High Priest in a state of filthiness would result in being cut off from God and from Israel (Lev 22:3–6). At this moment, Joshua was utterly disqualified to serve the Lord. In that respect, Satan had a legitimate accusation to bring against him. Stained with sin, Joshua was unfit to enter the Lord's presence. As a result, Israel had no qualified mortal priest to mediate between them and God. This scene provides a descriptive picture of the nature of sin, which is repulsive and vile before the divine Judge (cf. Isa 64:6; Phil 3:8).

Because they have been stained and defiled, sinners are not qualified to serve God, enter His presence, or enjoy fellowship with Him. They are guilty and deserving of condemnation. Nevertheless, Joshua was still **standing before the angel**, as he had been earlier. Just as Joshua was absolutely dependent on the Angel of Yahweh to intercede for him and his people Israel (see discussion on Zech 3:1), so Joshua also depended upon the Angel of Yahweh for his righteousness before God (cf. Heb 5:2–3). For God to fulfill His promises to His people—to commune with them and dwell in their midst (cf. Zech 2:5)—they needed to be holy as He is holy (Lev 11:44–45). This fourth vision demonstrated that this cannot occur by the power of any sinful human priest, but that it is achieved only by the sinless Messiah's priestly work of imputation. Joshua was **standing before the angel of Yahweh**, trusting in Him to do what he could not do for himself.

Just as before (see Zech 3:2), the Angel of Yahweh was neither passive nor silent, but rather **He answered**. The pre-incarnate Christ **spoke to those who were standing before him**. These were most likely angels, the heavenly hosts who do God's bidding and carry out His providential plan (cf. Heb 1:7). God committed all of heaven to serve those who will inherit salvation (cf. Isa 6:6; Heb 1:14; 1 Pet 1:12). With sovereign authority, Christ issued the command: **"Remove the filthy garments from him."** If Joshua was to be acceptable to God, putting new clean clothes on top of filthy ones would not be sufficient. He would still be unclean, and his new clothes would become contaminated. Instead, what was required was for Joshua's **filthy garments** to be **removed** completely. Every scrap of dirty clothing needed to be stripped away. Thus, the Angel of Yahweh commanded that these garments be removed **from him**. If Joshua had temporarily discarded these garments simply to put them on again later, it would have been self-defeating. These unclean garments were to be totally and permanently separated from the High Priest.

Such comprehensive removal was required not merely for Joshua's filthy garments, but for the sin they symbolized. Thus, the Angel of Yahweh said, **"See, I have made your iniquity pass away from you."** In a judicial and positional sense, everything that happened to Joshua's clothes happened to his sin, thereby illustrating the wondrous nature of forgiveness and justification. The Angel of Yahweh made Joshua's guilt **pass away.** Just like Joshua's dirty garments, the guilt of his sin was abolished completely and permanently.

When the Lord graciously forgives the sinner, He does not superficially mask or partially remove the guilt of sin. Forgiven sin is removed as far as the east is from the west (cf. Ps 103:11–12). The Angel of Yahweh declared He had fully dealt with Joshua's **iniquity**, including its guilt. The Lord's forgiveness is not partial or temporary so that it fades or falters, leaving the sinner to make up for it on his own. Rather, Christ's sacrifice is fully sufficient once and for all (cf. Heb 9:12; 10:10). The forgiveness God grants is both complete and final.

With the pronoun I, the Angel of Yahweh claimed personal responsibility for making Joshua's sins pass away. It is a reminder that God alone has the authority and prerogative to forgive sin (cf. Mark 2:7–9). The work of atonement is entirely a divine work (cf. 10:45), to which neither Joshua nor any other sinner contributes. No self-righteous work plays a part in making the sinner right with God (cf. Rom 3:27–28; Eph 2:8–10). Joshua was unworthy because of his sin. Yet, because of the work of the great High Priest, Joshua's filthy garments were removed so that he might be pardoned by God.

But the removal of sin and impurity is only half of what must be done. To be clean, dirty clothes must not only be removed, but clean clothes must also be put on. This points to the nature of justification: the guilt of sin is not only taken away from the sinner, but the sinner is clothed in the imputed righteousness of Christ. So the Angel of Yahweh told Joshua that He would **clothe** him **with festal robes.** Importantly, **it was** the Angel of Yahweh who **clothed** Joshua in these robes. The verb is causative, stressing that the Angel placed these new clothes on the High Priest, as opposed to Joshua doing this himself. The picture is similar to what transpired in the garden of Eden when Adam and Eve tried to make their own garments but failed. God, in His grace, clothed them in garments of His own making (cf. Gen 3:7, 21). Just as Joshua could not remove his own filth and sin, so he also could not procure or put on his own righteous garments.

Joshua's new garments were thoroughly clean. As the text said, Joshua was clothed with **festal robes**. Fundamentally, these garments were fine and white. They stood in vivid contrast to Joshua's filth. His brilliant new attire did not come from his own efforts but was a gift of God's grace. Though in practice Joshua was still a sinner, in position he was now righteous, having been clothed in the impeccable righteousness of Christ. Isaiah 53:11 prophesied of the Messiah, that "by His knowledge the Righteous One, My Servant, will justify the many." The way God declares people righteous is by covering them in the righteousness of His Son. As Paul said in 2 Corinthians 5:21, "He made Him who knew no sin *to be* sin on our behalf, so that we might become the righteousness of God in Him." Paul elsewhere explained his desire to "be found in Him, not having a righteousness of my own which is from *the* Law, but that which is through faith in Christ, the righteousness which *is* from God upon faith" (Phil 3:9). Even the most religious acts of self-righteous sinners are filthy garments (Isa 64:6), but in salvation, the sinner's filthy clothes are replaced with the garments of Christ's righteousness.

These **festal robes** were not only pure, but also designed for feasting and celebration. As the Lord Jesus stated in the parable of the wedding feast, those who do not have the proper clothes cannot attend the wedding feast of the Son (cf. Matt 22:11–14). Only when people are made right with God, being clothed with Christ's righteousness, can they enjoy fellowship with Him. Since Joshua had been given such garments, there was a future not only for Joshua, but also for those he represented. Through His work of substitutionary atonement, the Messiah would not only strip away the filth that sullied His people, but He would also clothe them with a righteousness they could never achieve on their own.

In a surprising turn, verse 5 opened with the clause **then I said**, as

Zechariah started talking and thus participating in the vision. But this was no intrusion. In other visions, God had His prophets participate to show that what God was revealing would affect His people. For example, in Isaiah's vision, the prophet was touched by a burning coal to show that Israel's sin would be atoned for (cf. Isa 6:7; 53:1–12). Likewise, in Ezekiel's vision (Ezek 2:1–2), the Spirit entered into Ezekiel to foreshadow His indwelling ministry in the hearts of God's people (36:27). In this case, the Lord prompted Zechariah to urge the angels to **put a clean turban on his** [Joshua's] **head**. The turban was the last item of clothing the priest would don at his ordination (Lev 8:9). In calling for this, Zechariah expressed his desire to see the priest's consecration completed. Such enthusiasm prefigured that the people would one day unite with the priest in following God. This scene anticipates the future time when "all Israel will be saved" (Rom 11:26), being justified by God on account of the Messiah's work.

As soon as Zechariah spoke the word, the angelic helpers **put a clean turban on his head**, not merely because this was the last piece of attire to put on the priest (see above), but for two additional reasons. First, the **clean** turban starkly contrasted the filth Joshua had previously been wearing. It was a vivid reminder that he was now clothed in a righteousness not his own, but that which comes from the Lord (Phil 3:9). Second, the **turban** indicated that Joshua was truly ordained and ready for priestly service (cf. Exod 29:6; 39:31; Lev 8:9). In the Old Testament, the priest's turban had a sign that read "Holy to Yahweh" (Exod 28:36; 39:30), designating that the priest was set apart, consecrated, dedicated to Yahweh, and totally belonging to Him. Putting the **turban on** Joshua's **head** signified that Joshua was officially consecrated for the work of leading the people in worship.

To that end, Zechariah also mentioned that Joshua was **clothed with garments**. Joshua did not merely have a clean robe and turban; he was dressed in holy fashion from head to toe. He was not clean in part, but in whole. The term **garments** here is the same word that earlier described Joshua's filthy attire (cf. Zech 3:3–4). All of Joshua's filth was replaced, showing that God had changed Joshua's status from unclean (guilty) to clean (righteous). In this way, Joshua was justified in the courtroom of heaven and commissioned for service to the Lord, a picture of what will happen for Israel and its priests in the future (cf. Isa 61:6).

One additional aspect of Joshua's attire is also significant. The word for **turban** in Hebrew is not the usual term used to describe the priest's garb. In another usage, it refers to a royal diadem or crown (cf. Isa 62:3), indicating that it was not only priestly but also royal. Accordingly, this vision portrayed Joshua as a Priest-King, which is a surprising image since no Israelite priest could also be king. Priests and kings were from two different tribes (Heb 7:13–17). But this depiction of Joshua as a Priest-King was critical. It is the first time this dual role appears in the book of Zechariah, but it is not the last. The very next chapter also presents this imagery (Zech 4:14), and in Zechariah 6:9–15, Joshua the High Priest received a crown on his head. The Lord intended this image of a priest and king to show that, while no mere man could assume both offices, the Messiah could and in fact did. The Messiah is the culmination of these combined roles: He is the King who sits at the right hand of His Father (Ps 110:1–3) and He is the great High Priest who is of the order of Melchizedek (110:4; cf. Gen 14:18).

At this point in Zechariah's vision, Joshua was not merely presented as a recipient of Christ's work; he was also recast to prefigure Christ. Joshua pointed to the Messiah as the only One who, as both King and High Priest, can accomplish the salvation that His people need. As the author of Hebrews later proclaimed, those in the line of Levi could never achieve forgiveness for sin (cf. Heb 10:1–4). Only the great High Priest and King, the One who is of the order of Melchizedek, is able to do so (cf. Heb 7:11–17; 10:12).

This explains why verse 5 concludes with the statement **"while the angel of Yahweh was standing by."** The word "stand" has been used repeatedly in this fourth vision. Joshua stood before the Angel of Yahweh for both intercession (Zech 3:1) and imputed righteousness (3:3). Now, the Angel of Yahweh **was standing by** as a reminder that He was the One who accomplished all of this for Joshua and for His people. Although Joshua was a major figure in this fourth vision, he was not the central person. Rather, the Angel of Yahweh, the Messiah, was the main character all along. In this way, God showed Zechariah (and all

Israel) that He had not forgotten His promises about the Messiah, the ultimate High Priest and King. He is the One who ever intercedes for His own, clothing them in His righteousness so they might offer acceptable worship and service to God.

The Fourth Night Vision, Part 2: God's Relationship with Israel

Zechariah 3:6–7

And the angel of Yahweh testified to Joshua, saying, "Thus says Yahweh of hosts, 'If you will walk in My ways and if you will keep the responsibility *given by* **Me, then you will also render justice in My house and also keep My courts, and I will grant you access to walk among these who are standing here.'"**

Worship is God's ultimate priority. The Father seeks true worshipers (John 4:23), those who offer themselves to Him as living sacrifices (Rom 12:1–2), viewing even the most routine activities as opportunities to give God glory (1 Cor 10:31). It is not surprising, then, that having cleansed Joshua, clothing him in righteous garments, the Angel of Yahweh commanded him to take up his responsibility as High Priest and lead Israel in worship.

In God's plan, the Lord raised up Israel to be a kingdom of priests (Exod 19:5–6), a nation to lead other nations in the worship of the one true God (Deut 4:6–8; Zech 8:23). With their tabernacle/temple, sacrificial system, yearly festivals, and psalms of praise, Israel was to be a nation of worshipers inviting other nations to join with them in serving the Lord (cf. Ps 117:1). Within this, God used priests to lead His kingdom of priests in worship. They maintained the tabernacle/temple, led the congregation in praise, administered the sacrifices, and taught the Scriptures. God called His people to worship Him not only as individuals but also as a community, doing so corporately, publicly, and nationally. His worthiness was to be proclaimed and adored on every level. The priests were privileged to lead the people in this activity, which is the reason the priesthood was to be characterized by joy and celebration. The psalmist declared, "Let Your priests be clothed with righteousness, and let Your holy ones sing for joy" (Ps 132:9). The psalmist also said of the priests, "May Yahweh bless you from Zion, who made heaven and earth" (134:3). Israel looked forward to the time when such worship would be fully realized and when the priests would lead the world in pure and passionate praise. Such a time would represent the culmination of God's relationship, not only with the nation of Israel but also with the priests.

That culmination never took place in Israel's history. The priests consistently abandoned their responsibilities and perverted their God-given role. The prophet Hosea indicted them for their failure, stating:

> Yet let no man contend, and let no man offer reproof;
> Indeed, your people are like those who contend with the priest.
> So you will stumble by day,
> And the prophet also will stumble with you by night;
> And I will destroy your mother.
> My people are destroyed for lack of knowledge.
> Because you have rejected knowledge,
> I also will reject you from ministering as My priest.
> Since you have forgotten the law of your God,
> I Myself also will forget your children. (Hos 4:4–6)

Priests were supposed to teach the knowledge of God to the people, but they could not do so if they themselves did not know Him. Many of the priests rejected the law they were ordained to uphold. So, God declared that He rejected them, stating that both they and their offspring would be spurned from serving Him. Subsequently, in Israel's history, the Babylonians conquered Judah and destroyed the temple, taking the priests into captivity (2 Kgs 25:8–21). The nation, by continuing in its sin, forfeited God's blessing and experienced His judgment (Ezek 44:10–14).

However, that was not the end of the story. God did not forget His promises to His remnant nor to the priests. The Lord's promise of an unending priesthood was set by the priestly covenant in Numbers 25:10–13:

> Then Yahweh spoke to Moses, saying, "Phinehas the son of Eleazar, the son of Aaron the priest, has turned away My wrath from the sons of Israel in that he was jealous with My jealousy among them, so that I did not consume the sons of Israel in My jealousy. Therefore say, 'Behold, I give him My covenant of peace; and it shall be for him and his seed after him, a covenant of a perpetual priesthood, because he was jealous for his God and made atonement for the sons of Israel.'"

That covenant given to Phinehas and his descendants promised an enduring priesthood until the fulfillment of God's full promise to bless both priests and people. The prophet Jeremiah revealed that the priesthood would continue when he wrote: "The Levitical priests shall not have a man cut off from before Me who is to offer burnt offerings, to offer up grain offerings in smoke, and to perform sacrifices continually" (Jer 33:18). This priestly activity will continue into Christ's future kingdom and the millennial temple. In Ezekiel 44:15, God announced, "But the Levitical priests, the sons of Zadok, who kept the responsibility of My sanctuary when the sons of Israel went astray from Me, shall come near to Me to minister to Me; and they shall stand before Me to bring near to Me the fat and the blood." God declared that though some of the Levites were unfaithful in days past, the tribe of Levi would still minister in the future temple (Ezek 44:10–11). However, not all the Levites will make offerings or enter the most Holy Place (44:10–14) since only the line of Zadok will be given these privileges (44:15–16; cf. 48:11). The reason for this is the value God placed on Zadok's faithfulness (1 Sam 2:35; 2 Sam 15:24ff; 1 Kgs 1:32–40; 2:26–35). So, God will keep His promises to the priestly line of Israel.

In these passages related to the millennial temple, the priests' activity will not be atoning. The burnt and grain offerings that the priests offer will be used for worship and thanksgiving, commemorating and celebrating the once-for-all work that Christ completed on the cross. During the millennial kingdom, God will once again use the priests of Israel to lead the world in worship. In doing so, the priests will enjoy the privilege and blessing that the Lord promised them in the priestly covenant (Num 25:10–13).[1]

This helps explain the significance of the divine commands from the Angel of Yahweh to Joshua the High Priest, directing Joshua to fulfill his responsibility to lead God's people in worship. These commands not only teach about worship generally, but also point to the specific promise that Israel will not be cut off from serving the Lord in His future kingdom. One day, Israel's priests will be given the honor of leading Israel and the world in true and full worship. Though the Levites deserved to be cast aside for their unfaithfulness, God will cleanse them and invite them to serve in His presence. As improbable as it may seem in this world, a time will come when all the nations will join Israel in worshiping Yahweh.

Believers today can marvel that God will remember His promises to the undeserving line of Levi. Their participation in worship during the millennial kingdom will be a compelling testimony to the faithful goodness and mercy of God. The Lord will graciously overcome Israel's sin in order to save His people and equip them for service. In this passage, the Messiah Himself reiterated the responsibility to worship (Zech 3:6–7a), the reward for worship (3:7b), and the relationship within worship (3:7c).

THE RESPONSIBILITY TO WORSHIP

And the angel of Yahweh testified to Joshua, saying, "Thus says Yahweh of hosts, 'If you will walk in My ways and if you will keep the responsibility given by Me...'" (3:6–7a)

---

1 "The perpetual nature of the priestly covenant suggests that it stands as a separate covenant and not as a part of the Mosaic Covenant, which is temporary. First, the terminology employed is similar to the covenants made with Noah, Abraham, David, and the new covenant. Second, that it remains when the Mosaic covenant was rendered obsolete speaks even louder for its standing as a separate covenant. The Mosaic covenant was abrogated by the new covenant, but the promise given to Phinehas continues into the millennium. Third, the language of Jeremiah 33:20–21 places its permanence alongside the Davidic covenant, contending that it remains in force as long as the cycle of day and night remains." John MacArthur, ed., *Essential Christian Doctrine: A Handbook on Biblical Truth* (Wheaton, IL: Crossway, 2021), 451.

Having clothed and cleansed the High Priest and made him fit for service, **the angel of Yahweh testified to Joshua**. The term **testified** is often used in affirming a solemn warning. It is to bear witness to the full weight, authority, and accountability brought by the demands of a law or command (cf. Deut 4:26; 8:19; 30:19; 31:28; I Sam 8:9; I Kgs 2:42). Contrary to the shallowness of modern church trends and fads, worship is the most serious responsibility. For that reason, the Lord often gave a weighty charge to those who sought to worship Him in an acceptable manner (Lev 10:1–3; Eccl 5:1; John 4:21–24; I Cor 11:23–34). Just as a Christian is freed from sin not for licentiousness but to walk in righteousness (cf. Rom 6:18), so God cleansed the High Priest to make him useful for service and ready to discharge his duties. With that in view, the Angel of Yahweh impressed upon Joshua the gravitas of what he was called to do to fulfill his God-given role.

Joshua's responsibility was first to **walk in My ways**. The language of **walk** depicts life as a road or path. Summing up Enoch's godly life, Moses wrote in Genesis 5:24, "Enoch walked with God." In contrast to this, Paul described unbelievers as those who walk in their transgressions and sins (Eph 2:1–2). The language of transgressions and trespass describes people deliberately deviating from the path prescribed by God, and instead choosing to walk on their own road of sin. When Christ commanded Joshua to walk in **My ways**, He was demanding what God always requires of His people—a life conformed to His Word. In the New Testament, Paul particularly presented the characteristics of a worthy walk in his letter to the Ephesians. He noted that the Lord calls believers to walk worthy of the gospel (Eph 4:1), to walk differently than unbelievers (4:17), to walk in love (5:1), to walk in light (5:8), and to walk in wisdom (5:15).

The Lord's exhortation in verse 6 was not just for Joshua but for all who lead. Because spiritual leadership is so important, God requires those in such positions to exhibit a life of continual consecration and consistent obedience. New Testament elders are not qualified to serve in that leadership role simply because they can teach. Rather, the Lord requires that their lives be honoring to Him in every respect (cf. I Tim 3:1–6). Indeed, walking in God's ways is the standard for all believers who desire to worship the Lord in spirit and in truth.

Still, Joshua needed to **keep the responsibility given by Me.** The Hebrew root behind the term **responsibility** is the word "keep" or "pay attention." A responsibility is a task entrusted into one's care. The word was often used to describe the job of the priests and the tribe of Levi (Lev 8:35; 22:9; Num 1:53; 3:7, 8, 25, 28, 31, 32, 36, 38). In the millennial kingdom, the priests will have the responsibility to maintain the temple grounds (Ezek 40:45) and the altar (40:46), as well as many of the worship activities that take place in and around the temple (44:14).

These commands to Joshua were a symbol of a glorious future. Throughout Israel's history, the priests were never able to carry out their responsibilities with perfect faithfulness. But a time will come, in the millennial kingdom, when they will be transformed by the Messiah, just as Christ cleansed Joshua in this vision. In that day, the Lord will give Israel's priests the weighty charge pronounced here to Joshua. Having been transformed by Him, they will finally be able to fulfill the calling given to them: to lead the people in true and full worship.

God's charge of responsibility to Joshua serves as a reminder that while no work of man can contribute to salvation, God's work of salvation enables every believer to respond in obedience and good works (cf. Eph 2:10). Though not everyone was a High Priest like Joshua, Israel was a kingdom of priests (Exod 19:5–6). In giving this charge to Joshua, the Lord showed that He remembered what He had promised to the line of priests and to the entire nation. In the Millennium, He will not only give Israel an opportunity to fulfill and enjoy this glorious honor, but He will transform them so that they are able to do so effectively.

THE REWARD FOR WORSHIP

"'...then you will also render justice in My house and also keep My courts...'" (3:7b)

In general, priests had two major roles in Israel. They served as mediators from God to man as they taught people to understand the law of the Lord (cf. Deut 17:8–13). Conversely, they also functioned as mediators from man to God as they led the people in worship through the sacrificial system (Lev 1–7). If the priests faithfully fulfilled their God-given responsibilities, they would experience divine blessing. Sadly, throughout Israel's history, the priests never fully realized that blessing, due to their sin and unfaithfulness. However, in the millennial kingdom, God will equip them to serve Him faithfully. They will then enjoy the full privileges and rich blessings He promised to them.

At that future time, the priesthood will fulfill its role in explaining God's law to man. Thus, the Angel of Yahweh explained to Joshua, **"Then you will also render justice in My house."** To **render justice** is not merely to govern or rule, but specifically to give judicial counsel and pronounce decisions. In Israel's history, priests were often consulted to settle difficult legal cases (cf. Deut 17:8–13). The prophet confirmed here that this will happen during the Millennium as well. Isaiah prophesied that at that time, many nations will come to Jerusalem to learn God's commands, and the Lord will rule over every nation, rendering decisions for them (Isa 2:2–4). And Ezekiel foretold that the priests will play a role in this process: "In a dispute, they shall take their stand to judge; they shall judge it according to My judgments. They shall also keep My laws and My statutes in all My appointed times and keep My sabbaths holy" (Ezek 44:24). In the millennial kingdom, Israel's priests will serve under the Priest-King, the Messiah, to aid in maintaining justice. Such is the ultimate priestly honor, to serve alongside the Angel of Yahweh—the Lord Jesus Christ.

God further declared that in the future the priests would lead not only in justice but also in worship. The Lord promised Joshua that he would **"also keep My courts."** The word **keep** generates a word play in the immediate context. The priests could "keep" God's court because they had "kept" their God-given responsibilities (see Zech 3:7a). This play on words emphasized the tight connection between obedience and the priests' rich reward and privilege of leading in worship. The term **courts** refers to the area surrounding the temple building itself (1 Chr 28:6). Historically, and tragically, the courts were where Israel's unfaithfulness to Yahweh was often manifested. In Isaiah, God condemned the faulty sacrifices that took place in those courts (Isa 1:12). Ezekiel too noted how idolatry was practiced in that area (Ezek 8:16). For this reason, the courts were the place where God's judgment began (9:7).

By contrast, the courts described in Zechariah's vision are the courts in the millennial temple described by Ezekiel (Ezek 40–48) and alluded to by Isaiah (Isa 2:2–4), Jeremiah (Jer 33:18), and Zechariah himself (Zech 2:5). These courts will be an architectural marvel with massive pillars (Ezek 40:14), paved stones (40:17), formidable gates (40:23), and vast spaces (40:19–20). The priests will be the stewards of that exquisite and expansive area. It would be a great privilege simply to gain access to such a glorious place. But the priests will do more. They will lead in the activities that occur in that part of the temple complex. Formerly the location of spiritual infidelity, the courts will be filled with genuine worship, and the priests will be at the head of the exuberant assembly. They will finally fulfill their duties without compromise or failure (44:21), as they lead people in offering sacrifices of thankfulness to Yahweh. To be in the center of such joyous celebration will be an unparalleled honor. On that day, because of the work of the Messiah on their behalf, the priests will finally realize the profound blessings and joy God promised them long ago.

Such is the beautiful ending to the story of God's relationship with the tribe of Levi. Throughout Israel's history, the priests were sinful, failing to serve the Lord, at times acting with extreme wickedness, and even rejecting the Lord for idols. They deserved to be rejected by God because they truly were a priesthood with dirty robes (like Joshua in the vision). Nevertheless, the Lord did not negate His promises to them. Rather, in the future, He will raise up a cleansed priesthood, purged by the work of their Messiah. As a result, they will experience the honor and privilege that God designed for them as they lead the world in worship.

All of this testifies to the truth that the Lord will fulfill every promise He gave to His priests. For the Israelites of Zechariah's day, that truth would have been greatly encouraging, as they worked to rebuild the temple. Indeed, for all believers from every nation, faith and hope are built on this foundation: that God always remembers His promises to His people.

THE RELATIONSHIP IN WORSHIP

"'...and I will grant you access to walk among these who are standing here.'" (3:7c)

In Israel's history, the priests not only experienced the privilege of serving God, but also enjoyed the blessing of standing in special relationship to Him. Priestly privilege was entirely a gift of divine grace, a truth punctuated by what the Angel of Yahweh said to Joshua: **"I will grant you."** The Lord's blessings—whether to the Levitical priests, to Israel, or to the church—are not in any way deserved. No one can claim to have merited God's blessings. On the other hand, no one can assert it is unfair for the Lord to give a privilege to one person and not to another. God's blessings are based solely upon His loving and gracious choice (Exod 33:19; Rom 9:14–18; cf. 1 Cor 12:4–6).

For the priests, God promised that one day they will have **access to walk among these who are standing *here*.** The clause **these who are standing here** referred to the angels who were involved in the vision (cf. Zech 3:4, 5). These angels ministered before the Lord Himself. Therefore, to have **access to walk** among them implies that the priests will move freely in the presence of God. The Lord promised that in the millennial kingdom He will dwell with His people, and that His glory will be in their midst (cf. Isa 4:2–3; Ezek 43:1–5; Zech 2:5). The priests will draw near to Him without any hesitation, just like the angels who are constantly before Him (Isa 6:1–2; Rev 4:1–5). In this way, the Angel of Yahweh told the High Priest that if he would **walk** in God's ways, he would ultimately walk among angels in the presence of God in heaven. In the Millennium, the ultimate blessing of worship for the priests will be the intimate communion they enjoy with God in His presence.

As distinctive as they are, the priests are not the only ones who will enjoy such close access to the Lord. As Scripture reveals, God already indwells the heart of every believer (cf. Ezek 36:26; cf. 2 Cor 6:16–18). Though the priests may experience this in some unique way during the millennial kingdom, all believers already enjoy intimate fellowship with God because He lives within them. The object of worship—God

Himself—is the highest reward of worship. Though His presence is a present reward, in the glory to come such fellowship will involve intensified communion with Him (cf. 1 John 3:2; Rev 22:1–4). What a glorious day that will be, when the world gathers with the priests in Jerusalem to worship Yahweh with pure hearts and unbridled affection.

The Fourth Night Vision, Part 3: The Priest-King Messiah

Zechariah 3:8–10

"'Now listen, Joshua the high priest, you and your friends who are sitting in front of you—indeed they are men who are a wondrous sign, for behold, I am going to bring in My servant the Branch. For behold, the stone that I have put before Joshua; on one stone are seven eyes. Behold, I will engrave an inscription on it,' declares Yahweh of hosts, 'and I will remove the iniquity of that land in one day. In that day,' declares Yahweh of hosts, 'every one of you will call for his neighbor to *sit* under *his* vine and under *his* fig tree.'"

No theme in Scripture is more central than Christ. He is the subject of God's first promise (Gen 3:15), a promise that set the trajectory for God's plan of redemption. From the beginning, all of history flows from Christ and leads to Him. Eve anticipated the Messiah when she hoped her firstborn child would be the one obtained from the Lord to defeat the devil (4:1). The patriarchs looked for Him as God revealed that kings were to come from Abraham (17:6), and that the ultimate King would be like Melchizedek, a King of righteousness who was also a priest (Gen 14:18; cf. Psa 110:1–4). Jacob declared that the scepter (a symbol of authority) would not depart from Judah, and that the Messiah would come from that tribe, having the title "Shiloh," or peace (Gen 49:10; cf. Isa 9:6).

In the time of David, greater detail was revealed about the Messiah. The Davidic covenant included precious promises about His coming reign (2 Sam 7:1–14), indicating that the weight of Israel's destiny—and thereby the blessing of the whole world—would rest on the Messiah's shoulders. The Psalms resonated with that same theme. They recounted Christ's suffering (Ps 22), resurrection (Ps 16), vindication (Ps 6:8), triumph (Ps 110), and reign (Pss 2; 24; 72).

The portrayal of the Messiah continued in the time of Solomon whose reign foreshadowed the blessings of the millennial kingdom. Solomon's rule was characterized by peace, as each person dwelt under his own vine and fig tree (1 Kgs 4:25; cf. Zech 3:10), Israel was filled with prosperity, and the surrounding nations came and were blessed (1 Kgs 10:8–9). Under Solomon, Israel had a preview of the fulfillment of what God promised to Abraham long before: "In you all the families of the earth will be blessed" (Gen 12:3).

As the history of Israel progressed, the kings failed and Israel constantly faced dark periods of disobedience. However, the prophets remained steadfast in declaring the hope of the coming Messiah. Isaiah prophesied that Christ would be virgin born (Isa 7:14), that His name would be Mighty God and the Prince of Peace (9:6), and that His reign would last forever (9:7). Ezekiel declared that the Messiah would be the Good Shepherd who leads His people safely home (cf. Ezek 34:1–24). Jeremiah stated that Christ would be the Prophet, Priest, and King who is able to succeed where Israel's entire leadership failed (cf. Jer 23:5–22). These and many other Old Testament texts demonstrate the centrality of Christ within the redemptive plan of God. The Messiah is the One who fulfills all history and theology, prophecy, and covenant.

It is therefore fitting that this theme would be found near the end of Old Testament history, in the book of Zechariah, whose prophecy assured Israel that God remembers His promises. Significantly, at the very center of Zechariah's eight night visions, God focused on the central figure of redemptive history: His Son, the Messiah. This fourth vision had already indicated that Christ is the One who intercedes for (cf. Zech 3:2), cleanses (cf. 3:4–5), and restores His people (cf. 3:6–7). In verses 8–10, the Lord made it crystal clear that this vision was indeed about the Messiah (3:8). After noting the significance of Joshua and his friends (3:8a), He described the service (3:8b), supremacy (3:9a), salvation (3:9b), and success (3:10) of Israel's great High Priest and ultimate King.

THE SIGNIFICANCE OF JOSHUA AND HIS FRIENDS

"'Now listen, Joshua the high priest, you and your friends who are sitting in front of you—indeed they are men who are a wondrous sign...'" (3:8a)

In the vision, the Angel of Yahweh continued to speak, and His words took an urgent tone. He exclaimed, **"Now listen, Joshua the high priest, you and your friends who are sitting in front of you."** The imperative **now listen** conveyed a passionate command to stop talking and pay full attention to what was going to be said. The directive punctuated the importance of the truth about to be revealed.

The people addressed were **Joshua the high priest, you and your friends who are sitting in front of you.** At the beginning of this vision, **Joshua** stood before the Angel of Yahweh and depended on the Angel to intercede for him (cf. Zech 3:2–3) and to cleanse him (cf. 3:4–5). He needed spiritual transformation and the very righteousness of Christ (cf. 2 Cor 5:21). As **high priest,** he was the leader of all the priests of Israel, having the distinctive privilege, once a year on the Day of Atonement, to offer the sacrifice at the mercy seat on behalf of the priesthood and the entire nation (cf. Lev 16:11–19). In this vision, Joshua was even uniquely clothed in garments of a royal priest to accomplish this role (cf. Zech 3:4–5). As the vision continued to unfold in verse 8, Joshua was seen with his **friends who** were **sitting in front of** him. The term **friends** can also mean "companions" to denote someone who is a peer. These individuals were not to be confused with the angelic helpers involved earlier in the vision (cf. Zech 3:4, 5, 7). The angels were standing before the Angel of Yahweh, but those mentioned here were **sitting in front of** Joshua. The implication is that these individuals were fellow priests, those who similarly represented Israel by virtue of their office (see discussion on 3:1).

The significance of Joshua and his friends is stated in the description: **"indeed they are men who are a wondrous sign."** A

wondrous sign refers to a miraculous act or mighty work of God, either in history (cf. Exod 4:21; 7:3, 9; Neh 9:10) or the future (cf. 1 Kgs 13:3; 2 Chr 32:24; Isa 8:18). This scene portrayed a future reality related to Christ's return and the establishment of His earthly kingdom. Joshua, clothed in pure and festal robes (Zech 3:4) with a royal and priestly turban (3:5), prefigured the ultimate Priest-King, the Messiah. He demonstrated that the Messiah will not only be the great High Priest, but also the ultimate King (cf. 6:11, 13; Ps 110:1, 3–4; Ezek 21:26). This Priest-King Messiah will be the culmination of all of Israel's leadership, both royal and religious.

The men sitting in front of Joshua prefigured the day when Israel and its priests will sit before the Messiah in eager adherence and humble submission to Him. Just as the Angel of Yahweh stripped Joshua's filth and gave him new clothes so that he would be fit to serve (Zech 3:4–5), so the Messiah will redeem the priests and the nation when He returns (cf. Isa 61:6; Jer 33:18–22; Ezek 44:15–31). In this way, Joshua standing in front of his fellow priests provided a symbolic image of the future day when the Messiah will save and sanctify His people Israel (cf. Rom 11:26).

THE SERVICE OF THE PRIEST-KING MESSIAH

"'...for behold, I am going to bring in My servant the Branch.'" (3:8b)

With the word **for**, God explained that Israel will be cleansed because of the Person and work of the Messiah. In the rest of this passage, the Lord revealed wonderful truths about Christ, declaring, **"behold, I am going to bring."** The language of **behold** with the verb **I am going to bring** not only drew attention to what the Lord was saying, but also emphasized the certainty and imminence of His actions.

In introducing His Messiah, God used two titles. The first was **"My servant."** Throughout Scripture, the title **"servant"** is used to refer to those whom God uses in a special way to fulfill His purposes. This included individuals like Abraham (Gen 26:24), Moses (Num 12:7), Caleb (Num 14:24), and David (2 Sam 3:18), all of whom were called "my servant" by God. However, the ultimate usage of this title was in reference to the Messiah. He had the critical distinction of being the One who would accomplish God's salvation (Isa 49:4–6), by providing the perfect righteousness that God requires and that sinners desperately need (cf. 50:1–4). The Servant of Yahweh would do this by offering Himself as the final sacrifice for sin (cf. Isa 52:13–53:12; Mark 10:45). The title "Servant" in Isaiah points to the seminal importance of the Messiah and His work of atonement, justification, and salvation. Because of His redemptive work, Israel could be cleansed.

The second title is **"the Branch."** In the Old Testament, "the Branch" was used of the Messiah in four ways. First, the Messiah was called a Branch of David, which speaks of His place as King (Isa 11:1; Jer 23:5). That became a theme in the gospel of Matthew. Second, this very verse in Zechariah emphasized the Branch as God's Suffering Servant (see above). The gospel of Mark featured Jesus in such a light. Third, in Zechariah 6:12–13, the Messiah was called the Man whose name is the Branch, thereby highlighting His humanity. The gospel of Luke emphasized Christ as the perfect man. Finally, in Isaiah 4:2, the deity of the Messiah was declared in His title "the Branch of Yahweh." John's gospel was written to reveal that Christ Jesus is truly God and man. Thus, the rich theology encompassed within the term Branch can be seen in detail in the New Testament gospels.

The Lord also called the Messiah **"the Branch"** because this title emphasized His incarnation and humility. Just as a branch sprouts from a plant, so the Messiah would descend from the royal line as the lowly **Branch** (Isa 11:1). Though He is God (4:2; 7:14; 9:6), He would come as a baby (7:14; 9:6). And as a humble tender shoot, He would die for His people (52:13–53:12). The title **"Branch"** identifies Jesus as the humble, rejected priest, who would offer Himself as the once-for-all sacrifice for the sins of His people.

With that, God reiterated the saving role of the Messiah. As the Servant of Yahweh, He would perfectly fulfill the work of atonement and justification. And as the messianic Branch, He would accomplish this salvation through His humiliation and sacrifice. He would give Himself up to endure the wrath of God in the place of His people, to secure their eternal forgiveness, cleansing, and salvation.

THE SUPREMACY OF THE PRIEST-KING MESSIAH

"'For behold, the stone that I have put before Joshua; on one stone are seven eyes.'" (3:9a)

Having discussed the Messiah as Servant and Branch, God focused **(for behold)** upon another title for the Messiah: **"the stone."** Earlier, Joshua stood *before* the Angel of Yahweh, the Messiah (Zech 3:3). Here, the stone was **put before** Joshua. In placing the stone in a parallel position with the Angel of Yahweh, the Lord indicated that **the stone** was a symbol of the Messiah.

Stone and its synonyms are used as a title for Christ throughout Scripture. In Isaiah 8:14, the Messiah was called a stone of stumbling and a rock of offense. In Isaiah 28:16, He was called a stone of refuge. For those who rejected Him, He was a stone of stumbling; but for those who embraced Him in faith, He became a stone of refuge. Additionally, the imagery of a stone pertains to the Messiah's sovereignty over the nations. In Daniel 2:34–35 and 44–45 the Messiah is the stone cut out without hands that smashes the Gentile world powers. In the New Testament, the term "stone" also relates to the Messiah's role in the church as the chief cornerstone (Eph 2:20). As these examples illustrate, "stone" is a prevalent title for Christ.

As the great High Priest, the Messiah is called **the stone** because He makes His people a temple or sanctuary, for which He serves as the foundation (cf. 1 Cor 3:11). The prophet Isaiah explained that Christ is both Israel's sanctuary and its stone. In Isaiah 8:14, Isaiah declared, "Then He shall become a sanctuary; but to both the houses of Israel, a stone to strike and a rock to stumble over, *and* a snare and a trap for the inhabitants of Jerusalem." Later, Isaiah said, "Therefore thus says Lord Yahweh, 'Behold, I am laying in Zion a stone, a tested stone, a costly cornerstone *for* the foundation, firmly placed. He who believes *in it* will not be disturbed'" (28:16). Likewise, Psalm 118 declared, "The stone which the builders rejected has become the chief corner *stone*" (Ps 118:22). The Old Testament declared the Messiah to be the foundation of Zion and even its central structure, the temple (cf. John 2:19). Both Paul and Peter described our Lord as the cornerstone of believers who are built up into a temple for God (cf. Eph 2:20; 1 Pet 2:5–8). In Zechariah's day, Israel was struggling to rebuild the temple (Ezra 4–5). With the title **"stone,"** Zechariah reminded the nation that the Messiah will not merely build a temple (cf. Zech 2:10), but that He will make His people the temple, the very dwelling place of God (cf. Ezek 3:1–2; 1 Cor 6:19; Eph 2:20; 1 Pet 2:5–8). All of this takes place only because Christ the stumbling **stone** was first rejected but then exalted as the cornerstone (cf. Ps 118:22).

In this vision, God further described that **on one stone are seven eyes.** The symbolism of **seven eyes** refers to God's omniscience—that He sees and knows everything perfectly. The next night vision (Zech 4:1–14) confirmed this interpretation by depicting God's seven eyes roaming to and fro throughout the earth (cf. 4:10). That vision also associated God's omniscient activity with the Holy Spirit (4:6). So, the symbol of a stone with seven eyes revealed two fundamental truths: that the Messiah is God Himself, all-knowing and all-seeing, and that He is empowered by the Holy Spirit. The Spirit's empowerment of the Messiah is reiterated elsewhere in Scripture. Earlier in the Old Testament, Isaiah declared that there would be a sevenfold ministry of the Spirit with the Messiah (Isa 11:1–2). The book of Revelation also made this association, describing a "Lamb standing, as if slain, having seven horns and seven eyes, which are the seven Spirits of God, sent out into all the earth" (Rev 5:6; cf. 1:4). Prior to Christ's first advent, the Holy Spirit empowered other select individuals for service (cf. Exod 31:3; 1 Sam 11:6; 19:23; Ps 51:11), but this sevenfold anointing demonstrated that the Messiah was in a category all His own. He was and is the ultimate and unequalled great High Priest and King of Israel (Isa 11:1–2). As such, the divine Messiah is authenticated and empowered by the Spirit of God to accomplish His mission as the Stone, to make His people a holy sanctuary.

THE SALVATION OF THE PRIEST-KING MESSIAH

"'Behold, I will engrave an inscription on it,' declares Yahweh of hosts, 'and I will remove the iniquity of that land in one day.'" (3:9b)

The word **behold** is used here to draw attention to the work God promised to do through the messianic Stone. The Lord declared, "**I will engrave an inscription on it.**" In Israel's history, a craftsman engraved the names of the tribes of Israel on two stones of the High Priest's uniform (cf. Exod 28:11, 21, 36; 39:6, 14). These engravings symbolized his role as a mediator for the nation. In the same way, God declared He would **engrave** on Christ, the Stone, the names of the elect to show the certainty of their salvation. The Apostle Paul articulated this reality in Romans 8, "Those whom He predestined, He also called; and those whom He called, He also justified; and those whom He justified, He also glorified" (Rom 8:30). Christ's redemptive work is not potential but particular. The names of His elect are engraved on His heart, and He will secure their salvation by an unbreakable chain of redemption.

So, in the future, Christ will accomplish the full deliverance of those He came to save. Yahweh further revealed to Zechariah: "**I will remove the iniquity of that land in one day.**" The word **remove** denotes complete elimination, while the term **iniquity** not only refers to one's wrongdoing but to all the guilt and harmful consequences that ensue from sin. Just as the Angel of Yahweh cleansed Joshua from his filthy clothes and iniquity (cf. Zech 3:4), so in the future, Yahweh will erase the stain of sin from His people. God's purifying work will be so great that even the **land** will be cleansed, a point on which the next verse elaborates. Such atonement does not come by Israel's merit or accomplishment; rather, God explicitly stated that He ("I") will take away the transgressions of His people, accomplishing their salvation solely through the Messiah's priestly work.

This redemption will take place **in one day**. The basis for this great salvation is what God did in one day at Calvary, when the Lamb of God took away the sins of the world. But the specific **one day** referred to here is described in greater detail in the prophets and later in the book of Zechariah. This will be that day when the nation that rejected their Messiah looks on the One whom they have pierced and mourns for Him as one mourns for an only son (Zech 12:10). "In that day," Zechariah declared, "a fountain will be opened for the house of David and for the inhabitants of Jerusalem, for sin and for impurity" (13:1). While there have been thousands of festival days in Israel's history, there will be one day in the future when the entire nation, every Jewish person within the surviving remnant, will be saved (13:9; 14:2; cf. Rom 11:26). That will be the greatest single day of Israel's history. On that day, it will be unmistakably clear that the Lord Jesus Christ is the One depicted in this passage: the Servant who perfectly fulfills God's promises, the Branch who suffered and died for sin, and the Stone who mediates for His people and makes them into the dwelling place of God.

THE SUCCESS OF THE PRIEST-KING MESSIAH

"'In that day,' declares Yahweh of hosts, 'every one of you will call for his neighbor to sit under his vine and under his fig tree.'" (3:10)

The phrase **in that day** builds upon what the prophet spoke about in the previous verse. It refers to the future day when Israel will repent, believe, and be forgiven. At that time, God will not only grant forgiveness, but also provide all the blessings of salvation. Those wondrous benefits only come through the atoning work of the great High Priest, the Messiah.

When that day comes, **every one of you will call for his neighbor.** To **call** expresses the idea of an invitation, welcoming others to have fellowship and join in celebration (Job 1:4). The description implies that the Israelites will be at peace with one another and with the nations around them. This was certainly not true throughout Israel's history (cf. Judg 19:1–21:25; 2 Kgs 18:1–19:37). However, when Christ returns and establishes His earthly kingdom, Israel will experience lasting tranquility with no more enemies. They will truly enjoy peace and fellowship with each other and with other nations. Such peace and joy will not only characterize the nation as a whole but will also be experienced by each person individually, by **every one of you** (cf. Zech 12:10–14). When the stain of sin is removed from Israel, and the Prince of Peace rules the world, the earth will enjoy true peace.

This peace will extend to all creation. The prophecy states that a man will **sit under his vine and under his fig tree.** The **vine** is often

associated with both creation and a renewed creation. After God flooded
the earth, Noah planted a vine, and despite the effects of the curse (cf.
Gen 3:17; 5:29), that vine grew (cf. 9:20). Its growth demonstrated that to a
certain degree, the Lord had restrained His curse on the earth (cf. 8:21–
22). Later in Genesis, the vine reappeared in a prophecy about creation
being made new. In Genesis 49:10–11, Jacob foretold that one day the
Messiah (Shiloh) will come and tie His donkey to the vine. Jacob was
speaking about the abundance of the Messiah's future kingdom. At that
time, a vine will become so robust that it will be strong enough to hold an
animal tied to it. The vine appeared again in the book of 1 Kings, where
the author described Solomon's kingdom. Solomon "had dominion over
everything west of the River, from Tiphsah even to Gaza, over all the
kings west of the River; and he had peace on all sides around about him.
So Judah and Israel lived in security, every man under his vine and his
fig tree, from Dan even to Beersheba, all the days of Solomon" (1 Kgs
4:24–25). The golden age of Solomon was characterized by peace and
prosperity on both a national and international level. The symbol of this
well-being was that every person was "under his vine and his fig tree."

The language of the **vine** and **fig tree** in Zechariah anticipates a
future time of renewed creation, an epoch that will surpass the golden
age of Solomon. This will take place because the millennial kingdom
will be ruled by One greater than Solomon, the Lord Jesus Christ (Matt
12:42). Such an era of peace and prosperity will only be possible because
of His priestly work for His people, by which He removed their sins and
reconciled them to God.

Zechariah's fourth vision unveiled to Israel a spectacular drama
focused on their great High Priest. Though Satan is relentless as an
accuser, Christ stands always ready to intercede for His people (Zech
3:1–2). He secures their justification because He has cleansed them and
clothed them in His righteousness (3:3–5). The Messiah is no ordinary
priest. He is the Servant, the Branch, and the Stone. As the God-man,
He is both divine and divinely empowered. And as the perfect Priest-
King, He is able both to redeem and to reign. In the middle of these eight
amazing visions, God focused the attention on the most important figure
of history. By featuring the Messiah as the centerpiece of Zechariah's

visions, the Lord emphasized that Christ's saving work is at the center of God's redemptive plan.

The Fifth Night Vision, Part 1: The Light of the World

12

Zechariah 4:1–3

> Then the angel who was speaking with me returned and roused me, as a man who is roused from his sleep. And he said to me, "What do you see?" And I said, "I see, and behold, a lampstand all of gold with its bowl on the top of it, and its seven lamps on it with seven spouts belonging to each of the lamps which are on the top of it, also two olive trees by it, one on the right side of the bowl and the other on its left side."

Light is a powerful and pervasive reality in Scripture. The first words God spoke were, "Let there be light" (Gen 1:3), and so light was at the beginning of creation, and it will continue to shine into the eternal state (Rev 22:5). The brilliance of light, often used in the Bible to illustrate scriptural enlightenment (cf. Ps 119:105), is at times best understood in contrast with its opposite, darkness. God's Word uses darkness to symbolize the depths of sin and ignorance. Because of sin, the world plunged itself into spiritual, moral, and theological darkness (cf. Isa 5:20; Eph 5:8, 11; 1 John 2:9), experiencing the resulting darkness of God's judgment as its consequence (Zeph 1:15; cf. Isa 8:22).

Nevertheless, as the circuit of the sun consistently runs its orbit whether seen or not (cf. Ps 19:4), God's light constantly shines. It was

Yahweh who appeared as the flaming fire in the darkness to secure His promises to Abram (cf. Gen 15:17). He also appeared in the fire of the burning bush to commission Moses and deliver His people (Exod 3:3). It was God who dwelt among the Israelites as a pillar of fire by night, emanating light to guide His people through the wilderness (13:21). Spiritually speaking, God promised that His light will overcome the darkness. This promise extended to the faithful remnant of the exile (Isa 9:2), and also to believers in the church age who formerly walked in darkness (2 Cor 4:6; Eph 5:8–14). The Lord has called His people out of darkness into His marvelous light (1 Pet 2:9). In the new heavens and the new earth, there will be the everlasting light, not of the sun or the moon, but of God's glory (Rev 21:23–25). The theme of light extends from the beginning of Scripture to the end, symbolizing the presence and power of God, and giving His people the assurance that He has not forsaken them (cf. Ps 27:1).

When a lampstand appeared in Zechariah's fifth vision, the prophet would have immediately recognized the symbolism. The lampstand conveyed the breadth of God's plan concerning His glorious light (Zech 4:1–2a). It not only symbolized the presence of God, but also expressed the part Israel and the temple would play in God's plan to overcome all darkness. The lampstand also pointed to the one true Light of the world, the Lord Jesus Christ (Zech 4:2b–3; cf. Isa 49:5–6). The lampstand that Zechariah described was no ordinary lampstand. Its uniqueness pointed to the extraordinary Messiah by whom God would fill the earth with His glory. Christ is the light that pierces the darkness (Isa 9:2; Matt 4:12–17), the light that gives life (John 8:12), and the light that gives both physical and spiritual sight to the blind (John 9; Acts 9:3–19; 2 Cor 4:4–6). The revelation in this vision presents the glorious theme of God's light and, specifically, the brilliant radiance of Jesus Christ.

THE LAMPSTAND

Then the angel who was speaking with me returned and roused me, as a man who is roused from his sleep. And he said to me, "What do you see?" And I said, "I see, and behold, a lampstand all of gold..." (4:1–2a)

Like the previous one (cf. Zech 3:1–10), the fifth vision began differently than the other six of Zechariah's night visions. Instead of saying he lifted his eyes and saw, Zechariah wrote: **"Then the angel who was speaking with me returned and roused me, as a man who is roused from his sleep."** The **angel who was speaking with me** was the same interpreting angel who appeared previously in Zechariah's visions (1:9, 13, 14, 19, 2:3). He was noticeably absent in the previous chapter, as the emphasis was on the Angel of Yahweh, the Messiah. For this vision, however, the interpreting angel **returned**, indicating that there was still more revelation for Zechariah to receive and comprehend. It is possible that this same angel may have helped earlier prophets understand their visions as well (cf. Ezek 40:3; Dan 7:16). The angel not only returned but also **roused** the prophet to stir him to action. **As a man who is roused from his sleep** becomes awake and alert, so the prophet was brought to a peak level of attentiveness and clarity. The activity of the angel demonstrated that Zechariah needed to be fully aware of all that this vision entailed. Like the previous vision, this fifth scene pertained to God's promises regarding the Person and work of the Messiah. It therefore warranted the prophet's full attention.

What Zechariah saw was complex. The angel even drew attention to this by asking, **"What do you see?"** He invited the prophet to scrutinize and describe what he was observing. Thus, Zechariah began to look **(I see)** and to concentrate on the features of this intricate vision **(behold)**. The unfolding scene focused on **a lampstand** (*menorah* in Hebrew), which had a base and a centerpiece going straight up with multiple branching arms, each with a lamp at its top. Each lamp provided light by burning oil. In Scripture, such a lampstand, similar to a candelabra, was found primarily in the tabernacle (Exod 25:31) and later in the temple (1 Chr 28:15). Since the light given by the lampstand symbolized God's continual presence with His people, the lamps were always lit (2 Chr 13:11). The lampstand held out the hope that, though the people could not fully see God at present (Exod 33:20), one day He would dwell with them face to face (cf. 1 Cor 13:12; 1 John 3:2). It also served as a symbol of Israel's witness to the world, that they mediated God's presence to the nations as a kingdom of priests (Exod 19:6) and a light to the Gentiles (cf. Isa 42:6). Accordingly, the lampstand that was in the temple, as well as the one that was in Zechariah's vision, was made **all of gold**. It represented the precious value of the glorious and brilliant light of God's glory among His people. Even in the New Testament, the church is described as a lampstand (Rev 2:1, 5). Believers are instructed to live as those who were called out of darkness into the clarity and holiness of righteous light (cf. Acts 26:18; Eph 5:9; Phil 2:15; 1 Thess 5:5; 1 John 1:7). The Lord Jesus reiterated this responsibility in the Sermon on the Mount when He said: "You are the light of the world. A city set on a hill cannot be hidden; nor does *anyone* light a lamp and put it under a basket, but on the lampstand, and it gives light to all who are in the house. Let your light shine before men in such a way that they may see your good works, and glorify your Father who is in heaven" (Matt 5:14–16). As noted above, the theme of God's glorious light extends from the beginning of creation to its culmination in the eternal state. The lampstand vividly encapsulates that theme as it portrays both God's radiant presence and His purposeful plan to overcome darkness and fill the earth with the light of His glory (Hab 2:14; Num 14:21; Isa 40:5; Ps 72:19).

THE LIGHT OF THE WORLD

"...with its bowl on the top of it, and its seven lamps on it with seven spouts belonging to each of the lamps which are on the top of it, also two olive trees by it, one on the right side of the bowl and the other on its left side." (4:2b–3)

Zechariah highlighted three features that differentiated the unique lampstand of this vision from any lampstand he had seen before. These three distinctives show that the lampstand was perfectly self-sufficient, illustrating the reality that God will fill the earth with His glory by His power alone. He requires no external aid or assistance to accomplish His purposes.

First, the lampstand was self-supplying with a **bowl on the top of it.** That bowl served as a reservoir of oil, allowing for a constant flow of fuel so the lamps could burn continually. In the lampstand found in the tabernacle or the temple, the oil had to be constantly supplied by the priests who would refill each lamp regularly (Lev 24:4; 2 Chr 13:11). A normal ancient lamp was far from automatic, but the lampstand in Zechariah's vision had a bowl which rendered such priestly assistance unnecessary.

Second, the lampstand was self-operating. It had **seven lamps on it with seven spouts belonging to each of the lamps which are on the top of it.** The lampstand in the tabernacle also had **seven lamps** (Exod 25:37). The number seven corresponded to completeness and fullness, as in the seven days of the creation week (Gen 1–2). With its seven lamps, the lampstand in this vision, like the one in the temple or tabernacle, brilliantly lit up its respective space, symbolizing the fullness of God's presence. Zechariah's unusual menorah also had **seven spouts belonging to each of the lamps which are on the top of it.** This made the lamp operate in a self-filling fashion. No priest was needed to bring oil from storage to light each lamp. Each distributing **spout** was a conduit that channeled the oil from the reservoir bowl to the lamps. The Hebrew is specific that for each of the seven lamps, there were **seven** pipes feeding oil from the central bowl, resulting in forty-nine spouts total. While the lampstands in the tabernacle and temple were designed to show the fullness of God's presence, Zechariah's lampstand, with an additional seven spouts for each of the seven lamps, was meant to show the complete perfection—truly the fullness of the fullness—of God's brilliant glory.

Finally, the lampstand was not only self-supplying and self-operating but also self-sustaining. It had **two olive trees by it, one on the right side of the bowl and the other on its left side.** The particular significance of the olive tree and the reason for two of them would be revealed later by the angel (cf. Zech 4:12–14). However, at this stage of the vision, everything was related to the operation of the lampstand, and the **olive trees** completed the picture of its self-sufficiency. Zechariah had observed how each of the seven lamps drew their oil through seven pipes, which provided the most plentiful flow from the abundant reservoir in the bowl of oil. However, if the reservoir were to run dry, there would soon be no light. Without oil, the seven pipes were purposeless, and the lampstand would cease to function. The prophet knew, as did everyone in ancient Israel, that an olive tree could yield olives and olive oil for centuries. In fact, the oldest olive trees in the world today are estimated to be more than 3,000 years old. Thus, the **olive trees** served a crucial function—they demonstrated that the supply of oil was endless, and that the operation of the lampstand would not cease. Further, Zechariah described one tree to be **on the right side of the bowl and the other on its left side.** They stood on both sides of the bowl strategically to supply oil in abundance (cf. Zech 4:12). In effect, the lampstand would burn brightly, automatically, and perpetually.

Two major observations come from all of this. First, the lampstand was truly exceptional, superior to every other lampstand in Israel's history. It was completely self-sufficient. Its description repeated the number seven to accentuate its fullness. This lampstand visibly illustrated the brilliant splendor of God's presence and His unstoppable power to display His glory. Just as the lampstand in Zechariah's vision was brighter than any former lampstand, so God's presence will outshine any potential competitor. The sun will cease, but God's light will never go out (cf. Isa 24:23; 60:19–20; Ezek 43:2–4), filling not only the world but also the hearts of His people (cf. Ezek 36:26–27; 2 Cor 4:6). On every level, God's light will triumph over all darkness. The lampstand Zechariah beheld was a stunning symbol that God will certainly accomplish His plan for redemption history, since the penetrating light of His glory will always prevail.

Another key feature of this lampstand was its full autonomy. It did not rely on man's assistance for any part of its operational process. There were olive trees to supply the oil, a bowl to store the fuel, and a network of pipes to distribute the necessary resources to each lamp. It operated entirely apart from priests or any other human power. This showed that God alone, without help from anyone else, will fully accomplish the triumphant unveiling of His glory.

Who will specifically achieve this? The answer is God's Son, the Lord Jesus Christ. Isaiah declared that God gave His Servant not only as salvation for the Jews but also as a light for the Gentiles (Isa 49:5–6). Earlier in Isaiah's prophecy, the Servant was presented as the light that shines in the darkness (9:2). Simeon recounted that majestic truth, when he said of baby Jesus, "A Light for revelation to the Gentiles, and for the glory of Your people Israel" (Luke 2:32). Most explicitly, Jesus Himself declared, "I am the Light of the world" (John 8:12), making that declaration while standing in the temple where a large candelabra would have been lit (7:28). At the time Jesus spoke, the Feast of Booths had just ended, and the massive lampstand was lit to commemorate the glory of God in the wilderness. While Israel had their physical lampstand, a mere symbol of God's presence, Jesus declared Himself to be the true light, God incarnate. Christ exclaimed that He is the eternal light and that all who are in Him possess the light of life (Ps 36:9; John 8:12). The lampstand that Zechariah saw ultimately pointed to the Lord Jesus, the divine Messiah and the Light of the world.

In presenting this vision to Zechariah, the Lord revealed to the prophet and to His people that the light of God's glory continues to shine. His presence is with His people, and His glory will ultimately fill the earth. The lampstand demonstrated that God's sovereign purpose does not depend on any outside aid. Its light is the eternal, divine Messiah who is the fullness of God's glory (John 1:14). Christ came the first time as the Light of the world to save sinners from their sin. He will come again in unveiled glory to fill the earth with the light of His presence (Matt 24:29, 30; 25:31–34; Rev 1:12–17).

The Fifth Night Vision, Part 2: Not by Power but by My Spirit

13

Zechariah 4:4–10

Then I answered and said to the angel who was speaking with me saying, "What are these, my lord?" So the angel who was speaking with me answered and said to me, "Do you not know what these are?" And I said, "No, my lord." Then he answered and spoke to me, saying, "This is the word of Yahweh to Zerubbabel, saying, 'Not by might nor by power, but by My Spirit,' says Yahweh of hosts. 'What are you, O great mountain? Before Zerubbabel *you will become* a plain; and he will bring forth the top stone with shouts of "Grace, grace to it!"'" Also the word of Yahweh came to me, saying, "The hands of Zerubbabel have laid the foundation of this house, and his hands will finish *it*. Then you will know that Yahweh of hosts has sent me to you. For who has despised the day of small things? But these seven will be glad when they see the plumb line in the hand of Zerubbabel—*these are the eyes of Yahweh which roam to and fro throughout the earth.*"

The confident declaration of the Apostle Paul in Philippians 4:13 is well-known to most believers. There he wrote, "I can do all things through Him who strengthens me." Though that familiar statement expresses wonderful truth, it can also be taken out of context and misused. Far too often, its meaning is twisted to justify the notion that

God gives believers the power to do whatever they want. But that is the opposite of what Paul was saying. His point was that God gave him the strength to endure trials and tribulations, the kind of circumstances no one would choose for themselves. Paul had learned to live a life of contentment and to persevere even through overwhelming difficulties (cf. 2 Cor 11:23–29). He stated this explicitly in the preceding verse (Phil 4:12): "I know how to get along with humble means, and I also know how to live in abundance; in any and all things I have learned the secret of being filled and going hungry, both of having abundance and suffering need." In verse 12, the apostle spoke of "all things" as the full range of his experiences, troubling or triumphant, in which he had learned to be content in God's will. So when he repeated the phrase "all things" in verse 13, he was affirming that the Lord would provide him with the strength to be faithful, no matter how challenging life might become.

The encouragement of Philippians 4:13, then, is not found in having the power to change one's circumstances, but in receiving the grace to endure difficult seasons. God faithfully supplies sustaining strength for His children to persevere in obedience to Him even in the most challenging experiences. For those wanting to live godly lives, to walk in contentment, and to serve the Lord wholeheartedly, this verse is a great comfort. It reminds believers that God truly does empower His children to endure trials as He works in them for His plan and glory (cf. Rom 8:28; Jas 1:1–3). As Paul affirmed earlier in Philippians: "For it is God who is at work in you, both to will and to work for His good pleasure" (Phil 2:13).

This very truth was revealed to Zechariah through the fifth night vision. As explained in the previous chapter of this volume (on Zech 4:1–3), the lampstand symbolized God's glorious presence. It signified that God was powerfully present and active with His people. This would have been tremendously encouraging for Zechariah and his fellow Israelites, to know that the Lord was with them as they worked to reconstruct the temple (4:4–7). His Spirit ensured that the people, under the leadership of their governor Zerubbabel, would be able to finish the task. However, the message went beyond the immediate events of Zechariah's lifetime. Zerubbabel's successful completion of the temple in his day prefigured the Spirit-empowered work of the Messiah, who will one day return to build the final house of God, the millennial temple (Zech 4:8–10; cf. 2 Sam 7:13; 1 Chr 17:12). As this vision clearly reveals, God's presence is not hypothetical or abstract. Rather, His Spirit is active to empower His people and to accomplish His promises.

THE POWER OF GOD

Then I answered and said to the angel who was speaking with me saying, "What are these, my lord?" So the angel who was speaking with me answered and said to me, "Do you not know what these are?" And I said, "No, my lord." Then he answered and spoke to me, saying, "This is the word of Yahweh to Zerubbabel, saying, 'Not by might nor by power, but by My Spirit,' says Yahweh of hosts. 'What are you, O great mountain? Before Zerubbabel *you will become* **a plain; and he will bring forth the top stone with shouts of "Grace, grace to it!"''"** (4:4–7)

The lampstand Zechariah saw was so impressive that again, the prophet addressed the **angel who was speaking** with him, asking, **"What are these, my lord?"** The prophet was not inquiring about the identity of the images he saw (cf. Zech 1:9, 19), but rather about their meaning. His description of the lampstand and its components (in vv. 2–3) indicated that he understood their general function. However, he remained curious about their significance (cf. 4:4, 11–12), and so he requested additional explanation.

The angel welcomed Zechariah's questions. He replied to the prophet, **"Do you not know what these are?"** Previously, with earlier visions, the interpreting angel had directly provided an explanation (cf. 1:9, 19). This time, however, he asked a follow-up question. The angel's question was not a rebuke but an encouragement for Zechariah to pursue the answers he sought. The prophet's confession, **"No, my lord,"** humbly acknowledged both his ignorance and his earnest desire to receive what the angel was about to reveal.

The angel responded by declaring the divine origin of his message, **"This is the word of Yahweh to Zerubbabel."** While Joshua, the High

Priest, was the focus of the previous vision (Zech 3:1–10), **Zerubbabel**, the royal governor, was featured in this setting. The previous vision focused on Joshua to prefigure Messiah's priestly ministry. This current vision featured Zerubbabel to point to Christ's kingly ministry. As a descendent of David, Zerubbabel was a member of the royal line and an ancestor of Christ (cf. Matt 1:12–13; Luke 3:27). He was also the dominant leader of the Jewish people who returned from exile (Ezra 2:2). God gave a revelation for Zerubbabel, both to encourage him personally and to provide a picture of the greater Son of David, the Messiah.

The specific encouragement that God gave was expressed in the words, **"Not by might nor by power, but by My Spirit,"** says **Yahweh of hosts**. The name **Yahweh of hosts**, the prophet's favorite designation for God, reflected the promise that the Lord will use all His heavenly resources **(hosts)** to fulfill His promises to His people (see discussion on Zech 1:8). The work to rebuild the temple could not be achieved merely through mortal strength, and Yahweh stated this explicitly: **"Not by might nor by power."** When these terms are used together, **might** refers to one's resources—like wealth (2 Kgs 15:20) or military assets (1 Kgs 5:13–18)—that could be deployed to overcome an obstacle or accomplish a goal. By contrast, **power** speaks of personal strength and inner fortitude. The Lord's point was that no material resource nor human strength could do what God alone can achieve.

The clear implication of the text is that spiritual work can only be accomplished **by** the power of the **Spirit** of God. The whole of Scripture shows this to be true. The Spirit is the One who regenerates the spiritually dead heart, causing the sinner to believe and embrace the message of salvation (cf. Ezek 36:26; Titus 3:5). The Spirit dwells in the hearts of God's children (Ezek 36:26–27), empowering them to live in obedience and shine as lights in the world (Matt 5:16; Eph 5:18). The Spirit preserves God's people for the day when Christ will return (Eph 1:13–14), and His indwelling ministry previews the intimate fellowship with God they will enjoy in the coming kingdom (cf. Ezek 36:26–27; 37:1–28; 40–48). The Spirit's work extends God's glory not only throughout creation, but also in the hearts of His people. In calling Zerubbabel and his fellow Israelites to finish their God-given task, the Lord reminded them to rely not on their own power and ingenuity, but on the strength provided by His Spirit.

The image of the lampstand powerfully illustrated this truth. The oil was essential for its operation, since without fuel, it would cease to function. Throughout Scripture, oil also served as a symbol to signify being anointed and empowered by the Holy Spirit (cf. 1 Sam 16:13; Isa 61:1; Luke 4:18; Acts 10:38). The connection to Zechariah's vision is clear. If Zerubbabel and his fellow Israelites failed to rely on the power of the Spirit, their finite reservoir of human strength would quickly run dry, and they would be unable to complete the task. But if they relied on the Spirit's power, they would enjoy an unending Source of unstoppable strength (cf. Zech 4:1–3).

Yahweh punctuated that point by saying, "**What are you, O great mountain? Before Zerubbabel** *you will become* **a plain.**" The Bible uses mountains to illustrate that which is strong and immovable (cf. Ps 36:6; Prov 8:25). Accordingly, they can represent obstacles or problems that seem insurmountable and unassailable (cf. Mark 11:23). In the days of Zechariah, Zerubbabel faced such challenges in rebuilding the temple. But the Lord encouraged His people by putting those obstacles in proper perspective. He addressed those seemingly insurmountable difficulties with a rhetorical question, "**What are you?**" The challenges Zerubbabel faced were nothing for God to overcome. Hence, the Lord proclaimed, "**Before Zerubbabel** *you will become* **a plain,**" a flat and level surface. God pledged to smooth the way for Zerubbabel and His people. If they would depend on Him in obedience, He would remove any obstacle in their path.

Declaring victory, Yahweh said of Zerubbabel, "**He will bring forth the top stone with shouts of 'Grace, grace to it!'**" The **top stone** is the stone at the pinnacle of a building, the final stone that would complete the temple. Though Israel faced overwhelming odds, God confirmed that His Holy Spirit would enable and empower Zerubbabel to overcome all adversity and finish the task. Once the temple was complete, great joy would follow, marked by **shouts of "Grace, grace to it!"** Used to denote loud thunder (cf. Job 36:29) and a noisy town (Isa 22:2), the term **shouts** described the exuberant and deafening response of the people. In their enthusiasm, they would repeatedly exclaim **grace, grace**. The word **grace** in Hebrew signifies divine favor and kindness. Recognizing their success came from God's empowerment, Zerubbabel and his fellow Israelites would give all the glory and credit to the Lord. They would express their exhilaration and gratitude for God's faithfulness and favor towards them. For Zerubbabel and those around him, the anticipation of that joyful moment provided great motivation and encouragement.

The prophecy of verses 6–7 not only points to Zerubbabel and his labors, but also anticipates the ultimate work of the Messiah. The language of a **mountain** becoming a **plain** is reminiscent of Isaiah 40:4: "Let every valley be lifted up, and every mountain and hill be made low; and let the rough ground become a plain." This verse in Isaiah described the coming of the Messiah to rebuild the temple (cf. Isa 2:2; Ezek 40–48; Dan 9:24) just as Zerubbabel was doing in Zechariah's day. Zechariah's allusion to Isaiah's prophecy connects Zerubbabel with the Messiah, showing that the former prefigured the latter. Thus, Zechariah's prophecy about Zerubbabel was designed to recall greater prophecies about the coming of Christ and His glorious kingdom. If the Lord was faithful to Zerubbabel, He would certainly be faithful to fulfill His promises regarding the ultimate Governor and King, the Messiah (cf. Isa 9:6).

THE PICTURE OF CHRIST

Also the word of Yahweh came to me, saying, "The hands of Zerubbabel have laid the foundation of this house, and his hands will finish *it*. **Then you will know that Yahweh of hosts has sent me to you. For who has despised the day of small things? But these seven will be glad when they see the plumb line in the hand of Zerubbabel—**these are **the eyes of Yahweh which roam to and fro throughout the earth."** (4:8–10)

The message of verses 6–7 strongly implied that the prophecy about Zerubbabel pertained to more than just him and his time. In verses 8–10, the implicit was made explicit when **the word of Yahweh** again came to

Zechariah. This word from the Lord focused on the work of Zerubbabel, portraying it as the work of a Davidic king: **"The hands of Zerubbabel have laid the foundation of this house."** This statement described the work of a royal official. In ancient times, a leader would lay a symbolic brick into the foundation of a building to launch its construction. The fact that **Zerubbabel** was involved in this work depicted him as both the builder and the chief of state, especially since only an individual from David's line was authorized by God to build **this house**, the temple. In His promises to David about the royal line of the Messiah, God said, "He shall build a house for My name, and I will establish the throne of his kingdom forever" (2 Sam 7:13; 1 Chr 17:12). Related to this promise, the psalmist recounted David's desire for the Lord to have His temple established, starting with the ark of the covenant being brought to Jerusalem (see 2 Sam 6):

> Remember, O Yahweh, on David's behalf, all his affliction; how he swore to Yahweh and vowed to the Mighty One of Jacob, "Surely I will not come into my house, nor lie in the comfort of my bed; I will not give sleep to my eyes or slumber to my eyelids, until I find a place for Yahweh, a dwelling place for the Mighty One of Jacob." (Ps 132:1–5)

While the descendants of David did not serve in the role of Levitical priests (cf. 2 Chr 26:18–21; Heb 7:12–14), they did play a vital role in constructing the temple and supporting its work. When Zerubbabel laid the foundation stone of this building, he was not merely acting as any royal leader. He was functioning specifically in the capacity of a Davidic king.

The Lord emphasized that the **hands of Zerubbabel** which began this process would be the same **hands** that **will finish it**. The repetition of the term **hands** shows that Zerubbabel was personally involved in leading the process from beginning to end. That was no small feat. Very few in Israel's history had the honor of building the temple (cf. 1 Kgs 8:12–13) or even renovating it (2 Kgs 12:14–16, cf. vv. 17–18; 22:5). Zerubbabel's personal effort in this work is noteworthy, placing him in a category with former kings like Solomon, Joash, and Josiah. In a preliminary way, he would fulfill God's promise to David; and in so doing, he serves as a picture of the Messiah.

Zerubbabel's triumph would lead the people to one conclusion: **"Then you will know that Yahweh of hosts has sent me to you."** This statement should be understood as messianic for at least two reasons. First, it was spoken by **the word of Yahweh** (4:8), the Messiah, the pre-incarnate Christ (see discussion on Zech 1:1). Second, elsewhere in Scripture, the phrasing "He has sent me" consistently refers to Messiah. Such language was used earlier in Zechariah 2:8 and 11, and there it described that the Messiah would accomplish His mission (see discussion on Zech 2:8, 11). The wording also appeared in Isaiah 61:1 which described the Suffering Servant, a fact confirmed by Jesus in the New Testament (Luke 4:18). In light of this, when the people saw the temple completed, they would not only **know** that the revelation Zechariah had received was indeed from the Lord, but they would also be reassured that God would certainly send His Messiah, exactly as He had promised. The people responded with joy and celebration when Zerubbabel completed his building efforts (cf. Zech 4:7). To a far greater degree, a future generation of Israelites will know abundant joy and amazing grace when the Messiah returns and builds the ultimate house for God (2 Sam 7:13; cf. Rom 11:26). Zerubbabel's success in rebuilding the temple foreshadowed that final messianic glory. When Israel beheld the former, they could be confident that the Lord would certainly accomplish the latter. As illustrated by the vision of the lampstand, Yahweh will one day fill the earth with His glory, through the work of His Son and the power of His Spirit.

All of this gave a new and triumphant perspective to those in Zechariah's day. As the Lord pointed out, **"For who has despised the day of small things?"** The rhetorical question addressed those in Zechariah's audience who were saddened and discouraged as they compared Zerubbabel's construction project to the memory of Solomon's majestic temple (cf. Ezra 3:12; Hag 2:3). Because Zerubbabel's temple seemed so meager, some in Zechariah's time **despised** it, showing contempt at the **day** when the reconstruction work began. They viewed these efforts as **small things**.

However, Yahweh confronted such disdain: **"But these seven will be glad when they see the plumb line in the hand of Zerubbabel."** The text depicts Zerubbabel during the construction of the temple holding a **plumb line**, a Hebrew word that may denote a dedication stone commemorating the completion of the temple or, more traditionally and preferably, the rock tied to the end of a plumb line. This rock would pull the string of the plumb line down, creating a straight vertical line used to ensure that the angles of a building were straight. The fact that the plumb line was in Zerubbabel's **hand** emphasized his efforts in this endeavor. Just as Zerubbabel's hands laid the stone to begin the project (Zech 4:9a), and just as his hands would finish the project (4:9b), so his **hand** was involved during the project as well. The leader of Israel was not merely leading the construction work but was engaged in it himself. Though some might have thought that Zerubbabel's efforts were pathetic, the Lord celebrated the governor's hard work, saying, **"These seven will be glad."** The number **seven** is connected to the lampstand, which had seven lamps as well as seven spouts for each of those lamps (4:2). The sevens of the lampstand represented the fullness of God's presence and His pledge to shine the light of His glory throughout the world. The very presence of God was with Zerubbabel. The Lord saw his efforts, and He rejoiced over them. God celebrated the work of rebuilding the temple, knowing that this moment represented a step toward the fulfillment of His sovereign plan. Israel needed to see this event the way God saw it.

The Lord added further definition to **these seven** just mentioned, stating that **these are the eyes of Yahweh which roam to and fro throughout the earth**. The number seven does not merely refer to the lampstand but more specifically to the **eyes of Yahweh**, signifying the very omniscience and omnipresence of God. Indeed, God is all knowing and all present as His eyes **roam to and fro throughout the earth**. This is not the first time that Zechariah connected the number seven with eyes. Such a connection was also found in the prophet's previous vision in chapter 3. In 3:9, the stone, the Messiah, had seven eyes, which represented the seven-fold ministry of the Spirit through the Messiah (cf. Isa 11:1–3). The Apostle John also defined the "seven eyes" as the work of the Spirit. He saw a "Lamb standing, as if slain, having seven horns and seven eyes, which are the seven Spirits of God, sent out into all the earth" (Rev 5:6). Based on this pattern, the association in this passage between seven and eyes also points to the Holy Spirit. This fits the context of Zechariah 4, since the text indicated that the lampstand was supplied by the Spirit (Zech 4:6). Thus, while the seven generally referred to the lampstand and God's presence (see above), the Lord specified here that the number related to the presence and power of the Spirit.

Some of his fellow Israelites may have underestimated the value of Zerubbabel's obedience, but God did not. He had sovereignly ordained this moment in keeping with His perfect purposes. The Holy Spirit empowered Zerubbabel's efforts, and rejoiced over them, because they contributed to the divine plan for the coming of the Messiah and the display of God's glory. Thus, the Lord charged Zerubbabel and all the people to live not by might nor by power, but by His Spirit.

The Fifth Night Vision, Part 3: The King-Priest Messiah

14

Zechariah 4:11–14

Then I answered and said to him, "What are these two olive trees on the right of the lampstand and on its left?" And I answered the second time and said to him, "What are the two olive branches which are beside the two golden pipes, which empty the golden *oil* from themselves?" So he spoke to me, saying, "Do you not know what these are?" And I said, "No, my lord." Then he said, "These are the two anointed ones who are standing by the Lord of the whole earth."

Throughout Israel's history, the offices of king and priest were distinct and separate. The priests came from the tribe of Levi, but the kings from the tribe of Judah. While priests administrated the law (Deut 17:8–13), they did not have the authority of a king. Likewise, while kings facilitated sacrifice (cf. 1 Kgs 3:4), they were forbidden to offer the sacrifices themselves. Thus, when King Uzziah attempted to burn incense as a priest before the Lord, God struck him with leprosy (2 Chr 26:19–21). Uzziah thought he could draw near to God as a priest. In response, the Lord rejected him and turned him into an outcast. His leprosy served as a vivid reminder of how strictly God kept these two roles separate (cf. Heb 7:12–14). Even then, the kings and priests of Israel never perfectly fulfilled their respective offices. As sinners, they were finite and fallible.

The Old Testament, however, held out hope that there would be One who would flawlessly fulfill both of these functions. Early on, God showed that He intended His Messiah to be both king and priest by introducing the godly Melchizedek to Abraham. One of the distinguishing traits of Melchizedek was that he was both a king and a priest (Gen 14:18). Though mentioned only briefly, he was not forgotten. Later on, David revealed that the Messiah would be of the order of Melchizedek (Ps 110:4); He would be both a king and a priest. Ezekiel's prophecy also affirmed this dual role and privilege. In Ezekiel 21:26–27, the prophet foretold that there would be One who would possess the right to both the priestly turban and the royal crown. Only He would be worthy and capable of bearing the weight of both offices.

The future of Israel, and of the entire human race, depends on the Messiah's ability to do what no one else can—to be both the ultimate King and the great High Priest. That messianic role is depicted in the final portion of Zechariah's fifth vision. The angel directed Zechariah's attention to the lampstand one last time to establish an important truth about the Messiah. Only He is able to mediate God's glorious presence to the world. As King, He can represent God to men; and as Priest, He can represent men to God. Zechariah's fifth vision ended on a majestic note of messianic hope, announcing that Christ would fulfill the mediatorial role no one else could.

TWO OLIVE TREES

Then I answered and said to him, "What are these two olive trees on the right of the lampstand and on its left?" And I answered the second time and said to him, "What are the two olive branches which are beside the two golden pipes, which empty the golden *oil* **from themselves?"** (4:11–12)

Awestruck by all that had been revealed about the lampstand and its component parts (cf. 4:1–10), Zechariah summoned one final question for the angel: **Then I answered and said to him, "What are**

these two olive trees on the right of the lampstand and on its left?"
The interpreting angel had already explained the lampstand, which
symbolized the fullness of God's glorious presence. The flow of oil in the
lampstand, from the bowl through the seven spouts for each of the seven
lamps, signified the work of the Spirit who would empower His people,
and ultimately the Messiah. But one vital feature of the lampstand still
needed to be explained: the **two olive trees.** Zechariah's initial question
about these trees was not very detailed. In describing the lampstand
earlier, he had noted that the olive trees were on the right and the left of
the bowl of the lampstand (v 3). At this point of the passage, he did not
mention the bowl, but simply spoke of **these two olive trees** which were
on the **right** and **left** of the **lampstand.**

Though his query was simple and straightforward, the prophet
received no response from the angel. So, Zechariah was forced to **answer
the second time,** inquiring about the vision yet again. To need to ask a
question a second time is highly unusual in prophecy and completely
exceptional in Zechariah's visions. Why did the angel require this of
the prophet? While Zechariah understood the olive trees generally,
his initial question was not specific enough. The angel, by his silence,
compelled Zechariah to look again at the olive trees with greater focus
and to reword his inquiry more precisely.

As Zechariah studied the **two olive trees** further, he framed
his question in a more detailed way, asking: "**What are the two olive
branches which are beside the two golden pipes which empty the
golden** *oil* **from themselves?**" Zechariah had already observed that the
olive trees provided an unending source of oil for the lampstand. But the
angel did not want him to stop there. The prophet needed to focus more
intensely on the flow of oil from the olive branches to the lampstand.
This was significant because it was the means by which the lampstand
was fueled.

The flow of oil to the lampstand involved several elements: two
trees, two branches, and two pipes. Having identified the two trees in
verse 11, the prophet further specified **two olive branches which are
beside the two golden pipes.** The term **branches** describes a cluster of
olive-ladened boughs woven together (cf. Ruth 2:2; Isa 17:5). They were

extensions of the olive trees, and the conduit by which the oil dripped into the **pipes** of the lampstand. The word **pipes** is different in Hebrew from the term "spouts" used earlier (cf. Zech 4:2). Though the pipes were distinct from the spouts, they similarly channeled the oil dripping from the branches to the lampstand. Significantly, the number **two** was repeated to emphasize the presence of **two** olive trees (4:3), with **two** branches (4:12), and **two** corresponding pipes (4:12). Moreover, Zechariah had to ask his question **two** times (4:12). The emphasis on **two** set the stage for an important theological truth to be revealed. Just as oil poured from two branches and two pipes into one lampstand, so God would merge two realities into one. As will be defined in more detail shortly, this symbolized the two offices of priest and king being brought together in the one Person of the Messiah. He alone would be able to fulfill these two offices simultaneously and perfectly.

A major emphasis within Zechariah's final description of the lampstand is its **golden** material and color. The pipes which carried the oil from the olive branches were **golden**, complementing the entire lampstand which was also made of gold (cf. Zech 4:2). Zechariah even described the oil as being **golden oil**. The golden brilliance of the lampstand is a symbol of God's divine presence and glory, especially the **golden oil**, since the Holy Spirit is associated with oil and anointing in Scripture (1 Sam 16:13; 1 John 2:27). Thus, just as everything about the lampstand was golden—the golden oil flowed perfectly through the golden pipes to a golden lampstand—so the One who mediates God's presence must be perfectly divine. While many priests and kings mediated God's presence and power in the past, none of them adequately fulfilled this task. Only the incarnate Messiah could achieve the perfection required, since He is both truly God (John 1:1; Col 1:15; 2:9; Heb 1:3) and truly Man (John 1:14; Phil 2:6–8; 1 John 4:2–3).

Zechariah saw that the olive branches **empty** oil **from themselves** to supply the lampstand. This detail reiterated the main point of the vision, focusing on how the lampstand was fueled, and by extension, how the theology symbolized by the lampstand would be fulfilled. According to His perfect plan, God would mediate His glorious presence to the world through the Messiah, His Son, the One who is uniquely able to be both King and Priest.

TWO OFFICES

So he spoke to me, saying, "Do you not know what these are?" And I said, "No, my lord." Then he said, "These are the two anointed ones who are standing by the Lord of the whole earth." (4:13–14)

Once again, the interpreting angel asked, **"Do you not know what these are?"** to which Zechariah answered in the negative, **"No, my lord."** The intricate imagery of the lampstand required much illumination to comprehend its meaning. So, the prophet again humbly acknowledged his ignorance as he had done earlier in the vision (4:5).

This culmination of the scene revolved around **two anointed ones**, or more literally in Hebrew, "two sons of oil." In this case, however, the word for "oil" is different from the one used earlier in the vision. The word here refers to oil that is not processed by anyone, but that is taken fresh from the tree. Such oil is a highly appropriate metaphor for the pure presence of God. In Israel, the positions of king and priest were **two** major offices that involved being anointed with oil at the point of inauguration (cf. Lev 8:12; 1 Sam 16:13). Both offices were tasked with mediating God's presence to His people. The kings represented God before the nation. They helped construct or renovate God's house, the temple (2 Sam 7:13; 1 Kgs 8:12–13), and they conveyed divine authority based on God's law (cf. Deut 17:18–20). By contrast, priests represented the nation to God. They maintained temple services, facilitated the sacrificial system, and led Israel in worship before the Lord (cf. Exod 28:12). In essence, the king brought God before the people, and the priest brought the people before God. Both king and priest were fundamentally involved in mediating God's presence, and both attempted to do so throughout Israel's history (cf. Exod 28:30; 1 Kgs 8:1–61). The **anointed ones** in Zechariah's vision represent these two offices, and both of their functions were vital in fulfilling the theology of the lampstand, by mediating the presence of God to His people.

By God's design, no single person in Israel could be both king and priest. No one could hold both roles of representing God to man and man to God. The kings and priests came from separate tribes—Judah and

Levi. As noted above, God strictly maintained the separateness of these distinct offices. In 1 Samuel 13, King Saul attempted to offer sacrifices to God. Consequently, he was punished for assuming a priestly duty he was not permitted to fulfill. Likewise, in 2 Chronicles 26:16–23, as noted above, King Uzziah presumptuously offered incense in the temple. As a result, God turned him into a leper for violating the priestly office. In instances when David (2 Sam 6:13) and Solomon (1 Kgs 3:4) offered sacrifices, they did so presumably through a priest.

Furthermore, no Old Testament king or priest ever fulfilled his singular office perfectly. Israel's past was marked by a litany of kings and priests who had failed in their God-given responsibilities (cf. Jer 22:24–30; Hos 4:4–6; Mal 2:1–9). As a result, the nation fell under God's judgment. According to Ezekiel, God punished Israel's royal line (Ezek 19:1–14) and negated the mediatorial role of its priests (cf. 14:12–23). Likewise, Jeremiah declared that, due to the sins of Israel, Yahweh would devastate the offices of the priest (Jer 20:1–6; 21:1–7) and the king (22:24–30). The collapse of Israel's leadership occurred in its exile to Babylon. In the time of Zechariah, the effects of this punishment were still present. While there were priests in Zechariah's day, there was no king in Israel (cf. Hag 1:1), only a governor (cf. Zech 4:6–10). The record of Israel's history demonstrated that no mere mortal could carry the full mantle of leadership for the nation.

However, the Old Testament prophesied that the Messiah would function as both the ultimate King and perfect Priest. In Psalm 110, David spoke of the Messiah coming from the order of Melchizedek, a man who was both king and priest (cf. Gen 14:18). Ezekiel also wrote of One who would wear the turban and the crown (cf. Ezek 21:26–27). While the Old Testament recounted Israel's inability to fulfill these distinct offices, it also held out hope that the Messiah would succeed where all others had failed. He would merge the two offices together in Himself and fulfill them perfectly.

That is why the angel declared that the anointed ones **are standing** by the Lord. In the previous vision, Joshua stood before the Angel of Yahweh, depending on Him for intercession (Zech 3:1) and righteousness (3:3). That vision indicated that Joshua could not fulfill his role on his own; he needed the Angel of Yahweh to intercede and atone for him. Similarly, in this fifth vision, the interpreting angel explained that **the two anointed ones**—the king and the priest—were standing by the Lord in utter reliance on Him, trusting Him that He would accomplish what they could never do on their own. Just as the oil flowed from two branches and pipes into one lampstand, so these two anointed roles would come together in one Person—the Lord Jesus Christ.

Christ is able and worthy to unite these roles, for He is the **Lord of the whole earth**. While this title fundamentally expresses the Messiah's complete sovereignty over everything in the created order, it was reserved in the Old Testament to describe the unique dominion He will have when He returns and reigns in the millennial kingdom (Ps 97:5; Mic 4:13; Zech 6:5; cf. 6:8). That is why the two offices of priest and king depend upon Him. He alone has the supreme sovereignty and perfect purity to unite these two roles. Moreover, the title "**Lord of the whole earth**" is used elsewhere in Scripture to describe the presence of God (cf. Ps 97:5; Mic 4:13; Zech 6:5; cf. 6:8). For example, Joshua 3:13 speaks of "the ark of Yahweh, the Lord of all the earth" (cf. Josh 3:11; cf. Num 10:35–36; 1 Sam 4:4). Christ will fulfill not only the offices of priest and king, but also the message revealed by the vision of the lampstand. As **Lord of the whole earth**, He is the very presence and light of God, and He will fill the earth with His glory.

Because of their messianic significance, it becomes clear why this vision and the previous one were placed in the center of Zechariah's eight night visions. The prophet's visions revealed divine promises about Israel and the nations, and they depicted God's presence, salvation, judgment, restoration, and reign. They unveiled details about His activity in the past, the present, and the future. But at the center of them all stands the Messiah because He is able to do what no other king or priest can do. The conclusion of the vision of the lampstand powerfully reveals that the Light of the world is coming, and as the ultimate King and Priest, He will fulfill God's promise to display His glory through all creation.

The Sixth Night Vision: God Enforces the Covenant

15

Zechariah 5:1–4

Then I lifted up my eyes again and saw, and behold, a flying scroll. And he said to me, "What do you see?" And I said, "I see a flying scroll; its length is twenty cubits and its width ten cubits." Then he said to me, "This is the curse that is going forth over the face of the whole land; surely everyone who steals will be purged away according to the writing on one side, and everyone who swears will be purged away according to the writing on the other side. I will make it go forth," declares Yahweh of hosts, "and it will enter the house of the thief and the house of the one who swears falsely by My name; and it will spend the night within that house and consume it with its timber and stones."

The sixth of Zechariah's eight visions (see discussion on Zech 1:7) parallels his third vision (cf. 2:1–13) in that both visions feature God's plans for Israel (cf. 2:1–5; 5:3). The third vision revealed that God will one day rebuild the temple, restore the city of Jerusalem, dwell as a wall of fire around it, and usher in the Messiah's kingdom over the whole earth. But a vital question remains: what will God do with the ungodly and unrepentant? The Lord answered that question in this vision, revealing that He will not only fulfill His promises of blessing for the redeemed, but that He will also enforce His promises of condemnation against the reprobate. God will punish impenitent sinners, and by that judgment He will keep His covenant and advance His purposes.

Judgment is a major theme in Scripture, necessitated by the holiness and righteousness of God. As the psalmist proclaimed to Israel, "Exalt Yahweh our God and worship at His holy mountain, for holy is Yahweh our God" (Ps 99:9). David also exclaimed, "You are not a God who delights in wickedness; evil does not sojourn with You" (5:4). The prophet Habakkuk declared, "Are You not from everlasting, O Yahweh, my God, my Holy One?.... *Your* eyes are too pure to see evil, and You cannot look on trouble" (Hab 1:12–13). From the nation's beginning, the Lord revealed His holiness and called His people to walk accordingly: "For I am Yahweh who brought you up from the land of Egypt to be your God; thus you shall be holy, for I am holy" (Lev 11:45).

Some may question God's resolve to bring holy judgment, because they watch the wicked flourish and prosper in this world (cf. Job 21:7–9; Pss 10:2–6; 73:3; Hab 1:12b; Rev 6:9). Scripture is clear, however, that the Lord will execute His wrath against the wicked, bringing judgment to bear in His own time. As the Psalmist declared, "Yahweh reigns, let the earth rejoice; let the many coastlands be glad. Clouds and thick darkness are all around Him; righteousness and justice are the foundation of His throne. Fire goes before Him and burns up His adversaries all around" (Ps 97:1–3). In Isaiah 42:13, the prophet wrote about the coming of the Lord in judgment, saying, "Yahweh will go forth like a warrior; He will awaken *His* zeal like a man of war. He will make a loud shout, indeed, He will raise a war cry. He will prevail against His enemies." The Lord Jesus confirmed that God will unleash eschatological judgment during the Tribulation (Matt 24–25). In the book of Revelation, the Apostle John detailed that Tribulation judgment (Rev 6–19), describing how God's wrath will be poured out on the nations prior to the establishment of the millennial kingdom (20:4–6).

The culminating scenes of human history will include both the outpouring of God's wrath on the wicked, and the establishment of His kingdom for the redeemed. The message of this vision in Zechariah 5 captures both realities. As one commentator explained:

> Sin must be purged away, iniquity must be stamped out in the city of God; and when the sinner is so wedded to his sin that he is no longer separable from it, he becomes the object of God's curse, and must be "cleansed away" from the earth. In short, then, the two visions in chapter five give us the reverse side of the truth unfolded in the first four chapters.[1]

God's judgment and blessing are complementary realities, with the one leading to the other. By purging the wicked from the earth in judgment, the Lord will prepare the world for His rule of righteousness during which His promised blessings will be fulfilled. As Zechariah revealed in this passage, God will judge sin based on clear criteria (Zech 5:1–2), with comprehensive completeness (5:3), and with certain calamity as its result (5:4). The Lord's commitment to condemn and punish iniquity serves both as a warning for sinners to repent, and as a comfort for believers to rest in God's promises (Rom 12:19), knowing He will fulfill all of them in His perfect time, including His promise to judge the world in righteousness (cf. Gen 18:25; Ps 9:8).

THE CRITERIA FOR GOD'S JUDGMENT

Then I lifted up my eyes again and saw, and saw, and behold, a flying scroll. And he said to me, "What do you see?" And I said, "I see a flying scroll; its length is twenty cubits and its width ten cubits." (5:1–2)

The sixth vision began with Zechariah saying, **"I lifted up my eyes again."** This was the normal transition between visions, and in this case, it demonstrated that Zechariah had moved from the central and heightened visions about the Messiah (visions four and five) to visions regarding God's plan for Israel and the nations. As noted above (see discussion on Zech 1:7), this sixth vision specifically paralleled the prophet's third vision, because both focused on God's plan for Israel. The third vision described millennial Jerusalem and noted that the Lord will

---

1 David Baron, *The Visions and Prophecies of Zechariah: The Prophet of Hope and Glory* (London, England: Morgan and Scott, 1918), 144.

one day dwell among His people as a wall of fire (cf. 2:1–13). The current vision, by contrast, featured **a flying scroll**. Such a scroll consisted of a long piece of papyrus or animal hide wound up on two sticks. In Scripture, the predominant use of the scroll was to contain God's Word (Ps 40:7; Jer 36:2; Ezek 3:1). That the scroll was **flying** indicated that its divine message was living and active (cf. Heb 4:12), and that it moved with speed, swiftness, and effectiveness. As the Lord declared in Isaiah 55:11, "So will My word be which goes forth from My mouth; it will not return to Me empty, without accomplishing what pleases Me, and without succeeding *in the matter* for which I sent it."

As in the previous vision, the interpreting angel asked Zechariah, **"What do you see?"** Scrutinizing the object further, Zechariah replied, **"I see a flying scroll; its length is twenty cubits and its width ten cubits."** In giving these dimensions, Zechariah implied that the scroll was unrolled; its message was not hidden or dormant but clear and actively in force. In modern measurements, the scroll was about thirty feet by fifteen feet, or nine meters by three meters. Because it was large and visible, its contents were readily available for all to see. Furthermore, these measurements—twenty cubits long and ten cubits wide—were the same dimensions as the porch in front of Solomon's temple (1 Kgs 6:3) and also the entrance into the millennial temple (Ezek 41:2). This connection was intentional, showing that the contents of the scroll related to entry into God's house.

On the one hand, these measurements reminded Israel of God's holiness, and that no unrepentant sinner will be granted access into His presence. Just as there is a porch before one enters the temple, so there is a standard of holiness for those who wish to fellowship with the Lord. That standard is not based on a relative moral code; rather, it is objectively laid out in the scroll of God's Word. Israel needed to deal with sin according to the law of God. This was particularly imperative since the scroll was flying to implement and execute judgment.

On the other hand, the scroll carried not only the threat of punishment, but also the hope of purification. Its connection to the temple was fitting given the situation of Zechariah's audience, as they worked to rebuild the temple under Zerubbabel. This vision reassured them that one day God will purify the nation, purging the rebellious and reprobate from among His people, so that He might establish the righteous reign of the Messiah. In that future kingdom, the purified remnant will enjoy intimate fellowship with the Lord in His millennial temple.

Because God's final judgment is yet future, the image of this scroll appears again in the book of Revelation (Rev 5:1–10). There, the Apostle John described the Lord Jesus taking the scroll of divine judgment and beginning to unroll it. The subsequent calamities unleased on the world will include the judgments of the seven seals, the seven trumpets, and the seven bowls (6–16). These expressions of divine wrath will occur during the Tribulation, prior to Christ's return and the establishment of His earthly kingdom (19–20). In this way, the book of Revelation represents the culmination of what Zechariah saw—namely, that God will one day judge the world according to the righteous standard of His Word.

THE COMPLETENESS OF GOD'S JUDGMENT

Then he said to me, "This is the curse that is going forth over the face of the whole land; surely everyone who steals will be purged away according to the writing on one side, and everyone who swears will be purged away according to the writing on the other side." (5:3)

The interpreting angel further defined the scroll with the words, **this is the curse**. The Hebrew word for **curse** conveys an extreme punishment brought about when one breaks an oath or violates a covenant (Gen 24:41; Num 5:23; Deut 19:12, 14). In His covenant with Israel, God promised blessings for obedience, but curses for disobedience. In Deuteronomy 29:19–20, Moses used the same Hebrew term for **curse** to summarize all the judgments listed earlier in Deuteronomy, including divine destruction in every place (28:15–20), pestilence, famine, defeat before an enemy, boils, shame, and exile (28:21–37). The flying scroll in Zechariah's vision depicted divine and devastating curses being unleashed on those who had violated the covenant they had promised to keep.

In the rest of the verse, the angel demonstrated how overwhelming and comprehensive such a curse will be, as it **is going forth over the face of the whole land**. Primarily, this referred to the land of Israel. God's judgment was going to cover the entire country. At times in Israel's history, there were crises in one part of the land, but not in another (cf. Judg 3:15, 31; 12:8–15). However, when His judgment falls at the end of the age, no part of the nation will be exempt. At the same time, the word **land** is also used to refer to the whole earth, suggesting that the curse on Israel will be part of a larger, global judgment (cf. Isa 24:1–6). This corresponds to the Tribulation judgments described in the book of Revelation, which will involve the entire world (cf. Rev 6–16).

The angel continued by specifying the objects of such judgment: **"Surely everyone who steals will be purged away according to the writing on one side, and everyone who swears will be purged away according to the writing on the other side."** The warning, appearing in two parallel lines, was directed to those who **steal** and those who **swear** falsely. Both sins were prohibited by the Ten Commandments, the heart and summary of the law (cf. Exod 20; Deut 5). In the Decalogue, stealing was prohibited by the third command of the latter five commandments (Exod 20:15; Deut 5:19), while swearing falsely by the name of Yahweh was prohibited by the third command of the first five commandments (Exod 20:7; Deut 5:11). In that way, stealing represented the set of commands concerning love for one's neighbor (cf. Mark 12:31; Rom 13:9), and swearing represented the set of commands concerning love for the Lord (cf. Mark 12:30). Accordingly, God's curse will fall on those who broke any of His commandments, whether it regards love for Him or love for one's neighbor. The word **everyone** is repeated in verse 3 for both kinds of sinners, those who steal and those who swear falsely, to show that no one will escape His notice. Every violator of God's law will be punished (cf. Ps 14:1; Rom 3:23; Jas 2:10), except those who have been pardoned through the work of His Son, the Messiah (cf. Zech 3:3–4; Rom 6:23; 2 Cor 5:21).

The nature and extent of this judgment is described in the expression **purged away**. The verb *naqah* means "to be emptied." For example, in Isaiah 3:26, the prophet described Jerusalem as completely deserted because everyone in it had been annihilated. In a similar way,

Zechariah's message was that the guilty will be entirely wiped out and cut off from the realm of God's blessing.

All of this was to take place **according to the writing on one side** and also **on the other side**, meaning the front and the back, of the flying scroll. This description coincides with the depiction of the scroll in Revelation 5:1, which also had text written on the front and the back. This unique feature further links these two scrolls together, indicating that the work of judgment which began in Zechariah will culminate in Revelation. Additionally, the description of the scroll also coincides with the stone tablets that contained the Ten Commandments, which also had writing "on one *side* and the other" (Exod 32:15). That connection confirmed that the flying scroll represented the covenant the Lord made with His people at Sinai. It was a reminder that God would execute His entire covenant to its fullest extent, both in blessing the redeemed and in judging the unrepentant.

THE CERTAINTY OF GOD'S JUDGMENT

"I will make it go forth," declares Yahweh of hosts, "and it will enter the house of the thief and the house of the one who swears falsely by My name; and it will spend the night within that house and consume it with its timber and stones." (5:4)

The angel had already said that the flying scroll of covenant judgment will "go forth" (cf. Zech 5:3). In verse 4, he added that such judgment will happen because **Yahweh of hosts** Himself declared, **"I will make it go forth." Yahweh of hosts**, who has every resource and who commands all the armies of heaven, guaranteed that He would **make** His judgment **go forth** according to His sovereign will. The Lord emphasized the absolute certainty of this future reality by formally and personally announcing His involvement.

Accordingly, God will ensure that judgment will transpire exactly as He promised. The Lord's covenant curse **will enter the house of the thief and the house of the one who swears falsely by My name**. In the previous verse, the angel warned sinners of the coming curse of divine punishment. Here, the Lord Himself described the execution of that judgment, as His wrath enters the house of the **thief** and of the **one who swears falsely by My name**. The vivid picture portrays Yahweh doing exactly what He promised to do. The wording here (for **thief** and for **the one who swears falsely**) is singular, stressing that God's judgment will seek and destroy every unrepentant sinner. No one will be missed when He enacts His eschatological judgment.

God's judgment will be both comprehensive and complete. The Lord earlier declared that the curse would purge the wicked from among His people (Zech 5:3), and here He showed how that would be accomplished. God's wrath, represented by the flying scroll, **will spend the night within that house and consume it with its timber and stones**. The idea of **spending the night** is that God's judgment will remain until it achieves its full effect. The unredeemed sinner will not be safe, even in his own home. Divine wrath will find him and **consume** him along with his possessions. The word **consume** conveys bringing something to a complete and utter end. Since **timber and stones** were the building materials for a house at that time, the annihilation of those things expressed the total destruction of both the sinner and all he possessed (cf. Mark 8:37; Luke 12:13–21).

One further observation can be made about this vision—the focus, three times in one verse, on the **house** of the unredeemed sinner. Why did the Lord concentrate so heavily on the sinner's **house**? While this certainly shows that God will devastate the total person and estate of the reprobate, there is an additional reflection to ponder. In Zechariah, the temple of Israel is called God's house (Zech 1:16; 3:7; 4:9; cf. 1 Kgs 6:1; Ezra 3). Haggai, a contemporary of Zechariah, rebuked the people for building their own houses when the house of God was yet unfinished (cf. Hag 1:2–4). The focus on houses in Zechariah's prophecy would have similarly motivated the people to prioritize the house of God. Though His judgment will one day level the houses of the wicked, there is one house that will certainly remain when the Messiah's kingdom is established—that is, the house of the Lord (cf. Ezek 40–48).

In summary, the vision of the flying scroll teaches profound prophetic truth about God's plan for Israel and the world. God's judgment is holy, active, exhaustive, and sure. All should tremble before His Word (cf. Isa 66:1–2) and warn the unrepentant of the wrath to come (cf. Acts 2:37–40). At the same time, the redeemed can rest assured that God will one day judge the wicked in righteousness. He will do so to fulfill His covenant promises, purge the chaff from the wheat, and usher His saints into His holy kingdom where they will enjoy the infinite blessings of His glorious presence.

The Seventh Night Vision: God Remembers His Plan for the Nations

Zechariah 5:5–11

Then the angel who was speaking with me went out and said to me, "Lift up now your eyes and see what this is going forth." So I said, "What is it?" And he said, "This is the ephah going forth." Again he said, "This is their appearance in all the land" (and behold, a lead cover was lifted up); and this is a woman sitting inside the ephah. Then he said, "This is Wickedness!" And he threw her down into the middle of the ephah and threw the lead weight on its opening. Then I lifted up my eyes and saw, and behold, two women were coming out with the wind in their wings; and they had wings like the wings of a stork, and they lifted up the ephah between the earth and the heavens. And I said to the angel who was speaking with me, "Where are they taking the ephah?" Then he said to me, "To build a house for her in the land of Shinar; and when it is prepared, she will be set there on her own pedestal."

In Revelation 17 and 18, God disclosed details about the eschatological harlot of Babylon, the ultimate symbol of worldliness and the wickedness that flows from it. In Revelation 17:4–5, John described the harlot as follows: "The woman was clothed in purple and scarlet, and adorned with gold and precious stones and pearls, having in her hand a gold cup full of abominations and of the unclean things of her sexual immorality, and on her forehead a name *was* written, a mystery, 'BABYLON THE GREAT, THE MOTHER OF HARLOTS AND OF THE ABOMINATIONS OF THE EARTH.'" Scripture often equates false religion and worldliness with spiritual adultery and harlotry (cf. Ezek 16; Hos 1–3; Jas 4:4). But all of that corruption will culminate in a final Babylon, which will be both the hub of global commerce (cf. Rev 18:12–13) and the seat of false religion. As John prophesied in Revelation 18:2, "She has become a dwelling place of demons and a prison of every unclean spirit, and a prison of every unclean bird and a prison of every unclean and hateful beast." That future Babylon will be the climax and epicenter of ungodliness, seducing "all the nations" of the world as they eagerly engage in the false system of sensuality and secularism she represents (18:1–3, 7). Despite its power, and due to its wickedness, it will be thoroughly and suddenly destroyed by the judgment of God (cf. 18:7–19).

Roughly 600 years before John described Babylon in the book of Revelation, the Lord showed Zechariah a similar vision also featuring the harlot of Babylon. This seventh vision primarily revealed two truths about God's plan for the nations. First, it demonstrated that God sovereignly constrains evil, even as wickedness continues to grow throughout the world (Zech 5:5–8). Second, it revealed that God has set the course for this wicked world system (5:9–11). Because its destruction has been predetermined by Him, God's people should not grow anxious but rejoice in hope.

THE SOVEREIGN CONSTRAINT ON GLOBAL EVIL

Then the angel who was speaking with me went out and said to me, "Lift up now your eyes and see what this is going forth." So I said, "What is it?" And he said, "This is the ephah going forth." Again he said, "This is their appearance in all the land" (and behold, a lead cover was lifted up); and this is a woman sitting inside the ephah. Then he said, "This is Wickedness!" And he threw her down into the middle of the ephah and threw the lead weight on its opening. (5:5–8)

The prophet introduced this vision with the statement **then the angel who was speaking with me went out.** Throughout this chapter, "go out" or "going forth" have been used repeatedly. Zechariah observed that the flying scroll went forth (5:3) because God caused it to go forth (5:4). In like manner, the angel here **went out,** perhaps following the path of the scroll of God's judgment. The scroll and the angel were not the only things in this passage that went forth. The angel directed Zechariah to **lift up now your eyes and see what this is going forth.** The expression **lift up now your eyes** appeared in earlier visions (1:18; 2:1; 5:1). In this instance, it signaled to Zechariah that he needed to fix his concentration on another object that was **going forth.** The repetition of the verb **going forth** establishes the theme of this vision. Like the previous vision in which the scroll went forth in judgment (see discussion on 5:3–4), this vision pictured God's plan for history, including the wickedness of the world, moving steadily forward to the day of His judgment. However, while the previous vision centered on Israel, this vision focused on the nations (cf. 5:11; see also discussion on 1:7). Both are joined together to trace how God's judgment will move through Israel to the entire world.

Though he obeyed the angel's command, Zechariah was not able to discern exactly what he was seeing, so he asked the angel, **"What is it?"** In earlier visions, the prophet had sometimes asked what he was seeing to learn the significance of what was before him (1:9; 2:2; 4:4, 5, 11–12). Other times, the interpreting angel asked Zechariah what he saw to prompt the prophet toward further investigation (4:2). Here, however, Zechariah asked simply because he was unable to identify the object presented in the vision. The interpreting angel had to tell him that **this is the ephah,** a basket that could hold 1.05 bushels or 8 gallons of grain. The prophet had difficulty seeing it because the basket was small, a feature related to God's message in this vision (see discussion below). In answering Zechariah's question, the angel was emphatic that **this** basket **going forth** was the item the prophet was intended to observe.

Having identified the basket, the angel proceeded to reveal its significance. Speaking **again he said, "This is their appearance in all the land."** The interpreting angel equated the basket with **their appearance,** meaning the **appearance** of the people of Israel. In Hebrew, the word for "appearance" literally means "eye." The language sets up a contrast between God's eyes, which Zechariah mentioned earlier in the book, and the eyes of the people. Unlike God's eyes which roamed to and fro throughout the earth to advance His plan (cf. 3:9; 4:10), the eyes of the people were like an empty basket, craving to be filled with grain and material wealth. The people's **appearance** was visibly greedy. While the exile in Babylon purged the Israelites of idolatry externally, it had not purged them of materialism. Rather, during their time in captivity, they became ensnared by the foreign commercial emporium of Babylon which exposed them to a new level of avarice and secularism.

Self-centered materialism had sunk deep into their hearts and stayed with them even after they returned to Judah. The prophet Haggai, Zechariah's contemporary, rebuked Israel for focusing on their wealth and houses instead of prioritizing God's house (cf. Hag 1:2-4). In Nehemiah 5, Nehemiah confronted Israel's leaders for their selfish materialism. Similarly, in Malachi 3:8-9, the prophet asserted that Israel had robbed God by their covetousness. Greed had spread to the leaders and lay people, affecting their worship and every other area of life. This sin of avarice was Israel's **appearance in all the land**. Though there was no more worship of pagan idols in Israel, the people had filled their homeland with a new form of idolatry—greed (cf. Col 3:5). But, as noted in Zechariah 5:3, the term **land** does not solely denote the land of one specific nation, such as Israel. The term can also refer to the entire earth, as it does in this context. The rest of the passage supports this interpretation because the ephah basket went out from Israel to Shinar, a distant land far outside of Israel (Zech 5:11; cf. Gen 10:10). This prophetic vision established that the sin of worldly materialism was not limited to Israel but was common to the nations.

Recognizing the pervasive nature of worldliness, the writers of the New Testament repeatedly warned believers against greed (Col 3:5), the love of money (1 Tim 6:10), and the love of the world (1 John 2:15-16; 2 Tim 4:10). So the sin of materialism symbolized by the ephah basket was not limited to Zechariah's day. Just as the basket went forth in the prophet's vision, so the sin of greed has continued to operate throughout world history and will remain dominant until the end times. Nevertheless, while the ephah basket depicted the greedy desire of sinful people to idolize earthly goods and material riches, God simultaneously demonstrated that He was sovereignly in control. The very fact that the basket was small signified that the Lord has set limits on its wicked influence.

The theme of God's restraint of evil continued as the prophet observed that, **behold, a lead cover was lifted up.** Zechariah noticed a circular piece of heavy lead that functioned as a lid for the basket. This cover represented God's constraining control over evil, containing the wickedness inside the basket. For Zechariah's sake in the vision, the cover **was lifted up** to allow the prophet to peer inside. There he saw **a woman sitting inside the ephah.** The basket itself was a symbol of sinful materialism. Based on Zechariah's explanation (cf. Zech 5:8, 11), as well as on the book of Revelation (Rev 17:1–7), the woman symbolized religious perversion. Her place in the basket depicted the relationship between greed (the love of material riches) and idolatry (the love of something other than God). Remarkably, the woman fit inside the small basket, both **sitting** and remaining **inside** the ephah. In the book of Revelation, the harlot of Babylon, the final form of worldly false religion, is depicted sitting on a great beast out in the open (17:3). But in Zechariah's vision, the harlot of Babylon was still very small, illustrating that God had confined the spread of her wickedness at that time.

The angel's actions against the woman evidenced the forcefulness of God's restraint against the evil she represented. The angel exclaimed, **"This is Wickedness!" And he threw her down into the middle of the ephah and threw the lead weight on its opening.** The angel's reference to **wickedness** describes the terrible abomination of worldliness and moral corruption represented by the harlot. In Revelation 17:4, John portrayed such wickedness as whoring after worldly pleasure, wealth, intoxication, and sexual immorality. Though she symbolized abhorrent evil, Zechariah saw that she was constrained by the Lord. This was evidenced by the angel's ability to throw **her down** into the basket. She was also small in size, since she fit in **the middle of the ephah.** Her containment was completed when the angel **threw the lead weight on its opening,** thereby incarcerating her wickedness inside. Controlled by God and caged in by the basket and the heavy lid, the harlot was confined. The Lord had placed limits on the extent of her evil influence.

Thus, while God will judge evil with finality in the future, Zechariah's vision showed that until then, He restricts evil in keeping with His sovereign purposes. Such restraint is nothing new. God restrained evil after the Flood (Gen 8:20–22) and by scattering the nations (11:6–9). In the New Testament, Paul reminded the Thessalonian church that the Lord continues to restrain evil during the church age (2 Thess 2:6–7). Because God constrains evil, His people need not fear the wickedness of the world around them. As the Apostle John reminded his readers, "Greater is He who is in you than he who is in the world" (1 John 4:4).

THE SET COURSE FOR GLOBAL EVIL

Then I lifted up my eyes and saw, and behold, two women were coming out with the wind in their wings; and they had wings like the wings of a stork, and they lifted up the ephah between the earth and the heavens. And I said to the angel who was speaking with me, "Where are they taking the ephah?" Then he said to me, "To build a house for her in the land of Shinar; and when it is prepared, she will be set there on her own pedestal." (5:9–11)

The words **then I lifted up my eyes and saw** introduced one more feature about the ephah and the woman inside it. As Zechariah looked, a new image caught his attention—**behold, two women were coming out with the wind in their wings; and they had wings like the wings of a stork.** The **two women** had wings like angels, but the context suggests that they were demonic figures, not holy angels. That interpretation is supported by the fact that they assisted the ephah basket and the wicked woman inside it. Zechariah revealed that these **women** would build a house for the woman and establish her on a pedestal (cf. 5:11). Their willingness to aid the harlot evidenced their wicked intentions. In addition, the prophet described these women as having **wings like the wings of a stork.** Storks were unclean birds (Lev 11:19; Deut 14:18).

By comparing these women to such birds, Zechariah depicted them as impure harbingers of unclean things.

The prophet observed that these winged figures **were coming out**. The concept of "going forth" or "coming out" was repeated throughout this section of Zechariah's prophecy. The flying scroll went out, as did God's curse (Zech 5:3), the interpreting angel (5:5), and the ephah (5:6). Everything was in motion, and the motion of the text emphasized that God's judgment was moving forward against the wicked. By describing these figures as **coming out**, the text placed them in the same divine flow of judgment. Though they were agents of evil, these demonic angels were operating according to God's sovereign purposes. The description that **the wind** was **in their wings** indicated that they were flying at a high rate of speed. The pieces of God's sovereign plan were moving rapidly into place.

As the angels moved, they **lifted up the ephah between the earth and the heavens**. This exact phrase, **between the earth and the heavens**, occurs only three times in the Old Testament, each time depicting God's supernatural judgment. In 1 Chronicles 21:16, an angel was standing between earth and heaven to strike down Jerusalem because of David's sinful census. To appease God's wrath, David purchased the threshing floor of Ornan (1 Chr 21:18), which later became the site of the temple (cf. 2 Chr 3:1). The phrase next occurred when Ezekiel was lifted up between earth and heaven in a vision to behold Jerusalem's abominations (Ezek 8:3). In judgment for this idolatry, God's glory departed from the temple (10:18–22), but Ezekiel prophesied that His glory would one day return (43:1–3). This passage in Zechariah is the third time the phrase **between the earth and the heavens** appeared, and here it also involved divine judgment. Like the other two occurrences, the context connected it to the temple, since Zechariah's prophecy addressed the task of completing the temple's construction. That the ephah was lifted up **between the earth and the heavens** signaled that God would judge the wickedness it represented (Rev 18:2). The Lord will judge the evil angels and the wicked harlot they accompanied, even while establishing His own temple in righteousness.

Seeing the two demonic figures moving away with the basket,

Zechariah **said to the angel who was speaking with** him, **"Where are they taking the ephah?"** The prophet's question emphasized that the wicked angels and the ephah were leaving the land of Israel to go to another location. As noted above, this vision addressed God's plan not merely for Israel but also for the nations (see discussion on Zech 1:17; and also the parallel vision in 1:18–21). The interpreting angel's response confirmed that this was happening according to God's sovereign purposes. **Then he said to me, "To build a house for her in the land of Shinar; and when it is prepared, she will be set there on her own pedestal."** **To build a house for her** denotes the construction of a pagan temple, which was fitting since the woman in the basket symbolized false religion. As the angel explained, that pagan temple would be located **in the land of Shinar**, the very location of the tower of Babel (Gen 10:10; 11:2), where humanity once united in rebellion against God. Furthermore, Shinar was the location not only of the tower of Babel, but also of the city of Babylon. Zechariah's vision revealed that history was moving from the tower of Babel in Genesis 11 to the harlot of Babylon in Revelation 17–18. Though the harlot was small enough to fit in a basket at the time of Zechariah, God has sovereignly allowed her wicked influence to grow.

At the end of the age, the evil system she symbolizes will dominate the entire world. As the angel explained, **when** her house **is prepared, she will be set there on her own pedestal.** The task of the demons was to facilitate and develop the world system of idolatry and immorality represented by the wicked woman. The end result of their efforts is described by John in Revelation 17–18. At the end of history, the false religion of Babylon will be on its own **pedestal**, established as the dominant center of world religion and global blasphemy. Zechariah's vision revealed that evil would progress throughout the course of history, finally culminating in the events described in the book of Revelation. At the end of the age, the Lord will judge this wicked world system, crushing it completely before establishing the righteous reign of the Messiah. To that end, God's sovereign plan is moving forward.

For this reason, Zechariah's use of the word **house** in this passage must not be overlooked. The term **house** not only indicates that the temple of false religion would arise, but also contrasts Zechariah's emphasis that God's house would be built and would prevail (Zech 1:16; 3:7; 4:9). Just as the previous vision revealed that God's wrath would destroy the houses of the impenitent (cf. 5:4), so this vision depicted the final house of false religion to demonstrate that it too will be destroyed. By contrast, when the Messiah returns and establishes His earthly kingdom, only the true and glorious house of God will stand. While sinful society moves from bad to worse (2 Tim 3:1), Zechariah's vision revealed that this world system is constrained by God and moving along the course He has ordained. In the end, the Lord will destroy the wicked world and fulfill His plan for the salvation of His people.

The Eighth Night Vision: God Remembers to Implement His Plan

17

Zechariah 6:1–8

Then I lifted up my eyes again and saw, and behold, four chariots were coming forth from between the two mountains; and the mountains were bronze mountains. With the first chariot were red horses, with the second chariot black horses, with the third chariot white horses, and with the fourth chariot dappled horses—*all of them* mighty. Then I answered and said to the angel who was speaking with me, "What are these, my lord?" And the angel answered and said to me, "These are the four spirits of heaven, going forth after standing before the Lord of all the earth, with one of which the black horses are going forth to the north country; and the white ones go forth after them, and the dappled ones go forth to the south country." Now the mighty ones went out, and they sought to go to patrol the earth. And He said, "Go, patrol the earth. So they patrolled the earth." Then He cried out to me and spoke to me saying, "See, those who are going to the land of the north have caused My Spirit to have rest in the land of the north."

In a single night, the Lord unveiled a series of revelatory dramas to the prophet Zechariah. The first seven conveyed that God not only remembered all His promises but that He would also fulfill all He had declared, ultimately by the coming of His Messiah. These astonishing disclosures were meant to comfort the people of God's beleaguered nation (cf. Zech 1:13), who were wondering if the Lord intended to keep His Word. To cap all of this, Zechariah's eighth and final vision specifically revealed God's readiness to set His plan in motion. Yahweh demonstrated to the prophet that His heavenly hosts were prepared for action (6:1–3), and that He would deploy them to implement His plan, precisely as He had depicted it to Zechariah (6:4–8). This final scene provided the perfect conclusion to Zechariah's visions. It testified in stunning form that God will faithfully remember and fulfill all He has determined to do.

GOD SETS HIS PLAN IN MOTION

Then I lifted up my eyes again and saw, and behold, four chariots were coming forth from between the two mountains; and the mountains *were* bronze mountains. With the first chariot *were* red horses, with the second chariot black horses, with the third chariot white horses, and with the fourth chariot dappled horses—*all of them* mighty. (6:1–3)

Zechariah's eighth and final vision began in a similar fashion to his former visions. He stated, **"Then I lifted up my eyes again and saw."** Paralleling the first vision with colored horses (Zech 1:8), this eighth vision also employed horses to depict the way God was moving His plan swiftly forward. However, whereas the first vision featured three horses, this final vision portrayed **four**. In this context, the number four conveys universality, since these horses will be sent to patrol the whole earth (cf. v. 7). The number four is used similarly in other passages. For example, Isaiah spoke of the four corners of the earth (Isa 11:12), and Daniel described the four winds of heaven (cf. Dan 7:2; 8:8; 11:4; Jer 49:36; Zech 2:6; and Mark 13:27). Ezekiel's vision repeated the number four in reference to various objects—living creatures, faces, wings, and directions—to refer to the four cardinal directions and to emphasize God's omnipresence (Ezek 1:5, 6, 8, 10, 15, 16, 17). Additionally, Zechariah's second vision also displayed four horns that symbolized the major nations of history (Zech 1:18–21). In the eighth vision, God's **four** horses illustrated His intent to act globally to accomplish His purposes.

Beyond the difference in number (three horses in vison one, but four in vision eight), the two visions also differed in content—whereas the first vision had only horses, the eighth vision had **horses** and **chariots**, demonstrating God's readiness to act. Previously, the horses were patrolling the earth and bringing a report (1:10–11). But in the final vision, the presence of chariots indicated that the reconnaissance was complete and that God was advancing His forces into battle. Thus, Zechariah stated that these chariots **were coming forth**. Echoing the description of the flying scroll, curse, angels, and ephah in the previous chapter, all of which also were "coming" or "going forth," this language revealed that God's plan was in motion. He was actively moving to implement judgment (cf. 5:3, 4, 5, 6, 9). The Lord was deploying the chariots of His heavenly host to accomplish that eschatological plan.

Additionally, in the first vision the horses were in a ravine (1:8), but in this final vision the chariots and horses came **from between the two mountains** (6:1–3). The definite article **the** indicates that these two mountains were specific and familiar to Zechariah's audience. Beginning with the early church father Eusebius, many Bible scholars have believed that the two mountains represent Mount Zion and the Mount of Olives.[1] This conclusion is warranted since the ravine mentioned earlier was the Kidron Valley (see discussion on Zech 1:8), the valley between Mount Zion and the Mount of Olives. While the first vision spoke of the valley between the mountains, the final vision looked to the mountains on either side of the valley, the location where God's triumph will take place. That is why the prophet observed that **the mountains were bronze mountains**. Since bronze often symbolized strength and holiness (Dan 10:6; Rev 1:15–16), these mountains showcased the indomitable power and purity of God's victory. Such will be the case when the final temple is built on Mount Zion, fulfilling many prophecies described in Zechariah's visions (cf. Zech 1:16; 2:5, 10, 11; 3:7; 5:4, 11; 6:13). Moreover, when the Messiah returns, He will come down on the Mount of Olives to redeem His people (cf. Zech 14:4). These mountains will

---

1 Eusebius Pamphill, *The Proof of the Gospel*, trans. and ed. W. J. Ferrar, 2 vols. (Grand Rapids: Baker Books, 1981), 2:26–27.

be the location of God's victory over His enemies and for His people, and this vision emphasized that God was committed to such triumph, commissioning His angelic hosts to secure it.

There is a third difference between Zechariah's first vision and this final scene. While both of Zechariah's visions described horses with specific colors, the colors themselves were not all the same. The first vision had red, sorrel, and white horses (Zech 1:8). But in the last vision, **with the first chariot were red horses, with the second chariot black horses, with the third chariot white horses, and with the fourth chariot dappled horses**. Each color was significant. As noted above (see discussion on 1:8), the red horse represented war. The black horse depicted famine (cf. Rev 6:5–6). The white horse portrayed victory (see discussion on Zech 1:8). The dappled horse—a horse that had spots and discolorations—symbolized death (cf. Rev 6:8). The dappled horse related to the pale horse in Revelation 6:8, which was associated with Death and Hades. Zechariah concluded by noting that the supernatural chariots and horses were **all of them mighty**, having the strength to overcome and destroy all opposition. At the end of the age, the Lord will engage in war, famine, victory, and even death, in order to confront, curse, conquer, and crush His adversaries. He will exert all power necessary to gain total triumph. Though the opening vision depicted things at a seeming standstill (cf. Zech 1:11), in this final vision, God revealed that His chariots of war will one day fan out across the world to dramatically complete His program and bring Him glory.

These same horses also appear in John's apocalyptic and eschatological vision in Revelation 6. The Apostle John saw red, black, white, and dappled or pale horses, just like Zechariah did. In revealing the same vision to John, the Lord demonstrated that His plan had not changed. God confirmed to John that He will use His angels to judge the world and exalt His Son just as Zechariah beheld in his eighth vision. God remembered what He revealed to Zechariah, and He will fulfill every detail of that promise.

GOD SETS EVERY PROMISE IN MOTION

Then I answered and said to the angel who was speaking with me, "What are these, my lord?" And the angel answered and said to me, "These are the four spirits of heaven, going forth after standing before the Lord of all the earth, with one of which the black horses are going forth to the north country; and the white ones go forth after them, and the dappled ones go forth to the south country." Now the mighty ones went out, and they sought to go to patrol the earth. And He said, "Go, patrol the earth. So they patrolled the earth." Then He cried out to me and spoke to me saying, "See, those who are going to the land of the north have caused My Spirit to have rest in the land of the north." (6:4–8)

As in other visions, Zechariah desired further explanation. So, he **answered and said to the angel who was speaking** with him, **"What are these, my lord?"** (cf. Zech 1:9; 4:4–5, 13). **The angel answered** Zechariah's question by explaining that these chariots will implement all that God had disclosed to His prophet in the night visions. The angel began with the fact that **these** chariots **are the four spirits of heaven**, meaning that they represented angels who were divine instruments of judgment. The Hebrew word for **spirit** (*ruach*), can also be translated as "wind," as is found in Zechariah's earlier visions. In the third vision, Israel was scattered to the "four winds" (2:6), and in the seventh vision a "wind" filled the wings of the two angelic figures (5:9). In calling His angels "winds" or "spirits," God indicated that He would use His angels to drive forth what He had disclosed in those visions. He would send these angels to help restore Israel from exile, and to assist in judging the nations. The Apostle John also described these four angels as being engaged in this very activity in Revelation 7:1: "After this I saw four angels standing at the four corners of the earth, holding back the four winds of the earth, so that no wind would blow on the earth or on the sea or on any tree."

The interpreting angel also noted that these angelic agents were **going forth**, a verb used repeatedly in the sixth and seventh visions (cf. Zech 5:3, 5, 6). Just as the scroll and the ephah went forth, so these chariots went forth in keeping with God's purposes. The previous two visions revealed truth about God's impending judgment. In this vision, the Lord dispatched these angels to ensure that judgment was executed.

The angels were sent to do this from their post of **standing before the Lord of all the earth**. Angels are servants of God, and they stand before Him, worshiping and waiting to do His bidding (Dan 7:10; Luke 1:19). The Hebrew word for **standing** has the notion of standing at attention or officially presenting oneself for service (cf. Job 1:6). So while the angels pictured in Zechariah were working to drive God's plan onward, it was Yahweh Himself who sovereignly deployed them. He is **the Lord of all the earth**, the ruler over the entire created order, both supernatural and natural. This grand title was used in Zechariah's fifth vision for the Messiah, the One who would possess all authority as the ultimate King and great High Priest (Zech 4:14). Given this connection with Zechariah's fifth vision, the divine title shows that the Messiah is the One commanding the angels with the purpose to fulfill what was revealed in that vision. Christ commissioned these angels to exact judgment so that at His second coming, His glorious light would prevail as He exercised dominion over **all the earth** (cf. 4:14). Micah reflected this identity in his magnificent picture of the Lord Jesus Christ:

> Now muster yourselves in troops, daughter of troops; they have laid siege against us; with a rod they will strike the judge of Israel on the cheek. But as for you, Bethlehem Ephrathah, *too* little to be among the clans of Judah, from you One will go forth for Me to be ruler in Israel. His goings forth are from everlasting, from the ancient days. Therefore He will give them *up* until the time when she who is in childbirth has borne a child. Then the remainder of His brothers will return to the sons of Israel. And He will stand and shepherd *His flock* in the strength of Yahweh, in the majesty of the name of Yahweh His God. And they will remain because at that time He will be great to the ends of the earth. And this One will be peace. (Mic 5:1–5a)

The Lord assigned these chariots to go forth in specific directions, starting with **the black horses going forth to the north country** to bring famine and devastation. For Israel's enemies, the most effective way to attack Israel was from the north, and many invading armies, such as Assyria and Babylon, or later in history, the Seleucids (Greeks) and the Romans, came from that direction. In this specific context, the **north country** refers to Babylon, and relates to Zechariah's seventh vision of judgment against the harlot of Babylon (cf. Zech 5:11). Thus, God will send **the black horses** to judge Babylon. But to ensure that wicked Babylon will be utterly destroyed as prophesied, God will send a second set of horses, **the white ones**, symbolizing victory. They will **go forth after** the black horses of famine as the Lord crushes the enemies of the north in absolute triumph.

The land of the north is not the only direction God's judgment will move. The interpreting angel stated that **the dappled ones** will **go forth to the south country**. This primarily referred to Egypt, which opposed Israel from the very beginning of the nation (cf. Exod 1:8–22) and throughout its history (1 Kgs 11:17–40; 14:25; 2 Kgs 18:21–24; 23:29). The dappled or pale horses, symbolizing death, went out to curse this nation which had previously cursed Israel (cf. Gen 12:1–3). Zechariah's vision predicted that Egypt will one day be broken in eschatological judgment (cf. Isa 19:1–15).

In attacking both **north** and **south**, God will ultimately bring judgment, death, and punishment on all of Israel's foes. Neither the west nor the east were mentioned because attacks against Israel did not generally come from those directions. Israel was buttressed by the Mediterranean Sea to the west and vast deserts to the east. The nation faced military threats mainly from the north and the south. By sending angels in those directions, God indicated that He would eliminate every enemy who had come against His people. This final judgment of nations to the north and the south fulfills part of Zechariah's second vision as well, which depicted nations destroying nations.

So far, three groups of horses have been mentioned—black, white, and dappled. But what about the red ones (cf. 6:2)? The red horses, symbolizing war and bloodshed, remained in Israel, for there will be war throughout the entire nation with blood splashing up to the horses' bridles (Rev 14:20). As mentioned in Daniel (Dan 11:1–35) and Zechariah (Zech 13:8–9; 14:1–3), this final and epic battle will not only destroy Israel's enemies but also purge unbelievers from the nation itself. Zechariah saw the same event in his sixth vision, which prophesied that God's covenant curse and judgment will fall on the rebellious among His own people (cf. 5:1–4). God had commissioned His angelic host to bring this about as well.

In verse 7, the interpreting angel indicated that God will also accomplish what He had revealed in the first vision. He said: **"Now the mighty ones went out, and they sought to go to patrol the earth. And He said, 'Go, patrol the earth.' So they patrolled the earth."** In the first vision, the angelic horses were designated for reconnaissance, but the angels here are called **mighty ones**, able to execute and overcome. In the first vision, the angels came in, but in this vision, these chariots **went out**. In the first vision, the angels gave a report, but here, they **sought to go to patrol the earth**, to assess the situation and execute divine judgment. In the first vision, the Lord made promises to comfort His people (1:13), in this final vision, He commissioned the implementation of those promises. **He said** to these angels, **"Go, patrol the earth,"** and in obedience, **they patrolled the earth**, carrying out His will. The plans Yahweh revealed in the first vision, He began to carry out in the last.

Having demonstrated that He will accomplish the promises found in Zechariah's first, second, third, fifth, sixth, and seventh visions, the Lord concluded by demonstrating that He will also fulfill the revelation of Zechariah's fourth vision. The prophet recounted: **"Then He cried out to me and spoke to me saying, 'See, those who are going to the land of the north have caused My Spirit to have rest in the land of the north.'"** At the end of this final vision, Zechariah recorded that the Lord **cried out to me and spoke to me**, conveying the Lord's triumphant joy and enthusiasm for what will result from His work. Yahweh's angelic agents will **go forth** to punish one of Israel's fiercest enemies, Babylon, in the **land of the north** (cf. discussion on Zech 5:6, 11; Rev 17–18).

Such judgment will ultimately **cause My** [God's] **Spirit to have rest in the land of the north**. The language of **rest** connects with Zechariah's fourth vision, where God's people were depicted sitting under their respective vines and fig trees, experiencing the Edenic rest of Christ's coming kingdom (see discussion on Zech 4:10). At that time, the Lord will exhaustively accomplish the millennial rest that He had promised, and not only in Israel but **even in the land of the north**, the land of Israel's archenemies (cf. 5:11).

That the **Spirit** of God will **rest** at this future time is significant. Zechariah's earlier visions already emphasized the role of the Holy Spirit. For example, the Spirit was mentioned in the context of the lampstand (4:1–5) as He communed with God's people. The Spirit also empowered Zerubbabel to complete the temple, prefiguring His empowerment of the Messiah to build the millennial temple (see note on 4:6–10). According to Zechariah's visions, the Spirit is active in all divine efforts of communing, empowering, and governing. So when the Spirit rests, all that God has determined and revealed in vision and prophecy will be fulfilled. Then there will be true rest.

The kingdom of the Messiah will be so restful that not only will there be world peace, but God Himself will rest, as He did after creation (cf. Gen 2:2). The kingdom will be paradise recovered—the earth restored to the peace that will be established by the reign of the Prince of Peace. As Isaiah wrote:

> For a child will be born to us, a son will be given to us; and the government will rest on His shoulders; and His name will be called Wonderful Counselor, Mighty God, Eternal Father, Prince of Peace. There will be no end to the increase of *His* government or of peace, on the throne of David and over his kingdom, to establish it and to uphold it with justice and righteousness from then on and forevermore. The zeal of Yahweh of hosts will accomplish this. (Isa 9:6–7)

This will be the fullest triumph, and in this last vision, God commissioned His angelic messengers to that end.

The eighth and final vision of Zechariah is the sum of all the other visions, dramatically demonstrating that God remembers His promises, and that He secures their fulfillment by His immutable character and Word. Though His people cannot always see His invisible power, God reminded them that He rules every material and spiritual reality in existence. In the future, Yahweh of hosts will send His angelic hosts throughout Israel and the world to execute judgment and implement salvation, just as He had shown to Zechariah on the twenty-fourth day of the month of Shebat in the second year of Darius (Zech 1:7).

To all who still wonder, "Where is the promise of His coming?" (2 Pet 3:4), the answer was given more than twenty-five hundred years ago in God's revelation to Zechariah, the grandson of Iddo. For he heard Yahweh saying, "Yahweh was very wrathful against your fathers. Therefore say to them, 'Thus says Yahweh of hosts, "Return to Me," declares Yahweh of hosts, "that I may return to you," says Yahweh of hosts'" (Zech 1:2–3). With that, Zechariah was given visions to comfort God's people of all generations, revealing that Israel will one day return to God in repentance and faith in their Messiah (Rom 11:26). Then they will be given all the blessings of God's covenant salvation, and those salvation blessings will extend to all who believe (John 3:16). As God showed Zechariah, these promises come only through Christ, "for as many as are the promises of God, in Him they are yes" (2 Cor 1:20).

The Coronation
of the Coming King

18

Zechariah 6:9–15

And the word of Yahweh came to me, saying, "Take *an offering* from the exiles, from Heldai, Tobijah, and Jedaiah; and you come the same day and come into the house of Josiah the son of Zephaniah, where they have come from Babylon. And take silver and gold, make an *ornate* crown, and set *it* on the head of Joshua the son of Jehozadak, the high priest. Then you will say to him, 'Thus says Yahweh of hosts, "Behold, a man whose name is Branch, and He will branch out from where He is; and He will build the temple of Yahweh. Indeed, it is He who will build the temple of Yahweh, and He who will bear the splendor and sit and rule on His throne. Thus, He will be a priest on His throne, and the counsel of peace will be between the two offices."' Now the crown will become a memorial in the temple of Yahweh to Helem, Tobijah, Jedaiah, and Hen the son of Zephaniah. And those who are far off will come and build the temple of Yahweh." Then you will know that Yahweh of hosts has sent me to you. And it will happen if you utterly listen to the voice of Yahweh your God.

Coronations and inaugurations are among the most impressive and weighty events in any society, ancient or modern. For example, on June 2, 1953, over 20 million people tuned in via television to watch the coronation of Queen Elizabeth II of England. The event captured the attention not only of people in the United Kingdom, but also in the United States, as 85 million Americans would later watch the highlights. The broadcast of the event was so massive it helped solidify the BBC as the UK's major media outlet for televising national events.

In a single night, God gave Zechariah eight spectacular visions. On the next day, the Lord directed His prophet to participate in a dramatic portrayal of the Messiah's coronation at the inauguration of the millennial kingdom (cf. Dan 12:11–12; Matt 24:29–31; Rev 19:11–21). When that day comes, the promises of Zechariah's visions will be completely fulfilled. In this passage, Yahweh began by setting the scene for the ceremony that would symbolize Christ's future coronation (Zech 6:9–11). God then revealed the significance of that future moment (6:12–13). Finally, He called Zechariah and those with him to strive faithfully in the present in view of the messianic glories to come (6:14–15).

THE SCENE OF THE CORONATION

And the word of Yahweh came to me, saying, "Take *an offering* **from the exiles, from Heldai, Tobijah, and Jedaiah; and you come the same day and come into the house of Josiah the son of Zephaniah, where they have come from Babylon. And take silver and gold, make an** *ornate* **crown, and set** *it* **on the head of Joshua the son of Jehozadak, the high priest."** (6:9–11)

Although a remnant of the Jews had returned to Israel from exile, there were still many who remained in Babylon. Occasionally, more of God's people would return to their homeland. In this passage, Zechariah noted that one such caravan had arrived on the same day the prophet's night visions concluded (Zech 6:10). At this providential moment, **the word of Yahweh came to** Zechariah. God used this occasion to orchestrate a scene prefiguring the future coronation of the Messiah in the millennial kingdom. This symbolic ceremony served as the perfect epilogue to Zechariah's visions since it previewed the culmination of the realities revealed during the previous night.

God meticulously directed this scene, carefully arranging every element to foreshadow the grandeur of the Messiah's millennial coronation. In verse 10, the Lord began by describing five key characteristics of the people who attended the ceremony. First, they were generous and supportive, which is why the Lord instructed Zechariah to **take an offering** from them. Those returning from Babylon in Zechariah's day had not come back empty-handed. They returned with gold and silver, which contributed to the rebuilding of the temple (cf. Ezra 7:11–20) and to crafting a crown for Joshua (Zech 6:11). Second, as **exiles** returning from Babylon, this group was part of the faithful remnant who journeyed home to Israel. Third, they were men of godly character. The Lord listed their names—**Heldai, Tobijah, and Jedaiah.** The meaning of these names is significant, describing the God-centered character of these men. The name **Heldai** likely means "the Lord's world." **Tobijah** means "Yahweh is good." **Jedaiah** means "Yahweh knows." Together, their names bore witness to the dominion, goodness, and omniscience of God. Fourth, they were part of Israel's priesthood. Zechariah was to join the other men and come the same day and **come into the house of Josiah the son of Zephaniah**, who likely belonged to the priestly line (cf. 2 Kgs 25:18; Jer 21:1). His **house** provided a gathering place for these exiles, including **Heldai, Tobijah, and Jedaiah**, who were also associated with the priesthood (cf. Ezra 2:36, 59–60). The priests apparently gathered in the household of a fellow priest to begin preparations to serve the Lord. On this occasion, they gathered for a very special coronation ceremony. Fifth, those in attendance had **come from Babylon.** This statement not only reiterated that they were returning from exile, but also recalled God's command to leave the worldliness and wickedness of Babylon behind (cf. Zech 2:6–7).

Each of these five features anticipated the future generation of Israelites who will celebrate the Messiah's coronation at the outset of His millennial reign. First, they too will bring an offering to build the millennial temple (Isa 60:10–14; 61:4; 62:6–9; Hag 2:7–9) and to honor their Messiah (Mic 4:13). As the prophets described, this offering will encompass the treasures of the world (cf. Mic 4:13; Hag 2:7–9). One day, the nation which neglected the temple (cf. Hag 1:2) and rejected their

Messiah (Zech 11:12–14) will offer vast riches in their enthusiasm for God's house and God's Son. Second, they will return as exiles from the ends of the earth (Deut 30:3–4; Isa 60:4–9). Though a small remnant returned from Babylon at the time of Zechariah, their homecoming foreshadowed the day when an entire generation of Jewish people will come back to Israel and heed God's salvation call, becoming the nation's supreme generation (Deut 30:3–6, 19; Isa 61:9; Rom 11:23–27). Third, that future generation of Israelites will love and fear the Lord. As they walk in devotion and obedience to Him, the people will be strong (Isa 60:22), righteous (61:3), joyful (61:7), and full of life and blessing (Deut 30:19). Fourth, they will be led in worship by a line of millennial priests. As depicted in Zechariah's fourth vision, Israel's line of priests will be restored to lead the world in the worship of Christ (cf. Zech 3:7). At the time of the Messiah's coronation, the godly remnant will stand ready to worship and serve their King with love and loyalty. Fifth, and finally, the future remnant of Israel will consist of those who rejected the worldliness and wickedness of eschatological Babylon. They will leave its godless system behind in order to honor and serve the Lord. As these five characteristics demonstrate, that future generation of believing Jews will be fit for Christ's kingdom and will enjoy its blessings and fullness. As the most upstanding generation in Israel's history, they will assemble to celebrate the coming of Christ and the inauguration of His earthly millennial reign (cf. Rev 20:4–6).

Having described the characteristics of the remnant, the focus of the narrative turned to the glorious King (Zech 6:11). The symbol of royal sovereignty at every coronation is the crown since it represents both authority and grandeur (2 Sam 12:30; Jer 13:18; Ezek 23:42). Accordingly, God directed Zechariah to **take silver and gold**, the most precious metals of the day, and **make an ornate crown**. The term is actually plural **(crowns)**, emphasizing the elaborate, beautiful, and ornate design, exceeding the majesty of every other headpiece. The crown Zechariah prepared pictured the crown that will be given to Christ in the future. The crown in Zechariah's time was crafted from whatever **silver and gold** was available. But the crown at Christ's coronation will be fashioned from the vast treasures that will pour into Jerusalem from the entire world (Hag 2:7–9). It will be the most valuable and exquisite crown ever made, a crown of crowns to match the King of Kings and the Lord of Lords (Rev 19:12).

A majestic crown would be a scandal if the king himself were not worthy of it. God symbolized the Messiah's worthiness by instructing Zechariah to **set the crown on the head of Joshua the son of Jehozadak, the high priest.** To the Israelites in Zechariah's day, placing a royal crown on the **head of the high priest** was unthinkable. As discussed earlier, in Israel, kings could not be priests and priests could not be kings. God strongly enforced the separation of these powers through the threat of a divine curse (cf. 2 Chr 26:18–19; see discussion on Zech 4:14). Therefore, the crown placed on Joshua's head was not intended for Joshua. Instead, it was symbolic of something beyond Zechariah's time, as demonstrated by the juxtaposition of a kingly **crown** and **the head** of **the high priest.** As noted above, the scene pointed to the future Messiah, who alone is King and Priest (cf. Ps 110:1–3; Ezek 21:26–27). On the day of Christ's future coronation, there will be no question about His worthiness. It will be clear that He alone unites and fulfills that which could never be joined in Israel's history (cf. Zech 3:5; 4:13–14). He is the culminating Sovereign and divine Intercessor, the eternal King and great High Priest. So, with the best crowd, the best crown, and the best King, this future coronation will be unparalleled in all history. Its wonder will be unmatched, and its glory paramount.

THE SIGNIFICANCE OF THE CORONATION

"Then you will say to him, 'Thus says Yahweh of hosts, "Behold, a man whose name is Branch, and He will branch out from where He is; and He will build the temple of Yahweh. Indeed, it is He who will build the temple of Yahweh, and He who will bear the splendor and sit and rule on His throne. Thus, He will be a priest on His throne, and the counsel of peace will be between the two offices."'" (6:12–13)

Yahweh then commanded Zechariah to **say to him**—to Joshua— the words explaining the significance of what had just been symbolized.

In describing the glory of the Messiah's future coronation ceremony, the Lord revealed six features of that eschatological event.

First, it will display and celebrate the ultimate Sovereign. Zechariah declared: **Thus says Yahweh of hosts, "Behold, a man..."** This language recalls that the prophet in an earlier vision saw a **man** (cf. Zech 1:8) identified as the final Adam, the Messiah. By referring to the Messiah as a **man**, Zechariah portrayed Christ as the One who will fulfill and reclaim Adam's role of dominion over the whole earth (Gen 1:28; cf. 2:23–25; Zech 1:8; 14:9–21; and Dan 7:13–14). His inauguration will announce not only that He is King of the Jews, but that He is King of all creation. Unwittingly, with no knowledge of Zechariah, Pilate referred to Jesus similarly when he said in John 19:5, "Behold, the man!" If the Jewish leaders assembled before Pilate had been paying attention, rather than closing their hearts in unbelief, they might have recalled this scene from Zechariah's messianic drama. Nevertheless, what the religious leaders in Jesus' day failed to recognize, a future generation of Israel will understand when Christ returns as the final Adam, the inheritor of all the earth.

Second, the coronation will honor the achievements of the Messiah. Zechariah announced that this man's **name is Branch**, a messianic title mentioned in Zechariah's visions (cf. Zech 3:8) and by other prophets (cf. Isa 4:2; 11:1; Jer 23:5). In those contexts, it was made clear that no mortal man could perfectly fulfill the offices of either king (cf. Isa 4:2; 11:1; Jer 23:5) or priest (cf. Zech 3:8), but that the messianic Branch would one day do so. Christ's coronation will recognize that from His humble birth, He overcame all barriers to take the throne and fulfill all divine intentions (Isa 4:2; 11:1; Rev 3:21).

Third, the Messiah's future coronation will honor His sacrificial and saving work. As discussed earlier (see Zech 3:8), the title "Branch" was inextricably linked with the Messiah's incarnation and suffering as a substitutionary sacrifice for His people. Zechariah referred to this when he declared that the Branch **will branch out from where He is**. This language echoes the words of Isaiah 53:2, "For He grew up before Him like a tender plant and like a root out of parched ground," as well as Isaiah 61:11, "So Yahweh will cause righteousness and praise to branch out before all nations." As the Branch, the Messiah would not only suffer and die at the hands of His people, but He would also overcome death to be their atoning sacrifice and the Righteous One who justifies the many (Isa 53:11–12). The branching out of the Branch describes the entire saving work of Christ. He who begins humbly in His incarnation and affliction **(from where He is) will branch** out to redeem sinners and reconcile them to God (cf. Isa 53:11; Mark 10:45), as His righteousness extends to the nations (cf. Isa 61:11).

Fourth, Christ's coronation will honor His faithfulness to fulfill God's purposes for Israel. The Lord announced, **"And He will build the temple of Yahweh."** For the people in Zechariah's day, the mention of the temple was significant, since they themselves were struggling to rebuild God's house (cf. Ezra 5:1; Hag 1:2). Knowing that the Messiah would one day rebuild the future millennial temple assured the people that their labors were not in vain but were part of God's sovereign plan for His house (cf. Matt 21:13). The temple not only mattered to those in Zechariah's day but to God Himself. Having directed His people to build a first temple (1 Kgs 5–9) and a second temple (in Zechariah's day), Christ will one day build a third temple during His millennial reign. It will be the epicenter of God's glory (Isa 60:7; Ezek 40–48), the pinnacle of world rule (Isa 2:2; Mic 4:1–2), the global house of worship (Isa 62:9; Jer 33:11; Dan 9:24), and the ultimate place of peace (Hag 2:9). Zechariah's visions themselves revealed that the completion of the temple after the Messiah returns will mark the full restoration of Israel and Jerusalem (Zech 1:16), the full dwelling of God with His people (2:5), and the enjoyment of His gracious privileges in worship (3:7). In the plan of God, the building of the final temple of Yahweh represents the apex of the fulfillment of God's blessings upon Israel. Because of its importance, only the final and true Davidic King will be able to build it (Zech 4:9; cf. 2 Sam 7:13; Ps 132:3–5, 13–17). At His coronation, the Son of God will be celebrated as the One who alone is worthy to accomplish that spectacular task and all it represents.

Fifth, the Messiah's future coronation will display His singular dominion. God declared: **"Indeed, it is He who will build the temple of Yahweh and He who will bear the splendor and sit and rule on His throne."** By saying **"Indeed, it is He,"** Zechariah stressed the worthiness of the Messiah alone to drive and direct the work of rebuilding the millennial temple. In His kingdom, Christ will not only be the center of this glorious achievement but the center of all glory as **He will bear the splendor.** The term **splendor** expresses the personal holiness and divine majesty Christ exclusively possesses. In such resplendent magnificence, He will **sit and rule on His throne** as the sole and stable ruler whose throne is established forever (2 Sam 7:13). From that throne, He will reign over all creation as the final Adam (see above). The future coronation of the Messiah will announce the exaltedness of His work, worth, and worldwide reign.

Sixth, Christ's coronation will proclaim His supreme office. The Lord pronounced, **"Thus, He will be a priest on His throne."** In setting up the scene, Zechariah had already placed a crown on the head of Joshua the priest (cf. Zech 6:11). The Lord explicitly stated here that this symbolism was essential because it depicted the Messiah in His unmatched preeminence. As discussed above, no king of Israel could be a priest, and no priest could be a king. Only the Messiah can and will unite these two offices. David prophesied in Psalm 110:4, "You are a priest forever according to the order of Melchizedek." Melchizedek was an ancient priest who was also a king (Gen 14:18). Though David was never a priest, he understood that the one who would fulfill the Davidic covenant needed to be like Melchizedek, both king and priest. Likewise, Jeremiah (Jer 20:1–6; 22:1–23:12) and Ezekiel (Ezek 21:27), who beheld the collapse of Israel's leadership, prophesied that only the Messiah would restore all of this in Himself. The preview of the Messiah's coronation in Zechariah displayed that Christ will be the divine King-Priest. He will be the ultimate ruler, governing righteously and mediating perfectly between God and man.

Thus God declared in Zechariah's prophecy: **"And the counsel of peace will be between the two offices."** In the past, **the two offices** of king and priest produced conflict, not **peace.** The kings were mostly evil, while the priests were frequently corrupt, and often these offices counteracted each other (cf. 1 Sam 22:18; 2 Kgs 11:1–21; 2 Chr 23:16–23; 24:20–22). However, united in Christ, the power and function of both roles will finally produce the **counsel of peace. Counsel** refers to the exercise of authority in planning, decision-making, and the execution of one's intentions. Isaiah used the word to describe the Messiah as the "Wonderful Counselor" (Isa 9:6). The word also expresses God's infallible ordination of judgment (19:17; 23:9) and salvation (25:1; 46:10). Accordingly, counsel does not refer to advice, but to a plan that is formed and enacted to shape the world. This divine plan is for global **peace** (*shalom*), which describes a state of wholeness, unity, rest, joy, and calm. Because the curse on creation will be curtailed, Christ's kingdom will be characterized by the Edenic rest portrayed earlier in Zechariah's visions (cf. Zech 3:10; 6:6). The Wonderful Counselor is the Prince of Peace, and His coronation will set Him on His throne as His people celebrate the immeasurable blessings of His kingdom. Its motto will be "peace on earth" (Luke 2:14). Its subjects will live in peace. Its ruler will be the Prince of Peace. As Paul said of the kingdom in Romans 14:17: it is "righteousness and peace and joy"—so it will finally be.

THE STRIVING BASED ON THE CORONATION

"Now the crown will become a memorial in the temple of Yahweh to Helem, Tobijah, Jedaiah, and Hen the son of Zephaniah. And those who are far off will come and build the temple of Yahweh." Then you will know that Yahweh of hosts has sent me to you. And it will happen if you utterly listen to the voice of Yahweh your God. (6:14–15)

Now the crown will become a memorial of this prophecy of Christ's coronation. The reference to a **memorial** is very fitting for the book of Zechariah. In Hebrew, the word "memorial" is *zikaron*, which has the same root as the name Zechariah, and the name "Zechariah" means "Yahweh remembers." The crown that Zechariah placed on Joshua's head (cf. Zech 6:11) symbolized the precious truth that God remembers His promises regarding the coming kingdom of His Son. In Old Testament times, memorials were set up to aid people in recalling certain truths (cf. Exod 12:14), actions (cf. 13:9), or even promises (cf. 17:14). God had this memorial crown placed **in the temple of Yahweh** to signify that He would never forget what He promised His people. Whenever the Israelites saw this crown, they too would be reminded of God's commitment to fulfill His plan for His Son, the messianic King.

In symbolizing God's dedication to His plan, the crown specifically commemorated **Helem, Tobijah, Jedaiah, and Hen the son of Zephaniah.** The Lord desired His people to reflect on these men in two ways. First, they were eager and sacrificial supporters of God's work. Their generosity in giving was commendable. Second, they were men of godly character, depicting the meanings of their names. The names **Tobijah** ("Yahweh is good") and **Jedaiah** ("Yahweh knows") were used earlier (cf. Zech 6:10) and reminded God's people to hope in the goodness and understanding of Yahweh. The other two names, **Helem** and **Hen the son of Zephaniah**, were most likely alternative names for Heldai and Josiah the son of Zephaniah, respectively (cf. 6:10). As in modern times, people in the ancient world often had more than one name. By using their alternative names, Zechariah brought attention to their meaning. **Helem** means "strength" (cf. Job 39:4) and reminded God's people that He has the power to fulfill His promises. **Hen** means "grace" or "kindness," the very word the people shouted when the temple was completed by Zerubbabel (Zech 4:7). The future remnant of Israel will also respond with shouts of "grace" when the millennial temple is constructed by the Messiah (see discussion on 4:7). Thus, the crown in God's temple not only displayed that Yahweh remembered His promises but also declared what kind of people Israel ought to be. They were to imitate the service and godly character and hope of Helem, Tobijah, Jedaiah, and Hen the son of Zephaniah.

In verse 15, Zechariah concluded with three ways Israel needed to respond as they considered the devotion and diligence of these four Israelites. First, God called His people to hope in His promises. The Lord painted a beautiful future scene by saying: "**And those who are far off will come and build the temple of Yahweh.**" Those who are far off referred to Israelites dispersed throughout distant lands in exile (cf. Isa 57:19; Acts 2:39). At the end of the age, God promised to regather His people no matter how far away they may be (cf. Deut 30:4). However, **those who are far off** will include not merely the Israelites but also the saints among the Gentiles (cf. Zech 2:11; Eph 2:13) who will help Israel return home (cf. Isa 60:4). So, Zechariah's words indicated that the exiles **who are far off**, scattered and solitary, will one day find themselves surrounded by nations that delight in God. Ushered by these eager people, beleaguered Israel **will come** full of joy back to their homeland. Under the leadership of the Messiah (cf. Zech 6:12), they, with believing Gentiles, will **build the temple of Yahweh** to herald the return of God's glory. With these words of comfort, the Lord assured His people that everything Helem, Tobijah, Jedaiah, and Hen hoped for would one day be fulfilled.

Second, the Lord called His people to exercise faith in the Messiah. As verse 15 continued to explain, when the Messiah returns, regathers His people, and builds His millennial temple, **then you** (Israel) **will know that Yahweh of hosts has sent me to you.** This statement was exclaimed earlier (cf. Zech 2:11; 4:9) and is messianic in nature. It proclaimed not only that the people of Israel will recognize and acknowledge their Messiah in repentant faith (12:10), but that they will also enjoy a personal relationship with Him. Those characterized by the faith of Helem and his associates will embrace the Messiah for who He truly is, the Anointed One of Yahweh.

Third, God called His people to respond in love and obedience. Simply being an Israelite was insufficient to enter the Messiah's coming kingdom (cf. Matt 3:8–9; John 8:39–44). Rather, the Lord explained, **"And it will happen if you utterly listen to the voice of Yahweh your God."** Only those who heed **the voice of Yahweh** (the Word of God) will inherit the blessings of His kingdom. Conversely, those who reject or ignore His Word will not be permitted to enter. The Apostle Paul made this point emphatically clear when he said, "Or do you not know that the unrighteous will not inherit the kingdom of God? Do not be deceived; neither *the* sexually immoral, nor idolaters, nor adulterers, nor effeminate, nor homosexuals, nor thieves, nor *the* greedy, nor drunkards, nor revilers, nor swindlers, will inherit the kingdom of God" (1 Cor 6:9–10). By contrast, Christ's kingdom will consist only of those who love, honor, and obey the King—as they **utterly listen to the voice of Yahweh their God.**

External acts of obedience do not earn the sinner a place in the kingdom (cf. Phil 3:3–9). Rather, true obedience is the result of a heart that has been justified and regenerated by God's grace, based solely on the work of His Son (cf. John 8:43–47; Titus 3:4–7). As Paul continued, "Such were some of you; but you were washed, but you were sanctified, but you were justified in the name of the Lord Jesus Christ and in the Spirit of our God" (1 Cor 6:11). Only those who have been clothed in the righteousness of Christ, having been saved by grace through faith (Acts 16:31; Eph 2:8), will be admitted into His kingdom (cf. Zech 4:3–5; Matt 22:1–14; 2 Cor 5:21). Having been transformed by the Holy Spirit, they now act in accordance with their love for the Lord (cf. Mark 12:30–31; John 14:15). So, as they anticipated their future place in the Messiah's kingdom, the righteous remnant of Israel was called to **listen** submissively to **Yahweh**. They were to respond in obedience **utterly**, eagerly and from the heart, as they served **God** out of loyal love for Him (cf. Deut 6:5).

Thus, Israel was to emulate the hope, faith, and love of Helem, Tobijah, Jedaiah, and Hen, because the kingdom of God belongs to people such as these. Having been redeemed by God's grace, they eagerly responded with devotion, diligence, and delight in the Lord. The right response to what God revealed in this chapter is succinctly summarized by Peter: "Therefore, beloved, since you are looking for these things, be diligent to be found by Him in peace, spotless and blameless" (2 Pet 3:14).

Ritual Versus Reality

Zechariah 7:1–14

19

Now it happened that in the fourth year of King Darius, the word of Yahweh came to Zechariah on the fourth *day* of the ninth month, *which is* Chislev. And *the town* of Bethel sent Sharezer and Regemmelech and their men to entreat the favor of Yahweh, speaking to the priests, who belong to the house of Yahweh of hosts, and to the prophets, saying, "Shall I weep in the fifth month and abstain, as I have done these many years?" Then the word of Yahweh of hosts came to me, saying, "Speak to all the people of the land and to the priests, saying, 'When you fasted and mourned in the fifth and seventh months these seventy years, was it actually for Me that you fasted? And when you eat and when you drink, are you not eating for yourselves and are you not drinking for yourselves? Are not *these* the words which Yahweh called out by the hand of the former prophets, when Jerusalem was inhabited and at ease along with its cities around it, and the Negev and the Shephelah were inhabited?'" Then the word of Yahweh came to Zechariah saying, "Thus has Yahweh of hosts said, 'Judge with true justice and show lovingkindness and compassion each to his brother; and do not oppress the widow or the orphan, the sojourner or the afflicted; and do not devise evil in your hearts against one another.' But they refused to give heed and turned a stubborn shoulder and dulled their ears from hearing. And they made their hearts diamond-hard so that they could not hear the law and the words which Yahweh of hosts had sent by His Spirit by the hand of the former prophets; therefore great wrath came from Yahweh of hosts. And it happened that just as He called and they would not listen, so they called and I would not listen," says Yahweh of hosts; "but I scattered them with a storm wind among all the nations whom they have not known. Thus the land is desolated behind them so that no one was passing through and returning, for they made the pleasant land desolate."

Superficial, self-righteous religion was the primary issue the Lord Jesus confronted and condemned during His earthly ministry. Though Christ compassionately offered salvation to repentant sinners, He attacked the religious establishment and their legalism head on. Jesus vividly illustrated the distinction between the hypocrisy of self-righteousness and the humility of sincere repentance in Luke 18:9–14:

> He also told this parable to some people who trusted in themselves that they were righteous, and viewed others with contempt: "Two men went up into the temple to pray, one a Pharisee and the other a tax collector. The Pharisee stood and was praying these things to himself: 'God, I thank You that I am not like other people: swindlers, unjust, adulterers, or even like this tax collector. But I fast twice a week; I pay tithes of all that I get.' But the tax collector, standing some distance away, was even unwilling to lift up his eyes to heaven, but was beating his chest, saying, 'God, be merciful to me, the sinner!' I tell you, this man went down to his house justified rather than the other, for everyone who exalts himself will be humbled, but he who humbles himself will be exalted."

For the self-righteous Pharisee, religion was legalistic and superficial, consisting entirely of external rituals like fasting and tithing. He had no interest in genuine sorrow, repentance, or worship. By contrast, the tax collector was deeply distraught over his sin. Recognizing the reality of his spiritual bankruptcy, he responded with sincere humility, guilt, and sorrow, saying, "God, be merciful to me, the sinner!" (Luke 18:13). He offered to God only a broken and contrite heart. Of these two men, Jesus noted that only the tax collector went to his house justified.

Ritualism and hypocrisy were the major features of the apostate religion of first-century Judaism. The Lord Jesus came to Israel at a time when superficial religious tradition had reached its pinnacle. He exposed such legalistic externalism as a deadly deception and preached a gospel of genuine repentance and faith (cf. Mark 1:15). The Apostle Paul also challenged the ritualism of apostate Judaism (cf. Phil 3:3–9). He wrote to the Corinthians that there were some "who boast in appearance and not in heart" (2 Cor 5:12). In Romans, speaking of unbelieving Israel, he declared that though they received the law and claimed to be instructors and correctors of the foolish (Rom 2:20), they had in fact broken God's law to such an extent that His name was blasphemed because of them (2:23–24). Paul addressed the issue again in Colossians 2:20–23, where he wrote:

> If you have died with Christ to the elementary principles of the world, why, as if you were living in the world, do you submit yourself to decrees: "Do not handle, nor taste, nor touch"? Which deal with everything destined to perish with use, *which are* in accordance with the commands and teachings of men; which are matters having, to be sure, a word of wisdom in self-made religion and self-abasement and severe treatment of the body, *but are* of no value against fleshly indulgence.

Throughout biblical history, the Lord's messengers consistently warned against superficial, ritualistic, and self-righteous approaches to God. That warning is needed in the church age, and it was also needed in Old Testament Israel during Zechariah's time. Accordingly, it is the theme of chapter 7, where God exhorted His people to abandon superficial forms of ritualism and instead to worship Him from the heart. This text addresses this issue by describing ritualistic reasoning (Zech 7:1–2), repulsive worship (7:3–6), real obedience (7:7–11), and the ramifications for religious hypocrisy (7:12–14).

RITUALISTIC REASONING

Now it happened that in the fourth year of King Darius, the word of Yahweh came to Zechariah on the fourth *day* of the ninth month, *which is* Chislev. And *the town of* Bethel sent Sharezer and Regemmelech and their men to entreat the favor of Yahweh, speaking to the priests, who belong to the house of Yahweh of hosts, and to the prophets, saying, "Shall I weep in the fifth month and abstain, as I have done these many years?" (7:1–3)

Now it happened introduces the next section in the prophet's revelation from God. In the preceding context, the Lord had shown through a series of visions that He remembered all His promises to Israel (Zech 1–6). He vividly depicted the glory of Christ's future kingdom, the era when those promises will be fulfilled (6:9–15). In chapters seven and eight, God expressed what He required of His people in response to His promises for them.

The timing of this message was in **the fourth year of King Darius**, two years after Zechariah received his visions (1:7). **Darius** was the pagan ruler of the Persian Empire, of which Israel was a part. Previously, Zechariah mentioned only Darius's name (1:7), but this time he added that he was **king**. It underscored that though God promised that the Messiah would one day reign, that time had not yet come. A different king was ruling over Israel and the surrounding regions—**King Darius**. Though God had already instructed His people that delay did not mean He was slow to carry out His promises (cf. Zech 1:7–17; 2 Pet 3:9), some might have wondered what they were supposed to do while waiting.

To give clarity on what He required, **the word of Yahweh came to Zechariah on the fourth day of the ninth month, which is Chislev**. At that time, the people were nearing the midpoint of their work to reconstruct the temple. Two years had passed, and the project would be completed within another two years and three months (cf. Ezra 6:15). This rapid progress undoubtedly thrilled the people, who perceived it as evidence of God's blessing. But in their enthusiasm for the temple and its ceremonies, they faced a familiar danger. The people could easily lapse into patterns of ritualism so common throughout Israel's history (cf. Isa

65:3–4; 66:1–2; Jer 7:1–7). Such danger also threatened those who were
baffled by the fact that they were still under foreign rule, still having to
call the ninth month by its Babylonian name, **Chislev**. In their frustration
and impatience, they wondered if there was something more they could
do to accelerate God's plan. So, divine revelation was sent to warn both
the eager and the frustrated not to fall into the trap of ritualism.

Whether motivated by enthusiasm or frustration, **the town of
Bethel sent Sharezer and Regemmelech and their men to entreat
the favor of Yahweh**. The name **Bethel** means "house of God," and
the names **Sharezer and Regemmelech**, the leaders of the **men** who
came to Zechariah, respectively mean the "prince of the treasury" and
"messenger of the king." In God's providence, these names related
to the temple and the things Yahweh had revealed about the coming
Messiah. Out of concern for those subjects (the temple and the timing
of God's promises), these men came **to entreat the favor of Yahweh**. To
entreat favor was not only to ask God to look kindly on them, but to
seek His immediate deliverance (Exod 32:11; 1 Kgs 13:6; 2 Kgs 13:4). Thus,
the delegation from Bethel journeyed to Jerusalem to inquire about the
temple, and to see what they could do to expedite the fulfillment of God's
messianic promises.

The men who were sent were **speaking to the priests, who belong
to the house of Yahweh of hosts, and to the prophets**. In their sincerity,
the members of the delegation addressed their inquiries to the right
people—the priests and the prophets of God. Because their pressing
questions related to the temple, it followed that they would speak with
the **priests**, who belonged **to the house of Yahweh of hosts**. The priests
were familiar with the temple and knew what the Lord had promised to
do for His house. Additionally, the delegation spoke with the **prophets**,
those who received divine revelation and declared it to the people (cf.
Isa 8:19–20). The delegation was not merely seeking human wisdom, but
truth from God Himself.

However, despite their fundamental sincerity, the delegation's
line of inquiry was flawed. They asked the question: **"Shall I weep in
the fifth month and abstain, as I have done these many years?"** The
question may seem honest and pure, but it carried the marks of ritualism.

It betrayed a faulty assumption that they could prompt a response from God through ceremonial observances. In Israel's history, during Nebuchadnezzar's conquest, the city of Jerusalem fell during the **fifth month** (2 Kgs 25:8). In subsequent years, the people **wept** in mourning on that date and even **abstained** from routine practices and luxuries to show their grief. While there was nothing inherently wrong with such a commemoration, over time the practice had become rote tradition. The spokesman for the delegation even said, **"as I have done these many years,"** emphasizing the routine nature of this annual practice. The clear assumption was that such external traditions would entreat God's favor (cf. Zech 7:2), earning His kindness through religious rituals and ceremonial works. But the Lord was about to show that this superficial externalism is not what pleases Him (cf. Matt 5:21–48).

REPULSIVE WORSHIP

Then the word of Yahweh of hosts came to me, saying, "Speak to all the people of the land and to the priests, saying, 'When you fasted and mourned in the fifth and seventh months these seventy years, was it actually for Me that you fasted? And when you eat and when you drink, are you not eating for yourselves and are you not drinking for yourselves? Are not *these* the words which Yahweh called out by the hand of the former prophets, when Jerusalem was inhabited and at ease along with its cities around it, and the Negev and the Shephelah were inhabited?'" (7:4–7)

God answered Israel's question about ritualism pointedly. Zechariah said, **"Then the word of Yahweh of hosts came to me."** In His personal relationship to Israel as **Yahweh**, and in His powerful character as **Yahweh of hosts**, God provided a corrective to the delegation's honest but errant question. The Lord said to Zechariah, **"Speak to all the people of the land and to the priests."** While a specific delegation posed the question, the Lord made it clear that His answer was for **all the people of the land** to hear. God desired to warn everyone about the dangers of hypocritical religion and false worship. He particularly addressed **the priests** because they led His people in worship. In so doing, they needed to be careful to avoid empty rituals and superficiality, the kind of worship God rejects. More than 500 years later, Jesus proclaimed similar warnings to Israel's leadership in His day (cf. Matt 23:1–12; Luke 10:37–54), as did Paul to the church (cf. Col 2:16–19). The warning against ritualism did not just apply to those of Zechariah's time; it remains relevant for every age.

God's declaration revealed six characteristics of ritualism, exposing its counterfeit nature and the reason God finds it so repulsive. First, ritualism is deceptive since it has only the appearance of godliness. The Lord's response began with the statement, **"When you fasted and mourned in the fifth and seventh months." Fasting** was part of the practice of "abstaining" that was mentioned earlier in the text (cf. Zech 7:3). **Mourning** denoted public displays of grief, often over the death of a loved one (cf. Gen 23:2; 50:10; 1 Sam 25:1; 28:3; 2 Sam 1:12). Israel fasted and mourned to commemorate the fall of Jerusalem in the **fifth** month (2 Kgs 25:8) and the assassination of Gedaliah in the **seventh** month (25:25). Those ceremonies were dramatic and visible, having the appearance of piety as the people forfeited comfort and engaged in outward expressions of sorrow. But, as the Lord will soon explain through His prophet, when true grief over sin and genuine awe of God are absent from these practices, the external actions become superficial and meaningless. They are like tombs that have been cleansed on the outside, but are rotten with death on the inside (Matt 23:27). Indeed, God pointed out the irony that Israel showed piety only twice a year. How could that be considered meritorious before Him?

Second, ritualism misses what God requires. The Lord said that these acts of fasting and mourning had been occurring **these seventy years.** This time period recalled the seven decades Israel spent in Babylon (cf. Jer 25:11; 29:10; Dan 9:2), a time when God was calling them to repentance. The Lord declared through Jeremiah that at the end of the seventy years, Israel was to "call upon Me and come and pray to Me, and I will listen to you. You will seek Me and find Me when you search for Me with all your heart" (Jer 29:12–13). In that passage, God referred to Himself five times, emphasizing that Israel should seek Him from the heart. However, instead of doing that, Israel persisted in superficial ritualism for seventy years. The Lord was not impressed. While the delegation described their dutiful efforts over "these many years" (cf. Zech 7:3), God knew the exact number—**seventy years**—that they had been carrying on. During all those years, God saw His people perform fast after fast, but none of those ceremonies fulfilled the heartfelt obedience He desired. So, while Israel thought they were accumulating divine favor over the decades, the Lord was counting each year of their disobedience.

Third, ritualism is insincere. If Israel had not yet realized that God's response was a rebuke, the final part of His statement made that unmistakably clear. The Lord's words came in the form of a harrowing question: "**Was it actually for Me that you fasted?**" Mourning and fasting have the appearance of religious devotion, but God knows the heart (cf. 1 Sam 16:7). Proverbs 16:2 says: "All the ways of a man are pure in his own sight, but Yahweh weighs the motives." True **fasting** takes place because one is so distraught over his sin and so focused on the Lord, that he foregoes even the basic needs of life such as eating (cf. Jonah 3:4–9). Because God knew the insincerity of their hearts when they fasted and mourned, He asked, "**Was it actually for Me?**" This question was designed to pierce their self-righteous shell and reveal that their worship was hypocritical. Though their actions appeared noble, religious, and even righteous, they were displeasing to God because they were not truly for Him. Their fasting was a meaningless form of ritualism. By contrast, genuine worship seeks the Lord in spirit and in truth (John 4:23–24).

Fourth, ritualism is self-centered and self-serving. God stated to the people, "**And when you eat and when you drink, are you not eating for yourselves and are you not drinking for yourselves?**" In confronting Israel's hypocrisy, God switched from behaviors related to restraint and sadness to occasions **when you eat and when you drink**. Israel not only observed fasts and times of mourning, but also held feasts and celebrations in their yearly calendar. God declared to the people that even in those activities they had failed to honor Him. His line of interrogation exposed their duplicity: "**Are you not eating for yourselves and are you not drinking for yourselves?**" The people were not only *not* offering God worship that satisfied Him, but worse yet, they were engaged in satisfying themselves in His name. Every part of their feasts, whether **eating** or **drinking**, was all for their own gratification. The shift from past to present tense **(are you not eating** and **drinking)** was a reminder that such perversion was not merely a past problem in Israel's history, but that it was a present problem in the hearts of the people. Even as Zechariah spoke to them, the Israelites had made themselves the object of their worship. Their ritualism led them into idolatry.

Fifth, ritualism is condemned by God. The Lord reminded the people of prior revelation He had given to Israel throughout the nation's history: "**Are not** *these* **the words which Yahweh called out by the hand of the former prophets?**" The truth God revealed through Zechariah was not new, but the very **words which Yahweh called out by the hand** of His messengers, the **former prophets** (cf. Exod 9:3; 9:35; 10:21; 1 Kgs 18:46; 2 Kgs 4:34). Zechariah was not the first to confront the wickedness and idolatry of ritualism. Isaiah (Isa 1:10–15), Joel (Joel 2:12–17), Jeremiah (Jer 7:21–23), and Samuel (1 Sam 15:22–23) all preached against the blasphemy of legalism and hypocrisy. The Lord's standard had not changed. The people in Zechariah's time were without excuse.

Sixth, ritualism carries heavy consequences. The Lord sent previous warnings to Israel at a time when **Jerusalem was inhabited and at ease along with its cities around it, and the Negev and the Shephelah were inhabited.** At the time of David and Solomon, the situation was tranquil as Israel's capital **(Jerusalem)** and its environs **(along with its cities around it)** were at peace. In fact, that peace extended across the entire land of Israel, from the **Negev**, in the far south of the nation, to the **Shephelah** in the west. It was a time when the citizens of the nation had **inhabited** the land, settled down, and were **at ease**, secure from any significant threat. The land of Israel was filled with a flourishing people. However, the scene in Zechariah's day was completely different. Jerusalem was barely inhabited, there were essentially no established cities around it, and the people were in a state of constant alert, rather than at ease. Even more, the Negev and Shephelah were essentially empty because only a fraction of the Jewish people had returned to the land. What caused such a dramatic change? The answer was directly related to the nation's history of religious hypocrisy. Israel had been warned by the former prophets, but the people had failed to heed the warning (cf. Isa 1:10–15). Jeremiah described Israel's attitude: "I spoke to you in your prosperity, but you said, 'I will not listen!' This has been your way from your youth, that you have not listened to My voice" (Jer 22:21). Israel's ritualism brought swift and devastating judgment from God. Zechariah demonstrated that such empty externalism was not harmless, so he called the people to be vigilant against it, and instead to do all things from the heart for God's glory (1 Cor 10:31; Col 3:17).

REAL OBEDIENCE

Then the word of Yahweh came to Zechariah saying, "Thus has Yahweh of hosts said, 'Judge with true justice and show lovingkindness and compassion each to his brother; and do not oppress the widow or the orphan, the sojourner or the afflicted; and do not devise evil in your hearts against one another.'" (7:8–10)

Harkening back to his opening call (Zech 1:4) and to the warnings of earlier prophets (cf. Isa 1:11–17; 58:1–7; Amos 5:10–15), Zechariah exhorted Israel to produce authentic fruit of righteousness. The **word of Yahweh came to Zechariah** yet again and with a parallel message to what had just been revealed (cf. Zech 7:4–7). Godly sincerity was required not only in Israel's religious practices, but also in daily life. The Lord Jesus addressed this issue for the people of His day (cf. Matt 5–7). He even asked the Pharisees, "Why do you yourselves transgress the commandment of God for the sake of your tradition?" (Matt 15:3). Because they did not genuinely love God, the Pharisees replaced heartfelt obedience with a set of extrabiblical rules that were inconsistent and burdensome. As Jesus informed them, they had elevated their manmade traditions and legalistic rituals above the Word of God.

In the previous verse, the prophet used the preceding generations of Israel to illustrate the need for genuine worship (cf. Zech 7:7). Zechariah continued that approach here in discussing righteous living. The past tense verb in **"Thus has Yahweh of hosts said"** indicates that the prophet was still discussing what God had said throughout Israel's history. Zechariah referred to prior generations to demonstrate the nature and importance of real obedience in his own day.

The Lord revealed four characteristics of authentic obedience, the kind that honors and pleases Him. First, real obedience required Israel to **judge with true justice**. As noted above, none of the commands spoken by Zechariah were new. This first imperative was uttered by various prophets throughout the Old Testament (cf. Deut 16:18; Jer 5:28; Ezek 7:27). The call to **judge** relates to the practice of pronouncing a legal verdict or making a legal decision. This certainly pertained to leadership in the courts of Israel. However, it also applied to lay people as they made decisions related to treating others justly in day-to-day society. The prophet Micah said, "He has told you, O man, what is good; and what does Yahweh require of you but to do justice, to love lovingkindness, and to walk humbly with your God?" (Mic 6:8). When Yahweh specified that the people were to judge with **true justice**, He was requiring them to show no partiality. Concerning this principle, James said, "My brothers, do not hold your faith in our glorious Lord Jesus Christ with an attitude of personal favoritism" (Jas 2:1). James pointed out that partiality is incompatible with true faith in Christ. It is not true justice. To judge others with true justice is to do for others exactly what God's Word commands.

Second, real obedience required God's people to **show lovingkindness and compassion each to his brother. Lovingkindness** called for using all of one's might to extend mercy or benevolence to another person. In the New Testament, the idea is captured by the word "grace" (John 1:17; cf. Exod 34:6–8). Just as God graciously intervened in their lives (Eph 1:4–5; 2:1–10; Titus 3:5–6; 2 Tim 1:9–10), so God's people are to engage with grace and kindness in the lives of others. Zechariah also called the Israelites to have **compassion**, a word in Hebrew related to a mother's womb. This word conveys the idea of showing immense care and concern, as a mother does toward her child. God desires not merely that His people treat others fairly or do the minimum the law requires, but that they extend genuine love and compassionate care to their **brother**. This admonition applies not just to some, but to **each** individual.

Third, real obedience does not take advantage of others. Zechariah exclaimed this categorically: **"Do not oppress the widow or the orphan, the sojourner or the afflicted."** The word **oppress** deals with harsh treatment and pressure used to coerce weaker people to fulfill one's own desires. This could be manipulation for financial gain (Lev 5:21) or actions that severely burden or beat down the helpless or vulnerable in society (Deut 28:33). **Widows** and **orphans** lacked husbands and fathers, respectively, to protect and provide for them. The **sojourner** was a foreigner who settled in Israel, and who could easily be neglected as an outsider, lacking any support from the community. Likewise, the **afflicted** and suffering Israelite would have been an easy target, not possessing the strength or resources to defend himself. These were the people to whom Israel was commanded to show lovingkindness and compassion, the kind of attitude reflecting the character of God. In Deuteronomy 10:18–19, speaking of God, Moses said, "He executes justice for the orphan and the widow, and shows love for the sojourner by giving him food and clothing. So show love for the sojourner, for you were sojourners in the land of Egypt." Because God loves the downtrodden, He called His people to do the same. This reveals a foundational principle of genuine spiritual life—it seeks to reflect the moral character of God. Scriptural commands about morality are based on God's law, but that law is a reflection of God's holy nature. Obedience to the Word of God is devotion to God Himself. That is precisely why James exclaimed: "Pure and undefiled religion before *our* God and Father is this: to visit orphans and widows in their affliction, *and* to keep oneself unstained by the world" (Jas 1:27). Most in Israel were bound to traditions and rituals, thinking such practices would find favor with the Lord. Zechariah, however, reminded the people that no religious ritual or performance would please Yahweh unless it came from a heart of love for Him and for others (cf. Matt 22:39–40).

Fourth, real obedience refuses to entertain evil in the heart. The Lord commanded, **"and do not devise evil in your hearts against one another."** **Devise** refers to imagining, plotting, or planning. Coupled with **evil**, it denotes how one intends harm toward others. Zechariah's words pointed out that such destructive planning is formed **in your**

hearts, the seat of volition and will, hidden from man, but known to God (cf. 1 Sam 16:7). It was fitting that a command dealing with the heart was the capstone exhortation from Zechariah in this passage. The remedy to superficial ritualism is a transformed heart that loves the Lord (Deut 6:4–6; 30:1–6) and seeks to serve Him while also seeking the good of others (cf. Luke 6:35–36).

God's command for sincere obedience from the heart is reminiscent of Isaiah 58:3–7:

> Why have we fasted and You do not see? *Why* have we afflicted our souls and You do not know? Behold, on the day of your fast you find *your* desire, and oppress all your workers. Behold, you fast for contention and quarreling and to strike with a wicked fist. You do not fast like *you* do today to make your voice heard on high. Is it a fast like this which I choose, a day for a man to afflict himself? Is it for bowing one's head like a reed and for spreading out sackcloth and ashes as a bed? Will you call this a fast, even an acceptable day to Yahweh? Is this not the fast which I choose, to loosen the bonds of wickedness, to release the bands of the yoke, and to let the oppressed go free and break every yoke? Is it not to divide your bread with the hungry and bring the afflicted homeless into the house; when you see the naked, you cover him; and not to hide yourself from your own flesh?

The "fast" that God accepts as worship is not a hypocritical ritual, but a life of righteousness and self-sacrifice characterized by love for Him and compassion for others.

RUINOUS RAMIFICATIONS

"But they refused to give heed and turned a stubborn shoulder and dulled their ears from hearing. And they made their hearts diamond-hard so that they could not hear the law and the words which Yahweh of hosts had sent by His Spirit by the hand of the former prophets; therefore great wrath came from Yahweh of hosts. And it happened that just as He called and they would not listen, so they called and I would not listen," says Yahweh of hosts; "but I scattered them with a storm wind among all the nations whom they have not known. Thus the land is desolated behind them so that no one was passing through and returning, for they made the pleasant land desolate." (7:11–14)

As noted, these exhortations did not originate with Zechariah but were the same commands Yahweh had given to previous generations. The tragic truth is that when the Israelites' ancestors heard these same instructions, they openly rejected them. Zechariah bluntly recounted: **"But they refused to give heed and turned a stubborn shoulder and dulled their ears from hearing."** That the previous generations **refused to give heed** meant not that they were confused or unclear about God's will, but that they made a deliberate choice to reject His Word. Then, they put that settled intention into action as they **turned a stubborn shoulder.** This expression, also used in Nehemiah 9:29, described Israel's persistence in turning their back on God as they deliberately moved away from Him in rebellion. Israel's ancestors were also resistant to the Lord as they **dulled their ears from hearing.** Like petulant children, past generations plugged their ears to shut out God's unwanted instruction. Entrenched in their sin, Israel refused to hear His voice.

Zechariah declared that Israel's stubborn rebellion came from the heart. The statement **and they made their hearts diamond-hard** reveals that Israel's resistance to God came from deep within. The pathology is chilling—**they made** their hearts hard. They set their minds, including their thinking, perspective, and attitude, against the Lord, hardening their hearts to the point of absolute recalcitrance **(diamond-hard).** Diamonds are so dense that to cut a diamond requires another diamond. A heart as hard as a diamond is impenetrable.

Israel's past generations had so thoroughly fortified their hearts against God **that they could not hear the law and the words which Yahweh of hosts had sent by His Spirit by the hand of the former prophets.** Sin, so deeply buried, produced a deadly condition of spiritual self-destruction. The people of Israel resolved themselves to resist the Word of God, refusing to **hear** it, much less obey it. They rejected all of it, both **the law and the words,** the first five books of Moses along with the rest of the Old Testament. Israel did this while knowing full well that the source of the Scripture was **Yahweh of hosts**, the One who commands all the powers of heaven. They ignored His Word, even though they understood it was **sent by His Spirit**, every word inspired (cf. 2 Tim 3:16; 2 Pet 1:20–21). They callously repudiated God's Word though it came **by the hand of the former prophets** who worked signs and wonders to confirm the authenticity of Scripture (cf. Heb 2:4). Instead of trembling before God's Word (cf. Isa 66:1–2), Israel hardened their hearts and closed their ears. Throughout Israel's history, the Lord repeatedly called the nation to sincere worship and heart-filled obedience, but what they offered God instead consisted of superficial rituals and hard-hearted rebellion.

The consequences of Israel's hypocrisy were that **therefore great wrath came from Yahweh of hosts** (cf. Zech 1:2, 15). God, who controls the hosts of heaven, expressed severe displeasure toward His people for their apostasy. He responded with **great wrath**, and the result was an onslaught of fury that leveled the nation and sent the people into exile (cf. Deut 29:27). Incredibly, such divine punishment was directed toward a people who appeared highly religious. Israel never ceased holding on to external rituals even while their hearts wandered far from God. The Lord demonstrated that He reserves the greatest wrath for such blatant duplicity.

In judging past generations, God did to them as they had done to Him. "**And it happened that just as He called and they would not listen, so they called and I would not listen,**" says Yahweh of hosts. In the past, the Lord **called** out for Israel's ancestors to obey Him from the heart (cf. Deut 6:4–6). But those past generations **would not listen**. Instead, they responded with empty ceremonies and heartless rituals which were nothing but disobedience in disguise. So, when God unleashed His wrath, Israel **called** out in prayer to God, desperately asking for help and deliverance. But Yahweh **would not listen** to them. Because they had ignored His Word, the Lord ignored their cries in their day of distress. His people experienced the emptiness of their own hollow ritualism.

Instead of answering Israel's pleas, God said, "**I [Yahweh] scattered them with a storm wind.**" This is the language of Jonah 1:11–13 in which a storm raged with gale-force winds that nearly destroyed Jonah's ship.

God was not only scattering His people, but doing so with violent intensity. As a result, the Lord dispersed the Israelites **among all the nations whom they have not known.** Exactly as He promised (cf. Deut 29:25), God swept His people to places so foreign they were essentially unknown to the nation. By scattering Israel far away from Jerusalem and the temple (cf. Deut 12:1–14; 1 Kgs 8:33–34), God separated His people from Himself. To those who may think their religious ritualism brings them close to God, this judgment proved otherwise. God casts out those whose religion is purely external; they have no genuine relationship with Him (cf. Matt 7:21–23).

The outcome of the Lord's judgment was severe: **"Thus the land is desolated behind them so that no one was passing through and returning, for they made the pleasant land desolate."** To be **desolate** is to be deserted and to become a wasteland without any inhabitant, where **no one was passing through and returning.** Truly, Israel's enemies **made the pleasant land desolate.** The destruction of the Promised Land exhibited the fury God unleashed against Israel's superficial obedience. It also illustrated the nature of their externalism. Israel gave God empty worship, so God gave them an empty land. The lesson to be learned is simple: never substitute ritualism for reality.

Psalm 95 recalled an earlier generation of God's people who came out of Egypt. But because of the same kind of hard-heartedness, they perished in the wilderness and never entered the Promised Land:

> Oh come, let us sing for joy to Yahweh, let us make a loud shout to the rock of our salvation. Let us come before His presence with thanksgiving, let us make a loud shout to Him with songs of praise. For Yahweh is a great God and a great King above all gods, in whose hand are the depths of the earth, the peaks of the mountains are His also. The sea is His, for it was He who made it, and His hands formed the dry land. Come, let us worship and bow down, let us kneel before Yahweh our Maker. For He is our God, and we are the people of His pasture and the sheep of His hand. Today, if you hear His voice, do not harden your hearts, as at Meribah, as in the day of Massah in the wilderness, "When your fathers tried Me, they tested Me, though they had seen My work. For forty years I loathed

that generation, and said they are a people who wander in their heart, and they do not know My ways. Therefore I swore in My anger, they shall never enter into My rest."

The Holy Spirit drew that Psalm into a warning in the book of Hebrews. This warning extends to all generations, urging the reader to guard against developing a heart that is diamond hard:

> Therefore, just as the Holy Spirit says, "TODAY IF YOU HEAR HIS VOICE, DO NOT HARDEN YOUR HEARTS AS WHEN THEY PROVOKED ME, AS IN THE DAY OF TRIAL IN THE WILDERNESS, WHERE YOUR FATHERS TRIED *ME* BY TESTING *ME*, AND SAW MY WORKS FOR FORTY YEARS. THEREFORE I WAS ANGRY WITH THIS GENERATION, AND SAID, 'THEY ALWAYS GO ASTRAY IN THEIR HEART, AND THEY DID NOT KNOW MY WAYS'; AS I SWORE IN MY WRATH, 'THEY SHALL NOT ENTER MY REST.'" See to *it* brothers, that there not be in any one of you an evil, unbelieving heart that falls away from the living God. But encourage one another day after day, as long as it is *still* called "TODAY," so that none of you will be hardened by the deceitfulness of sin. For we have become partakers of Christ, if we hold fast the beginning of our assurance firm until the end, while it is said, "TODAY IF YOU HEAR HIS VOICE, DO NOT HARDEN YOUR HEARTS, AS WHEN THEY PROVOKED ME." For who provoked *Him* when they had heard? Indeed, did not all those who came out of Egypt *led* by Moses? And with whom was He angry for forty years? Was it not with those who sinned, whose corpses fell in the wilderness? And to whom did He swear that they would not enter His rest, but to those who were disobedient? (Heb 3:7–18)

Looking to the
Future Kingdom

20

Zechariah 8:1–8

Then the word of Yahweh of hosts came, saying, "Thus says Yahweh of hosts, 'I am jealous with great jealousy for Zion, and with great wrath I am jealous for her.' Thus says Yahweh, 'I will return to Zion and will dwell in the midst of Jerusalem. Then Jerusalem will be called the City of Truth, and the mountain of Yahweh of hosts *will be called* the Holy Mountain.' Thus says Yahweh of hosts, 'Old men and old women will again sit in the streets of Jerusalem, each man with his staff in his hand because of age. And the streets of the city will be filled with boys and girls playing in its streets.' Thus says Yahweh of hosts, 'If it is too difficult in the sight of the remnant of this people in those days, will it also be too difficult in My sight?' declares Yahweh of hosts. Thus says Yahweh of hosts, 'Behold, I am going to save My people from the land where the *sun* rises and from the land where the sun sets; and I will bring them *back*, and they will dwell in the midst of Jerusalem; and they shall be My people, and I will be their God in truth and righteousness.'"

The pages of Scripture resound with the glorious hope of Christ's future kingdom. Passage after passage promises that one day Messiah will reign physically from Jerusalem, over both the nation of Israel and the entire world (cf. 2 Sam 7:16; Pss 72:8; 89:20–37; Isa 2:1–4; 9:6–7; 11:1–16; 16:5; 24:23; 32:1; 40:1–11; 42:3–4; 52:7–15; 55:4; Jer 31:12; 33:19–21; Ezek 34:25–29; Dan 2:44; 7:27; Joel 2:21–27; Amos 9:13–14; Mic 4:1–8; 5:2–5; Zech 9:9; 14:16–17). The inhabitants of the nations will serve the Lord and submit to His absolute rule (Pss 2:6–9; 72:8–11; Isa 11:4; Dan 2:35; 7:14; Mic 4:1–2; Zech 9:10; Rev 19:16). During His reign, the effects of the curse will be mitigated and curtailed (Isa 30:23; 32:14–15; 35:1–2, 7). The world will be characterized by righteousness and justice (Isa 2:4; 11:3–5, 9; 12:3–4; Jer 31:33–34; Ps 72:7), peace and prosperity (Jer 31:12; Ezek 34:25–29; Joel 2:21–27; Amos 9:13–14), flourishing and fruitfulness (Isa 65:20, 23; Jer 30:19–20; Ezek 37:25; Zech 8:5), physical health and long life (Isa 29:18; 33:24; 35:5–6; 65:20). The capital city of Jerusalem will be expanded and enlarged (Jer 30:18b; 31:38–40; 37:13; Zech 14:10). From there, Messiah will reign in holiness, exercising sovereign judgment against those who practice iniquity (Ps 2:9; Zech 14:16–19; Ezek 44:25, 27; Rev 19:5; 20:7–10). The unsurpassed blessing of Messiah's future kingdom will last for a thousand years (Rev 20:1–7), providing the climactic conclusion to human history before the inauguration of the eternal state (Rev 21:1–22:5; cf. 1 Cor 15:28).

The opening verses of Zechariah 8 focus on this very theme, the coming kingdom of the Messiah. While Zechariah's previous visions also revealed aspects of the millennial kingdom, the declarations in this vision expound upon those truths in greater detail. This passage (Zech 8:1–8) provides an in-depth look at the time when Christ will rule from Jerusalem over the whole earth.

Our Lord instructed us to pray, "Your kingdom come. Your will be done, on earth as it is in heaven" (Matt 6:10; cf. v. 33). Why do believers long for God's kingdom to come? What will life be like when Messiah reigns on the earth? This prophetic word from Yahweh to Zechariah features five powerful pronouncements about that future golden age. The hope of the kingdom reminds God's people of His loving pursuit (Zech 8:1–2), abiding presence (8:3), enduring peace (8:4–5), limitless power (8:6), and saving plan (8:7–8).

GOD'S PURSUIT OF HIS PEOPLE

Then the word of Yahweh of hosts came, saying, "Thus says Yahweh of hosts, 'I am jealous with great jealousy for Zion, and with great wrath I am jealous for her.'" (8:1–2)

Once again, **the word of Yahweh of hosts came**. In chapter 7, divine revelation came to rebuke the people for their ritualism and religious externalism. Here, God's message is one of encouragement and exhortation. Instead of emphasizing what they were doing wrong, this chapter provides instruction for how to do what is right. If the nation was to respond rightly to the Lord's admonition, they needed to begin by focusing on and rejoicing in the hope of the Messiah's future kingdom.

In disclosing Israel's future hope, this section is structured around a series of introductory statements declaring **thus says Yahweh of hosts**. To those who might question if there will be a future kingdom for Israel, Zechariah 8 offers a powerful rebuttal. The phrase **thus says Yahweh** or **thus says Yahweh of hosts** is repeated ten times in this chapter, reinforcing the reality that the promise of a future kingdom comes from God Himself. The repeated refrain provides the reader with complete assurance that Yahweh will keep His promises for His people Israel. Just as there are Ten Commandments, these ten declarations depict the wholeness and certainty of God's program for the nation. For the people of Zechariah's day, this repeated reminder served as a wake-up call to focus their attention on being in right relationship with God. Instead of preoccupying themselves with external rituals, they needed to fix their hope and their hearts on the Lord and His promises.

Yahweh's message in verse 2 underscored His zeal for Israel: **"I am jealous with great jealousy for Zion."** The Lord had already declared this earlier in the book (Zech 1:14). In both passages, the statement described how God was passionately committed to His people. In this context, the phrase **jealous with great jealousy** does not deal with envy but with love. Like a husband is rightfully jealous for his wife, so God was jealous to have Israel as His own. Because God loved Israel, He made commitments to His people and to the city of Jerusalem, the place He chose for His name to dwell (cf. Deut 12:5, 11; Ps 135:21). Out of love for His people, He refused to be apathetic towards them or indifferent to their idolatry. Instead, He determined to do whatever was necessary to fulfill His good purposes for Israel.

The message from Yahweh continued with this sobering statement: **"and with great wrath I am jealous for her."** God's jealousy for Israel **(her)** not only explained His passionate pursuit of His people; it also indicated His readiness to unleash **great wrath** against Israel's enemies. In Zechariah 1:15, the Lord declared, "I am very wrathful with the nations who are at ease." God's disposition toward the unbelieving nations is one of destructive fury. In Genesis 12, God warned that any nation that curses Israel will be cursed, and any nation that blesses Israel will be blessed. A day will come when that divine threat will be fully carried out. God's jealousy will be unfurled in vengeance against those nations that persecuted His people. As the prophets foretold, this day of reckoning will be the day of Yahweh, when He establishes His earthly dominion by conquering His enemies and inflicting fearful judgment on the world. Jesus will come with vengeance out of heaven (2 Thess 1:7–10) to destroy His enemies at Armageddon (Rev 19:11–19) and to judge all the Gentiles in the Valley of Jehoshaphat (Joel 3:12). He will separate the sheep from the goats, and cast the goats into eternal punishment (Matt 25:46).

These words not only served as a warning to Israel's enemies. They were also a powerful reminder to God's people of His jealous love for them. His covenant commitment to Israel was evident both in His passionate pursuit of the nation and in His great wrath toward her enemies. He would not only help His chosen people but would also bring down those who opposed them. Israel needed to stop focusing on themselves and their religious rituals, turning their eyes instead to behold the glory and goodness of God.

GOD'S PRESENCE WITH HIS PEOPLE

"Thus says Yahweh, 'I will return to Zion and will dwell in the midst of Jerusalem. Then Jerusalem will be called the City of Truth, and the mountain of Yahweh of hosts *will be called* the Holy Mountain.'" (8:3)

The next appearance of the statement **thus says Yahweh** shifts the focus to God's abiding presence during the millennial kingdom. The glory of His presence will transform Jerusalem. As He declared, **"I will return to Zion."** This statement reiterated the promise made earlier in Zechariah 1:16 (cf. Ezek 43:2–5), that although the glory of God had departed from Jerusalem because of Israel's sin (cf. Ezek 10:18), His glory will one day return in all its majesty and fiery brilliance (Zech 2:5; cf. Ezek 40–48). With that, the capital will truly be **Zion**, the political and doxological center of all the earth (cf. Ps 48:2; Isa 2:2). The word **return** highlights a significant point for Israel. God will return to His people as they return to Him in repentance (Zech 1:3–4).

The Lord's abiding presence in Jerusalem signifies the intimate communion He will share with His people. This is evident from the remainder of His statement: **"I will dwell in the midst of Jerusalem."** The word **dwell** denotes the idea of abiding or residing and is related to the image of God dwelling in both the tabernacle (Exod 40:35) and the temple (1 Kgs 8:12). This term also contains the same root as the word for God's Shekinah glory. In that day, the glory of God will dwell among His people in a way reminiscent of His glory in the pillar of cloud (cf. Exod 13:21–22; 40:34–38). At that future time, Yahweh will return to His people, restoring the nation and their relationship with Him.

The location, **in the midst of Jerusalem**, identifies God's focus on the city of Zion and His close communion with its inhabitants. His people will surround Him in worship even as He will surround them with His presence (see discussion on Zech 2:5). Unlike earlier times, when the people were not permitted to be in the presence of His glory (cf. Exod 40:35; 1 Kgs 8:11), at this time, they will enjoy intimate communion with God through the Messiah, as they engage in vibrant worship at the millennial temple (Ezek 40–48; Zech 2:5; 3:7; 6:12–13). God's people will experience perfect fellowship with Him (cf. 1 John 3:2), a kind of intimacy that had previously existed only in the Garden of Eden (Gen 1–2). There, God walked with man in the cool of the day (cf. 3:8). But when Adam fell, that closeness ended. Nevertheless, one day God will once again walk among a holy people (cf. Lev 26:12). That hope will be realized when the Lord returns to Jerusalem to establish His earthly kingdom. His people will know Him as He had always intended.

In keeping with that reality, the Lord declared to Zechariah, **"Then Jerusalem will be called the City of Truth."** The return of God's glorious presence will transform Jerusalem. Though it is God's chosen city, Jerusalem's past is marked by wickedness and rebellion. Scripture calls the city a harlot (Isa 1:21), compares it to Sodom and Egypt (Rev 11:8), and condemns it for its lack of truth seekers (Jer 5:1). Historically, it has not been a city of truth. But when Yahweh returns and resides with His people, the situation will be altogether different. The capital of Israel will finally be the **City of Truth**. Jerusalem will be the place where people will know God's Word and live in light of it (cf. John 17:17). Even more, it will be the place where the Way, the Truth, and the Life, the Faithful and True will reign in messianic glory (cf. John 14:1–6; Rev 19:11; 20:1–6).

The transformation of Jerusalem will not stop there, for **the mountain of Yahweh of hosts will be called the Holy Mountain**. The phrase **the mountain of Yahweh of hosts** is an eschatological title for Jerusalem (Isa 2:3; 30:29; Mic 4:2). This title identifies Jerusalem as the place from which the Lord will reign with a rod of iron and command His heavenly forces (cf. Ps 2:9; Rev 2:27; 12:5). All the nations will stream to the mountain of Yahweh to learn and submit to His law (cf. Isa 2:1–4). Jerusalem will serve as the capital city of all creation, just like Eden was long ago. In fact, Ezekiel described Eden as the mountain of God and the holy mountain (Ezek 28:14, 16), just as Jerusalem is described here in Zechariah. Because God's presence will return to His people, Jerusalem will become the new Eden. The city in Zechariah's time was in disrepair, having been ravaged by invading armies. What a contrast that was to the picture of hope painted in these verses, of a future kingdom in which Jerusalem shines as the epicenter of the world.

As impressive as that future city will be, the primary point of the text is that the mountain of Yahweh **will be called the Holy Mountain**. Holiness deals with God's otherness—His perfection, loftiness, and distinction from all others. The rest of the Old Testament anticipates this designation (cf. Pss 2:6; 48:1; Isa 11:9; 27:13; 66:20; Ezek 20:40; Joel 2:32) and articulates several reasons why Jerusalem will be described as God's holy mountain. Psalm 2:6 states that Jerusalem will be a holy mountain, unique and set apart from all others, because the Messiah will reign from there. Ezekiel 20:40 further explains that Jerusalem will be called a holy mountain because Israel will serve God there in holiness. In Isaiah 11:9, Jerusalem is called the holy mountain because it conforms to God's perfect character. Because the Lord will be on His holy mountain, the cow and the bear will graze, the leopard will lie down with the goat, the lion will eat straw, the wolf will be with the lamb, and the nursing child will play with the cobra (Isa 11:6–9). As these passages reveal, Jerusalem will be God's holy mountain because it radiates His glorious presence and reflects His perfect character. From Jerusalem, His holiness will permeate the entire earth, so that peace will prevail in every aspect of life. As Isaiah proclaimed, "They will do no evil nor act corruptly in all My holy mountain, for the earth will be full of the knowledge of Yahweh as the waters cover the sea" (Isa 11:9; cf. 65:25).

GOD'S PEACE FOR HIS PEOPLE

"Thus says Yahweh of hosts, 'Old men and old women will again sit in the streets of Jerusalem, each man with his staff in his hand because of age. And the streets of the city will be filled with boys and girls playing in its streets.'" (8:4–5)

For a third time, the declaration is repeated: **thus says Yahweh of hosts.** Here it introduces a discussion about the pervasive peace that will prevail during the millennial kingdom. This peace is a result of God's presence among His people. As Yahweh's words explain, **"Old men and old women will again sit in the streets of Jerusalem, each man with his staff in his hand because of age."** The scene described here depicts a lasting peace, as even the elderly sit in the streets without care or concern. Streets can be a dangerous place, whether in the present or in Israel's past. According to Lamentations 4:18, the people of Jerusalem were once unable to enter the streets for fear of their enemies. However, in the future kingdom, even the most vulnerable members of society, the elderly, will feel completely safe in those same Jerusalem streets. They will not only walk the streets, but even **sit** and relax in tranquility.

The peace described in this scene is unprecedented in human history. The elderly will each have **his staff in his hand because of age**. Such a posture denotes an exceedingly old age, as these individuals require a staff even to sit down. Life expectancy during the millennial kingdom will increase dramatically. Isaiah stated that a person who dies at one hundred years of age would be considered young in the kingdom (Isa 65:20). The significance of this is that the effects of sin—including the brevity of life—will be severely curtailed because of Christ's reign. That is partly why Messiah's earthly kingdom will last for one thousand years (Rev 20:1–4). Early in human history, Methuselah lived nine hundred sixty-nine years, longer than any other person (Gen 5:27). However, in the Millennium people will live even longer than Methuselah did. The text explicitly states that both **old men and old women** will age gracefully in this way. With the effects of the curse mitigated, and with no threat of war or crime, life in the millennial kingdom will be characterized by both quantity and quality. The peace that characterizes Christ's earthly reign not only prevents conflict in the political realm but also restrains the effect of the curse on the natural world. This prevailing peace is consistent with the character of our Lord, who is the Prince of Peace (Isa 9:6).

The Lord continued by noting that **the streets of the city will be filled with boys and girls playing in its streets**. This too contrasts the scene described in Lamentations, in which little ones and infants fainted with hunger in the streets of Jerusalem (Lam 2:11–12). In the millennial kingdom, the streets will again be **filled** with children, but they will be playing rather than starving. Families will grow to be large because of the length of life and the security and prosperity of this time. The peace of Messiah's kingdom will extend not only to the old (see above), but also to the young. As these **boys and girls** play, they exhibit the busyness of joyful activity and laughter—indicators of a long and good life in the land. God had promised such blessings for Israel's children if they walked in obedience, both to Him and to their parents (cf. Exod 20:12).

The peace that characterizes Christ's future reign encompasses nations and individuals, old and young, men and women, parents and children. Its blessings include both quantity of life (exceedingly old age) and quality of life (security and stability), as the citizens of the kingdom walk in obedience to the Lord. For a thousand years, life on this earth will again be like Eden. This is the hope God's people have as they anticipate His coming reign.

GOD'S POWER FOR HIS PEOPLE

"Thus says Yahweh of hosts, 'If it is too difficult in the sight of the remnant of this people in those days, will it also be too difficult in My sight?' declares Yahweh of hosts." (8:6)

For a fourth time the text asserts, **thus says Yahweh of hosts**. The preceding verses identified marvelous realities about Messiah's kingdom, to the extent that someone might wonder if those prophetic details will truly come to pass. God's answer to any doubters takes the form of a rhetorical question: **"If it is too difficult in the sight of the remnant of this people in those days, will it also be too difficult in My sight?"** The clear answer to that question is no. Nothing God promised about the future kingdom is hyperbole. All will be fulfilled, just as it had been foretold.

The Lord's rhetorical statement provided the people of Zechariah's day with absolute assurance that He possesses the power to do what He says. Though His promises may seem impossibly **difficult** from a human perspective, they are no problem for Him to fulfill. To be sure, God's promises are so lofty they stretch the limits of human imagination, especially when one begins to contrast divine promises with present circumstances. For the Jewish people in Zechariah's day, being small in number, the promise that God would overflow Jerusalem with inhabitants may have seemed incredible. The Lord's promise sounded too good to be true at a time when Israel was struggling to rebuild Jerusalem and the temple. Given the scarcity of the people and the magnitude of the challenges they faced, it is no wonder they could not fathom the way God's presence and peace would one day transform the world.

But what seems impossible from a human perspective is by no means difficult for God. **"Will it also be too difficult in My sight?"**

declares Yahweh of hosts. By repeating the word **difficult** from the previous phrase, the Lord formed a direct contrast between man's finite weakness and His limitless power. The point was simple: nothing is impossible for the Lord. As Jeremiah 32:17 states, "Ah Lord Yahweh! Behold, You have made the heavens and the earth by Your great power and by Your outstretched arm! Nothing is too difficult for You." Later in that same passage, the Lord echoed those words, "Behold, I am Yahweh, the God of all flesh; is anything too difficult for Me?" (Jer 32:27). In Genesis 18:14, when Sarah thought it impossible for her to have a child, God reminded her of His omnipotence. The God who spoke the world into existence, and who blessed a barren woman with a child, will transform the barren city of Jerusalem into an Edenic paradise (cf. Isa 54:1). Because God's power guarantees His promises, the people of Israel could have certainty that all He foretold would come to pass.

The truth of divine omnipotence brings great comfort to the people of God. To those in Zechariah's day who saw Jerusalem and the temple in shambles, this message reminded them they were part of God's kingdom plan (cf. Zech 4:6–7). To the future generation living in the end times, at the peak of judgment and chaos during the Great Tribulation, this proclamation will provide assurance of God's power to deliver them. For any of God's people living between these two points in history, while they might not see a way out of their present difficulties, true hope is found in remembering that nothing is impossible with God (Luke 1:37).

God's power ensures that His promises will be fulfilled with precision and completeness. All obstacles will be overcome, so that every outcome conforms exactly to what He has said. The future kingdom will be established precisely as He has revealed it. To emphasize the divine source behind these promises, the text reiterates that these declarations come from **Yahweh of hosts,** the sovereign Commander over the forces of heaven. The word **declares** denotes an official announcement, a decree that is formal and fixed. God has codified His commitment in His Word. He will not change, so His kingdom promises are sure.

GOD'S PLAN FOR HIS PEOPLE

"Thus says Yahweh of hosts, 'Behold, I am going to save My people from
the land where the *sun* rises and from the land where the sun sets; and I will
bring them *back*, and they will dwell in the midst of Jerusalem; and they
shall be My people, and I will be their God in truth and righteousness.'"
(8:7-8)

With the fifth recurrence of the phrase **thus says Yahweh of host**s,
the Lord announced His plan for each Israelite person alive at His return.
To begin, He said, **"Behold, I am going to save My people."** The Hebrew
grammar indicates this action is imminent, an event already set on God's
eschatological timeline. His promised plan is not in doubt, nor will it
change, because it has already been determined by the Lord.

God has purposed to **save** His **people**. The word **save** denotes the
overarching act of deliverance from beginning to end. It includes God's
spiritual work of salvation (cf. Zech 12:10) but focuses in this context
on the physical rescue of His repentant people from their exile. This
deliverance is accomplished by God's initiative and intervention. Yahweh
will not allow Israel's faithless wandering and physical oppression to
continue indefinitely. He will intervene to save them **from the land
where the sun rises and from the land where the sun sets.** This
language describes the entire globe, from one end of the world to the
other. Some may argue this refers only to Israel being regathered from
Babylon, but the text is far more expansive than that. This terminology
includes a country like Babylon in the east **(where the sun rises)**, but
it also includes other Gentile nations in the west **(where the sun sets)**.
The idea is that wherever the people of Israel may be scattered, God will
overcome their captors and enable them to come home. No place will be
too far away or exempt from His reach. A deliverance of such magnitude
has never occurred in Israel's history. Therefore, this promise is yet to
come.

In addition to delivering His people, the Lord further promised,
"I will bring them back." God will not only save His people spiritually
and rescue them physically in their locations across the world. He

will regather His people by bringing them back to the Promised Land. As Isaiah 43:5–7 declared, "I will bring your seed from the east, and gather you from the west. I will say to the north, 'Give them up!' And to the south, 'Do not hold them back.' Bring My sons from afar and My daughters from the ends of the earth, everyone who is called by My name, and whom I have created for My glory, whom I have formed, even whom I have made." The nation that was dispersed will be reconstituted and repopulated. For the first time since the initial deportation of Israel to exile (cf. 2 Kgs 24:14), every Israelite scattered across the world will be brought back to one place. This will not merely be a restoration of the nation, but a restoration of the nation to what it was always intended to be (cf. Rom 11:26).

God will gather His people so that **they will dwell in the midst of Jerusalem**. Fundamentally, this statement reminded the people that **Jerusalem** would once again be a vibrant and populated city (cf. Zech 2:4). As noted earlier, not many people lived in Jerusalem at the time of Zechariah (cf. Neh 11:1–2), but God would change that in the future. The word **dwell** does not merely emphasize the physical residence of the people, but also the way they will relate to God. The same word was used earlier in this chapter to describe how God's presence will **dwell** intimately with His people (cf. Zech 8:3). In this way, the reciprocating nature of intimate fellowship between God and His redeemed people is emphasized. Not only will God dwell with His people; His people will also dwell with Him. Even as He will love and abide with them, so they will pursue, embrace, and enjoy their relationship with Him. Many will live in Jerusalem and delight in God's manifest presence, and even those who do not live in Jerusalem (for it will be too full, cf. Zech 10:10) will frequent the city to fellowship with the Lord and to worship Him. God will gather His people not only so they live in the Promised Land, and specifically in Jerusalem, but also so they can express their love for the Lord and abide in His presence. This will be the nation as it was always intended to be.

The result of this will be, as God declared, that **"they shall be My people, and I will be their God in truth and righteousness."** In accordance with the rest of the Old Testament (cf. Ezek 11:20; Jer 31:33),

Zechariah expressed here the pinnacle of God's relationship with Israel. On the one hand, God will fully draw near to His own, as He said, **"they shall be My people."** Israel will become everything the Lord intended them to be. They will be cleansed, forgiven, justified, sanctified, and redeemed. They will truly be His own people. On the other hand, the people will utterly draw near to God, as He declared, **"I will be their God."** Israel, which had always been idolatrous (cf. Jer 7:22–25), never truly knew God as a nation (cf. Rom 9:6). The people invariably strayed after other gods instead of worshiping Yahweh alone. However, in the future kingdom, God will occupy a singular place of devotion in their lives and hearts. Yahweh will be their God in **truth and righteousness.** In other texts, this phrase speaks of sincere and upright conduct (1 Kgs 3:6; Jer 4:2). Although the nation never attained this in history (Isa 48:1), Israel will exhibit such worship and obedience in the end. They will know God **in truth**, as their love for Him flows from sincere hearts. They will also know God in **righteousness**, as their thoughts and deeds conform to Him in complete obedience. They will love God as He had always desired.

A day is coming when God's glory will return, Jerusalem will be transformed, peace will blanket the earth, and God's people will love Him in truth and righteousness. That is what Yahweh has in store for His people Israel. For those in Zechariah's day, the promises highlighted in this passage provided a needed corrective. They sought to earn God's favor through external actions and religious rituals (cf. Zech 7:2–3). In response, Zechariah reminded them that their starting point should never be their works, efforts, or merit. Instead, they needed to begin by looking to the Lord and His promises, fixing their hope in Him, and resting in His grace.

Present Faithfulness in View of Future Promises

21

Zechariah 8:9–17

"Thus says Yahweh of hosts, 'Let your hands be strong, you who are listening in these days to these words from the mouth of the prophets, *those who spoke* in the day that the foundation of the house of Yahweh of hosts was laid, to the end that the temple might be built. For before those days there was no wage for man or any wage for animal; and for him who went out or came in there was no peace because of the adversary, and I set all men one against another. But now I will not treat the remnant of this people as in the former days,' declares Yahweh of hosts. 'For *there* will be peace for the seed: the vine will yield its fruit, the land will yield its produce, and the heavens will give their dew; and I will cause the remnant of this people to inherit all these *things*. And it will be that just as you were a curse among the nations, O house of Judah and house of Israel, so I will save you that you may become a blessing. Do not fear; let your hands be strong.' For thus says Yahweh of hosts, 'Just as I purposed to bring about evil to you when your fathers provoked Me to wrath,' says Yahweh of hosts, 'and I have not relented, so I have again purposed in these days to do good to Jerusalem and to the house of Judah. Do not fear! These are the things which you should do: speak the truth to one another; judge with truth and judgment for peace in your gates. Also let none of you devise evil in your heart against another, and do not love false oaths; for all these are what I hate,' declares Yahweh."

"Some people are so heavenly minded that they are no earthly good." That familiar adage, credited to Oliver Wendell Holmes, expresses a popular notion: that those who focus their attention on future glory will be of little value in the present. For the Israelites who heard Zechariah's prophecies, it may have been tempting to share such a concern. Though they marveled at the majesty of Messiah's coming kingdom, some likely wondered, "What good does thinking on the future do for us right now?" The Lord Himself answered that question in this passage.

God's Word is clear that hope for the future is essential for endurance and effectiveness in the present. Throughout Scripture, the believer's future hope is presented with immediate objectives in mind: to provide perspective (2 Cor 4:17–18), produce perseverance (Rom 5:3–5; 8:25), and promote holiness in this life (1 John 3:3). Believers are therefore instructed to set their minds on the things above (Col 3:1) and to fix their hope on the grace to come (1 Pet 1:13). When they do, they simultaneously grow in holiness (1 Pet 1:16), reverence (v. 17), and fervent love for others (v. 22). By reflecting on their heavenly citizenship (Phil 3:20–21) and the Lord's promises of future glory (John 14:2–3; Rom 8:18), believers are equipped to walk in righteousness despite the darkness of this present age (1 Thess 5:4–10; cf. Eph 5:15–17).

The theme of hope permeates the eighth chapter of Zechariah's prophecy. Instead of trusting in the false hope of religious ritualism (Zech 7), Israel was called to embrace the true hope of Messiah and His future kingdom. The glory of that kingdom was described in verses 1–8. In this section (vv. 9–17), the Lord continued by calling His people to obedience based on their messianic hope. In view of Israel's future glory, the people were charged to be strong in four vital areas: in God's work (Zech 8:9), God's grace (8:10–12), God's promises (8:13–15), and God's truth (8:16–17).

BE STRONG IN GOD'S WORK

"Thus says Yahweh of hosts, 'Let your hands be strong, you who are listening in these days to these words from the mouth of the prophets, *those* who *spoke* in the day that the foundation of the house of Yahweh of hosts was laid, to the end that the temple might be built.'" (8:9)

Throughout verses 1–8, the Lord revealed a series of glorious realities about Messiah's future kingdom. In verse 9, with the sixth occurrence of the phrase **thus says Yahweh of hosts**, He introduced the practical implications of those kingdom promises. For those who wondered how their future hope should impact their present conduct, God exhorted them, **"Let your hands be strong."** Instead of growing slack, becoming apathetic, or losing heart, the Israelites were to take courage as they worked to complete their God-given task. The right response to God's kingdom promises was neither laziness nor indifference. Rather, the people were to actively engage in their present work, rejoicing in God's unfailing plan for Israel's future.

In calling His people to be strong, the Lord focused on those who gave heed to His Word: **"you who are listening in these days to these words from the mouth of the prophets."** Throughout Israel's history, most did not listen to what God revealed through His prophets (cf. 1 Kgs 19:10; Neh 9:26; Jer 2:30; Matt 23:37; Rom 11:3). By contrast, the righteous remnant (cf. Zech 8:6) heeded the words of prophetic revelation. Their submissive attention to divine truth set them apart as the redeemed (cf. John 10:27). A consistent characteristic of God's people is that they love and cling to His Word (cf. Isa 8:19–20; Pss 1; 19; 119; Eph 2:20; Jas 1:19–25). In this passage, the Lord commended the righteous remnant for **listening to these words** of exhortation and encouragement **from the mouth of the prophets in these days**, like Zechariah and Haggai.

The Lord continued by reminding His people of what the prophets said, when they **spoke in the day that the foundation of the house of Yahweh of hosts was laid, to the end that the temple might be built.** Through the prophets, God instructed Israel to rebuild the temple. But completing that assignment was no easy task, which is why the Lord encouraged His people to stand strong and persevere.

The time when **the foundation of the house of Yahweh of hosts was laid**—the point when reconstruction of the temple began—was a major milestone in Israel's history. However, it also involved significant challenges since the footprint of the temple was relatively small (Ezra 3:12), and the people surrounding Israel were vigorously opposed to any rebuilding effort (cf. 4:1–24). Despite these difficulties, the exhortations of Zechariah and his contemporary Haggai were clear: **to the end that the temple might be built.** The prophets' message did not waver from the beginning. The remnant of Israel had been charged with a single task to complete no matter the obstacles or opposition. They were commanded to rebuild the temple.

In the face of difficulty and repeated challenges, these faithful believers needed to be reminded about both the future hope God promised and the present work He called them to accomplish. The majesty of Messiah's millennial kingdom, including the transformation of Jerusalem and the glory of the future temple, served as a powerful encouragement and motivation. Confident that their efforts were part of God's unfailing plan for Israel—a plan that would one day culminate in a glorious kingdom—the people of Zechariah's day could persevere in their present work. They did so knowing that God would empower their efforts and prevail over their enemies (cf. Rom 8:31).

BE STRONG IN GOD'S GRACE

"'For before those days there was no wage for man or any wage for animal; and for him who went out or came in there was no peace because of the adversary, and I set all men one against another. But now I will not treat the remnant of this people as in the former days,' declares Yahweh of hosts. 'For *there will be* peace for the seed: the vine will yield its fruit, the land will yield its produce, and the heavens will give their dew; and I will cause the remnant of this people to inherit all these *things.*'" (8:10–12)

The opening word **for** (v. 10) introduces the reason why the people should continue to strengthen their hands and persevere in their work (cf. v. 9). Though God had previously stood in judgment against Israel, those days were past. He now stood ready to bless and sustain the remnant of His people. That knowledge gave them confidence that God would protect and preserve them, just as He promised to do. In the New Testament, the Apostle Paul encouraged the Philippian believers with a similar truth. Speaking of progressive sanctification, Paul wrote, "He who began a good work in you will perfect it until the day of Christ

Jesus" (Phil 1:6). Fortified by the promise of divine enablement, believers find the resolve to persevere by looking to the Lord and resting in His power (cf. Phil 2:12–13).

In explaining this to the people of Zechariah's day, the Lord first recounted that **before those days there was no wage for man or any wage for animal.** The designation **before those days** referred to the events of verse 9, leading up to and culminating in the prophetic ministries of Haggai and Zechariah. Speaking of that time, Haggai noted there was not enough money to pay the people, and the harvest was insufficient to feed the animals. Such scarcity was the result of Israel's complacent disobedience and God's consequent judgment, which came in the form of severe drought (Hag 1:9–11).

In addition to economic struggles, Israel also experienced political instability, so that **for him who went out or came in there was no peace because of the adversary.** The primary source of this opposition came from the nearby Samaritans, who violently opposed Israel's rebuilding efforts. In addition to external threats from their adversaries, the people also suffered from internal strife and division. As God explained, "I **set all men one against another."** Both from without and within, the remnant of God's people faced severe challenges.

To Israel's great relief, the Lord revealed He was about to change the situation. He declared, **"But now I will not treat the remnant of this people as in the former days," declares Yahweh of hosts.** The divine judgment unleashed on Israel during the **former days**—the time from the initial return of the Israelites to Jerusalem under Zerubbabel (sometime after 538 BC) until Zechariah uttered these words (around 518 BC)—would no longer continue. In the past, they had experienced God's displeasure for neglecting the temple (Hag 1:2–4). But now the Lord promised to bless **the remnant of this people** as they worked to complete that unfinished task. The **remnant** (cf. Zech 8:6, 9) consisted of the faithful and obedient Israelites who listened and responded obediently to God's Word (v. 9; Hag 1:14; cf. Zeph 3:13).

This dramatic difference between God's former judgment and His unfolding blessing would be immediately felt by His people. As Yahweh explained, **"For there will be peace for the seed: the vine will yield its** fruit, the land will yield its produce, and the heavens will give their dew; and I will cause the remnant of this people to inherit all these things." The blessings described in this verse contrasted greatly with the prior experience of the people. To this point in time, the returning Israelites had sowed much, yet reaped little (Hag 1:6); but soon there would be peace for the seed as God secured the harvest cycle. To this point, "the vine, the fig tree, the pomegranate and the olive tree" had not yielded fruit (Hag 2:19); but soon the vine will yield its fruit, the land will yield its produce. God promised to bless both the quantity and quality of the harvest; it would not only be plentiful, but every kind of tree would also be fruitful. To this point, the land had been plagued by severe drought (Hag 1:11); but soon the heavens will give their dew. Rain would finally fall, and the ground would soak up the dew. To this point, the Israelites struggled to keep the little they gathered from the harvest (Hag 1:9); but soon, Yahweh would cause the remnant of this people to inherit all these things. The Lord Himself would personally intervene (I will cause) to ensure His people enjoyed the fullness of His blessings.

The promise that Israel would inherit all these things served as a clear reminder that the abundance they received was a gift from the Lord. An inheritance is not something earned or merited, but a gift that is bestowed. As the remnant enjoyed such a dramatic improvement to their circumstances, they would have no doubt it was all due to God's grace. The word inherit though is rarely used in the Old Testament to describe the blessings of harvest. Instead, the word predominantly conveys the fact that Israel will inherit the land (Deut 1:38; 3:28; Josh 1:6) and the fullness of God's kingdom promises in the end (Exod 32:13; Isa 14:12; 49:8; 57:13; Ezek 47:13; Zeph 2:9). The repetition of the word remnant emphasizes that the faithful Israelites of Zechariah's day would receive more than God's temporal blessings in the present. Along with all the redeemed, they will enjoy God's kingdom promises in the future (cf. John 5:28–29; Rev 19:17–20:7). By emphasizing that His remnant would inherit His blessings, God used the immediate provision of an abundant harvest to assure His people that they will certainly receive the fullness of His grace in the end. For that reason, they could stand strong without fear.

BE STRONG IN GOD'S PROMISES

"'And it will be that just as you were a curse among the nations, O house
of Judah and house of Israel, so I will save you that you may become a
blessing. Do not fear; let your hands be strong.' For thus says Yahweh
of hosts, 'Just as I purposed to bring about evil to you when your fathers
provoked Me to wrath,' says Yahweh of hosts, 'and I have not relented, so
I have again purposed in these days to do good to Jerusalem and to the
house of Judah. Do not fear!'" (8:13–15)

Having described His present faithfulness in verses 11–12, the Lord
continued by addressing Israel's future with the phrase **and it will be.** By
assuring His people that their future was secure, God gave them reason
not to worry or grow anxious. The command **do not fear** is repeated
twice in this section, both near the beginning (v. 13) and at the end (v. 15).
The Lord's promises securing Israel's future meant the faithful remnant
had nothing to fear in the present.

The first of these promises was that Israel's global reputation would
be restored: **"just as you were a curse among the nations, O house of
Judah and house of Israel, so I will save you that you may become a
blessing."** In the past, Israel had become **a curse**, a term that refers not
only to God's judgment and wrath, but also to the accompanying scorn
and stigma Israel bore **among the nations** (cf. Deut 28:15–45; Jer 24:9).
This curse was not only against the northern kingdom, but against both
the **house of Judah and house of Israel.**

This reminder of past national shame elevated, by contrast, the
promise of Israel's future glory. In His abundant grace, God will not
abandon His people; rather, He declared that He **will save** them—
meaning that He will intervene and overcome the former judgment He
had carried out against them, by atoning for their sins, restoring them to
Himself, delivering them from their enemies, and ensuring their future
in His kingdom. On account of God's merciful intervention, the once
cursed nation will instead **become a blessing**. The people will not only
enjoy blessing where they previously experienced judgment—in their
places of residence (cf. Deut 28:16), productivity (cf. 28:17), personal lives

(cf. 28:18), and pursuits (cf. 28:19)—but they will also **become a blessing** to the world. The nation of Israel, once shameful and despised, will ultimately bring joy to the entire globe as the inhabitants of every other nation come to Jerusalem to exalt the Lord (cf. Isa 2:2–4; 19:23–25; Zech 2:11), exult in His presence (Isa 19:24), experience His peace (60:10–19), and enjoy His goodness in a restored world (cf. 11:8–10; Gen 1:22, 28; 2:3). In Genesis 12, God promised Abraham that in Israel all the nations of the earth would be blessed (cf. Gen 12:1–3). More than a thousand years later, through the prophecy of Zechariah, the Lord reiterated that promise. Even those nations that hated the Israelites would love them in the end (cf. Zech 8:23).

Because of His future promises for Israel (cf. vv. 1–8), God commanded His people, "**Do not fear; let your hands be strong.**" The Israelites were not to fear failure, for the Lord guaranteed their success. They were not to fear enemies or obstacles, because Yahweh assured them He would be with them. They were not to fear personal inability or lack of resources, for God promised to save, deliver, and make all things right for His people.

Compelled by their hope in the Lord, Israel was not to shrink back in cowardice but to push forward in confidence. The people were called to **let** their **hands be strong.** God issued this same exhortation earlier in this passage (cf. Zech 8:13), directing the people to complete the construction of the temple. Instead of giving up, the faithful remnant needed to take courage as they persevered in obedience. They could do this armed with the hope of both God's abiding presence in the present and His abundant promises for the future.

With the seventh occurrence of the phrase **thus says Yahweh of hosts** in this chapter (v. 14), the Lord reminded His people not to fear, not only because His future promises are glorious but because they are certain. The words of verses 14–15 underscore the absolute nature of God's promises to Israel: "**Just as I purposed to bring about evil to you when your fathers provoked Me to wrath,**" says Yahweh of hosts, "**and I have not relented, so I have again purposed in these days to do good to Jerusalem and to the house of Judah.**" Highlighting His sovereign prerogative, Yahweh explained that He **purposed**, or formed and established a plan in His sovereign will (cf. Zech 1:6), **to bring about evil to you when your fathers provoked Me to wrath**. What the Lord ordained before the foundation of the world and revealed hundreds of years in advance (cf. Lev 26; Deut 27–28) took place exactly as He had warned. As He stated, **"I have not relented."** God did not fail to accomplish all He intended, nor did He reduce the intensity of what He foreordained. He carried out everything to the very degree He planned. The Israelites knew this full well. They had experienced God's judgment throughout their history. Their ancestors continually **provoked** God **to wrath** (cf. 2 Kgs 17:7–23), eventually resulting in the calamity of exile. Everything God promised in the past, in terms of judgment for Israel's rebellion against Him, was fulfilled. Therefore, everything God ordained and promised for Israel's future, in terms of salvation and blessing, will also be fulfilled. As the Lord declared, **"So I have again purposed in these days to do good to Jerusalem and to the house of Judah."** The word **purposed** is the same term used in the previous statement. The same sovereign will that ordained Israel's historical judgment also ordained Israel's future blessing, and all that God has sovereignly ordained will certainly be accomplished.

The Lord **again** reiterated that purpose **in these days**, for those listening to Zechariah, to assure His people that even though Israel sinned in the past, God's sovereign plan for His people had not changed. As a result, the people could be sure that Yahweh would **do good to Jerusalem and to the house of Judah**. The use of **good** stands in direct contrast to the word "evil" used earlier (cf. v. 14). Reversing the total calamity His people had experienced, the Lord promised to save them and shower them with blessing—a promise that extended both **to Jerusalem and to the house of Judah**. When the capital of the nation and its royal house triumph (cf. Zeph 2:7; Zech 10:3, 6; 12:4), Israel, and by extension the entire world, will enjoy sustained peace and prosperity (cf. 12:1–9; 14:1–11).

Because His promises are sure, the Lord once again declared to Israel, **"Do not fear!"** Fear had paralyzed the Israelites in Zechariah's time from persevering in their God-given task to complete the temple. But there was no reason to be afraid. Yahweh reminded His people that

He would save them, do good to them, and make them a blessing to the world. For this reason, they were charged to take courage and not lose heart. Knowing the outcome was sure, they needed to press on in faithful obedience to the Lord.

BE STRONG IN GOD'S TRUTH

"'These are the things which you should do: speak the truth to one another; judge with truth and judgment for peace in your gates. Also let none of you devise evil in your heart against another, and do not love false oaths; for all these are what I hate,' declares Yahweh." (8:16–17)

In verses 16–17, God provided a final series of practical implications that flow from the promises He made to Israel. He introduced these expectations for His people with the statement: **"These are the things which you should do."** God's promises to Israel not only informed the faithful remnant about the future but also prompted immediate action in the present.

In light of God's truth about the coming kingdom, the people were to walk in truth in the present. This expectation began with their words. The Lord's instruction was clear: **"Speak the truth to one another."** Putting aside deception and dishonesty, the Israelites were to speak with integrity, in accordance with the truths and promises of God's Word (cf. Ps 15:1–2). In this way, the people of Israel would be properly built up in truth even as they worked together to build the temple—the place where they would worship the true God. The Apostle Paul cited this very command centuries later in Ephesians 4:25, when he wrote: "Therefore, laying aside falsehood, SPEAK TRUTH EACH ONE *of you* WITH HIS NEIGHBOR, for we are members of one another." From Zechariah to Paul to today, believers in every age are called to speak in ways characterized by integrity, honesty, and truthfulness.

Israel was not only commanded to speak the truth, but also to **judge with truth and judgment for peace in your gates.** The **gates** represented the location where major business and governing decisions were made. In addition to the words they spoke in conversation, the

Israelites were commanded to exhibit veracity and integrity in their politics and jurisprudence. Specifically, they were to **judge with truth**, to make decisions and render legal verdicts consistent with the perfect standard of God's law (cf. Ruth 4:1–12). Thus, Israel was to speak truth and to judge truthfully, in anticipation of God's promise that Jerusalem would be transformed into a City of Truth (cf. Zech 8:3). That future reality served as a powerful motivation for the people to walk in truth in the present. Their holiness was motivated by their hope (cf. 2 Pet 3:14; 1 John 3:2–3). By governing with honesty and integrity, the Israelites would render **judgment** that resulted in **peace** as they considered civil and legal matters while meeting at the city **gates**. God called Israel to execute judgments that were righteous, thereby promoting peace and stability in society. The consequent peace foreshadowed the coming of the Prince of Peace, who will render perfect judgments and bring true unity in the millennial kingdom (cf. Isa 9:6).

Having given Israel a pair of positive commands—to speak truth and judge righteously—the Lord continued with a pair of negative injunctions. He declared, **"Also let none of you devise evil in your heart against another; and do not love false oaths."** In Zechariah 7:10, Yahweh had already issued the first of these prohibitions: "Do not devise evil in your hearts against one another." For a nation of people preoccupied with superficial and ritualistic religion, the emphasis on the heart provided a vital reminder (cf. 1 Sam 16:7). God's promises were not intended to prompt merely external action. The practical implications were aimed at the heart, out of which flowed genuine worship and obedience (e.g., Ps 19:14). The Lord reminded His people that their inner thoughts and motives needed to be pure toward one another (cf. Matt 5:21–22).

The second injunction was to **not love false oaths**. A **false oath** occurs when a witness intentionally gives errant testimony in court (cf. Exod 20:16) or when one knowingly makes a promise or guarantee that is not true. By contrast, Scripture commands believers to speak truthfully (cf. Jas 5:12), and to watch their words carefully (3:1). The Lord's command to the people of Zechariah's day again went deeper than mere externals. The Israelites were not simply to avoid speaking what was untrue; they were not to **love** it. God commanded them to watch their hearts (where wicked words originate—cf. Mark 7:20–22) so that they would not be inclined to do or say what was false.

The Lord punctuated these injunctions against falsehood with a decisive declaration of divine disapproval: **"For all these are what I hate," declares Yahweh**. Falsehood is not an arbitrary matter to God. He abhors anything that is not true, because it is contrary to His nature. He is the God of truth (Ps 31:5; Isa 65:16) who cannot lie (cf. Titus 1:2; Heb 6:18). The Lord's words reminded His people that the call to moral integrity was based on His character. They were called to love what He loves and hate what He hates (cf. Prov 6:16–19).

In addition to motivating Israel's obedience, the Lord's statement reinforced the certainty of His promises to Israel. God's oaths can never be false. His promises are forever true (cf. 2 Cor 1:20). Therefore, they will always come to pass. The faithful remnant could rest confidently in the Lord's promises for Israel's future. As they walked in light of that future hope, they were expected to live in a way that reflected the character of the God of truth—the One who had declared those promises to them.

In this section (Zech 8:9–17), the Lord exhorted His people to stand strong in His work, His grace, His promises, and His truth. By doing this, Israel would be equipped to walk in obedience, rest in God's faithfulness, remain steadfast in hope, and speak the truth in love. By grounding these principles in His promises for Israel's future, Yahweh provided His people with the motivation they needed to persevere in the present. That motivation centered on the hope of Messiah's future kingdom; the temple they were called to complete anticipated the glorious temple that will one day stand in the heart of millennial Jerusalem. Armed with God's promises and emboldened by His presence, the faithful remnant had everything they needed to avoid both fear and falsehood. As these verses demonstrate, being kingdom minded does not render someone of no earthly good. Rather, a kingdom mindset is essential for anyone who desires to honor and please the Lord.

From Fasting to Feasting

22

Zechariah 8:18–23

Then the word of Yahweh of hosts came to me, saying, "Thus says Yahweh of hosts, 'The fast of the fourth, the fast of the fifth, the fast of the seventh, and the fast of the tenth *months* will become joy, gladness, and merry appointed feasts for the house of Judah; so love truth and peace.' Thus says Yahweh of hosts, '*It will* yet *be* that peoples will come, even the inhabitants of many cities. The inhabitants of one will go to another, saying, "Let us go at once to entreat the favor of Yahweh and to seek Yahweh of hosts; I will also go." So many peoples and mighty nations will come to seek Yahweh of hosts in Jerusalem and to entreat the favor of Yahweh.' Thus says Yahweh of hosts, 'In those days ten men from every tongue of the nations will take hold of the garment of a Jew, saying, "Let us go with you, for we have heard that God is with you."'"

The greatest enemy to true religion is self-righteousness. Every false religious system appeals to selfish pride, promising salvation through self-effort, self achievement, and self-reliance. But the self-focused legalism of works-based religion crumbles when compared to the unmerited grace of the gospel, in which self-righteousness is utterly abandoned for the justifying righteousness God alone provides (Phil 3:7–9).

Consider the contrast between legalism and grace. The two are diametrically opposed and mutually exclusive (Rom 11:6). Legalism is man's work. Grace is God's gift. Legalism seeks to earn God's favor through personal merit. Grace is God's unmerited favor given to those who know they cannot earn it. Legalism is external and superficial, manifested in outward adherence to rules and rituals. Grace transforms sinners from the inside, as God regenerates them through the power of the Holy Spirit so they walk in obedience. Legalism is founded on the sinking sands of self-effort. Grace is anchored in God's perfect work of redemption. Legalism begins and ends with self. Grace puts self to death and focuses on God.

As the context of this passage reveals, the Israelites were trying to obtain God's favor through their works. They thought religious rituals held the key to pleasing Yahweh (cf. Zech 7:2–3). In response, Zechariah condemned such superficial notions. Though the people observed certain fast days, they were not truly worshiping God. Instead, they had placed the focus on themselves and their self-righteousness (cf. 7:5–6).

Zechariah 8 contrasts Israel's legalism (described in chapter 7) with the glorious wonder of divine grace, inviting the people to embrace the goodness of God's promises. In chapter 7, the Israelites thought fasting would compel God to help them (cf. 7:2–4). In this passage (8:18–19), Yahweh instructed them to live in godly joy rather than self-centered sorrow. In chapter 7, the people assumed they could entreat God's favor through their works (cf. 7:2). In this passage (8:20–22), the Lord expressed a desire to hear entreaties from those who sincerely seek the Giver, not merely His gifts. In chapter 7, the people acted as though they had done great works for God (cf. 7:2–5). In this passage (8:23), the Lord reminded them that He is the One who will accomplish great things for them.

This chapter concludes with a climactic set of God's kingdom promises, designed to drive Israel to turn from their legalistic ways and to rest instead in the grace of God. These final verses (8:18–23) provide three powerful portraits of Israel's glory in the millennial kingdom. In that day, Israel's mourning will be turned into merriment (vv. 18–19), her enemies into entreaters (vv. 20–22), and her humiliation into honor (v. 23).

FROM MOURNING TO MERRIMENT

Then the word of Yahweh of hosts came to me, saying, "Thus says Yahweh of hosts, 'The fast of the fourth, the fast of the fifth, the fast of the seventh, and the fast of the tenth *months* **will become joy, gladness, and merry appointed feasts for the house of Judah; so love truth and peace.'"** (8:18–19)

In the preceding context (vv. 9–17), God explained how His people ought to live out His promises. As **the word of Yahweh of hosts came to** Zechariah again, the Lord revealed more about the Messiah's future kingdom. As with other divine promises, Zechariah introduced this prophecy with the declaration **thus says Yahweh of hosts**, making it impossible for the reader to miss the divine source behind its content (cf. vv. 2, 3, 4, 6, 7, 9, 14, 19, 20, 23). As the eighth of the ten occurrences in this chapter (see discussion on Zech 8:2), this declaration introduced another aspect of God's kingdom plan for Israel.

In verse 18, God listed **the fast of the fourth, the fast of the fifth, the fast of the seventh, and the fast of the tenth months**. These words echo what the people of Israel said in Zechariah 7:3–5. In those verses, the Israelites asked if they should seek God's favor by continuing to fast in the **fifth** and **seventh months**. Those dates commemorated the fall of Jerusalem (2 Kgs 25:8) and the assassination of Gedaliah (25:25), both of which represented low points in Israel's history. To those, God added the **fourth** month, when Nebuchadnezzar's armies broke through Jerusalem's defenses (25:3–4), and the **tenth** month, when the siege of Jerusalem began (25:1). These fasts remembered the events that led to Jerusalem's downfall, the temple's destruction, and Judah's exile to Babylon. By marking these events with fasts of mourning, the people of Zechariah's day assumed they could garner God's favor (cf. Zech 7:2).

After two chapters of discussion, the Lord returned to and answered the people's original question (7:3). In sum, God informed them that they had been thinking about the situation backwards. They were focused on the tragedies of the past, but the Lord called them to embrace His promises for the future. He directed their attention to a time when such sorrowful fasts **will become joy, gladness, and merry appointed feasts**

for the house of Judah. The days of mourning would be transformed into times of jubilation and joy. Their pain would become **gladness**—a reference to genuine and internal happiness, standing in contrast to Israel's sullen ceremonies. Yahweh would replace the somber fasts of these months with **merry appointed feasts**. The term **appointed feasts** refers to set national holidays and is used elsewhere to denote Israel's major festivals when the people gathered at Jerusalem three times per year (cf. Exod 23:15; Num 10:10; 2 Chr 2:4). The times of national grief that marked God's judgment in the past will become holidays of national celebration in the future, celebrating God's grace and favor. There will be no mourning on those days, for the people will be **merry**. Thus, God promised that in the millennial kingdom, all the sorrow, grief, and distress of the past will be changed into jubilation. For the people of Zechariah's day, these promises provided the hope they needed. Instead of mourning for the past and seeking to earn God's favor in the present through fasts and rituals, it was time for God's people to look to Yahweh's promises and trust in His goodness.

The Lord expressed the practical implications of this hope-filled perspective for His people: **"So love truth and peace."** This exhortation provided a clear corrective to any hint of legalism. The conjunction **so** demonstrates that obedience to God's commands follows and is the result of embracing God's promises. The acts of loving truth and pursuing peace do not entice God's favor or merit His goodness. Rather, these obedient actions flow from hearts anchored in the hope of God's promises for His people. They are not merely external patterns of behavior, but reflect the transforming power of God, a point the Lord emphasized with the word **love**. Earlier in this passage, God exhorted Israel not to love false oaths (cf. Zech 8:17). The people were not only to avoid falsehood in their words; they were to hate it in their hearts. In that way, they would reflect God's perfect character (cf. Zech 8:17; 1 Sam 13:14). A right response to God's grace is not merely external; it rather begins with a change in one's affections. In this context, God called Israel specifically to love **truth and peace**. Earlier in the chapter (Zech 8:3, 8, 16), these terms described the activities of being honest, not telling lies or falsehoods, promoting the truth of God's Word, and establishing harmony and wholeness among God's people. The pursuit of truth and peace transcends any fast or ceremony and seeks to imitate God's character in all of life (see discussion on 8:17). Those marked by such virtues in this life show themselves to be citizens of that future kingdom, in which both truth and peace prevail (cf. 8:3, 12). In contrast to superficial religious observances and sorrow-filled fast days, Zechariah called Israel to respond to God's gracious promises with unwavering hope, joy-filled anticipation, and a sincere love for truth and peace.

FROM ENEMIES TO ENTREATERS

"Thus says Yahweh of hosts, 'It will yet be that peoples will come, even the inhabitants of many cities. The inhabitants of one will go to another, saying, "Let us go at once to entreat the favor of Yahweh and to seek Yahweh of hosts; I will also go." So many peoples and mighty nations will come to seek Yahweh of hosts in Jerusalem and to entreat the favor of Yahweh.'" (8:20–22)

In verse 20, with the next occurrence of the phrase **thus says Yahweh of hosts**, God introduced another kingdom promise, one that pertains to the conversion of the Gentiles. The Lord explained to the Israelites that **peoples will come, even the inhabitants of many cities**. This image depicts a stream of people from every nation flooding into Jerusalem. Throughout Zechariah, the word "people" is primarily used to refer to God's own people Israel (cf. Zech 2:11; 7:5; 8:6, 7, 8, 11, 12). Here the term refers to the Gentiles living during the millennial kingdom. By calling them **peoples**, the Lord indicated the inhabitants of these nations will also be God's people; they will enjoy a saving relationship with Him. These peoples will not be few in number but **the inhabitants of many cities**—a sea of humanity from around the world. The residents of **many cities** will come to one city, Jerusalem, the capital city of Messiah's kingdom. They will come, not to invade or wage war, but to invoke the Lord in worship. Throughout history, the nations came to Jerusalem to besiege it (cf. 1 Kgs 14:25; 2 Kgs 18–19), but in the future, they will come for an entirely different reason. They will journey to Jerusalem to praise and exalt Yahweh from hearts that have been transformed by Him.

The earnestness of their hearts is seen in the eagerness of their actions: **"The inhabitants of one will go to another, saying, 'Let us go at once to entreat the favor of Yahweh and to seek Yahweh of hosts.'"** The Gentiles will unite in a desire to worship the Lord, as **the inhabitants of one** city **will go to another,** proactively urging one another to praise and exalt the true God. Consumed with worship, they will say to each other, **"Let us go at once to entreat the favor of Yahweh."** The verb rendered **entreat the favor** was used earlier in Zechariah 7:2. It refers to calling on God not merely for His goodwill, but also for His aid and deliverance. By entreating the Lord, the nations will confess their complete dependence on Him. They will **seek Yahweh of hosts,** not merely desiring the gifts God provides but the Giver Himself. They will pursue a relationship with Him, eager to know Him more deeply and honor Him in everything (Exod 33:7; Deut 4:29; Isa 45:19; 51:1; Zeph 2:3).

As the Gentiles invite one another to worship Yahweh, each person will respond, **"I will also go."** The focus on each individual is significant. In Scripture, one does not possess saving faith by proxy—because he belongs to a specific group, nation, or family. Rather, God elects individuals and works on the heart of each person, so that every believer personally embraces the Lord Jesus in saving faith (cf. Ezek 36:25–28; Jer 31:31–34; Acts 2:37–41; Rom 10:9–10; Eph 1:3–6). The nations depicted in verses 20–22 will be saved because each inhabitant is transformed by divine grace. The declaration **"I will also go"** conveys the heartfelt desire of every inhabitant: an eager and joyful determination to go and worship the Savior.

For the first time in world history, the residents of every city on earth will desire to worship Yahweh. How different that future reality will be from times of past apostasy. The words of Deuteronomy 13:13 describe such a time: "Some vile men have gone out from among you and have driven the inhabitants of their city astray, saying, 'Let us go and serve other gods.'" Jeremiah 11:12 depicts a similar scene: "The inhabitants of Jerusalem will go and cry to the gods to whom they burn incense." As those passages illustrate, Scripture identifies times when the inhabitants of various cities rebelled against the truth and worshiped false gods. By contrast, in the days of Messiah's earthly kingdom, the inhabitants of every city—not only in Israel but across the entire world—will travel to Jerusalem, entreat the favor of Yahweh, and seek to worship Him.

Thus, Christ's earthly reign will include the most extensive corporate worship in human history. After invoking one another to worship, **many peoples and mighty nations will come to seek Yahweh of hosts in Jerusalem and to entreat the favor of Yahweh**. This worship will be global, as **many peoples** from every corner of the world travel to Jerusalem. Even **mighty nations will come**, demonstrating that all political authority, economic might, and military power are subject to Yahweh (cf. Dan 7:13–14). They will come **to seek Yahweh of hosts in Jerusalem and to entreat the favor of Yahweh**. In the previous verse, the Gentiles called each other to worship in delight and dependence (see above). This verse depicts them responding to that call, honoring the Lord not only in word but also in deed (cf. 1 John 3:18).

In verse 21, the inhabitants of the nations called on one another to entreat and to seek God. In verse 22, the order is reversed. The Gentiles first seek God and then entreat Him. This reflects the right priority in worship—a deep desire to know God (to seek Him), not merely to receive His blessings (to entreat His favor). The repetition of God's covenant name **Yahweh** shows that the nations will worship and commune with the one true God. He will set His love on them, and they will eagerly respond with love and affection for Him.

This global corporate worship will take place **in Jerusalem**. True worship, as the Lord Jesus explained, is not bound to a place, but must be offered to God in spirit and truth (John 4:23–24). However, the singular focus on Jerusalem in this passage is significant. In Deuteronomy, the Lord required His people to worship in *one* city to reflect that He is the *one* true God (cf. Deut 6:4; 12:1–5). In light of this, as the world worships the Lord in Jerusalem, the entire earth will publicly confess Yahweh to be the one true God. To demonstrate that the nations will all turn to the true worship of Yahweh, the Lord prophesied that the nations will all stream to Jerusalem, the city He designated for that purpose (Isa 2:2–4; 56:7; 60:1–13; Mic 4:1–3).

God's future plan for the Gentile nations serves as a magnificent display of His grace. However, the Lord's primary purpose in revealing this truth was to illustrate a vital lesson for Israel. In Zechariah 7:2, it was the Israelites who came to entreat the favor of Yahweh. In these verses (8:21–22), the Lord spoke of a coming time when even the Gentiles will entreat the favor of the Lord. For the people in Zechariah's day who thought they could earn God's favor through the prescribed fasts and religious rituals, the thought that Gentiles might **entreat the favor** of Yahweh must have been shocking. The Gentiles did not observe the fasts or rituals that Israel did. But that was the point. In the same way that Gentiles in the kingdom will be granted divine favor because they seek the Lord from a redeemed heart, so the Jewish people of Zechariah's day were to seek Yahweh in love and truth. The future salvation of the nations served as a potent reminder to Israel that the favor of the Lord cannot be merited through religious observances, ceremonies, or rituals. It is only granted to those who love the Giver, not merely His gifts.

FROM HUMILIATION TO HONOR

"Thus says Yahweh of hosts, 'In those days ten men from every tongue of the nations will take hold of the garment of a Jew, saying, "Let us go with you, for we have heard that God is with you."'" (8:23)

The opening words, **thus says Yahweh of hosts,** mark the tenth and final time this introductory statement occurs in Zechariah 8. By focusing on the Messiah's future kingdom, this chapter revealed how Israel will be restored (8:2–19) and how the nations will be converted (8:20–22). But how will Jews and Gentiles relate to one another during that time? When the world comes to Jerusalem, what kind of peace and harmony will there be? The final verse of this chapter answers that question, thereby bringing this section about God's kingdom promises to its climactic conclusion.

Yahweh began by stating that **in those days,** at the climax of history in the millennial kingdom, **ten men** will seek to accompany each Israelite. The number **ten** is significant, a point reflected even in this chapter with the ten-fold repetition of the expression "Thus says Yahweh of hosts" (or

"Thus says Yahweh" in 8:3). The number ten conveys the idea of fullness even while communicating the actual number (cf. Gen 31:7; Lev 26:26). In the future, there will be **ten men** for each Jewish person, illustrating the vast number of Gentile people **from every tongue of the nations** who stream into Jerusalem. Israel will go from being despised by her neighbors, to being the most desired nation in the world. The use of **tongue** points back to Babel where God divided the tongues of the people (Gen 10:5, 20, 31; 11:1–9). At Babel, the Lord confused the languages of the people because of their rebellion against Him. This resulted in the division of the people into many nations (cf. Acts 17:26). In the millennial kingdom, this disunity will be undone as every tongue will be united in pleading with the Jewish people to go with them to worship the one true God.

The inhabitants of the nations **will take hold of the garment of a Jew**, demonstrating their enthusiasm for the God of Israel. The Hebrew text emphasizes this action and literally reads, "take hold...they will take hold." The picture in the Hebrew is that the Gentiles will be repeatedly reaching for the clothing of the Israelites. But this is not an act of hostility. It is an act of eagerness to join with the people of Israel as they worship the Lord. To **take hold of the garment**, or more precisely the corner of the garment, is to try to gain special favor by associating with someone. In the Gospels, a desperate woman with a hemorrhage made similar efforts simply to touch the garment of the Lord Jesus (Mark 5:29). The nations will repeatedly seek to associate with Israel in any way possible, even if it means they can only grasp the edge of their garments. With such affection, disrespect for the nation of Israel will disappear.

The text says the Gentiles will take hold of the garment of a **Jew**. The term **Jew**, derived from the name Judah, was often used by Israel's enemies in a derogatory manner (cf. Esth 3:4, 6, 10; Neh 4:1). However, in the millennial kingdom, the term will stand as a title of respect and esteem. While Israel may have been humiliated and rejected by the nations in the past, the Jews will be honored and treasured during the earthly reign of Christ.

At that time, the inhabitants of the nations will explain their eagerness to associate with Israel, saying, **"Let us go with you, for we have heard that God is with you."** As the Gentiles invite each other to worship in Jerusalem (cf. Zech 8:21), they will also ask to join and go with you, the people of Israel. The Jewish people will enjoy a place of special honor and esteem among the nations—for, as the Gentiles will declare, **"We have heard that God is with you."** The nations will recognize the Lord's unique relationship to Israel as He dwells with and blesses His people. Knowing that, the Gentiles will desire to join with Israel to enjoy those blessings (cf. Gen 12:1–3). As the early fifth-century theologian Theodore of Mopsuestia explained:

> God will make the return of the remainder so conspicuous that many people who are from different nations and have shared that calamity will perceive God's care for the people. They will lay hold of any one of them and use him as a guide for a return to Jerusalem, since everyone is sufficiently stirred up to that end from the clear realization that God is with them on the basis of the incredible deeds done for them.[1]

Throughout its history, Israel has often been rejected by the nations, but in the millennial kingdom Israel will be revered. The reason for this is that, though Israel was abhorred by God for their past sins, they will be adored by Him upon their repentance. Though the Lord will bless all the nations during that period (Zech 8:20–22), He will do exceedingly more for Israel, such that the other nations of the world will acknowledge that Israel's blessings far surpass their own. God will certainly do more than Israel could ever ask or think.

This vivid picture of Israel's future blessing serves as a fitting conclusion to the glorious kingdom promises detailed in Zechariah 8. The Israelites of Zechariah's day wondered what they should do for God (cf. 7:2–3), but God instead revealed what He will do for Israel. Yahweh Himself reminded His people that they could not obtain His favor through fasts and rituals. Rather, He called them to worship Him from the heart in response to His gracious and lavish promises. Consumed with His love and grace towards them, they could respond by loving what He loves: truth and peace (cf. 8:19). That kind of love flows from

---

1 Theodore of Mopsuestia, *Commentary on Zechariah*, 8.23 (PG 66:552); and see George L. Klein, *Zechariah*, New American Commentary (Nashville: B&H Publishing Group, 2008), 250.

within. It is neither legalistic nor ritualistic. It seeks not merely God's good gifts, but the Giver Himself. It is activated by God's grace (1 John 4:19), and it is the essence of true religion (Mark 12:30–31). As Zechariah 8 illustrates, that kind of love is the distinguishing mark of every true believer—whether Jew or Gentile, in this age or the next.

A Tale of Conquests

23

Zechariah 9:1–8

The oracle of the word of Yahweh is against the land of Hadrach, with Damascus as its resting place (for the eyes of men, especially of all the tribes of Israel, are toward Yahweh),

And Hamath also, which borders on it;
And Tyre and Sidon, because they are very wise.
So Tyre built herself a tight fortification
And tied up silver like dust
And fine gold like the mire of the streets.
Behold, the Lord will dispossess her
And strike her wealth down into the sea;
And she will be consumed with fire.
Ashkelon will see *it* and be afraid.
Gaza too will writhe in great pain;
Also Ekron, for her hope has been put to shame.
Moreover, the king will perish from Gaza,
And Ashkelon will not be inhabited.
And those of illegitimate birth will inhabit Ashdod,
And I will cut off the pride of the Philistines.
And I will remove their blood from their mouth
And their detestable things from between their teeth.

> Then they also will be a remnant for our God,
> And be like a clan in Judah,
> And Ekron like a Jebusite.
> But I will camp around My house because of an army,
> Because of him who passes by and returns;
> And no taskmaster will pass over them anymore,
> For now I have seen with My eyes.

Zechariah ministered at a critical time in Israel's history. The people, having returned from captivity in Babylon, found their homeland in ruin. They journeyed to Jerusalem intending to rebuild. But the work stalled, in part, because the task seemed overwhelming. Israel's former glory had been reduced to a distant memory. Compounding their discouragement, the Israelites also faced constant threats from the surrounding nations. The mounting challenges tempted the people to retreat in fear, rather than to continue rebuilding courageously. Through His prophets, Haggai and Zechariah, the Lord encouraged His people to hope confidently in Him and persevere in the work.

The themes of God's presence, protection, and provision reverberate throughout Zechariah's prophecy. Those themes culminate in the final portion of the book (chapters 9–14), focusing specifically on Messiah's future earthly kingdom. Throughout these chapters, the Lord reiterated His steadfast love and saving plan for Israel. Because His love will never fail, He will surely keep His promises to His people—both in the immediate future and at the end of the age. As He promised, Israel's enemies will be defeated and destroyed, while God's people will be defended and delivered by Him.

These final chapters (Zech 9–14) consist of a pair of divine oracles. The first oracle (in chapters 9–11) reveals God's coming judgment against His enemies. The second (in chapters 12–14) foretells the Lord's ultimate deliverance of His people, when He returns to conquer all enemies and reign supreme in Jerusalem.

The opening section of chapter 9 (vv. 1–8) predicts the military defeat of Israel's neighbors in Syria, Lebanon, and Philistia. Roughly 200 years after Zechariah delivered this prophecy, Alexander the Great (356–323 BC) conquered those regions in precisely the way Zechariah foretold. Yet, the prophecies in this passage go beyond Alexander, ultimately pointing to the messianic conqueror at the end of the age. Alexander's military campaign serves as a historic illustration foreshadowing Christ's future conquest when He returns (cf. Rev 19). Additionally, by predicting Alexander's movements with such accuracy, the Lord demonstrated both His sovereignty over the future and His faithfulness to fulfill His Word perfectly.

For the original hearers of Zechariah's prophecy, everything revealed in this passage, including the military exploits of Alexander the Great, was yet future. As God's people looked ahead, these words encouraged them to hope in the Lord and rest in His sovereign plan. That plan included both the destruction of His adversaries and the deliverance of His people. Accordingly, this passage (9:1–8) highlights three important themes: the Lord's unstoppable judgment on Israel's enemies (vv. 1–6), His undeserved grace toward the Gentiles (v. 7), and His unfailing protection of His chosen nation Israel (v. 8).

UNSTOPPABLE JUDGMENT

The oracle of the word of Yahweh is against the land of Hadrach, with Damascus as its resting place (for the eyes of men, especially of all the tribes of Israel, are toward Yahweh),

And Hamath also, which borders on it;
And Tyre and Sidon, because they are very wise.
So Tyre built herself a tight fortification
And tied up silver like dust
And fine gold like the mire of the streets.
Behold, the Lord will dispossess her
And strike her wealth down into the sea;
And she will be consumed with fire.
Ashkelon will see *it* and be afraid.
Gaza too will writhe in great pain;
Also Ekron, for her hope has been put to shame.

Moreover, the king will perish from Gaza,
And Ashkelon will not be inhabited.
And those of illegitimate birth will inhabit Ashdod,
And I will cut off the pride of the Philistines. (9:1–6)

The oracle of the word of Yahweh begins a new section in the book and serves as a heading for the contents of Zechariah 9–11. The word **oracle** is likely connected to the idea of a burden. It conveys how revelation, especially concerning divine judgment, weighs upon the prophet's heart, compelling him to proclaim what God has revealed. The word **oracle** is often used to introduce prophecies of judgment against nations and individuals. In the final chapters of Zechariah, the word occurs twice, each time to introduce prophecies of judgment given by **the word of Yahweh**. The first oracle (beginning in 9:1) introduces historic judgment and prophecy concerning the Gentiles, and the second (beginning in 12:1) introduces eschatological judgment and fulfillment for Israel. The Lord Jesus reiterated this paradigm by speaking about the times of the Gentiles (Luke 21:24), after which God's promises to Israel will be fulfilled. The oracles at the end of Zechariah demonstrate that God has foreordained a comprehensive plan for all nations and for all of history until the end.

This oracle of judgment begins by naming **the land of Hadrach**. While Hadrach is not mentioned elsewhere in Scripture, its location is attested in extra-biblical sources as the northern part of biblical Aram, or Syria. It is one of the districts of Hamath, a place regarded as the very northern edge of Israel's ideal territory (cf. 2 Chr 8:4).[1] In Zechariah's day, it was clearly outside the land of Israel, indicating these words were directed to Gentile peoples.

God's judgment will move from Hadrach to Damascus, to have **Damascus as its resting place**, or residence. The language pictures the very oracle of God settling on and taking up residence in Damascus, indicating the city would experience God's wrath in a sustained manner. This was vividly illustrated during the conquests of Alexander the

---

1 Mark J. Boda, *The Book of Zechariah*, New International Commentary on the Old Testament (Grand Rapids: Eerdmans, 2016), 536.

Great, who moved his armies into Syria after conquering Medo-Persia in 333 BC. Alexander's victory over Damascus foreshadows the end of the age, when the Messiah will conquer Damascus and put His enemies to shame (cf. Jer 49:23–27).

At the same time, the notion of rest is used throughout Scripture (cf. Gen 2:3; Exod 33:14; 2 Sam 7:11; 1 Kgs 5:4; Ps 95:11; Heb 3–4) and even earlier in this book (Zech 6:8) to anticipate the Edenic rest God will one day bring to the earth. The term **resting place** includes that idea. Though Damascus will be a target of divine judgment, it will subsequently become a place characterized by divine blessing. Ezekiel revealed that, in the millennial kingdom, Damascus will be present at the border of Israel (Ezek 47:18; 48:1). Though the city will be judged, it will be reconstituted to play a role in Christ's earthly reign, during which its inhabitants will find their rest in Yahweh.

The source of this rest is identified in the remainder of verse 1, which states that **the eyes of men, especially of all the tribes of Israel, are toward Yahweh.** Earlier in Zechariah, the word **eyes** described both the Spirit's presence in God's plan (Zech 4:10) and His empowerment of the Messiah (3:9). In this verse (9:1), it is not the eyes of the Lord, but the eyes of the people who are looking **toward Yahweh.** Throughout history, people have observed earthly conquerors, like Alexander, whom God raised up to execute His sovereign purposes. But at the end of the age, every eye will be fixed on the final conqueror, the Messiah (Rev 1:7). This will not only include the Gentiles, but also **all the tribes of Israel.** For the people of Zechariah's day, that eschatological prophecy served as a timely reminder to fix their eyes on the Lord, not only for the future but also in the present.

In verses 2–7, the Lord continued to detail the coming defeat of Israel's neighbors, those nations surrounding Israel whom the people feared. In Zechariah's second vision (cf. Zech 1:18–21), a series of craftsmen hammered a series of horns. The vision symbolized how nation would conquer nation throughout history, until the Messiah's final conquest and reign. In that vision, the craftsmen were all connected, with one craftsman following and emulating the others, ultimately culminating in Christ, the final craftsman. That same pattern can be seen in this passage (9:1–8). Because Alexander the Great is one of those craftsmen, in God's providential plan, he illustrates the conquest that Christ will carry out in the end.

Verse 2 described God's judgment against Syria, by noting that His wrath would fall on **Hamath.** Though the city was more than 100 miles north of Damascus, Zechariah emphasized that it still **borders on** Israel (cf. Num 34:8), indicating that conquest would spill into the area of the Promised Land. Historically, after conquering Medo-Persia, Alexander's Greek armies swept throughout Syria and conquered the entire region. Looking beyond Alexander to the end of the age, Jeremiah prophesied that Hamath will one day be conquered again by the Messiah (Jer 49:23). According to Ezekiel, this city, which was once on Israel's border, will become part of Israel's border during the millennial kingdom (Ezek 48:1).

Yahweh shifted His focus in the second part of verse 2 to **Tyre and Sidon,** cities located in modern-day Lebanon. In predicting their defeat, the Lord noted that Tyre and Sidon were **very wise** in terms of human ingenuity and economic savvy. Yet their earthly wisdom and worldly wealth proved to be no match for divine judgment, illustrating that the wisdom of man cannot overcome the power of God. Both cities were places of impressive maritime accomplishments and commercial prosperity. Ezekiel depicted Tyre's fortune as a masterpiece of human shrewdness (cf. Ezek 27:1–36). Nevertheless, God would overturn Tyre and Sidon. He would demonstrate the folly of their cleverness (cf. 1 Cor 1:20), contrasting it with the wisdom of the coming Messiah (cf. Zech 9:9).

The Lord guaranteed the downfall of these cities, even though **Tyre built herself a tight fortification.** The Hebrew word Zechariah used for fortification (*matzor*) is similar to the Hebrew word for Tyre (*tzor*), doubling down on the impregnable nature of the city. It was so heavily fortified that this feature essentially served as its name. Archaeological evidence confirms the impressive nature of Tyre's fortifications. The city was surrounded by water, being built about half a mile offshore, with massive walls. The Hebrew word for fortress describes a structure that is tightly enclosed, and thereby more easily defended. Because Tyre was a tight fortification, as verse 3 describes it, the city was seemingly impenetrable.

It was also lofty in affluence and abundance. It **tied up silver like dust and fine gold like the mire of the streets.** Such imagery surpassed even the riches of Solomon, when he made silver like stone (1 Kgs 10:27). Tyre was so wealthy that silver seemed as plentiful as specks of dust, and gold was treated as if it were dirt kicked up on the side of the road. But there was irony in this description. The term **tied up** was not often used in a positive way in the Old Testament. Elsewhere, it described the piling up of dead frogs (Exod 8:14) and also the amassing of rubble to capture a city (Hab 1:10). The people of Tyre thought they were piling up safety and success; in reality, they were piling up a false sense of security, which would become their undoing (cf. Ps 39:7).

Despite Tyre's wisdom and wealth, Zechariah exclaimed, **"Behold, the Lord will dispossess her."** Though it was a tightly fortified city, God promised to **dispossess her**—to remove her inhabitants forcibly from their land and possessions. Likewise, God declared He would **strike her wealth down into the sea.** The city's location offshore was her greatest defense. But it would become her grave. In the end, the city would be completely destroyed, as the Lord explained, **"she will be consumed with fire."** The city on the water would, ironically, be burned with fire.

This was precisely what happened in the days of Alexander the Great. After eliminating their enemies in Syria, Alexander's armies moved west into Lebanon. When Tyre refused to surrender, retreating to the supposed safety of their offshore fortress, Alexander's army piled up stones to build a causeway across the ocean. The construction took seven months, but in the end, Greek forces reached Tyre, torched it, and razed it to the ground.

Tyre's destruction illustrates the reality that no city or nation can withstand God's judgment. As verse 4 explained, it was **the Lord** who dispossessed her. The word **Lord** (Adonai) is distinct from the covenant name "Yahweh" or the title "God" (Elohim). The title "Adonai" stresses Yahweh's authority and rule over this world. This is the first of two times this title appears in the book of Zechariah (cf. 9:14). It describes the Lord's dominion and sovereign authority over every nation and people. The Lord put His sovereignty on vivid display by perfectly fulfilling these prophecies of judgment against Tyre, using a pagan conqueror like Alexander to do so.

In verse 5, the geographic focus of Zechariah's prophecy moves south into Philistia, following the path of God's judgment as it overwhelms city after city. The first Philistine city mentioned is **Ashkelon**, a prominent enemy citadel throughout Israel's history. Yet, as this verse predicts, the inhabitants there **will see** *it*, the destruction of Tyre, and **be afraid**. Upon learning that an impregnable fortress like Tyre had been reduced to ashes, the residents of Ashkelon will tremble with fear, knowing they are next. Similarly, **Gaza too will writhe in great pain**, experiencing agony like that of a woman in labor, due to the anticipation of imminent destruction. Another mighty Philistine city, **Ekron**, will also be destroyed, **for her hope has been put to shame**. Historically, Ekron looked to Tyre as a military ally for security and aid. But any hope for assistance was gone.

Returning to Gaza, the Lord declared, "**Moreover, the king will perish from Gaza.**" Again, this prediction accurately described the conquests of Alexander and his forces. When Gaza resisted his campaign, it took Alexander five months to conquer this city. After defeating Gaza, he seized the king, bored holes through his feet, wrapped cords through the holes, and dragged him through the streets until he died. In like manner, the Lord declared, "**Ashkelon will not be inhabited.**" Verse 5 began by describing Ashkelon's terror; it concludes with the city being left empty. The Lord's point was that all of Ashkelon's fears would be realized. Historically, those fears were in fact manifested when the city fell to Alexander.

According to verse 6, God promised not only to defeat Philistia but to bring shame upon her. He declared that **those of illegitimate birth will inhabit** the Philistine city of **Ashdod**. Though illegitimate birth can refer to a child born by incest or sexual immorality, the reference here likely points to the fact that the Philistine line would be greatly diminished, resulting in their cities being populated and dominated by foreigners. The heritage of Philistia would disappear, and the nation would be dissolved. In this way, the Lord declared, "**I will cut off the pride of the Philistines.**" With their cities destroyed, their numbers depleted, and their dignity gone, the national pride of the Philistine people will vanish. With the phrase **and I will**, God made emphatically clear that this would be His doing, according to His plan. As the collapse of Philistia illustrates, Yahweh is the One who causes nations to rise and fall (cf. Dan 2:21; 4:17). He alone is sovereign, and there is no hope and no security apart from Him.

When Alexander marched from Tyre and Sidon to Philistia, he conquered the cities of Ashkelon, Gaza, and Ekron. The historical details of his conquest match the predictions recorded in Zechariah 9:1–6. It should be repeated, however, that these events serve as a precursor to events that will occur at the end of the age. According to Amos 1:7–8, God will one day judge the four cities of Ashkelon, Gaza, Ekron, and Ashdod. Habakkuk 3:10 links the writhing of Gaza with the eschatological writhing of the mountains (cf. Zech 9:5). And Zephaniah declared that by removing the inhabitants from Ashkelon and other Philistine cities, God will pave the way for Israel to inhabit that area as they were originally promised (Zeph 2:4–7). Alexander's historic fulfillment of the prophecies in Zechariah 9:1–6 demonstrates that God prewrites history with promises that are fully trustworthy. It serves as a guarantee or pledge that the Lord will perfectly accomplish what He has promised to do. Just as He sovereignly ordained history to bring about Alexander's conquest, according to what He foretold, so will He orchestrate future events to ensure the Messiah's conquest and earthly reign.

UNDESERVED GRACE

And I will remove their blood from their mouth
And their detestable things from between their teeth.
Then they also will be a remnant for our God,
And be like a clan in Judah,
And Ekron like a Jebusite. (9:7)

Though God will make the Philistines an object lesson of judgment, He will equally make them a trophy of His grace. In verse 7, the Lord declared, "**And I will remove their blood from their mouth.**" Depicting the Philistines as people with **blood** in their mouth, God made it clear they were cut off from Him. Israel was strictly forbidden to consume blood in order to avoid pagan practices, to show respect for life, and to remember the price of atonement (cf. Lev 17:1–16). The Philistines, in their rebellion against God—which included violence, idolatry, and sexual immorality—were like those who consumed blood. They showed no regard for God's law and offended His holiness to the extreme. Nevertheless, the Lord explained that one day He **will remove** the blood from the Philistines' mouth, thereby removing their offense. Likewise, He will also remove **their detestable things from between their teeth**. The idea of **detestable things** is often associated with pagan idolatry (cf. Deut 29:16; 1 Kgs 11:5, 7; 2 Kgs 23:13), emphasizing the grotesque nature of the images, gods, and practices of paganism. The people of Philistia held these things, as it were, between their teeth. They not only imbibed such wickedness but also put it on display for all to see. Though the Philistines could not cleanse themselves of these despicable practices, God promised to **remove** them. In an act of incredible mercy, the Lord promised to one day rid the Philistines of their wickedness, so that they might be redeemed and transformed to worship and serve Him. That is the power of God's saving grace (Eph 2:1–10; 4:20–24).

As a result, **they also will be a remnant for our God**. Throughout Scripture, God promised to preserve a remnant, or a small group, of Israelites for Himself, who would be sustained through judgment and be faithful believers. In Zechariah 8, God explained how He maintained such a remnant among the people of Zechariah's time and how He will bless them in the end (Zech 8:6, 11–12). However, Israel will not be the only nation to be part of God's blessed remnant. Philistia, their former enemy, will be included as well. The text says they will be a remnant **for our God**, emphasizing not only their physical preservation but spiritual conversion. God had every right to judge Philistia, and based upon their bloodstained description, one might have expected Him to eradicate them completely. However, the Lord declared that He will save a remnant of Philistines and bring them to Himself. Though specifically addressing the inhabitants of Philistia, this verse foreshadows the salvation of all Gentiles—those from every tribe, tongue, nation, and people (Rev 7:9).

While Philistia would be reduced in judgment, its inhabitants will one day occupy a place of dignity because of God's saving grace.

They will **be like a clan in Judah**. On the one hand, God's judgment would decimate the nation. Philistia would become small, no longer an autonomous nation, and possessed by Israel (cf. Gen 15:18–21; Zeph 2:4–7). That is why they will be like a clan **in Judah**, for they will assimilate into Israel. On the other hand, they will still be **like a clan**. The word **clan** can refer to a tribal chief (cf. Gen 36:15–43) or a group within a tribe or nation that contributes to the military. As such, the term is used in reference to a group that has recognition, significance, and dignity within a nation. Thus, Philistia, though reduced and shamed, will not be irreparably disgraced. The remnant of the Philistines, though small in size, will be redeemed.

According to verse 7, **Ekron** will be **like a Jebusite**. The Jebusites were the people living in and around Jerusalem before the Israelites came and conquered the Promised Land. The Jebusites remained within Israel, and one of them, Araunah the Jebusite, became a respected and beloved friend of David (2 Sam 24:18–24). That friendship reflects how Israel will one day treat the Philistines (such as those from **Ekron**) who live within its borders. While the Philistines, like the Jebusites, were not Israelites and did not have every privilege Israel had before God, they will still become part of God's people. They will be allowed to worship alongside God's chosen people Israel and will not be shunned or ostracized, but embraced. From the time of Abraham, God had revealed that He would have a relationship not only with Israel but with the nations as well (cf. Gen 12:3; Isa 49:1–6). He will certainly bring that promise to realization (cf. Zech 2:11; 8:22–23), so that the eyes of all peoples will be on Him in the end (cf. 9:1). Ekron will no longer be without hope (Zech 9:5), but will find true hope in the Lord.

UNFAILING PROTECTION

But I will camp around My house because of an army,
Because of him who passes by and returns;
And no taskmaster will pass over them anymore,
For now I have seen with My eyes. (9:8)

The Lord's grace toward the Philistines is amazing to consider. Equally amazing is His unfailing commitment to preserve Israel. Through this tumultuous time of conquests, even to the end of the age, God will protect His chosen people. God declared, **"But I will camp around My house."** To **camp** is to set up a tent or a settlement. It can refer to the temporary dwellings of nomads (cf. Gen 26:17), but it can also refer to a military encampment (cf. Josh 10:31; 2 Sam 24:5). The latter is in view here. God will set up His military outpost around the temple (**My house**). Earlier, God described His defense of Jerusalem to be in the form of a wall of fire (cf. Zech 2:5); here, He will be a proactive military presence to guard the temple and, by extension, the city and the people (cf. 2 Kgs 6:16–17).

The reason God will take this stance is **because of an army, because of him who passes by and returns**. The events described in verses 1–6 encompassed significant military conquests and were representative of other conflicts during the time of the Gentiles (Luke 21:24). At times throughout their subsequent history, Israel would experience the presence of a foreign **army** or garrison of troops, as military forces would **pass by** and **return** through the Promised Land (cf. Dan 11:1–34). Yet the Israelites were not to fear (8:13, 15). Despite these continual campaigns and wars, God promised to preserve His people.

The Lord protected Israel in a remarkable way during the time of Alexander the Great. Josephus records that when Alexander was going to Jerusalem to conquer the city, the High Priest called Israel together to sacrifice to God and pray for deliverance. The next day, the High Priest met Alexander, showed him the book of Daniel, and pointed out the prophecies regarding him. As a result, Alexander departed from Jerusalem and did no harm to the city. That illustrates what Zechariah described in this text. However, God's promise to defend Israel was not limited to the time of Alexander. He has continued to preserve a remnant of His people throughout subsequent history (cf. Rom 11). In the last days, He will dwell among them and defend Jerusalem in a climactic way (cf. Ezek 38–39; Zech 12:1–9; 14:1–3; Rev 19:11–19). As this verse reiterates, God has not forgotten His people, but will keep His promise to care for and defend them.

The result of such protection will be Israel's ultimate deliverance, so that **no taskmaster will pass over them anymore.** The words **no** and **anymore** convey universal declarations of negation and time, depicting a permanent state of affairs. God promised that Israel would no longer have any **taskmaster,** a term that points back to the book of Exodus when Egypt was Israel's taskmaster (cf. Exod 3:7; 5:6, 10). The term was also used to describe Babylon (cf. Isa 14:4). For Israel to have **no taskmaster** means they will never be subjected to or abused by another nation. This promise was clearly not fulfilled by Alexander, but anticipated the conquest of someone far greater. After the battle of Armageddon and with the establishment of the millennial kingdom (Rev 19:1–20:6), all oppression against Israel will be broken.

Throughout history, military leaders, oppressors, and tyrants have passed through Israel, but God declared that in the end no such person **will pass over them anymore.** Because the nations will be conquered and judged, and because Israel itself will be protected by the Lord, God's chosen nation will no longer be a stomping ground for invading armies. The people of Israel will be safe and secure. The end will bring about a new era in which they will experience true deliverance and peace.

God proclaimed in the last phrase of this passage, **"For now I have seen with My eyes."** The beginning of this text referred to the eyes of the world and Israel looking to Yahweh (cf. Zech 9:1). The conclusion of verse 8 refers to God's own **eyes.** God's **eyes,** an anthropomorphic reference to His all-knowing presence, sovereignly guide all that happens in history, as His Spirit ensures that His divine plan is carried out (cf. Zech 4:10). Because God's eyes are on His people, one day all of His elect will fix their eyes on Him (9:1).

God precisely said in this text, **"I have seen."** With this past tense verb, Yahweh declared that He has already seen the end. He has decreed and foreordained the end from the beginning (Isa 46:10). Israel's eyes will most certainly look to God, because God's eyes have already seen that this will take place. It is guaranteed by Him, so that no other outcome is possible. Guarded by His unfailing protection, His people can place their hope in Him, knowing that if God is for them, no one can do them any harm (cf. Rom 8:31).

The Ultimate Conqueror

24

Zechariah 9:9–10

Rejoice greatly, O daughter of Zion!
Make a loud shout, O daughter of Jerusalem!
Behold, your king is coming to you;
He is righteous and endowed with salvation,
Lowly and mounted on a donkey,
Even on a colt, the foal of a pack animal.

I will cut off the chariot from Ephraim
And the horse from Jerusalem;
And the bow of war will be cut off.
And He will speak peace to the nations;
And His reign will be from sea to sea
And from the River to the ends of the earth.

Each year, one week prior to Resurrection Sunday, Christians gather to celebrate the triumphal entry of the Lord Jesus into Jerusalem. This celebration, known as Palm Sunday, commemorates Christ's public arrival in Jerusalem days prior to His crucifixion and resurrection. Most believers today are familiar with the basic details of that historic occasion—that Jesus rode into Jerusalem on a donkey and was welcomed by crowds of people who laid garments and palm branches on the road (Matt 21:1–11; Mark 11:1–11; Luke 19:28–40; John 12:12–16). But despite their general familiarity with the story, many Christians have never fully considered the significance of that moment in Jesus' ministry. They may be surprised to learn that, centuries before Christ rode into Jerusalem, Zechariah prophesied about this pivotal event and laid out God's profound purpose for it.

In the opening verses of Zechariah 9, the Lord revealed His plan to judge the nations surrounding Israel. From Syria to Lebanon to Philistia, Israel's neighbors would experience severe defeat and destruction. Historically, the military exploits depicted in verses 1–6 predict the conquests of Alexander the Great, whose armies swept through the Middle East roughly 200 years after Zechariah's prophecy. More generally, however, these verses reflect the political tumult that would characterize the times of the Gentiles (Luke 21:24), an era marked by conquerors and conquests (cf. Zech 1:18–21). Eschatologically, these verses point to the messianic conqueror who will one day secure final victory for His people, bringing salvation to Israel and even to the Gentiles (cf. 9:7–8). Military leaders throughout history, like Alexander, merely prefigure the ultimate conqueror, the Messiah Himself.

In Zechariah 9:9–10, God foretold the very moment when the Messiah would be publicly revealed to Israel. That epic moment came when Jesus rode into Jerusalem at the triumphal entry, roughly 550 years after this prophecy was given. That occasion was of monumental significance, not merely because the people laid palm branches on the road and rejoiced with shouts of jubilation, but because it marked a major milestone in God's redemptive plan: the unveiling of the one true King to His people.

As it anticipates the triumphal entry, this passage reveals both the humility and honor that would characterize that event. On the one hand, it was marked by humility, because the Messiah would ride into Jerusalem not as a military hero but as a Suffering Servant (Zech 9:9). On the other hand, the triumphal entry also anticipated the honor rightly due Him. Through His suffering, the Messiah would secure salvation both for Israel and the nations. His humble entry on a donkey would be the precursor to His second coming, when He will return on a white horse (Rev 19:11). At that time, He will conquer all enemies, end all wars, and reign with perfect peace (Zech 9:10). The triumphal entry encompasses both aspects of Messiah's ministry: the humility of His sufferings and the honor of His future reign.

For those in Zechariah's day, this prophecy alerted them to the character of their coming King. Worldly conquerors would come and go, typically with lavish display, but they needed to look for the One who would ride into Jerusalem on a donkey. Only He was their Messiah. For believers today, looking back at the events of Jesus' Passion Week, this passage provides clear prophetic confirmation of His ministry. The Messiah who died as the Suffering Servant, being humble and lowly, will one day return as the supreme Sovereign to conquer His enemies and reign in glory.

THE HUMILITY OF THE SUFFERING SERVANT

Rejoice greatly, O daughter of Zion!
Make a loud shout, O daughter of Jerusalem!
Behold, your king is coming to you;
He is righteous and endowed with salvation,
Lowly and mounted on a donkey,
Even on a colt, the foal of a pack animal. (9:9)

The concluding prophecy of verse 8, that "no taskmaster will pass over them anymore," predicted that one day Israel would be permanently free from foreign oppression. But that divine promise has not yet been fulfilled. Though Alexander and his armies conquered many of Israel's neighboring enemies (cf. 9:1–6), while leaving Jerusalem unscathed, the Greeks did not free Israel from foreign rule or aggression. The fulfillment of that promise, that Israel will never again be subjected to a foreign taskmaster, awaits the second coming of the Messiah—the final conquest. Accordingly, the focus of Zechariah's prophecy shifts in verses 9–10 away from miscellaneous conflicts and conquerors to the messianic conqueror who will exceed them all.

In verse 9, the prophetic depiction of Israel's ultimate King began with a call to celebrate: **"Rejoice greatly, O daughter of Zion!"** The language of **rejoice greatly** denoted not just an attitude of happiness, but an outburst of exuberance. As noted earlier (see discussion on Zech 2:14), the phrase **daughter of Zion** personified Jerusalem as a young woman, in this case, in the full gladness of meeting her bridegroom, the Messiah (cf. Isa 26:1–19; Rev 19:7–9). Overwhelmed with joy, the inhabitants of Jerusalem are compared to a bride on her wedding day. Their uncontainable jubilation is expressed with a **loud shout**— not merely a sound of happiness but an exclamation of total triumph (Isa 44:23) and loyal allegiance (1 Sam 10:24). The invitation to shout is addressed to the **daughter of Jerusalem**, a title that not only personified the city (see above), but also highlighted Jerusalem as the political capital of the entire kingdom (Lam 2:13). At the time Zechariah delivered his prophecy, Israel's capital had seen better days. Jerusalem had lost her beauty and stature in defeat (Lam 2:15), but God prophesied it would one day be restored to perpetual prominence (Mic 4:8; Zeph 3:14). Hence, the people could shout for joy as they anticipated the One who would secure Jerusalem's future glory.

Who would that One be? God answered that question with this promise: **"Behold, your king is coming to you."** The title **"your king"** was an unmistakable reference to Israel's Messiah. As illustrated in verses 1–6, pagan kings and foreign conquerors constantly passed through the Promised Land. However, none of them could ever be Israel's true king. Only a king from Israel could rightfully reign over God's chosen nation. As Moses commanded, "You shall surely set a king over you whom Yahweh your God chooses, one from among your brothers you shall set as king over yourselves; you may not put a foreigner over yourselves who is not your brother" (Deut 17:15). The messianic King would not be a Gentile ruler but **your king**, a ruler who came from Israel and was for Israel. Through the lips of His prophet, God further declared that the Messiah **is coming to you**. The implication of the text is that He would be revealed not in secret, but openly—to be welcomed by the people with shouts of acclamation and triumph.

This was clearly and completely fulfilled during the earthly ministry of the Lord Jesus. To reiterate that point, both Matthew (21:5) and John (12:15) cited Zechariah 9:9 in describing Christ's triumphal entry. When Jesus entered Jerusalem, crowds of people laid down garments and palm branches, a symbol of welcome to a king (Matt 21:7; John 12:13; cf. 2 Kgs 9:13). They affirmed this audibly by exclaiming, "Hosanna to the Son of David" (Matt 21:9), expressing their adoration for Jesus and recognizing His royal lineage and right to reign. The actions and acclamations of the people demonstrated that they understood Jesus to be the one true King.

What would this coming King be like? The messianic conqueror described in verse 9 would be distinctly different from other conquerors. As the Lord explained, **"He is righteous and endowed with salvation."** Unlike pagan leaders who were wicked and cruel, the Messiah would be **righteous**, characterized by moral purity and perfect justice. Unlike conquerors who terrorize and oppress, the Messiah would be **endowed with salvation**, coming to deliver His people, "to seek and to save the lost" (Luke 19:10). The prophet Isaiah provided an in-depth look at the righteousness and salvation of the Messiah, the Servant of Yahweh. As Isaiah declared, the Servant would demonstrate His righteousness through perfect obedience to God (50:1–4; cf. Phil 2:8). As the righteous One, the Servant would justify His people (Isa 53:11) and one day establish righteousness on earth (Isa 61:11; cf. Ps 98:9). The halls of history are replete with earthly conquerors who came to take things for themselves, but the heavenly conqueror, the Messiah, will come to bring righteousness, salvation, and blessing to His people and the world.

Having predicted the people's joy over the arrival of their Messiah, the Lord revealed an unexpected detail at the end of verse 9. At the time of His unveiling, the Messiah would be **lowly and mounted on a donkey.** The term **lowly**, meaning humble and afflicted (cf. Isa 53:4), was not what Zechariah's original audience would have expected to hear. Why would the righteous and noble Messiah be humble and afflicted? How could a triumphal entry include humiliation and suffering? Yet, Isaiah had already explained to Israel that the Servant would save His people through suffering (Isa 53:1–12). So, the One endowed with salvation must enter Jerusalem in humility and lowliness. Through His affliction, betrayal, and death, He would deliver His own (cf. Zech 11:12; 12:10). To accentuate that point, the Messiah would not even ride on a horse, like other conquerors, but on a **donkey**. Though earlier in history royalty sometimes rode on donkeys (cf. Judg 5:10; 10:4; 12:14; 2 Sam 16:2), by the time of Solomon, the import and export of horses made the horse the animal of choice for royalty (Esth 6:8). Riding on a donkey was unimpressive, reinforcing the humble circumstances in which this King would enter Jerusalem. The shocking description of verse 9 depicted a Messiah who would save, but not by sword—rather, by suffering and self-sacrifice.

The final phrase of verse 9 links the Messiah's humiliation with His exaltation. God revealed that the Messiah will ride **even on a colt, the foal of a pack animal**. The words **colt** and **foal** point back to Genesis 49:11, where Jacob blessed Judah and the tribe of his descendants. There, Jacob prophesied that in the end times, Shiloh, the Messiah, will tie "*his* foal to the vine, and his donkey's colt to the choice vine." Grape vines are generally too frail to restrain a tethered pack animal. But Jacob prophesied that when the Messiah comes at the end of the age, vines will be so strong they could easily secure a donkey. Jacob's prophecy anticipated the reality that during the millennial kingdom, the curse of sin will be largely removed, allowing creation to flourish (cf. Isa 11:1–10). By riding into Jerusalem **on a colt, the foal of a pack animal**, the Messiah would demonstrate that He is not only the Suffering Servant, but also Shiloh, the descendant of Judah who will fulfill the prophecy of Genesis 49:11. His triumphal entry prefigured His ultimate triumph: from His sacrificial victory over sin and death to His supreme and universal victory at the end of the age, when He establishes His kingdom on earth.

Again, the details of verse 9 were fulfilled by the Lord Jesus when He rode into Jerusalem two millennia ago. As the gospels record, Jesus entered Jerusalem humble and riding on a donkey (cf. Matt 21:1–7). His humiliation continued with His betrayal, arrest, sham trial, sentencing, and execution on a cross (cf. 27:33–56). His triumphal entry anticipated tragedy exactly as the book of Zechariah foretold. But Jesus' death was not the end. His resurrection three days later (cf. 28:1–15) was the first fruits of a new creation (cf. 1 Cor 15:20) and a preview of the glory of His coming kingdom. All of this was perfectly in keeping with what God revealed about the coming Messiah in Zechariah 9:9.

THE HONOR OF THE SUPREME SOVEREIGN

I will cut off the chariot from Ephraim
And the horse from Jerusalem;
And the bow of war will be cut off.
And He will speak peace to the nations;
And His reign will be from sea to sea
And from the River to the ends of the earth. (9:10)

The prophecy of verse 9 revealed that the Messiah would enter Jerusalem humbly to save. By contrast, in verse 10, the Lord looked forward to the end of the age to reveal the magnificent results of the Messiah's victory. In this verse, the timeframe shifted from Christ's first coming to His second. The original readers of this book, and even Zechariah himself, would not have known the timing of these events. The Apostle Peter described how the prophets did not know "what time or what kind of time" these things would take place (1 Pet 1:11). Nevertheless, they could discern that Christ would be humbled and afflicted (Zech 9:9) and then be honored and exalted (v. 10; cf. 1 Pet 1:11). Thus, these verses reveal that Jesus' triumphal entry truly was triumphant, providing a preview of the rightful and royal honor He is due as Israel's Messiah.

Christ's second coming will be glorious, for God Himself will go to war. As Yahweh declared, **"I will cut off the chariot from Ephraim and the horse from Jerusalem."** The pronoun I distinguished the speaker in this verse from the pronoun "He" (in v. 9 and later in v. 10), which referred to the Messiah. That distinction indicates that this promise was spoken by God the Father, regarding what He will do when His Son, the Messiah, returns. The Father loves His Son and will fight to give all things into His hand (cf. John 3:35; 1 Cor 15:24–28). The verb **cut off** does not merely have the idea of removal, but of a violent eradication resulting in complete termination. The verb was used when Moses spoke of God cutting off the nations in judgment (Deut 19:1) and when Saul cut off mediums by eliminating them from the land (1 Sam 28:9). When Christ returns, God the Father will forcefully and systematically destroy **chariot** and **horse**, the symbols of war, conquering every adversary and eradicating all resistance. Though Israel was never supposed to trust in horses (cf. Deut 17:16; Ps 20:7), they often failed in that regard (1 Kgs 4:26). But in the end, God will cut off any reliance on military weapons or equipment as He forcefully abolishes warfare, brings about a perfect peace (cf. Isa 2:4; Hos 2:18; Mic 4:2–4), and compels His people to look to Him alone (cf. Zech 12:10). During the Messiah's earthly reign, the situation will become so secure and stable that Israel will have no need for military defenses, from the very north of Israel (**Ephraim**) to its capital in the south (**Jerusalem**).

In this climactic conquest, God the Father will eliminate not only war but any opposition against His Son. In addition to cutting off chariot and horse, **the bow of war will be cut off**. The bow was often used in battle as a long-range weapon (Gen 49:24; Josh 24:12; 1 Sam 2:4; 2 Sam 1:22). God will fiercely **cut off** every **bow of war** so that there will be only one bow of war: His Son (cf. Zech 10:4). The Father will ensure that the Lord Jesus alone possesses all might, honor, and authority (cf. Dan 7:14; Rev 20:1–6).

Though He could decimate them with divine power, the Messiah **will speak peace to the nations**. He will soothe and console the peoples, drawing them to Himself (cf. Isa 60:1–10; Zech 2:11), uniting them with Israel (cf. Zech 8:23), and inviting them to worship together (Isa 19:23–25). According to Zechariah 14:16–19, people from all the nations will go up to Jerusalem to celebrate the Feast of Booths each year, rejoicing in the faithfulness and goodness of God. So, there will be peace between nations, peace between former enemies, and peace that cultivates and facilitates worship. Such global, lasting, and pristine peace will distinguish Christ's final conquest from all other campaigns in world history. The Lord Jesus truly is the Prince of Peace (cf. Isa 9:6).

At the end of verse 10, the Lord revealed the extent of Messiah's future kingdom: **"His reign will be from sea to sea and from the River to the ends of the earth."** These words, taken from Psalm 72:8, described the ideal kingdom of Israel. Through the mouth of Zechariah, God reminded His people that He had not forgotten His promise regarding the land Israel would one day possess. Messiah's future **reign**, meaning His total sovereign dominion, will extend globally, **from sea to sea**. His rule will fulfill the promises made to Israel as He reigns from **the River** Euphrates, which is the promised territorial boundary of Israel (cf. Gen 15:18), and as His power extends **to the ends of the earth**. This latter phrase encompasses every part of the globe and is reserved in the Old Testament to describe the Messiah's rule (cf. 1 Sam 2:10; Pss 2:8; 22:27; 72:8; Isa 52:10; Mic 5:4).

Throughout world history, there have been many conquerors who had the ambition to dominate the world. In the end, only Christ will achieve permanent global victory. His reign will be exhaustive and His rule ultimate. At His first coming, the Messiah rode into Jerusalem humbly on a donkey. But when He returns, He is depicted riding on a white horse in judgment and victory (Rev 19:11). As these verses from Zechariah 9 reveal, the triumphal entry represented both the humiliation and the glorification of the Messiah. Though His first coming was marked by suffering and affliction, His second coming will be characterized by victory and dominion. As the final conqueror, He will vanquish every enemy, cut off all power and authority, reign righteously over the entire world, and fulfill every covenant promise to Israel. Thus, His people can enthusiastically respond to the invitation of verse 9 to "rejoice greatly." The reason for such jubilation is found in the Messiah, both for what He accomplished in His humility and for what He will accomplish in His glory.

God's Commitment to His People

25

Zechariah 9:11–17

As for you also, because of the blood of your covenant,
I have set your prisoners free from the waterless pit.

Return to the stronghold, O prisoners who have the hope;
This very day I am declaring that I will return double to you.

For I will bend Judah as My bow;
I will fill the bow with Ephraim.
And I will rouse up your sons, O Zion, against your sons, O Greece;
And I will make you like a mighty man's sword.

Then Yahweh will appear over them,
And His arrow will go forth like lightning;
And Lord Yahweh will blow the trumpet
And will go in the storm winds of the south.

Yahweh of hosts will defend them.
And they will consume and trample on the stones of a sling;
And they will drink *and* roar as with wine;
And they will be filled like a *sacrificial* bowl,
Drenched like the corners of the altar.

And Yahweh their God will save them in that day
As the flock of His people;
For *they are as* the stones of a crown,
Sparkling in His land.

For what goodness and what beauty *will be* theirs!
Grain will make the choice men flourish, and new wine the virgins.

From the beginning of Genesis to the end of Revelation, Scripture clearly reveals the work of God in both the past and the future. But what about in the present? Believers may wonder how the Lord is working when the world around them descends into turmoil and chaos. At times, God's people may find themselves repeating the questions that David asked, "How long, O Yahweh? Will You forget me forever? How long will You hide Your face from me?" (Ps 13:1). Like David, believers yearn to know that God is committed to His people—not only in the past and in the future, but at all times in between.

In Zechariah 9:11–17, through the mouth of His prophet, the Lord assured His people He had not forgotten them. His loyal love for them was grounded in His covenant pledge to Abraham and Abraham's descendants (v. 11). It included the certain promise that He would bless His people (vv. 12–13). And it culminated with a reminder that His all-consuming power would one day eliminate all enemies and oppressors (vv. 14–17). For this reason, God called His people to fix their hope on Him (cf. 9:12). While they awaited the fulfillment of messianic and millennial prophecies (cf. vv. 9–10), they were not to lose hope. The Lord's commitment to Israel was not limited to the ancient past or reserved for the distant future. He remained faithful to them even in the present.

GOD'S COVENANT PLEDGE

As for you also, because of the blood of your covenant,
I have set your prisoners free from the waterless pit. (9:11)

With the opening words **as for you also**, Yahweh moved from discussing military conquerors (vv. 1–8), and particularly the messianic conqueror (vv. 9–10), to address the people of Israel directly. He reiterated His commitment to them, assuring them of His protection and provision. That divine encouragement provided Israel with the hope they needed in the face of the political upheaval foretold in the first half of Zechariah 9.

In explaining this, God recounted the grounds for His commitment to Israel—**because of the blood of your covenant.** The mention of **blood** recalled covenant ceremonies in which blood was shed, symbolizing the unbreakable seal of promise. In establishing His promises with Abram in Genesis 15, God instructed Abram to cut animals in half (Gen 15:9–10), thereby spilling their blood. Normally, both parties making such a covenant would walk through the pieces to show that if they failed to keep their part of the agreement, they would deserve to be cut up as well (cf. Jer 34:18–21). However, in the ceremony with Abram, God alone walked through the pieces (Gen 15:17). He did this to show His unconditional commitment to keep the covenant, demonstrating it was not contingent on the faithfulness of Abram or his offspring. This divine guarantee was reiterated in Exodus 24 where blood was sprinkled on the people (Exod 24:8) to symbolize that they were sealed by God's singular loyalty.

For the Israelites in Zechariah's day, **the blood of your** covenant not only pointed back to God's covenant promise to Abraham, but it also anticipated the blood sacrifice of the final Lamb of God (cf. 1 Pet 1:18–19). Ultimately, the grounds for God's commitment to save His faithful people is Christ's own blood, which is the seal of the New Covenant (Heb 9:13–22). God has sealed His promises to His people in blood, and they are therefore inviolable.

Out of His covenant love for His people, the Lord announced His plan to carry out a new exodus on their behalf. He declared, "**I have set your prisoners free from the waterless pit.**" The language of **setting** someone **free**, releasing them from bondage, was used to speak of liberating slaves (Deut 15:12). The most famous occurrence of that language appeared in Moses' demand to Pharaoh to let God's people go (Exod 3:20; 4:21, 23; 5:1). Though no longer in Egypt, the Israelites of Zechariah's day still felt like **prisoners**, subject to foreign powers and taskmasters (cf. Zech 9:8). But the subjugation Israel experienced was not the end of the story. As God pledged in this verse, He would liberate His people (cf. Isa 24:23; 27:12–13). He would lead them to freedom as He had done in the past.

In describing that future deliverance, Yahweh explained that He would set them free from **the waterless pit.** For Zechariah's audience, the imagery would have recalled the story of Joseph, who was sold into slavery after being thrown into a dry pit. According to Genesis 37:24, Joseph's brothers "took him and cast him into the pit. Now the pit was empty, without any water in it." Joseph was incarcerated initially by his brothers and then later in Egypt, until God delivered him. Centuries later, the prophet Jeremiah was similarly abandoned in an empty cistern (Jer 38:6; Lam 3:53). The Lord also rescued him from the wicked schemes of his enemies. Just as God delivered Joseph and Jeremiah, so He promised to accomplish the deliverance of His people. Significantly, the main verb is past tense **(I have set free)**—a prophetic perfect tense in Hebrew— highlighting the absolute certainty of everything God pledged to do. The unchanging One who made a unilateral covenant with Abraham and his descendants in the past would be faithful to keep it in both the present and the future.

GOD'S CERTAIN PROMISES

Return to the stronghold, O prisoners who have the hope;
This very day I am declaring that I will return double to you.

For I will bend Judah as My bow;
I will fill the bow with Ephraim.
And I will rouse up your sons, O Zion, against your sons, O Greece;
And I will make you like a mighty man's sword. (9:12–13)

The Lord continued by instructing His people to **return to the stronghold.** The Hebrew term for **stronghold** is found only here in the Old Testament. It may be related to the word for sheepfold (cf. Mic 2:12), which would be fitting since Zechariah 9:16 describes Israel as God's flock. The Hebrew word for **stronghold** (*bitzaron*) is similar in sound to the words for "daughter of Zion" (*bat tzion*). Zechariah's audience would have undoubtedly made that connection when they heard these words from the mouth of the prophet. That similarity suggests that the **stronghold** (*bitzaron*) in this verse refers to the city of Jerusalem, the "daughter of Zion" (*bat tzion*). Having been scattered across the world in exile, the Lord called His people—in Zechariah's time and beyond—to return to Jerusalem and the Promised Land. This return was both physical and spiritual (cf. Zech 1:3; 2:6–7), as they returned to Jerusalem to worship Yahweh. As God Himself promised, Zion would be the place where He would protect and care for His people.

God identified His people as **prisoners who have the hope**. This statement described Israel's experience during the times of the Gentiles (cf. Luke 21:24), as they endured the rule of various imperial powers—from Medo-Persia to Greece to Rome. The word **prisoner**, repeated from verse 11, described the condition in which Israel would be while it was bound up and oppressed by foreign invaders. Even in modern history, the state of Israel has continually faced military threats from surrounding enemies. But Zechariah prophesied that a time would come when "no taskmaster will pass over them anymore" (v. 8). By believing that promise for the future, along with the promises about the coming Messiah (in vv. 9–10), the Israelites could be characterized by unwavering **hope**. Despite the turmoil of world events, God called His people to carry a confident expectation in Him. Though they might feel like prisoners under the thumb of foreign rule, they were to set their minds on the promises of God, knowing that He would one day bring the final deliverance from all exile.

The Lord assured His people that, "**This very day I am declaring that I will return double to you.**" The language of **I am declaring** expresses a formal announcement (cf. Isa 48:20; Jer 5:20). This was an official pronouncement, underscoring the certainty and seriousness of God's commitment to His people. To emphasize that point, Yahweh added that He declared it **this very day**. This was not a promise merely rehearsed from "past days" (cf. Ezra 4:15), nor a guarantee to be made eventually "in that day" far into the future (cf. Zech 12:3, 4, 6). Rather, the Lord definitively declared it on **this very day**, the day Zechariah proclaimed these words, to a remnant of Israelites who were deeply discouraged by the challenges they faced. In so doing, God demonstrated that His commitment was not merely to Abraham or Moses in the former days, nor to the future generation of Israelites who will populate the millennial kingdom. Rather, His commitment was to His people in **this** time, to the righteous remnant of Israel during Zechariah's day and beyond. This promise from the Lord was directly for them.

In the subsequent phrase, the Lord articulated the substance of that promise: "**I will return double to you.**" The language of **double** conveys God's overwhelming grace, and it would have been a great encouragement for Zechariah's listeners. Almost two centuries earlier, the prophet Isaiah had already explained the meaning of such a promise, saying, "Instead of your shame *you will have* a double portion, and *instead of* dishonor they will shout for joy over their portion. Therefore, they will possess a double *portion* in their land; everlasting gladness will be theirs" (Isa 61:7). According to Isaiah's prediction, the **double** portion will overshadow all that Israel had lost and all that the people had endured. They will receive a double portion of the blessings God promised for them, not only in terms of land but also in the joy of experiencing God's everlasting goodness.

Included in this promise was God's assurance that He would **return** a double portion of blessing to Israel. As has been noted previously, the word **return** is a key term throughout the book of Zechariah. Earlier in this verse, God urged His people to return to the Promised Land (Zech 9:12). Throughout the book, God promised to return to Israel as the people returned in repentance to Him (1:3, 16; 8:3). The use of the word **return** here (in v. 12) reiterates that principle—God will pour out His blessings (even double) only on those who return to Him. Sadly, Israel has not yet returned to the Messiah, as the prophets (Isa 55:3; Zech 1:1–3) and the apostles (Acts 2:38; 3:19) called them to do. But one day they will return (cf. Hos 3:5), and when they do, God will give them a double portion of His blessing. He will demonstrate His unwavering commitment to giving them their blessing even as He declared on that day through Zechariah.

The Lord revealed a sign to His people to prove the veracity of

His commitment to them. In verse 13, God declared, "**For I will bend Judah as My bow; I will fill the bow with Ephraim. And I will rouse up your sons, O Zion, against your sons, O Greece; and I will make you like a mighty man's sword.**" The Lord promised to **bend Judah** for Himself as His **bow**. He would use Judah as a weapon, one of the most effective implements of war. Likewise, He promised to **fill the bow with Ephraim**. God would arm His bow with many arrows, namely the people of Ephraim. The nation would be sent as a lethal force against its foes. The combination of Judah and Ephraim, representing the southern and northern kingdoms respectively, indicates the entire nation of Israel was in view. The people would be empowered by God to overwhelm their enemies. As part of this, God promised to **rouse up your sons, O Zion**, strengthening and emboldening the inhabitants of Jerusalem for effective military victory.

The Lord revealed that this show of force by Israel would be **against your sons, O Greece**. Those words were fulfilled during the intertestamental period (the time between the ministry of Malachi and the birth of Jesus Christ). For much of that time, Israel suffered under the domination of the Seleucid empire, a Greek state formed after the death of Alexander the Great by one of his generals. In 167 BC, Judas Maccabaeus (or Judah Maccabee) and his brothers rebelled against their Greek oppressors. At that time, Antiochus Epiphanes (who reigned from 175–164 BC) oppressed Israel greatly, even contemptuously sacrificing a pig on the altar of the temple. In response, the people revolted. God raised up warriors from Israel to fight against their Greek adversaries. As the Lord declared to His people through Zechariah, "**I will make you like a mighty man's sword.**" The **mighty man** was a familiar image, used throughout the Old Testament to designate Israel's special forces. The most famous example was David's mighty men (2 Sam 10:7; 23:8). These elite soldiers were experts in combat, rendering them extremely lethal. The **sword** of the mighty man was a weapon that pierced its target with deadly precision. Empowered by God for such a fight, all of Israel would become like a deadly weapon in the hands of an elite warrior. This prophecy was fulfilled about 350 years after it was given by Zechariah, when the people of Israel shattered Greek oppression during the Maccabean Revolt.[1]

Israel's victory against Antiochus Epiphanes and his armies is celebrated annually in the Jewish holiday of Hanukkah. The Lord's fulfillment of this prophecy, like the predictions regarding Alexander in verses 1–6, proves that He always keeps His Word. It further illustrates His unwavering commitment to His people. Yahweh's faithfulness to them has never faltered. As a result, the hope they have in Him will not be disappointed.

GOD'S CONSUMING POWER

Then Yahweh will appear over them,
And His arrow will go forth like lightning;
And Lord Yahweh will blow the trumpet
And will go in the storm winds of the south.

Yahweh of hosts will defend them.
And they will consume and trample on the stones of a sling;
And they will drink *and* roar as with wine;
And they will be filled like a *sacrificial* bowl,
Drenched like the corners of the altar.

And Yahweh their God will save them in that day
As the flock of His people;
For *they are as* the stones of a crown,
Sparkling in His land.

For what goodness and what beauty *will be* theirs!
Grain will make the choice men flourish, and new wine the virgins. (9:14–17)

With the term **then**, the timeline of Zechariah's prophecy moves to the end of the age. The Hebrew conveys a sense of suddenness regarding

---

1 Kenneth L. Barker, "Zechariah," in *The Expositor's Bible Commentary: Daniel–Malachi*, rev. ed., ed. Tremper Longman III and David E. Garland (Grand Rapids: Zondervan, 2008), 8:799; George L. Klein, *Zechariah*, New American Commentary (Nashville: B & H Publishing Group, 2008), 280.

God's appearing to defend and deliver His people. What God promised to do for Israel against the Greek armies of the Seleucid Empire foreshadows what He will do for Israel in the future (cf. Dan 8:1–27; 11:1–45; Hab 3:11–15).

God's eschatological work for His people will far outshine what He did in history. Though God worked through hidden providence in Israel's conflict with Antiochus Epiphanes, in the end times, **Yahweh Himself will appear over them.** He will visibly manifest Himself to aid His people. During the Maccabean revolt, God used His people like deadly arrows (Zech 9:13). But in the future, **His arrow will go forth like lightning.** He will send forth His catastrophic judgment with the speed, terror, and deadliness of lightning (Ps 77:17). Though historically His people rose up to defeat the Greeks, in this final battle, **Lord Yahweh will blow the trumpet.** God Himself will lead the charge into battle. His trumpet blast will assemble His armies (Jer 4:5), signal the attack (Josh 6:4), and cause His foes to tremble (Amos 3:6). His presence will be noticed by all, for He **will go in the storm winds of the south.** Such storm winds were a familiar and formidable threat, violently whipping up dust that could be seen from a great distance. In this final battle, God will charge forward before His people, and no enemy will be able to withstand Him. He will demonstrate that He is not only Yahweh but **Lord Yahweh,** the Master of His people and their commanding general.

In this way, **Yahweh of hosts will defend them.** Zechariah once again declared the name **Yahweh of hosts,** a favorite name for God in this book. He will unleash the angelic armies of heaven as He moves to **defend** His own, meaning to enclose and protect them. The same root is used to describe a shield. God will be that shield for His people when they need Him most. He will absorb and repel any attack leveled against Israel (cf. Zech 12:8; 14:1–3).

On that future day, Yahweh will not merely be a defense for His people, but He will also be their offense. As verse 15 declares, "**They will consume and trample on the stones of a sling; and they will drink *and* roar as with wine.**" Because God will be for them, Israel will completely vanquish their enemies. Nothing will be able to slow their advance, nor will anyone be able to resist their attack. Empowered by the Lord, the people of Israel will **trample on the stones of a sling.** Slings were used in ancient times by many nations during combat. The Assyrians, Egyptians, Greeks, Romans, as well as the Israelites, all employed them. In the hands of a skilled marksman, they were lethal. It has been said that a slingshot was as deadly as a .44 Magnum when used by an expert, like David (1 Sam 17). Though enemy forces will hurl stones at them, such attacks will prove futile. God's people will trample on the projectiles of their adversaries.

As a result, **they will drink and roar as with wine.** God's people will not only consume their enemies (as if consuming a feast), but they will also **drink**, illustrating the full extent of their victory and its subsequent celebration (cf. Ps 110:7). They will even **roar as with wine.** Elsewhere, the concept of roaring is used to describe the loud sounds of the sea (Isa 17:12) or a boisterous city (22:2). When Israel achieves victory at the battle of Armageddon, the people will not be able to restrain their exuberance as they shout in triumph. They will make a deafening, unrestrained roar on account of God's work on their behalf (cf. Ezek 38–39; Zech 12:1–9; 14:1–3, 12–15; Rev 19:11–21).

The final line of verse 15 states that this will be the greatest, most triumphant, and final victory: **"They will be filled like a** *sacrificial* **bowl, drenched like the corners of the altar."** Initially, the picture is one of immense bloodshed. When priests would offer sacrifices, they would fill blood into specific bowls and sprinkle the blood on the altar. They would do so at each of the four corners so that the whole altar was splattered with blood. Here in this verse, the Lord conveyed that Israel will be filled and drenched with blood from the battle. Revelation 14:20 confirms this: "The wine press was trodden outside the city, and blood came out from the wine press, up to the horses' bridles, for a distance of 1,600 stadia." At the Battle of Armageddon, blood will flow for nearly the entire length of the Promised Land, pooling deep enough to splash up to a horse's bridle. That future conflict will result in massive destruction, the likes of which the world has never seen.

In this text, God depicted Israel specifically as a **sacrificial bowl** and **the corners of the altar.** He did this for a reason. Not only will they inflict heavy casualties, but they will also be the weapon through which

God enacts justice. The Old Testament at times portrayed a battle as a sacrifice to God, which satiated His judgment against sin (Isa 34:6; Ezek 39:17–20; Zeph 1:7). At Armageddon, God's enemies will not only be defeated, but destroyed with an intensity consistent with divine justice.

As a result, God's people will be delivered. Zechariah declared that **"Yahweh their God will save them in that day."** These words highlight the purpose behind such devastating eschatological judgment. The Lord does not wield His wrath capriciously but enacts His vengeance both to judge the wicked and to save the righteous.

Importantly, God will not merely deliver Israel *from* her enemies, but He will deliver them *to* Himself. They will be saved **as the flock of His people.** Throughout history, Israel had false shepherds whom the Lord condemned. As Ezekiel prophesied, "Thus says Lord Yahweh, 'Woe, shepherds of Israel who have been shepherding themselves! Should not the shepherds shepherd the flock?'" (Ezek 34:2). However, God also revealed: "I will save My flock, and they will no longer be plunder; and I will judge between one sheep and another. Then I will establish over them one shepherd, My servant David, and he will shepherd them; he will shepherd them himself and be their shepherd" (Ezek 34:22–23). The reference to David is actually to David's royal descendant, the Messiah, who will one day be Israel's Shepherd. He will fulfill Psalm 23 for them such that they will have no want (Ps 23:1). In the end, Israel's final conqueror will also be her King, her liberator, and her Good Shepherd (cf. John 10).

The Good Shepherd will love and care for Israel. Verse 16 describes the nation at that time as **the stones of a crown.** After so many foes had mistreated and manipulated Israel, the Messiah will treat His people like a treasure, as prized as the precious gems in a royal crown. This will fulfill what God announced to His people in Exodus 19:5: "Then you shall be My treasured possession among all the peoples" (cf. Mal 3:17). Israel will also radiate with the beauty of His holiness. As the people of God, they will be **sparkling in His land.** Psalm 60:4 uses the verb **sparkling** to refer to the unfurling of a banner. With equal elegance, this verse depicts the people of Israel dwelling throughout the land, glimmering and sparkling like treasured gemstones.

The prophet explained what that will look like, saying, **"For what goodness and what beauty *will be* theirs!"** **Goodness** refers to the benefits that Israel will receive from the Lord. They will enjoy tremendous prosperity and wealth because of God's blessing upon them. Likewise, they will exude **beauty**. The word is used to describe the loveliness of a woman (Ps 45:11) or the nobility of a king (Is 33:17). In addition to material blessings, the nation will enjoy the dignity, nobility, and honor bestowed on them by God.

Through Zechariah, the Lord further defined the notions of goodness and beauty by explaining that **grain will make the choice men flourish, and new wine the virgins. Grain** and the freshly pressed juice of **new wine** show the bounty of the land in terms of both food and drink. Israel will fully enjoy God's generous provision in this way. Likewise, **choice men** and **virgins** refer respectively to young men, representing strength, and young women, representing purity. These demographic groups consist of people in the prime of life, reflecting the health, vigor, exuberance, and devotion of the entire nation. Such a scene of youthful bliss captures the extent of Israel's future blessing. Isaiah 62 foretells how Jerusalem will be a crown of glory in Yahweh's hand (Isa 62:1–5). The city will be displayed to the whole earth as God's prized possession, so that all the world will admire its beauty and glorify God (62:6–12).

Zechariah 9 began with prophecies about God's judgment on the surrounding nations (vv. 1–6), predictions that were fulfilled in history by the armies of Alexander the Great. Yet, those prophecies also foreshadowed the future victories of Israel's ultimate conqueror, the Messiah (vv. 9–10). The chapter ends, in verses 11–17, by reminding Israel of their future hope, guaranteed by God Himself. As the Lord reiterated in these verses, He had not forgotten His promises to His people, but provided a sign that assured them of His final deliverance (v. 13). For that reason, they could fix their hope on Him, confident that Yahweh was committed to them both in the present and for the future.

False Substitutes and the True Shepherd

Zechariah 10:1–5

Ask rain from Yahweh at the time of the late rain—
Yahweh who makes the storm clouds;
And He will give them showers of rain, *the* plant in the field to *each* man.

For the teraphim speak wickedness,
And the diviners behold false visions
And speak worthless dreams;
They comfort in vain.
Therefore *the people* journey like sheep;
They are afflicted because there is no shepherd.

"My anger burns against the shepherds,
And I will visit *punishment* upon the male goats;
For Yahweh of hosts has visited His flock, the house of Judah,
And will make them like His splendid horse in battle.

From them will come the cornerstone,
From them the tent peg,
From them the bow of battle,
From them every *good* taskmaster, *all of them* together.

And they will be as mighty men,
Treading down *the enemy* in the mire of the streets in battle;
And they will battle, for Yahweh *will be* with them;
And the riders on horses will be put to shame."

No one wants to be fooled by a counterfeit. Whether it is a forged painting, a fraudulent email, or a form of fake currency, the world is full of deceivers whose scams are designed to trick the gullible and unsuspecting. For those who fall prey to such ploys, the consequences can be devastating, ranging from public embarrassment to massive loss and financial ruin.

As damaging as a counterfeit can be in the world of business and finance, the stakes are far higher when it comes to spiritual matters. False religion not only steals time, energy, and money from its victims, but also sets them on the path to eternal destruction. Luring in followers with empty promises, it offers hope and security that it cannot provide. Those who succumb to its deception not only waste their lives but also forfeit their souls. Tragically, many will not realize how badly they have been duped until it is too late (cf. Matt 7:21–23).

Because false religion poses such grave danger, Scripture condemns deceitful prophets and lying teachers to devastating judgment (cf. Deut 13:1–5; 18:20–22; Jer 14:14–16; 23:1–40; Ezek 13:9; 22:28–31; Mic 3:5–12). Purveyors of counterfeit religion are depicted as vipers (Matt 3:7), wolves (7:15), dogs (Phil 3:2), pigs (2 Pet 2:22), and unreasoning animals (Jude 10). Though they promise divine truth and spiritual life, in reality they offer only deceit and eternal death. Jude described these spiritual imposters as "clouds without water" (Jude 12), an image depicting the emptiness of their false promises. They claim to bring the rain of divine blessing, but they are never able to deliver, leaving the souls of those who trust in them parched and perishing.

Throughout Israel's history, false prophets and their religion represented a constant threat. The worship of pagan deities by the surrounding nations tempted the people to deviate from their singular devotion to Yahweh. That threat still existed even after the Babylonian captivity. Through His prophet Zechariah, the Lord warned His people not to be seduced by false shepherds, counterfeit religious leaders who would lead them astray. Instead, Zechariah called them to turn to Yahweh alone, looking ultimately to the Messiah, the Good Shepherd, who would care for His people and direct them in the truth.

In Zechariah 10, the prophet urged Israel to turn away from false substitutes and trust wholly in the Lord. He called the people to rely entirely on Yahweh, their sole sustainer (v. 1). They were to reject false shepherds who sought to mislead them (vv. 2–3), and instead to find their rest in the true Shepherd, the coming Messiah, through whom God promised ultimate victory (vv. 4–5).

THE SOLE SUSTAINER

Ask rain from Yahweh at the time of the late rain—
Yahweh who makes the storm clouds;
And He will give them showers of rain, *the* plant in the field to *each* man.
(10:1)

Chapter 9 ended with the glorious promise that Yahweh would protect His people and provide for them (cf. 9:11–17). In light of that divine assurance, Zechariah encouraged his listeners to look to the Lord to sustain them and meet their needs (10:1). In the ancient world, the most basic and vital necessity was rain, which brought food and life. Pagan religions worshiped deities like Baal and Hadad, hoping those storm gods would bring the much-needed precipitation. But the people of Israel were only to **ask rain from Yahweh**, the one true God and the Sovereign over all creation. The rain described in this verse is not spiritual but physical, as evidenced by the references to crops (cf. 9:17) and storm clouds (see below). The Hebrew word for **rain** does not denote a violent destructive downpour, but the kind of precipitation that is productive and ample. This rain would not flood the land but rejuvenate it. The timing of this rainfall was also important. It needed to come **at the time of the late rain**, in March or April, thereby enabling crops to reach their fullest potential before harvest.

Throughout Scripture, God promised to bless Israel with this kind of rain. In Deuteronomy, He assured His people that if they obeyed, He would send the early and the late rains (Deut 11:14). Through the prophet Joel, the Lord promised to provide the late rain as one of the first signs of His eschatological blessing (Joel 2:23). In Isaiah, He revealed that one day there would be rain of such magnitude that deserts would turn into fertile places (Isa 35:1–2). In this passage, Zechariah exhorted Israel to trust God to sustain them, both for the present and the future. They were to ask **Yahweh** and Him alone for the provision He had already promised.

Zechariah continued by giving two reasons the people should depend on God alone. First, the Lord was the only One able to help them. The prophet reminded them that **Yahweh** alone **makes the storm clouds**. As noted above, many of Israel's neighbors believed that pagan gods like Baal were responsible for storms and rain. But the Lord proved that notion false. At the time of Elijah, three centuries before Zechariah, God sent a drought to demonstrate that Baal had no ability to control the weather (cf. 1 Kgs 17:1; 18:20–46). Through Elijah, the Lord challenged Baal to send down fire from heaven, like a thunderbolt, to ignite a sacrifice (cf. 18:23–25, 38). This surely would have been an easy task for a god of storms and lightning. But when nothing happened, exposing Baal as impotent and false, the Lord dramatically demonstrated His exclusive power by sending fire like lighting from heaven to incinerate everything around the altar (cf. 18:38). The dramatic showdown proved that only Yahweh is God. He alone could break the drought and send a torrential downpour (cf. 18:41–46).

Testifying to God's complete control over clouds and rain, the book of Job records these words from Elihu:

> Behold, God is exalted, and we do not know *Him*; the number of His years is unsearchable. For He draws up the drops of water, they distill rain for His stream, which the clouds pour down, they drip upon man abundantly. Can anyone discern the spreading of the clouds, the thundering of His pavilion? Behold, He spreads His lightning about Him, and He covers the depths of the sea. (Job 36:26–30)

The Lord is the Creator and the Sustainer over all the natural world, including the rain, storm clouds, and lightning. In Zechariah 10:1, the Hebrew phrase **who makes** is a participle indicating that God is constantly in control of all the weather phenomena. This truth reminded Zechariah's audience why they needed to ask Yahweh alone for the rain. He was the only One who could answer them.

Second, Zechariah reminded his hearers that the Lord alone was faithful to them. The prophet proclaimed, **"And He will give them showers of rain, the plant in the field to *each* man."** The future-tense of **He will give** pointed beyond just the present, anticipating the eschatological rain of God's blessing in the millennial kingdom. This statement also underscored the certainty of God's promises: because He has guaranteed it, He certainly will give it. If Israel truly depends upon God for their sustenance, He will provide **showers of rain**. The word **rain** is the same word used throughout this passage to denote sufficient precipitation to sustain and cultivate Israel's crops. The term **showers** depicts abundant rainfall. Combined, these terms expressed God's provision of the perfect amount of rain for His people.

The Lord continued by describing the results of these showers, which produce **the plant in the field** for *each* man. The **plant in the field** is a generic phrase encompassing all of one's crops (cf. Gen 1:11–12, 29–30; 2:5; 3:18). By promising to send rain, both in the present and in the future, God assured His people that He would sustain them in the short term and preserve them to the end (cf. Zech 9:17). Because He would faithfully provide for them, they would not only survive but thrive (cf. Joel 2:24–25). They needed only look to the Lord, the one true God and their sole Sustainer, for their every need and daily provision. To look anywhere else was both foolish and futile.

THE FALSE SUBSTITUTES

For the teraphim speak wickedness,
And the diviners behold false visions
And speak worthless dreams;
They comfort in vain.

Therefore *the people* journey like sheep;
They are afflicted because there is no shepherd.

"My anger burns against the shepherds,
And I will visit *punishment* upon the male goats;
For Yahweh of hosts has visited His flock, the house of Judah,
And will make them like His splendid horse in battle." (10:2–3)

Zechariah not only illustrated the Lord's trustworthiness (v. 1) but also contrasted it with the worthlessness of every other alternative (vv. 2–3). Though Yahweh had demonstrated His faithfulness to Israel time after time, the people were constantly enticed to evil by idols and the false religious systems of their pagan neighbors. The Lord warned His people, through the mouth of His prophet, to repudiate such counterfeits and the false shepherds who promoted them.

One of these counterfeits was the **teraphim**. The term can refer to household idols (cf. Gen 31:19) as well as to the practice of using these idols in pagan rituals to commune with demonic forces (cf. 2 Kgs 23:24). For those engaged in such idolatry, the impact on their lives was entirely malevolent. The demonic forces behind the idols could only **speak wickedness**, giving harmful counsel and plunging their worshipers into depravity. The term **wickedness** includes the idea of misfortune, encompassing all the disastrous consequences of one's sin. The contrast Zechariah was making is clear. While Yahweh's promises provide life and joy, idolatry drives people to destruction.

Along with the teraphim, the prophet also condemned the **diviners**. Unlike the teraphim, which purported to connect with the spiritual realm for direction and guidance, the diviner claimed to derive omens and decipher signs from natural phenomena, including dreams. However, as Zechariah asserted, every message they allegedly relayed from the supernatural realm was a **false vision**. Though a **vision** was to provide supernatural sight, the supposed revelations received by these diviners were **false**, being both untrue and unreliable. Instead of providing insight, the diviner's vision only blinded people to the truth.

Zechariah further remarked that these diviners conveyed

worthless dreams. While God used **dreams** to reveal the future (cf. Gen 37:5–11; Num 12:6), the dreams of the diviner were **worthless**, empty, and futile. These false dreams did nothing for anyone, except to create empty expectations that would never be realized. Those who put their hope in diviners found their promises to be empty and useless. What a contrast this was to Yahweh's faithfulness.

As Zechariah went on to explain, lying religions and demonic forces **comfort in vain.** To **comfort** is to bring consolation and encouragement in difficult situations (cf. Gen 50:21; Ruth 2:13). Because their alleged insights were worthless, any comfort offered by idolaters or diviners was **in vain.** Zechariah used the same term for **vain** that Solomon employed throughout Ecclesiastes (cf. Eccl 1:2, 14; 2:1, 11, 15, 17, 21, 23, 26), picturing something as temporary as a breath and as aimless as dust blowing in the wind. The prophet's point was that false religion never grants any lasting consolation or sure direction. If the people sought help from idols, placing their hope in deceptive divinations, their pleas and prayers would come to nothing (cf. Isa 44:9–20).

Zechariah observed that, under the deadly misguidance of false religion, *the people* **journey** or wander **like sheep.** The imagery depicts a flock of lost lambs who cannot find their way. For any in Israel who would be lured by idolatry, Zechariah's warning rang out clearly: they would wander from place to place, never finding satisfying pastures or a safe haven of rest (cf. Jer 31:24). Though they would seek the stability of God's promises, it would be to no avail (cf. 44:15–19). Those clinging to idols would be **afflicted,** suffering, and abused, as well as exhausted from searching in vain for safety and stability (cf. Judg 10:14; Ps 115:4–8).

As the prophet explained, some in Israel had been afflicted **because there is no shepherd.** A faithful shepherd would attend to all the needs of his sheep (cf. Ps 23:1). He would lead the sheep to green pastures (cf. 23:2–3). He would protect the sheep from harm (cf. Ezek 34:4–8). But Zechariah indicated that Israel had suffered for lack of faithful shepherding. Since many of the people had been led astray, Zechariah called them to turn back to the Lord.

He used the word **shepherd** not only to talk about Israel's faulty religious leadership in the immediate context, but also to advance a grander theme developed in the latter half of the book. The prophet described the Messiah as a Shepherd in the previous chapter (cf. Zech 9:16) and will continue that designation in the next chapter (cf. 11:1–14). By emphasizing here (10:2) that Israel lacked faithful shepherds, Zechariah pointed to their need for the ultimate true and faithful Shepherd, the Messiah. He would truly comfort God's people, coming to Jerusalem to be afflicted (9:9) even as Israel was **afflicted** (10:2). As the Good Shepherd (John 10:1–21), He would bear His people's suffering and sacrifice Himself to save them and grant them eternal comfort.

The false shepherds were the complete opposite of the Good Shepherd, so the Lord expressed His displeasure towards them, saying, **"My anger burns against the shepherds."** With the statement **My anger burns**, God declared that His patience had run out; only a boiling zeal to punish wickedness remained. The God of Israel refused to tolerate the charlatans who had led His people astray. Thus, He declared, **"I will visit *punishment* upon the male goats."** The tense of the statement **I will visit *punishment*** indicates that the judgment described is future, and in this context, eschatological. While it is true that God punishes false shepherds in the present (cf. Zech 11:8), this text focuses on the end times. On that day, when the true Shepherd appears in judgment, He will not only conquer His enemies and deliver His people (cf. 9:14–17), but He will also personally **visit *punishment*** on His foes (cf. Exod 32:34; Lev 18:25; Isa 26:14; Zeph 1:8). Such punishment will not only be leveled against the shepherds (a reference to false religious leaders), but also against **the male goats** (a reference to every corrupt leader in Israel—cf. Ezek 34:17). Both in the present and the future, Yahweh's wrath is ever directed against false leaders.

The Lord will do this because of His great love for His people. While He will **visit *punishment*** on the wicked, He will visit the nation in a much different way: **"Yahweh of hosts has visited His flock, the house of Judah."** The Lord will appear to protect and support His people, since He is **Yahweh of hosts**, the One who commands myriads upon myriads of angels. Throughout Scripture, the title **"Yahweh of hosts"** is associated with God's sovereign control over the nations throughout history (cf. 1:7–17). Zechariah described Israel here as Yahweh's flock **(His** flock), emphasizing the reality that Yahweh will treat them as His own possession.

The Lord will also visit His people in triumph. The designation **the house of Judah** referred specifically to the royal tribe of Israel. Yahweh, the true King of Israel, **will make** the house of Judah **like His splendid horse in battle**. In ancient times, a horse functioned as a swift, strong, and strategic military weapon. The horse was so valuable in battle that Israel's kings were instructed not to multiply horses (Deut 17:16) lest they trust in their cavalry rather than the Lord (cf. Ps 20:7). The point here is that God will unleash the royal house of Judah like a choice weapon on the battlefield—His **splendid** horse. The term **splendid** described the dignity, resolve, and resilience of Judah, pictured as a valiant steed charging into battle (cf. Job 39:20). Though often characterized by weakness throughout their history, the Israelites will one day be transformed by the Lord into a mighty nation with strong, valiant leaders, in bold contrast to the false prophets and corrupt rulers whom the Lord condemned.

As Zechariah reminded the people, Yahweh alone was Israel's true leader. Only He could sustain and secure His people. To follow false shepherds was to take a destructive and futile path. But to follow the Lord was to take the path of blessing, both in the present and for the future. Ultimately, God will not tolerate the purveyors of spiritual deception. As the Lord Himself declared, He will remove all imposters and punish them for their wickedness.

THE TRUE SHEPHERD

"From them will come the cornerstone,
From them the tent peg,
From them the bow of battle,
From them every *good* taskmaster, *all of them* together.

And they will be as mighty men,
Treading down *the enemy* in the mire of the streets in battle;
And they will battle, for Yahweh *will be* with them;
And the riders on horses will be put to shame." (10:4–5)

Having declared His anger against the false shepherds (v. 3), the Lord turned to present Israel's true Shepherd, the Messiah (v. 4). Zechariah contains many portraits of Christ (cf. Zech 1:8, 20; 2:8; 3:2–3, 8; 4:7, 14; 6:11–12), with each having its own respective purpose. The portrait in this passage reveals the Messiah to be the perfect leader for His people.

The phrase **from them** is repeated four times in this verse, emphasizing that the Messiah will come **from** Judah. Yahweh visited the house of Judah to raise them up as Israel's leaders. But ultimately one leader would come from the house of leaders, one King from the house of kings, the Lord Jesus Christ. The repeated phrase **from them** highlights the Messiah's perfection, that He is the culmination of all rule and leadership. Each line depicts a distinct characteristic of Christ, demonstrating that He is Israel's ultimate leader.

First, the Messiah will uphold the nation, as He is called **the cornerstone** (*pinah*). This is not the first time He is called by this name. God foretold in Isaiah 28:16, "Behold, I am laying in Zion a stone, a tested stone, a costly cornerstone *for* the foundation, firmly placed. He who believes *in it* will not be disturbed." Likewise, Psalm 118 predicted that "the stone which the builders rejected Has become the chief corner *stone*" (Ps 118:22). Though initially rejected, the Messiah would be the most important part of the structure of Israel, providing the foundation stone that supports the nation. The New Testament writers further affirmed that Jesus is this stone. In Romans 9:32 and 1 Corinthians 1:23, Paul quoted from Isaiah 8, 28, and Psalm 118, and referred to Jesus as the stone. In Ephesians 2:20, Paul stated that the saints have been "built on the foundation of the apostles and prophets, Christ Jesus Himself being the corner *stone*." Like his predecessors, Paul articulated that Christ is the One who holds God's people together. He is the supporting stone on which His people are firmly established (cf. 1 Pet 2:4–10).

Second, the Lord revealed that the Messiah will be Israel's glory, as He is called the **tent peg**. There were two kinds of pegs in the Old Testament. One type was driven into the ground to secure a tent. This kind of tent peg is familiar to the modern-day reader. However, there was another kind of tent peg. It was driven into the central vertical pole of the tent and used to hang valuable ornaments. This latter peg was what the prophet had in view here, and Isaiah had spoken about this item earlier as well. In chapter 22, the prophet wrote that Eliakim would be a tent peg for the house of David. God said in verses 23–24, "I will drive *him* like a peg in a firm place, and he will become a throne of glory to his father's house. So they will hang on him all the glory of his father's house, offspring and issue, all the least of vessels, from bowls to all the jars." Eliakim was a tent peg for the royal household, on whom would hang all the weight of the royal house's majesty and nobility. In that way, he would for a time embody the grandeur and might of the royal line. But Eliakim's tenure was not to last. Isaiah concluded by saying that the peg would give way and the entire royal house would collapse (Isa 22:25). Although Eliakim would fail, Zechariah declared that the Messiah, the final **tent peg**, will never fall. All the government will rest on His shoulders (Isa 9:6). As Zechariah said earlier, "It is He who will build the temple of Yahweh, and He who will bear the splendor and sit and rule on His throne" (Zech 6:13). In describing Christ as the **tent peg**, Zechariah asserted that all the glory of Israel and its royal house will be displayed in Him.

Third, the Messiah will be Israel's warrior, as He is called the **bow of battle**. An identical Hebrew phrase was used earlier in Zechariah 9:10 (rendered as "bow of war"). In that context, the prophet stated that the bow of war would be cut off so that no one would have the power to engage in war again. By repeating that same language here, Zechariah indicated that in contrast to the bow in 9:10 that would be abolished, the Messiah, and no one else, will possess the power and prerogative for war and battle. No one will rival Him in any fashion, as He alone will reign over the earth. These truths are illustrated in Revelation 19 when Christ returns and destroys the armies of the world with a word. He will subsequently establish a time when swords are turned into plowshares (Isa 2:4). Because He will have all authority and power, He will be the perfect protector of Israel and enforcer of global peace.

Fourth, the Messiah will raise up true leaders from His people, as Zechariah expounded that **from them** will come **every *good* taskmaster, *all of them* together**. The term **taskmaster** was used earlier in Zechariah

9:8. The same word was employed in Exodus when Israel was in slavery and subjected to wicked taskmasters (cf. Exod 1:11; 3:7; 5:6, 10, 13, 14). In Zechariah 9:8, the prophet predicted a day when Israel will never again be subjugated to oppressive taskmasters. By contrast, the taskmasters in this passage (10:4) will not be like those in Israel's past. These will not be wicked, but righteous. While those in the past oppressed Israel, those in the future will use their positions of leadership to benefit the people and do them only good. That will be true of every single leader, for the text says, "*all of them* together."

In verse 5, Zechariah further described the nature of the future leaders whom the Messiah will raise up. They will not just care for their people but will also fight for them. The Lord revealed that **they will be as mighty men**. At times in Israel's history, the nation's leaders were weak-willed and vulnerable (cf. Isa 3:12). Corrupt and compromising leadership ushered the nation into moral decay and military defeat (Mic 2–3). However, during Messiah's kingdom, a new generation of leadership will arise, being characterized by truth, righteousness, and strength. These men will be **mighty**, a term used elsewhere to describe the fortitude of Israel's elite forces (cf. 2 Sam 23:8). The term **mighty** is also a key word in this chapter, appearing four times (cf. Zech 10:5, 6, 7, 12) and describing the powerful work that the Messiah will accomplish during His earthly reign.

Israel's future leaders will also prove to be relentless. Zechariah foretold that these leaders will be **treading down** *the enemy* **in the mire of the streets in battle**. To **tread down**, or stomp on repeatedly, represents unquestionable victory. It depicts complete domination, one so overwhelming that the foe is both defeated and disgraced (cf. Isa 14:19, 25; 63:6, 18; Ps 44:5). In this case, the enemy will be conquered **in the mire of the streets**. Other texts described Israel's enemies being trampled down like the mire of the streets (2 Sam 22:43; Mic 7:10). Zechariah, however, stated that Israel's foes will fall in defeat and lie *in* the mud of the road. The implication is that the slain enemy will not be given a proper burial, signifying their dishonor and the divine curse upon them (cf. Deut 21:22–23; 1 Kgs 13:29–30; 2 Kgs 9:10, 36–37). While the enemies fall **in battle**, the Lord declared that Israel's new leaders will prevail in

battle. The repetition of the word **battle**, once for Israel's foes and again for Israel's leaders, contrasts the defeat of the enemy with the dominance of the nation's leadership. In the same battle, one group will be disgraced in defeat and the other distinguished in victory.

Israel's leaders will enjoy total triumph because **Yahweh** *will be* **with them.** The people will not claim credit for their success in the battle. The victory of the Messiah will be solely the result of the power of Yahweh who will endow Israel with His strength and even fight alongside them (cf. 2 Thess 1:6–10; Rev 19). This future reality will reinforce the supremacy of the Messiah. He will raise up these leaders (cf. Zech 10:4), and under His leadership, they will triumph.

Overwhelmed by Yahweh and His armies, the opposing forces including **the riders on horses will be put to shame.** Horses represented a powerful weapon in battle (see discussion above). At the Battle of Armageddon, the horses and riders of the enemy will be **put to shame.** The strength of the foe will be countered and crushed. This decisive outcome, apparently unexpected by Israel's enemies, will send the riders fleeing in panic. Their dismay reflects the strength of Israel's future leaders and, more specifically, the power of Yahweh who appointed them and the Messiah who led them. He will prove to be the leader of all leaders, providing His people with eternal stability, splendor, and strength.

At a time when false shepherds deceived and seduced Israel to look to other gods for help, Zechariah reminded them of Yahweh's present provision (v. 1) and His future protection (vv. 4–5). He alone could sustain them, and He alone will ultimately save them. For Israel to turn to idols or any other supposed power would be to succumb to impotent imposters and sinister substitutes (vv. 3–4). Instead of wandering like confused sheep, the Lord called them to look to Him, resting in the promise of the coming Messiah who would shepherd His people with grace and truth and who would lead them to triumph.

The Messiah:
Mighty to Save

27

Zechariah 10:6–12

"I will make the house of Judah mighty,
And I will save the house of Joseph,
And I will cause them to return,
Because I have had compassion on them;
And they will be as though I had not rejected them,
For I am Yahweh their God, and I will answer them.

And Ephraim will be like a mighty man,
And their heart will be glad as if *from* wine;
Indeed, their children will see *it* and be glad;
Their heart will rejoice in Yahweh.

I will whistle for them to gather them together,
For I have redeemed them;
And they will be as numerous as they were before.

And I will sow them among the peoples,
And they will remember Me in far countries,
And they with their children will live and turn back.

Then I will cause them to return from the land of Egypt
And gather them from Assyria;
And I will bring them into the land of Gilead and Lebanon
Until no room can be found for them.

And they will pass through the sea of distress,
And He will strike the waves in the sea,
So that all the depths of the Nile will dry up;
And the pride of Assyria will be brought down,
And the scepter of Egypt will depart.

And I will make them mighty in Yahweh,
And in His name they will walk," declares Yahweh.

Having called Israel to turn to Yahweh (Zech 10:1, 4–5) and to reject all false substitutes (10:2–3), the Lord continued in the second half of chapter 10 to feature the Messiah's future work. The Messiah's power to save His people, as highlighted in this section, stands in stark contrast to the spiritual bankruptcy of all forms of counterfeit religion. A single word punctuates the truth that Christ is all that Israel needs. The adjective "mighty," repeated four times in this passage (cf. 10:5, 6, 7, 12), describes divine effectiveness and power. Its repetition in this context emphasizes that the Messiah alone possesses the strength His people need.

This passage (10:6–12) underscores that truth by considering three aspects of the Messiah's future work on behalf of Israel. First, Christ will rescue His people physically by gathering them from the nations (10:6–7). Second, He will save them spiritually by bringing them to repentance and faith (10:8–9). Third, He will deliver Israel definitively by establishing them permanently in the Promised Land (10:10–12). In accomplishing such glorious things for His people, Christ will demonstrate that divine strength and eternal salvation are found exclusively in Him.

MIGHTY TO SAVE PHYSICALLY

"I will make the house of Judah mighty,
And I will save the house of Joseph,
And I will cause them to return,
Because I have had compassion on them;
And they will be as though I had not rejected them,
For I am Yahweh their God, and I will answer them.

And Ephraim will be like a mighty man,
And their heart will be glad as if *from* wine;
Indeed, their children will see *it* and be glad;
Their heart will rejoice in Yahweh." (10:6–7)

The Lord employed the words **I will make** frequently throughout this passage to describe His messianic activity. The statement repeatedly and emphatically declared that the Messiah will personally accomplish a variety of tasks. He will strengthen (Zech 10:6, 12), regather (10:8), sow (10:9), and deliver His people (10:10). These divine declarations, issued in the first person, reminded God's people that the Messiah was taking full responsibility for Israel's triumph. Therefore, Israel needed to trust Him alone (cf. 10:1).

The text (vv. 6–7) delineates five major features of Israel's future deliverance from her enemies. First, it will be comprehensive. The Lord declared, "**I will make the house of Judah mighty and I will save the house of Joseph.**" Here, the Lord promised to strengthen the **house of Judah**, the royal dynasty and leadership of the southern kingdom. The Messiah will raise up true leadership within the tribe of Judah to usher in victory for the nation (cf. 10:3–4). In addition to Judah, He will also **save the house of Joseph**, a reference to the northern kingdom. The Messiah will secure both the southern and northern portions of Israel. Throughout Israel's history, its leadership struggled to defend the entirety of the nation. The judges of Israel could only deliver select tribes at certain times (cf. Judg 3:15–31; 7:19–8:21; 10:1–5). Only Saul, David, and Solomon were able to unite the entire kingdom, and even then, that unity was often tenuous (cf. 2 Sam 16:1–23; 19:8–43; 20:1–12; 1 Kgs 12:1–15). In contrast, the Messiah will strengthen and safeguard the entirety of Israel.

Second, His deliverance will not only be comprehensive but also complete. The Lord continued to say, **"And I will cause them to return."** The language of **return** throughout Zechariah and the prophets denoted the total restoration of Israel. It included the people's return from foreign nations (Zech 9:12), their return to the Promised Land (1:6), their turning back to God in repentance (1:3), and the return of all of God's promises upon them (1:3, 16). This verse emphasized the point that the Messiah **will cause** Israel to experience such a return. He will sovereignly orchestrate all these aspects of deliverance. Only in Christ will all blessings and promises be fulfilled (cf. 2 Cor 1:19–20).

Third, the Messiah's deliverance will be compassionate. The Lord declared that He will do all this **"because I [the Lord] have had compassion on them."** To be sure, since God cannot change, His promises are inviolable (cf. Rom 11:28–29). He must fulfill whatever He says He will do. Yet, the Lord is not complacent in keeping His promises. As He declared here, His commitment to restore His people flows out of His love and sympathy for them. The notion of **compassion** is linked with the mother's womb (cf. Zech 1:12, 16; 7:9), and describes the nurturing mercy and instinctive protection a mother provides for her child. The corrupt leaders of Israel lacked genuine affection for the nation. They sought to consume the people for their own benefit (cf. Ezek 34:3). By contrast, the Messiah will cherish His people. He will not spurn them in their distress but will care for them out of His faithful love.

Fourth, Christ's deliverance will be climactic. When He restores His people, **"they will be as though I had not rejected them."** This is a stunning statement of reversal. In the end, the transformation of Israel will be so great that the damage, distress, and dishonor of Israel's past failings will in essence be forgotten. The people's prosperity will be so abundant that no one would ever think they had endured God's judgment. The incredible goodness of God's future blessing on Israel will cause past difficulties to fade away. The glory of the future will eclipse the agony of the past.

Fifth, the Messiah's future deliverance will be divine. The Lord

declared, "For I am Yahweh their God, and I will answer them."
Fundamentally, this declaration makes clear that the Messiah is in fact
Yahweh, the one true God. He is not merely able to deliver His people,
but He also desires to do so because He is **their God** who loves them
and is faithful to them. Thus He declared, "**I will answer them.**" Because
of loyalty to His people, He did not cut off His relationship from them
nor will He ignore them when they call on Him in repentance (cf. Deut
4:29–31). Instead, He will respond to them as He had promised, and He
will do for them far more than they could ask or think in fulfilling all
His promises.

The Messiah will save not only Judah but also, as stated above,
the northern kingdom (Zech 10:6). Consequently, **Ephraim** (a reference
to the northern kingdom) **will be like a mighty man**. The tribes of the
northern kingdom were the first to be taken into exile (cf. 2 Kgs 17:1–23).
In the future, however, they will cease to be characterized by weakness
and defeat, but they will be **like a mighty man**. The phrase **mighty man**
refers to Israel's elite forces (cf. 2 Sam 23:8–17). Everyone in Ephraim and
the northern kingdom will have the skill and strength of the toughest
soldier. They will be able to defend their land in a way they never could
before; and they will do this through the power and strength given them
by the Messiah.

With such triumph, **their heart will be glad as if from wine**,
signifying that the subsequent joy of the northern kingdom will not be
superficial, but will rise from **their heart**. Moreover, the expression of
this gladness will be effusive, **as if from wine**, a reference to the nature
of their jubilation and celebration (cf. 2 Sam 13:28; Esth 1:10). Zechariah
specified that this joy will be only **as if** from wine. The inhabitants of
the northern kingdom will not need any stimulant to experience such
gladness. Their elation will flow from the victory they achieve through
Messiah's might and power.

The most telling result of Christ's mighty deliverance will be
that **indeed, their children will see it and be glad**. In the past, the
consequences of God's curse against Israel extended to their children (cf.
Deut 28:41, 53–57). Children often receive the worst of the horrors of war
and exile, and their suffering attests to the tragedy caused by military

conflict (cf. Lam 2:11). But Christ will turn the grief of Israel's children into joy. They will **see** what the Messiah accomplishes, and they will **be glad**. Their reaction will be instinctive, and it will demonstrate how magnificent His victory will be.

The repetition of the word **glad** indicates that every child will join with his parents in rejoicing on account of the Messiah's work. The entire nation, from the oldest warrior to the youngest child, will be filled with triumphant exuberance. Zechariah recounted that **their heart will rejoice in Yahweh**, not in superficial things or passing pleasures. In Messiah's kingdom, Israel's young ones will **rejoice**, or audibly express their excitement, **in Yahweh**. Their joy will be not in the gifts but in the Giver. Israel's children will turn to know and delight in the One who delivered them.

MIGHTY TO SAVE SPIRITUALLY

"I will whistle for them to gather them together,
For I have redeemed them;
And they will be as numerous as they were before.

And I will sow them among the peoples,
And they will remember Me in far countries,
And they with their children will live and turn back." (10:8–9)

Having discussed the physical deliverance of His people, the Lord then described how He will deliver them spiritually, saying, "**I will whistle for them to gather them together**." Previously, God **whistled** to gather nations to judge and exile His people (cf. Isa 5:26; 7:18). In the future, the Messiah **will whistle** to His people **to gather them together** like a shepherd gathering sheep (cf. Judg 5:16), a farmer gathering crops (cf. Gen 41:35), or a victorious king gathering the spoils of war (cf. Deut 13:17). This is precisely how God promised He would restore Israel. In Deuteronomy 30, Moses said that even though God would banish the nation far and wide, He "will gather you again from all the peoples where Yahweh your God has scattered you" (30:3). Christ will bring His people home and reverse the judgment of exile.

The Lord explained the reason behind this restoration with a direct statement: **"For I have redeemed them."** Fundamentally, redemption means to pay a price to purchase something or buy it back (cf. Exod 13:13; Lev 27:27). It can refer to God's physical rescue of Israel from Egypt (cf. Deut 7:8). However, it often carries a spiritual connotation, that God pays the price to save His people from their sins (cf. Pss 25:22; 26:11; 31:5; 34:23; 49:8; 130:8). In this passage, the reason the Lord will regather Israel is because He has redeemed them from bondage to sin and the penalty of His wrath.

As a result, **they will be as numerous as they were before.** The people will multiply, reversing any population loss resulting from war and exile (cf. Deut 28:62). Israel will be **as they were before**, as if the nation had never been depleted. The physical restoration of the nation is possible only because Christ secured spiritual redemption for His people. His redeeming work is the key to Israel's national recovery. In fact, the poetic structure of this verse testifies to that truth. The first line of the verse expresses God's reversal of judgment (Zech 10:8a) and the last line describes Israel's full restoration (10:8c). The middle of the verse highlights the central truth of redemption accomplished by the Messiah (10:8b).

Verse 9 recounts how God will carry out His plan of salvation for Israel. The Lord declared, **"And I will sow them among the peoples."** These words anticipated the dispersion of the Jewish people following the destruction of Jerusalem in AD 70. The Israelites would be scattered all over the world. However, this text does not say that God will scatter, but rather that He **will sow**. The emphasis is not on God's judgment in dispersing the people, but on His act of sowing Israel like one sows seed. The Jewish people, after being driven out of the land, would not die or become extinct. Instead, they would be purposefully planted like seed in a field. In effect, a day is coming when they will burst forth in life by turning to the Lord and being saved (Rom 11:15, 26). The Jewish people will embrace the Messiah in saving faith because the gospel will give them life (Ezek 37:14; Zech 12:10; Matt 23:39). In His perfect plan, God did not merely disperse His people from their land in judgment (cf. Deut 28:49–68; Isa 5:26–30). He scattered them with a redemptive purpose in mind. Like a seed planted in the ground, they will one day be transformed when they embrace Christ in saving faith as Messiah and Lord.

Because of this, Yahweh declared, **"they will remember Me in far countries."** To **remember** conveys not merely to recollect a fact, but to have deep and compelling focus upon that which is recalled. Deuteronomy taught that those who remember the Lord (cf. Deut 8:18) have a right relationship with and live for Him. Remembering is powerful in the life of God's people. Conversely, forgetting is dangerous and can lead to profound sin (cf. 6:12–13; 8:11–13). For Israel to remember the Lord means that they will be in a saving relationship with Him. They will be fixed upon Him in **far countries**, revealing that though Israel might be far from the Promised Land and from any remembrance of Jerusalem, they will never be too far away from God's grace. The Lord sowed them in these remote places knowing that He would gather them like a harvest to Himself. Zechariah's name means "Yahweh remembers." As this book reiterates, the Lord remembers His people and His promises so that His people will remember and return to Him.

The Lord continued by identifying three significant ramifications of this future salvation for Israel. First, it will affect the totality of the nation. Not only will the older generations experience salvation, but **they** will experience it along **with their children**. Both parents and **their children** will embrace Christ in saving faith. The entire nation will be transformed, as depicted in Deuteronomy 30:6, "Moreover Yahweh your God will circumcise your heart and the heart of your seed, to love Yahweh your God with all your heart and with all your soul, so that you may live." Moses also revealed that God will not only transform the hearts of the parents, but also "of your seed," that is their offspring. All the people will be redeemed, from parent to child, "and so all Israel will be saved" (Rom 11:26).

Second, as a result of this, the people will know the fullness of spiritual life, so that they **will** truly **live**. As evidenced by the context, the idea of "living" here refers to more than just physical life. It corresponds to the truth of Habakkuk 2:4, where Habakkuk stated that the righteous will live by faith. There, the word "live" encompassed the fullness of spiritual life—including justification, sanctification, and every blessing that comes from being in a saving relationship with God. The New Testament referred to Habakkuk 2:4 when speaking of life in this same way (Rom 1:17; Gal 3:11; Heb 10:38). One day, Israel will experience, to use the words of Paul, "that which is life indeed" (1 Tim 6:19). The people will enjoy a true knowledge of God the Father and His Son, the Messiah (John 17:3). Their lives will be long (cf. Zech 8:4), full (cf. 8:8), and in fellowship with the Lord (cf. 8:8).

Third, future Israelites will live because they will **turn back.** Turning is a significant term in the book of Zechariah and throughout the prophets (cf. Isa 55:7; Jer 15:19; 27:16; Hos 6:1). It denoted Israel's repentance (Zech 1:3), their return to the Promised Land (1:6), and the reversal of their situation (1:16). In the past, Israel refused to turn to God and even refused to return to the Promised Land (cf. Ezra 2:64; Jer 8:5; Hos 11:5). But in the future, the disposition of the people will change entirely. Scripture continually attests that while works do not save, true faith is always accompanied by life-changing works (Rom 6–8; Gal 3:1–5; Eph 2:8–10; Jas 2:14–26). The Messiah's work of salvation is not superficial; it will give to Israel repentance and a new life which causes the people to return, showing that their hearts have been regenerated and their lives transformed. Truly, there is no salvation in any other name than the name of Christ (Acts 4:12). He alone provides the full restoration His people need.

MIGHTY TO SAVE DEFINITIVELY

"Then I will cause them to return from the land of Egypt
And gather them from Assyria;
And I will bring them into the land of Gilead and Lebanon
Until no room can be found for them.

And they will pass through the sea of distress,
And He will strike the waves in the sea,
So that all the depths of the Nile will dry up;

And the pride of Assyria will be brought down,
And the scepter of Egypt will depart.

And I will make them mighty in Yahweh,
And in His name they will walk," declares Yahweh. (10:10–12)

To demonstrate Christ's sufficiency, Zechariah repeated that the Messiah will be the One who accomplishes Israel's final deliverance. The Lord announced, **"Then I will cause them to return from the land of Egypt."** By repeating the phrase **"I will cause"** (from v. 5), the Lord reiterated that He is the sole source of Israel's deliverance. At the end of the age, the Messiah will personally and exclusively lead His people **to return from the land of Egypt**, which recalls the events of Israel's original Exodus from Egypt. The Exodus was a seminal moment in the nation's history, dramatically demonstrating God's dedication and love for His people (cf. Hos 11:1). It sparked the Israelites' journey to the Promised Land and marked the beginning of the nation. With the language of a future return from Egypt (v. 10), the Lord revealed that what happened at the beginning will happen in the end. Just as the first Exodus inaugurated the nation, this second Exodus will establish the nation anew. But this will not merely be a second Exodus, but the final Exodus, ending all need for deliverance, and securing the nation permanently.

The rest of the passage provides three reasons why this will be the final Exodus. First, as the rest of verse 10 explains, this Exodus will mark the final homecoming of Israel. The Lord declared that He will **gather them from Assyria**. More than two centuries earlier, the prophet Hosea predicted that Israel would be sent into exile in both Assyria and Egypt (cf. Hos 8:9, 13), and that God will return them in the final Exodus (cf. Hos 11:11). That is precisely what Zechariah described here. The Israelites will not only return from their exile in the nations, but they will also be restored to their land in the fullest way. The Lord promised, **"I will bring them into the land of Gilead and Lebanon."** Gilead is a region northeast of Israel, and Lebanon is a country northwest of Israel. Technically, both of these areas are outside of the land of Israel proper. However, they are adjacent to the Promised Land and within the territory Israel was originally promised to have dominion over (cf. Gen 15:17–21). By mentioning these areas, the Lord showed that one day the land of Israel itself will be so full that the people will spill over into the neighboring regions. With no space left in the Promised Land itself, those returning will flood into these nearby areas. As Isaiah prophesied:

> The children of whom you were bereaved will yet say in your ears, "The place is too cramped for me; make room for me that I may live *here*." Then you will say in your heart, "Who has borne these for me? Indeed, I have been bereaved of my children, and am barren, an exile and a wanderer. And who has reared these? Behold, I remained alone; from where did these come?" (Isa 49:20–21)

Even with adjacent countries and regions used for overflow, still **no room can be found for them**. Israel will pack tightly into places like Gilead and Lebanon because the people will want to be as close to the Promised Land as possible. Yet even these nearby regions will ultimately become so full that there will be no space for others to settle there, necessitating that they move farther away. The abundance of Israel's future homecoming will truly be overwhelming.

Second, this final Exodus will manifest the ultimate triumph over all enemies and obstacles. The Lord announced, **"And they will pass through the sea *of* distress."** Some translations interpret the Hebrew to be referring not to Israel ("they") but to God Himself ("He"). That is likely the case here. The idea is that "He," that is the Lord, will pass through the sea as He leads His people to safety. The allusion is to the miraculous manner by which Israel crossed the Red Sea during the Exodus. Nothing will impede Israel's journey home, not even the sea of **distress**. The term **distress** describes a situation that confines and entraps someone, like the surrounding waters of the sea. More broadly, the word refers to the difficulties and pressures that tighten around God's people. Just as the Lord led His people through the Red Sea the first time, so will He cut through all barriers and dangers for Israel. Indeed, **He will strike the waves in the sea**. In Scripture, waves represent devastating forces that beat down believers (Ps 42:7) and even crush nations (Jer 51:42; Ezek

26:3). Though these waves are powerful and formidable, God Himself will strike them down so they are tamed and do no harm to His own (cf. Mark 4:39–41).

God will neutralize every threat and strike down all that impedes His people, to the point that **all the depths of the Nile will dry up**. The term **depths** refers to the lowest recesses of a body of water—locations where people drown. The term is reminiscent of Jonah (cf. Jonah 2:3) and the Egyptians who pursued Israel across the Red Sea (Exod 15:5). In the future Exodus, the darkest depths **will dry up** and pose no danger to Israel. In drying up the Nile, God will provide a straight road for Israel from Egypt back to the Promised Land. This reference illustrates the reality that God's people will go unimpeded all the way home. Through the prophet Isaiah, the Lord promised, "When you pass through the waters, I will be with you; and through the rivers, they will not overflow you. When you walk through the fire, you will not be scorched, nor will the flame burn you" (Isa 43:2; cf. Hab 3:8). God will eradicate anything that hinders His people from returning to their homeland.

Zechariah further stated that the Messiah will vanquish any nation that opposes Israel. The Lord declared, **"The pride of Assyria will be brought down."** Pride is that which is lofty or puffed up. As this verse indicates, the haughtiness of Israel's oppressors, specifically Assyria, **will be brought down** by the Messiah. Egypt will suffer the same consequence, as **the scepter of Egypt will depart**. The scepter represents political power and is often associated with royalty. In the first Exodus, Pharaoh oppressed Israel and resisted Yahweh. In the final Exodus, Egypt will have no Pharaoh because the **scepter** will depart. All of Israel's oppressors, represented from the north (Assyria) to the south (Egypt), will be utterly vanquished. Their decisive defeat demonstrates that no earthly power will be able to prevent Israel from fulfilling God's purposes for His chosen nation.

The language that the **scepter will depart** from Egypt both shows God's victory over Egypt and points to the Messiah's royal authority. Jacob prophesied in Genesis 49:10, "The scepter shall not depart from Judah." While the royal scepter will depart from Egypt, it will never depart from Judah. Rather, as the rest of Genesis 49:10 explains, Judah's royal line will instead culminate with the coming of Shiloh, the Messiah, who will reign forever and command all the peoples. The Messiah will humble Assyria and Egypt and all the nations not only to pave the way for His people, but also to consolidate all power and authority in Himself.

In the final verse of this passage, Zechariah provided a third reason why the Exodus described in this passage will be the final one. Having brought His people back from exile, the Messiah will make Israel all that God intended them to be. The prophet recorded Yahweh's words, **"And I will make them mighty in Yahweh and in His name they will walk,"** declares Yahweh. As noted, the word **mighty** was used previously in this passage, depicting the valiant strength of Israel's leaders (Zech 10:5) and the renewed military prowess of Judah (v. 6) and Ephraim (v. 7). But the might described in this verse is different because it refers specifically to being **mighty in Yahweh**. Beyond mere physical strength or military force, this depicted Israel's unshakable confidence in the Lord. Despite times of feeble faith throughout their history, in the end, Israel will be characterized by strength, not weakness. The people will be instilled with courage that flows from their fellowship with the Lord. As a result, **in His name they will walk**. The specific verb form of the word **walk** denotes a consistent pattern of life and communion with the Lord. It described how God walked with Adam in the Garden (Gen 3:8), how Enoch walked with the Lord (Gen 5:24), and how God promised to walk among His people if they were holy (Lev 26:12). To have such a walk **in His name** portrays an enduring lifestyle that conforms to God's very character (Col 3:17) and reflects His righteousness before the world (cf. Acts 9:15; 2 Thess 1:12).

At that future time, the people of Israel will have the relationship with God they should have always had. They will be used by Him to do what they should have always done (cf. Exod 19:5–6; 20:7). Of the kinds of **might** described in this chapter (vv. 5, 6, 7), being **mighty in Yahweh** is by far the most wonderful. This triumph is exclusively found in the Messiah. As the Lord declared, **"And I will make."** These words constitute a direct claim from the preincarnate Christ that strength in God, along with so many other divine promises (cf. Zech 10:6, 7, 8, 9, 10), will be realized only through Him. The final words of this chapter accentuate that point—

declares Yahweh. The marvelous truth revealed in this passage is divinely decreed and certified, and specifically articulated by the second Person of the Trinity. God the Son, the divine Messiah, will point His people to the Father, making them mighty in Him (cf. John 17:6–21).

Though the Israelites were tempted by idols, divination, and counterfeit religion (Zech 10:2–3), they needed to remember that only Yahweh could bring them true power and salvation. As Zechariah revealed in this passage, the Messiah alone has the might to save His people physically, spiritually, and definitively in a final Exodus. Though He will ride into Jerusalem on a donkey (cf. 9:9), He is the supreme Sovereign and only Savior. There is no salvation outside of Him (Acts 4:12). Therefore, if they desire lasting deliverance, the people of Israel must look to Christ (cf. Zech 12:10). He is the only hope, both for them and for the whole world (1 John 2:2).

The Rejected Shepherd

28

Zechariah 11:1–14

Open your doors, O Lebanon,
That a fire may consume your cedars.

Wail, O cypress, for the cedar has fallen,
Because the mighty *trees* have been destroyed;
Wail, O oaks of Bashan,
For the impenetrable forest has come down.

There is a sound of the shepherds' wail,
For their might is destroyed;
There is a sound of the young lions' roar,
For the pride of the Jordan is destroyed.

Thus says Yahweh my God, "Shepherd the flock *doomed* to slaughter. Those who buy them slaughter them and are not held guilty, and *each of* those who sell them says, 'Blessed be Yahweh. Indeed, I have become rich!' And their own shepherds do not spare them. For I will no longer spare the inhabitants of the land," declares Yahweh; "but behold, I will cause the men to fall, each into another's hand and into the hand of his king; and they will crush the land, and I will not deliver *them* from their hand." So I shepherded the flock *doomed* to slaughter—hence the afflicted of the flock. And I took for myself two staffs: the one I called Favor, and the other I called Union; so I shepherded the flock. Then I annihilated the three shepherds in one month, for my soul was impatient with them, and their soul also was weary of me. Then I said, "I will not shepherd you. What is to die, let it die, and what is to be annihilated, let it be annihilated; and let those who remain consume one another's flesh." And I took my staff Favor and cut it in pieces, to break my covenant which I had cut with all the peoples. So it was broken on that day, and thus the afflicted of the flock who were watching me knew that it was the word of Yahweh. And I said to them, "If it is good in your sight, give *me* my wages; but if not, never mind!" So they weighed out thirty *shekels* of silver as my wages. Then Yahweh said to me, "Throw it to the potter, *that* valuable price at which I was valued by them." So I took the thirty *shekels* of silver and threw them to the potter in the house of Yahweh. Then I cut in pieces my second staff Union, to break the brotherhood between Judah and Israel.

No event in human history is more important than the Cross, where the Lord Jesus Christ died as the final sacrifice for sin before rising in victory on the third day. As Paul explained in Romans, all were under God's wrath (Rom 1:18) until His righteousness was revealed in the propitiation of His Son (3:21). Christ's death and resurrection provide the basis by which God justifies sinners (Rom 4:25; 2 Cor 5:21) and offers them eternal life (cf. Rom 8:17, 30). If Jesus had not died to pay sin's penalty, sinners would have no hope of forgiveness. And if He had not risen from the dead, believers would have no hope of future glory (cf. 1 Cor 15).

The Old Testament anticipates the suffering and death of the Messiah. From the first book of Moses (cf. Gen 3:15; 22:1–14), to the Psalms of David (cf. Pss 16:10; 22:1–31), to the prophecies of Daniel (cf. Dan 9:26), God not only promised that the Savior would come, but that He would suffer and die. The most extensive prophecy regarding the Messiah's suffering is found in Isaiah 53. There, the prophet predicted that Christ would be "smitten of God, and afflicted" (v. 4), "pierced through for our transgressions" (v. 5), made to bear His people's iniquity (v. 6), "cut off from the land of the living" (v. 8), crushed and put to grief "as a guilt offering" (v. 10), and poured out to the point of death, being "numbered with the transgressors" (v. 12). The Servant of Yahweh was rejected, ridiculed, and killed. Yet this was necessary to bring salvation. God declared regarding His Son:

> As a result of the anguish of His soul,
> He will see *it and* be satisfied;
> By His knowledge the Righteous One,
> My Servant, will justify the many,
> As He will bear their iniquities. (Isa 53:11)

Two centuries after Isaiah, these familiar themes were echoed by the prophet Zechariah. Like his predecessor, he anticipated the suffering and humiliation that the Messiah would endure. Zechariah 9:9 predicted Christ's humble entry into Jerusalem: "Behold, your king is coming to you; He is righteous and endowed with salvation, lowly and mounted on a donkey, even on a colt, the foal of a pack animal." In Zechariah 12:10, the Lord reiterated how the people at the time of their salvation will recognize that they had mistreated their Messiah and they will repent: "They will look on Me whom they have pierced; and they will mourn for Him [the Messiah], as one mourns for an only son, and they will weep bitterly over Him like the bitter weeping over a firstborn."

In Zechariah 11:1–14, the prophet similarly addressed the rejection of the Messiah by His nation. Having drawn a contrast between Israel's false shepherds (10:2–3) and the Good Shepherd (10:4–12), the prophet continued in chapter 11 by providing a vivid illustration of Israel as a flock. In so doing, he predicted the consequences that would fall on Israel for rejecting their Messiah. Zechariah began in this passage by depicting the treacherous shepherds who were destined for destruction (11:1–3). Next, he portrayed the troubled flock of Israel which was doomed to die (11:4–6). Third, he described the career of Israel's true Shepherd, the Messiah, explaining that He would be detested and despised by His own (11:7–12). Finally, Zechariah noted the terrible consequences Israel would face for rejecting the Messiah; the nation would be severely disciplined by God for its deliberate disobedience (11:13–14).

The details of this passage (from a prophecy delivered in the 6th century BC) align perfectly with the life and ministry of the Lord Jesus. Jesus came and ministered to the nation of Israel, but was rejected by His people, betrayed for thirty pieces of silver, and crucified on the cross. As a result, God gave Israel over to destruction into the hands of the Romans in AD 70 and then in AD 135. Jerusalem and the temple were destroyed, and the Jewish people were slaughtered, sold into slavery, and scattered throughout the world for nearly two thousand years, until the reestablishment of Israel in 1948. The consequence of rejecting the Messiah was the outpouring of the wrath of God on the nation. The prophetic precision of this passage not only evidences its divine origin, but also puts the spotlight on the most pivotal event of human history: the tragedy of the Messiah's rejection.

THE TREACHEROUS SHEPHERDS:
DESTINED FOR DESTRUCTION

Open your doors, O Lebanon,
That a fire may consume your cedars.

Wail, O cypress, for the cedar has fallen,
Because the mighty *trees* have been destroyed;
Wail, O oaks of Bashan,
For the impenetrable forest has come down.

There is a sound of the shepherds' wail,
For their might is destroyed;
There is a sound of the young lions' roar,
For the pride of the Jordan is destroyed. (11:1–3)

The prophet's opening words mark a dramatic shift from the eschatological triumph of the Messiah portrayed in the previous chapter. Zechariah 11 begins with an open call for foreign invasion: "**Open your doors, O Lebanon.**" The term **door** in this context refers to the entrance to the nation and the gates of its cities. While a door is often shut to prevent intruders, Zechariah declared that Lebanon's **doors** would be **open** wide, signifying that this country would lose its protection, becoming vulnerable to foreign assault. An enemy from beyond Lebanon would effortlessly sweep through a massive swath of land, starting with Lebanon and extending southward. The picture painted in this verse stands in direct contrast to the security, stability, and victory described in the previous chapter, leaving the reader to wonder how this could happen.

Zechariah prophesied that this invasion would visibly devastate Lebanon as **a fire may consume your cedars.** Lebanon was known for its massive and beautiful cedar trees, which were a major contributor to its economy (cf. 1 Kgs 5:6–10). For Lebanon's cedars to be consumed by fire would be to destroy both its ecology and economy. However, the prophet also spoke of **cedar** trees because of their relation to Israel's temple. The most prevalent use of the term **cedar** in Scripture was in conjunction with the construction of Solomon's temple (cf. 2 Sam 7:2; 1 Kgs 5:6). Cedar was used to make the temple's planks (1 Kgs 6:9), framework (6:10, 36), and paneling (6:15–16), as well as the overlay of the altar (6:20). This attack on the cedars of Lebanon anticipated the enemy's attack on Jerusalem to the south of Lebanon. As the cedars of Lebanon would be destroyed, so the "house of cedar" (cf. 2 Sam 7:7)—the temple—would be destroyed.

The prophet focused not only on cedars, but also on Lebanon's cypress trees, as he cried out, **"Wail, O cypress."** Like the cedar, the cypress (a fir tree) was construction material for the temple, being used for the floorboards (1 Kgs 6:15) and doors (6:34). In Solomon's day, the two major materials Lebanon donated to Israel to construct the temple were cedar and cypress (5:10). By prophesying about the ruin of cedars and cypresses in this passage, Zechariah intensified the anticipation that Israel's temple would again be destroyed, just as Solomon's temple had been burned to the ground.

The cypress trees were summoned to wail because **the cedar has fallen.** If the most majestic tree in the forest—the cedar—was overcome by the enemy, none of the others would be able to withstand the assault. Two hundred years before Zechariah's prophecy, such destruction took place historically when Assyria invaded Israel and Judah around the

time of Hezekiah (2 Kgs 19:23). At that time, Israel could see the felling of
the forests, which demonstrated that region after region had collapsed
under the onslaught of the foreign foe. Recalling that historic image,
Zechariah prophesied that this would happen again. The enemy would
decimate the forests not just around Lebanon, but beyond, for Zechariah
foresaw that all **the mighty trees have been destroyed**. Once more,
forest after forest would be devastated, reflecting how a foreign invader
would systematically defeat city after city and nation after nation. The
word **destroyed**, which describes how an object is broken to pieces,
conveys the intense aggression of this attack. The enemy will not only
cut trees down, but violently shred them to pieces.

This military campaign would move from north to south, into
the territory of Israel. Zechariah declared, **"Wail, O oaks of Bashan."**
The word **wail** was already used earlier in reference to the cypress
trees. The repetition implies that the wailing would multiply as the
destruction increased. The **oaks of Bashan** were considered among
the most beautiful trees in biblical times (cf. Hos 4:13). They were also
used for construction to make items such as oars for ships (Ezek 27:6)
and idols for pagan worship (Isa 44:14). Since these trees were found in
northeastern Israel, the implication of the text is that the invasion would
reach Israel, destroying its beauty and defenses. As Zechariah explained,
"For the impenetrable forest has come down." The dense forest acted
as a fortification for the nation's northeastern border. At times, the forest
itself consumed the foe. As 2 Samuel 18:8 describes, "The battle there
was scattered over the whole countryside, and the forest devoured more
people that day than the sword devoured." The forest acted as a buffer
against Israel's enemies. But Zechariah indicated that such protection
would fail. In effect, the oaks of Bashan were called to **wail** not only
for their own demise, but also because the nation of Israel would be
overtaken by the enemy.

The invasion would spread from the oaks of Bashan to the rulers
of Israel. Zechariah prophesied, **"There is a sound of the shepherds'
wail, for their might is destroyed."** The word **wail** is the same word
used earlier to describe the wailing of the cypress and oak trees. All the
wailing in this passage crescendos with the **sound of the shepherds'**

wail. Might describes the "mighty trees" in the previous verse. The enemy would destroy the mighty trees of the nations just as it would crush the **might** of these false shepherds—namely, the corrupt leaders of Israel. The word **destroyed** here is also repeated from the previous verse. Zechariah declared that these shepherds would wail over their own destruction. They are the ultimate target of all the destruction God will bring through the enemy.

The prophet further described God's wrath against Israel's corrupt rulers by saying, **"There is a sound of the young lions' roar, for the pride of the Jordan is destroyed."** Israel's **young lions** were an image of royalty (cf. Ezek 19:1–9), and the **sound** of young lions **roaring** can either describe aggression (Isa 5:29; Ezek 19:7) or the desperation of a hungry predator (Job 4:10). These options are not mutually exclusive since a starving lion, desperate for food, might be the most aggressive. As Zechariah explained, the frustration and panic of the royal house would come in response to their realization that **the pride of the Jordan** had been **destroyed.** The **pride of the Jordan** referred to the natural defenses along the Jordan river, including dense thickets and wild animals. After the captivity of the northern kingdom, lions and other wild beasts multiplied in this area (cf. 2 Kgs 17:25, Jer 49:19; 50:44). When the forests to the north are destroyed (Zech 11:2), this area would also be ravaged, prompting the lions (both the animals and the royal house they represented) to roar in anguish. But **the pride of the Jordan** was not only a reference to dense foliage and large predators. It also referenced Jerusalem and the temple within it, which was made of wood from the forests described above. The desolation of the capital and the temple, marking the collapse of the nation and its leadership, would cause the royal house to moan vigorously.

In the previous chapter of Zechariah's prophecy, the Lord predicted that the nation would one day be reestablished, the temple rebuilt, and peace restored (cf. Zech 6:12–13; 10:9–12). So, why do these verses (11:1–3) foretell the nation's demise? The answer centers around one word. **shepherds.** Notably, this word is plural and not singular. The term does not refer to the Messiah, but to the false, treacherous shepherds Zechariah had warned about (10:3). God urged His people to accept the Messiah, the true Shepherd of the flock (9:16), and to reject corrupt leaders who would lead the people astray or abandon them altogether (cf. 10:2). Tragically, Israel embraced the false shepherds and rejected the true Shepherd. Consequently, the onslaught described above constituted God's judgment against Israel's false shepherds and the people who followed after them.

The fulfillment of the above prophecy demonstrates how clearly God linked His judgment on Israel with their rejection of the Messiah. Numerous scholars, including rabbis, have rightly held that this passage describes the destruction of Jerusalem and the temple in AD 70 during the First Jewish-Roman War. Josephus estimated that over a million Jews died in that catastrophic conflict.[1] The Romans enslaved nearly one hundred thousand people. The assault continued over the subsequent decades in additional conflagrations. In the Third Jewish-Roman War (also known as the Bar Kokhba Revolt) around AD 135, Roman Emperor Hadrian marched through the area and destroyed 985 towns and villages, crushing the state of Israel and scattering the people all over the world. For nearly two millennia after that, the Jewish people did not have a state until the rebirth of Israel in 1948. Significantly, the destruction of the temple occurred forty years after Jesus was crucified, and our Lord Himself connected that judgment with His death (cf. Luke 23:27–31). Jerusalem's prophesied destruction in AD 70 was explicitly tied to Israel's rejection of the Good Shepherd. It was this rejection, and the subsequent destruction, that Zechariah anticipated in the opening verses of this passage.

THE TROUBLED FLOCK:
DOOMED TO DIE

Thus says Yahweh my God, "Shepherd the flock *doomed* to slaughter. Those who buy them slaughter them and are not held guilty, and *each of* those who sell them says, 'Blessed be Yahweh. Indeed, I have become rich!' And their own shepherds do not spare them. For I will no longer spare the

---

1 Josephus, *The Jewish War: Books 1–7*, ed. Jeffrey Henderson et al., trans. H. St. J. Thackeray, Loeb Classical Library (Cambridge, MA: Harvard University Press, 1927–1928), 3:497.

inhabitants of the land," declares Yahweh; "but behold, I will cause the men
to fall, each into another's hand and into the hand of his king; and they
will crush the land, and I will not deliver *them* from their hand." (11:4–6)

Zechariah began to expound on why these catastrophic events
would take place by saying, **"Thus says Yahweh my God, 'Shepherd the
flock.'"** With these words, the Lord commissioned His prophet to engage
in role-play and act out his prophecy. This was not the first time God
had done this. The Lord instructed Isaiah to do something similar with
the naming of his children (Isa 8:1), and He commanded Ezekiel to do
this by dramatically portraying the siege of Jerusalem (Ezek 4). Earlier
in the book of Zechariah, God instructed His prophet to participate in
a scene in which Joshua the High Priest was coronated, depicting the
Messiah's coronation in the future (Zech 6:9–15). The Lord gave similar
instructions to Zechariah here to act out a role that projected the future.
That role was one of a **shepherd.** The previous verse mentioned multiple
false shepherds. In contrast, Zechariah was to prefigure the singular true
Shepherd, the Messiah.

Many prophets had foretold that the Messiah would be a
Shepherd, including David (Ps 23:1), Ezekiel (Ezek 34), and Micah (Mic
7:14). Israel needed a shepherd, for they had been without proper
direction or protection (cf. Zech 10:2; Isa 53:6). With God's command to
shepherd the flock, the Lord showed through Zechariah's actions that
Israel, the needy **flock,** would receive their true leader, one who would
truly care for them.

However, in the same sentence, Yahweh declared the ominous
reality that the flock of Israel was **doomed to slaughter.** The word
slaughter describes ruthless killing. This foreboding description
referred to what had already been established in this passage: one day
Israel would suffer massive devastation with Jerusalem destroyed, the
temple burned to the ground, and the entire region leveled in desolation
and death.

The Lord revealed three aspects of this coming slaughter. First, it
would be marked by ruthlessness. As God described, **"Those who buy
them slaughter them and are not held guilty."** The statement **those**

who buy them described the foreign nations who would take possession of Israel and her people. Israel was a flock doomed to slaughter, and these nations would be directly responsible for inflicting such violent destruction. Though these foreign nations would treat Israel with great brutality, they would not feel **guilty** for their atrocities, nor would they immediately experience judgment for their war crimes. Israel had already endured such mistreatment at the hands of the Assyrians and the Babylonians, but history was going to repeat itself again with the Romans.

Second, Israel's slaughter would be marked by betrayal. As Zechariah revealed, *"Each of* **those who sell them says, 'Blessed be Yahweh. Indeed, I have become rich!'"** Since the ones who buy Israel are the foreign nations, **those who sell them** must refer to the corrupt leaders of Israel—including apostate priests, elders, and scribes. These hypocritical leaders would exclaim, **"Blessed be Yahweh,"** evidencing their warped thinking. They would ascribe their treachery and the profit they made from it **(Indeed, I have become rich)** to God's favor. By crediting the Lord for their illicit gains, they exhibited the depths and depravity of their self-deception.

The Lord continued, in verse 5, to explain that **their own shepherds do not spare them.** Once again, the text uses the key term **shepherds.** Though shepherds inherently care, nurture, guide, and defend their flocks, these shepherds would do the opposite. They would **not spare them** from harm. At the time this prophecy was fulfilled, in the first century, Israel's leaders demonstrated they had no compassion or concern for God's people. Instead, they abused the people entrusted to them, using them for their own political and financial gain. The unsuspecting flock would be betrayed by its corrupt shepherds. That betrayal would climax with the destruction of the city and the temple in AD 70.

Third, Israel's slaughter would be marked by divine judgment. As verse 6 states, **"'For I will no longer spare the inhabitants of the land,' declares Yahweh."** The verb **spare** is used in the previous verse. Israel's wicked shepherds would not spare the people because they were driven by greed and self-interest. The Lord would also not spare the nation, but for a very different reason—because Israel rejected His Son, the Messiah. In keeping with God's sovereign purposes, the nation's judgment would reach a climactic point. It would be exactly as God prophesied, **"But behold, I will cause the men to fall, each into another's hand."** The Lord stated that He would cause an unavoidable destruction. For those attempting to escape, **each** of them would **fall** victim to slaughter, being caught in the **hand** of the enemy.

The Israelites would fall prey not only to their enemies; they would fall even **into the hand of** their **king.** Who was Israel's king? The nation did not have a king in AD 70. However, Israel's leaders had designated a king for themselves when they rejected their Messiah. John 19:15 records Israel's apostate leaders crying out for the execution of Christ, "'Away with *Him*! Away with *Him*! Crucify Him!' Pilate said to them, 'Shall I crucify your King?' The chief priests answered, 'We have no king but Caesar.'" In a single act, the nation's elite rejected the Good Shepherd and embraced a pagan king. Here in Zechariah 11:6, the Lord prophesied that He would bring this act on their heads. Ironically, instead of finding deliverance in Caesar, they were devastated by his hand. It was Caesar who ordered their destruction just decades later.

God designed this judgment to indict His people for their rejection of His Son, allowing Israel's foes to **crush the land.** The word **crush** depicts grinding something to bits (cf. 2 Kgs 18:4; Isa 2:4), which describes the way Rome would tear up Jerusalem and dismantle the temple. During Jesus' earthly ministry, Israel's leaders rejected their Messiah to salvage their political status with Rome (John 11:49–50). Ironically, by betraying Christ, they did not save the nation but ensured its destruction. As God said at the beginning of this verse that He would not spare His people, He reiterated at the end: **"And I will not deliver *them* from their hand."** Though Yahweh had rescued Israel in the past (cf. 2 Sam 5:17–25; 2 Kgs 19:1–37; 2 Chr 20:1–34), this time there would be no escape. The nation would fall into the hands of the enemy, and God would not snatch them from that judgment. With such finality, Israel became a flock destined for slaughter, doomed because they rejected their Defender and Deliverer.

THE TRUE SHEPHERD:
DETESTED AND DESPISED

So I shepherded the flock *doomed* to slaughter—hence the afflicted of the flock. And I took for myself two staffs: the one I called Favor, and the other I called Union; so I shepherded the flock. Then I annihilated the three shepherds in one month, for my soul was impatient with them, and their soul also was weary of me. Then I said, "I will not shepherd you. What is to die, let it die, and what is to be annihilated, let it be annihilated; and let those who remain consume one another's flesh." And I took my staff Favor and cut it in pieces, to break my covenant which I had cut with all the peoples. So it was broken on that day, and thus the afflicted of the flock who were watching me knew that it was the word of Yahweh. And I said to them, "If it is good in your sight, give *me* my wages; but if not, never mind!" So they weighed out thirty *shekels* of silver as my wages. (11:7–12)

The prophet heeded God's summons and **shepherded the flock doomed to slaughter.** In role-playing the part of a shepherd, the prophet depicted the positive effects of Christ's ministry. He would **shepherd** a flock, and though they were doomed to slaughter, He would nurture, care for, and feed them nonetheless. Within this doomed flock were **the afflicted of the flock,** which described the common people, those in Israel who were suffering, oppressed, and hurting. Often those who were so poor and lowly were part of the believing remnant (cf. Pss 10:12; 14:6; 18:27). Zechariah prophesied that, at His coming, the Messiah would minister to the afflicted and believing remnant who would receive His message. This was what happened during Jesus' earthly ministry. In the Sermon on the Mount, the Lord Jesus said, "Blessed are the poor in spirit" (Matt 5:3), and the gospel of Mark recounted, "The large crowd enjoyed listening to Him" (Mark 12:37). Just as Zechariah prophesied, though the political and religious leaders did not accept their Messiah, some among the lowly did.

In depicting the way the Messiah would minister to these people, Zechariah said, "**I took for myself two staffs.**" A staff is a stick or rod which was used to guide people and animals (cf. Num 22:27), and it was a symbol representing authority (cf. Jer 48:17). What Zechariah described here is similar to Ezekiel 37:16, which referred to the northern and southern kingdoms of Israel as separate sticks that the Messiah will ultimately join together. Zechariah alluded here to that earlier prophecy, showing that Christ, even in His first advent, would come to work toward unifying His people (cf. Matt 15:24; John 10:14–16; 11:51–52).

The two staffs in Zechariah's prophecy were designated as follows: **"The one I called Favor, and the other I called Union."** Favor speaks of God's kind, gracious, and tender care, and it describes that which is lovely and compassionate. This is certainly what defined the Messiah's ministry, for Christ was gentle, loving, kind, merciful, gracious, and forgiving. These were the characteristics the Lord Jesus demonstrated when He ministered to the sick and destitute, including needy people like the Syro-Phoenician woman, Jairus' daughter, the woman with an issue of blood, and the blind man by the Pool of Siloam. However, Christ did not only act with favor toward people, but brought people into favor with God. He explained how people can become right with God (cf. Mark 2:1–7; Luke 13:1–5) and be justified (Luke 18:9–14). He declared that only He is the way, the truth, and the life (John 14:6). Thus, **favor** refers to the fact that Christ ministered God's grace and goodness to man, and that He secured man's relationship with God.

Complementary to this, **union** refers to the relationship between man and man. Christ provided a foretaste of this when He came in His first advent and went throughout all of Israel, ministering to the people and gathering God's lost sheep into one fold (cf. John 10:14–16; 11:51–52). Thus, Zechariah prophesied that at His coming, the Messiah would show goodness to Israel and unite the sheep who were without a shepherd. As Zechariah said, **"So I shepherded the flock."** In this drama, Zechariah took the staff of favor and the staff of union and **shepherded the flock**, foreshadowing the Messiah's benevolent ministry toward Israel.

Though He came for the blessing of His people, the Messiah would encounter great opposition and difficulty. The prophet said on behalf of the Messiah, **"Then I annihilated the three shepherds in one month."** The idea of **annihilated** is to efface or erase completely. Zechariah prophesied that Christ would eradicate **three shepherds** from Israel.

The question of the identity of these shepherds is not an easy one to answer. However, throughout his prophecy, Zechariah has emphasized the three offices of prophet (cf. Zech 1:4–7; 7:3, 7, 12; 8:9; 13:2, 4–5), priest (cf. 3:1, 8; 6:11, 13; 7:3, 5), and king (cf. 9:9; 14:5, 9, 10, 16–17). But by the time of the Lord Jesus, these three roles were carried out by the scribes, priests, and elders of Israel. That is one of the oldest explanations for the identity of the **three shepherds** and is the most likely interpretation. Zechariah referred to these people as **shepherds** for two reasons: to connect these corrupt leaders with the false shepherds mentioned throughout this section (10:2–3; 11:3, 5, 15, 17), and to contrast them with the one true Shepherd, the Messiah (cf. 11:4, 7; 13:7). In His first advent, Christ soundly condemned Israel's faulty leaders (cf. Matt 23). Zechariah prophesied that their downfall would take place in **one month**, the same amount of time it took for Jerusalem to fall once the wall was breached by Babylon in 586 BC, a historic event commemorated by Israel's calendar (2 Kgs 25:3–9; Jer 39:2–4; cf. Zech 7:3–5). So, in speaking of **one month**, the prophet indicated that what had happened in the past would happen again. By early August of AD 70, the Romans had breached Jerusalem's final defenses and then destroyed the Temple by the end of August, burning it to the ground. By early September, they had quelled the remaining Jewish resistance and gained complete control of the city. For both Babylon and Rome, though each army began their assault with a longer siege, the time from their final breach of Jerusalem's defenses to the city's destruction was about a month. As Zechariah prophesied, God would bring Israel's corrupt system of leadership to an abrupt end.

Zechariah then expressed the reason the Good Shepherd opposed the false shepherds: **"for my soul was impatient with them."** These words anticipated Christ's attitude toward the first-century Jewish religious leaders. He openly rebuked them for their hypocrisy, wickedness, exploitation of the people, and rejection of Him (cf. Matt 21:12–16; Mark 11:15–18; Luke 19:45–47; John 2:13–16). As Zechariah said on behalf of the Messiah, **"Their soul also was weary of me."** Though the prophet commanded Israel to welcome the Messiah with open arms (Zech 9:9; 10:1, 7, 12), Israel's wicked leaders would quickly grow **weary** of Him, to the point of putting Him to death (cf. John 15:25).

Thus, the prophet, role-playing Christ, said, "**I will not shepherd you.**" The benevolent shepherding ministry of the Messiah, marked by favor and unity, would come to an end. That this occurred during the ministry of the Lord Jesus is clearly attested in the gospels. The Messiah's ministry started with many miracles but ended in judgment (cf. Matt 23:37–39; Luke 23:26–31). Having been rejected by the nation, Christ left the people to their decreed doom (Zech 11:4, 7). Zechariah, speaking on behalf of the Messiah, declared, "**What is to die, let it die.**" Christ would not intervene to deliver Israel. The prophet also proclaimed, "**What is to be annihilated, let it be annihilated.**" This same language described the judgment of the three false shepherds in verse 8, indicating that the demise of Israel's corrupt leaders would be both self-inflicted and unavoidable. Finally, the prophet declared, "**Let those who remain consume one another's flesh.**" The statement is reminiscent of verse 5 which prophesied that the corrupt rulers of Israel would betray their own people. But verse 9 describes a more violent scene, in which the sheep are not only sold but eaten. The prophetic picture depicts not only the buying and selling of captives, but a situation so desperate that people would even resort to cannibalism. The fulfillment of this in the first century was recorded by Josephus, the Jewish historian, in his description of what transpired in AD 70. Thus, Zechariah prophesied that Israel would reject their Messiah and that the Messiah would therefore hand them over to judgment.

Zechariah then portrayed the Messiah fulfilling what had just been declared. The prophet recounted, "**And I took my staff Favor and cut it in pieces.**" This dramatic action demonstrated that Israel's relationship with God would be severed. Because Israel would have no favor with God at this time, the Lord would **break** His **covenant which** He **had cut with all the peoples.** In the days of Moses, God promised Israel that if they were faithful to Him, He would not allow them to be overrun by any foreign enemy (Deut 28:1–14; cf. Gen 12:1–3). In effect, that divine guarantee **cut,** or firmly established, a covenant between God and **all the peoples.** Throughout history, even though Israel proved to be unfaithful, God has restrained enemy nations from annihilating His people. Though many other groups like the Canaanites, Hivites, Kenites, and Jebusites all perished, Israel survived under a form of divine protection. However, with the Messiah's rejection, God's favor was removed, and with it His hand of protection that had shielded His chosen nation. While the Jewish people were not totally annihilated, the temple was destroyed in AD 70, and after AD 135, the state of Israel ceased to exist for nearly two millennia.

By shattering the staff of God's favor, the Messiah would remove the shield of divine protection from Israel. Once the nation rejected the true Shepherd, God's covenant with the nations (involving a pledge of protection for Israel) would be shattered immediately. As Zechariah explained, **it was broken on that day**, indicating that the outworking of judgment began straightaway. This reality was reflected in the ministry of the Lord Jesus, whose preaching shifted from clear words to cryptic parables (Matt 13:10–17) and from public appearances to private encounters (Matt 23:38; Luke 13:35). Only forty years after His death, Jerusalem would be overrun, and the temple destroyed. While showing immediacy, the language of **on that day** also carries eschatological overtones in the prophets and especially in Zechariah (cf. Zech 2:15; 3:10; 9:16; 12:3, 4, 6). The ultimate and final shattering of God's protective covenant for Israel will take place when all the nations gather at Armageddon and invade Jerusalem "in that day," an event that Zechariah reveals later (cf. 12:1–3; 14:2). The prophet demonstrated that the effects of the Messiah's rejection would reverberate throughout Israel's history to the end of the age.

Continuing his role-play of the Messiah, Zechariah said, **"Thus the afflicted of the flock who were watching me knew that it was the word of Yahweh."** The **afflicted of the flock**, the poor and downtrodden among the sheep of Israel, included the followers of the Lord Jesus during His earthly ministry. They recognized their need for deliverance, and therefore **were watching** Jesus with great curiosity. As they observed His miraculous works and heard His marvelous teaching, they knew **the word of Yahweh** was being fulfilled. But not everyone who claimed to follow Jesus truly loved Him (cf. John 6:66). Even among the twelve disciples, one would prove to be a traitor—a point Zechariah makes clear in the next verse (v. 12). Judas Iscariot initially appeared to be part of the remnant (John 6:70–71), but was later exposed as a hypocrite. He too **was**

watching the Lord, but with nefarious intentions. He was "looking for a good opportunity to betray Jesus" (Matt 26:16). The treachery of Judas was compounded by the fact that he knew that Christ was fulfilling **the word of Yahweh**, but he turned against Him anyway.

In verse 12, Zechariah's drama moved to a point of decision. He exclaimed, **"If it is good in your sight, give *me* my wages; but if not, never mind!"** The prophet's request concerned his **wages**, the money owed in exchange for his work as a shepherd. The illustration was clear: a future time would come when Israel would convey how much or how little they thought the Messiah was worth. With the words **"If it is good in your sight,"** Zechariah expressed his lack of confidence (cf. 1 Kgs 21:2; Esth 5:8) that Israel would do right by their Messiah. And with the words **"but if not,"** he indicated his expectation that Israel would fail to value Christ at all (cf. Isa 53:3–4). In the face of such insult and hostility, the prophet, playing the role of the coming Messiah, simply said, **"Never mind,"** a phrase meaning to cease and desist. The Messiah would not demand His rights, wages, or honor (cf. 53:7; 1 Pet 2:21–25), but would rather confront the people for putting up pretenses. This was evident with Judas, as Jesus declared: "'Truly, truly, I say to you, that one of you will betray Me.... He is the one for whom I shall dip the piece of bread and give it to him.' So when He had dipped the piece of bread, He took and gave it to Judas, *the son* of Simon Iscariot. And after the piece of bread, Satan then entered into him. Therefore Jesus said to him, 'What you do, do quickly'" (John 13:21–27).

Having articulated the point of decision, Zechariah foretold what Israel would do in response as **they weighed out thirty shekels of silver as my wages.** From a strictly financial perspective, **thirty shekels of silver** constituted enough money to purchase prime real estate (cf. Matt 27:3–10; Acts 1:18–19). However, it was also the amount of compensation paid for a slave who had been gored by an ox (Exod 21:32). By setting this price for the Messiah, the nation showed that it viewed Him on the same level as a slave (cf. Phil 2:7), and not as their Good Shepherd and glorious King. So, though the sum of money is not inconsequential, it is nothing compared to the Messiah's infinite worth. Moreover, it signaled Israel's official decision about and disdain for the Messiah. Christ would be viewed as a slave, "despised and forsaken of men.... He was despised, and we did not esteem Him" (Isa 53:3). What Zechariah prophesied took place when Judas betrayed Jesus for this very amount of money (cf. Matt 26:15). With every phrase in this passage, the correspondence between Zechariah's prophecies and the life of Christ is astounding. All of it portrays the ministry of Israel's true Shepherd, who was detested by the nation.

THE TERRIBLE CONSEQUENCES: DISCIPLINED FOR DISOBEDIENCE

Then Yahweh said to me, "Throw it to the potter, *that* valuable price at which I was valued by them." So I took the thirty *shekels* of silver and threw them to the potter in the house of Yahweh. Then I cut in pieces my second staff Union, to break the brotherhood between Judah and Israel. (11:13–14)

Having previewed the Messiah's betrayal and rejection, God interjected His response to Israel's treachery. **Then Yahweh said to me, "Throw it to the potter."** These words predicted what would happen after Judas betrayed Jesus (cf. Matt 27:3–10). They also correspond to what God said in Jeremiah, the only other place in the Old Testament where the exact phrase **the potter** appears. In Jeremiah, the potter illustrates God's absolute right to do what He desires with Israel (Jer 18:1–6). Just as the potter smashes his clay, so Yahweh would smash the nation by sending Israel into exile in 586 BC (19:1–11). By again referencing **the potter** in Zechariah, God indicated that Israel would experience judgment and exile similar to what Jeremiah described concerning the generation of his day.

The Israelites always hoped to be fully free from exile. They prayed about this while they were in Babylon (Dan 9:1–19) and after a remnant returned to the land (cf. Neh 9:5–37). Even in the first century, they wished the Romans would be overthrown (Luke 24:21; Acts 1:6). However, because of their rejection of the Messiah, God decreed here that instead of ending, their exile would become worse.

The Lord made it clear that Israel's offense was directly against Him. He called the thirty pieces of silver **"that valuable price at which I was valued by them."** By devaluing the Messiah, the Israelites demonstrated how little they valued Yahweh Himself. The use of the first-person pronoun ("I") indicates that the Messiah is Yahweh, a point stated plainly in the next chapter (cf. Zech 12:10). The Lord's statement also exposed the treacherous depths of Israel's offense—they regarded God to be worth a mere thirty shekels of silver. For such a crime, Yahweh would take their money and have it hurled to the potter of judgment.

Thus, Zechariah **took the thirty shekels of silver and threw them to the potter in the house of Yahweh.** As directed, the prophet not only threw the money to the potter but did this **in the house of Yahweh,** emphasizing that God's wrath would not only be poured out against Israel or even against Jerusalem, but against the temple itself. At the time of Zechariah, the temple was being rebuilt, an event Israel might have interpreted to mean their time of exile was ending. But Yahweh revealed that a judgment was coming that would be worse than what had happened during Babylon's conquest. The enemy would destroy Israel's capital city and the temple once again, and the people would be hurled into an even more devastating state of exile.

Having thrown the silver to the potter, Zechariah then **cut in pieces my second staff Union.** The prophet had already cut the first staff Favor into pieces, symbolizing that Israel's relationship with God would be broken (cf. Zech 11:10–11). Now, Zechariah cut into pieces the second staff, and he did this to **break the brotherhood between Judah and Israel.** From its earliest days as a family even under Jacob, Israel was disunified (Gen 37:1–36). The nation under Saul, David, and Solomon enjoyed a degree of unity, but even that was tenuous (cf. 2 Sam 15:1–37). Hence, for most of Israel's history, the nation was not truly united. However, Ezekiel promised that the Messiah would join the nation together (cf. Ezek 37:16), and Zechariah's prophecy alluded to that truth (see discussion on Zech 11:7). But because Israel rejected the Messiah, the prophet here revealed that the time for Ezekiel's prophecy to be fulfilled was a long way off. The staffs that will one day be united (cf. Ezek 37:16–17) were cut into pieces by Zechariah. The unity and security that was promised to the nation, and all that they had hoped for, would be postponed. The fulfillment of those promised blessings to the nation still awaits a generation that will wholeheartedly embrace God's Son for who He is, the true Shepherd of Israel (cf. Zech 12:10; Matt 24:42–51).

Zechariah's prophecies in this passage were precisely fulfilled during the earthly ministry of the Lord Jesus. As Matthew records, Judas threw the thirty pieces on the ground of the sanctuary of God's house, and the religious leaders took it, went out, and gave it to a potter in order to buy his field (Matt 27:3–10). Forty years later, Jerusalem and the temple were razed to the ground similar to what had happened during the Babylonian conquest in 586 BC. When the Romans destroyed the temple and dispersed the people, Israel encountered the indignation of the divine Potter (Jer 18). From that time, the Jewish people have been scattered around the world. Even since the nation was reconstituted in 1948, the people are still unable to inhabit their own land peacefully. They have experienced ongoing oppression and hostility, a perpetual exile, suffering God's judgment for the sin of rejecting His Son. Even so, the day is coming when Israel will repent from unbelief and return to embrace the Lord Jesus in saving faith (Rom 11:26). Until then, the offer of the gospel extends to every person—both Jew and Gentile. Those who believe in Christ Jesus will be saved (Rom 10:9). They will find in Him the forgiveness, fellowship, and fulfillment that only the Good Shepherd can provide.

The False Shepherd

Zechariah 11:15–17

Then Yahweh said to me, "Take again for yourself the equipment of a foolish shepherd. For behold, I am going to raise up a shepherd in the land who will not care for those who face annihilation, seek the young, heal the broken, or sustain the one standing, but will consume the flesh of the fat *sheep* and tear off their hoofs.

Woe to the worthless shepherd
Who forsakes the flock!
A sword will be on his arm
And on his right eye!
His arm will be totally dried up,
And his right eye will be utterly dimmed."

Having revealed the rejection of the Messiah, Israel's true Shepherd, Zechariah continued by addressing the rise of the ultimate false shepherd, the anti-Messiah or Antichrist. Israel had many false shepherds throughout its history (cf. Ezek 34), and various antichrists have also arisen throughout church history (1 John 2:18; cf. 2 Pet 3:1–2). But at the end of the age, a final false shepherd, far worse than all the others, will arrive on the scene. Zechariah identified him as the foolish shepherd (Zech 11:15) and the worthless shepherd (11:17). Satan will elevate this satanic leader to be his instrument, intent on blaspheming God, destroying Israel, and persecuting all the saints.

Since the Fall, Satan has sought to thwart God's plan for the Messiah—the promised Seed who would come to crush the head of that serpent (Gen 3:15). The devil's failed efforts against the Messiah included attempts to pollute the messianic bloodline (cf. Gen 6:4) or eliminate it altogether (cf. Exod 1:15–22). At points, it seemed like his plots might succeed. More than once, the royal line of David from which the Messiah must come was nearly eliminated (cf. 2 Chr 21:4–7, 16–17; 22:1, 10–11), yet God faithfully preserved it.

Satan's attempts continued after Jesus was born, when Herod slaughtered the male children of Bethlehem in an effort to murder the Messiah (Matt 2:16–17). At the outset of Christ's ministry, the devil enticed Him with the full force of temptation to abandon the eternal plan (Matt 4:1–11). When that failed, Satan incited the people to kill Jesus before His appointed time (Luke 4:29; John 5:18; 10:31). The Cross itself represented a satanic effort to vanquish the Messiah (cf. John 13:27). Yet, it was through His death on the Cross that the Messiah destroyed the devil's power (cf. Heb 2:14–15).

Though soundly defeated (cf. Luke 10:18), the devil continues to war against the Messiah and His people (cf. 1 Pet 5:8). Satan's efforts to thwart God's purposes will culminate at the end of this age with the appearance of the Antichrist. This false messiah will be Satan's last-ditch effort to undermine God's plan for redemptive history, by controlling the world through a counterfeit christ. The Apostle Paul explained to the Thessalonians that the Antichrist will come prior to the Day of the Lord when Jesus returns: "Let no one in any way deceive you, for it [the return of Christ] *has not come* unless the apostasy comes first, and the man of lawlessness is revealed, the son of destruction, who opposes and exalts himself above every so-called god or object of worship, so that he takes his seat in the sanctuary of God, exhibiting himself as being God" (2 Thess 2:3–4). As Paul explained, before the Lord returns to establish His millennial kingdom, the Antichrist will set himself up as world ruler—the only god to be worshiped. The Apostle John, referring to the Antichrist as "the beast," revealed more details about his future reign of terror:

> I saw a beast coming up out of the sea, having ten horns and seven heads, and on his horns *were* ten diadems, and on his heads were blasphemous names. And the beast which I saw was like a leopard, and his feet were like *those* of a bear, and his mouth like the mouth of a lion. And the dragon [Satan] gave him his power and his throne and great authority. And *I saw* one of his heads as if it had been slain fatally, and his fatal wound was healed. And the whole earth marveled *and followed* after the beast. And they worshiped the dragon because he gave his authority to the beast, and they worshiped the beast, saying, "Who is like the beast, and who is able to wage war with him?" And there was given to him a mouth speaking great boasts and blasphemies, and authority to act for forty-two months was given to him. And he opened his mouth in blasphemies against God, to blaspheme His name and His tabernacle, *that is*, those who dwell in heaven. And it was also given to him to make war with the saints and to overcome them, and authority over every tribe and people and tongue and nation was given to him. And all who dwell on the earth will worship him, *everyone* whose name has not been written from the foundation of the world in the book of life of the Lamb who has been slain. (Rev 13:1–8)

A brief survey of Scripture reveals the characteristics of this coming diabolical despot. He will be a persuasive orator (Dan 7:8), political manipulator (Rev 6:2; 13:7), economic wizard (Dan 8:25), military commander (7:23), religious leader (2 Thess 2:4; cf. Dan 11:38), and brazen self-promoter (Rev 13:12). Amazed by his abilities, the fallen world will respond to the Antichrist with adulation and praise. The rulers of this world will bow to him and follow him into combat against the Messiah, resulting in their immediate destruction and eternal judgment (19:19–21).

The Lord Jesus, during His earthly ministry, alluded to the future arrival of this false messiah. In John 5:43, Jesus said, "I have come in

My Father's name, and you do not receive Me; if another comes in his own name, you will receive him." In that statement, Christ echoed the themes of Zechariah 11, that Israel would reject the true Shepherd while embracing a false shepherd instead. In Matthew 24, in His Olivet Discourse, Jesus referred to the Antichrist when He spoke of the abomination of desolation and said that "this was spoken of through Daniel the prophet" (Matt 24:15).

In chapter 9, Daniel prophesied about seventy weeks, or seventy sets of seven (490 years), that God had ordained specifically for Israel's future. The prophet explained that during the seventieth week, the Antichrist "will make a firm covenant with the many for one week" (Dan 9:27). During this period, known as the Great Tribulation (Matt 24:21; Rev 7:14), Israel will fall under the Antichrist's deception and make a treaty of protection with him. However, at the midpoint of this treaty, the Antichrist will violate the agreement and desecrate the temple, proclaiming himself to be God (2 Thess 2:4). Satan will inspire the Antichrist to organize a sinister global governmental system intent on killing the Jewish people and any Tribulation saints (Rev 13:7–10). This false messiah will be Satan's final attempt with all the demons to defeat the true Messiah. He will fail and be cast into the abyss for a thousand years (20:2–3), while the Lord Jesus Christ will reign over the whole world (20:4–6). His final sentence to judgment is described in Revelation 20:7–10:

> And when the thousand years are finished, Satan will be released from his prison, and will come out to deceive the nations which are in the four corners of the earth, Gog and Magog, to gather them together for the war; the number of them is like the sand of the seashore. And they came up on the broad plain of the earth and surrounded the camp of the saints and the beloved city, and fire came down from heaven and devoured them. And the devil who deceived them was thrown into the lake of fire and brimstone, where the beast and the false prophet are also, and they will be tormented day and night forever and ever.

As Zechariah 11 makes clear, Israel's rejection of the Messiah came with severe consequences, including extended exile, the destruction of Jerusalem, and the desolation of the temple. But no consequence is more shocking than the rise of the Antichrist. The rejection of the true Shepherd would pave the way for the coming of the ultimate false shepherd. Though his character and conduct are the essence of unprecedented wickedness (Zech 11:15–16), his subsequent collapse has already been determined (11:17). In these verses, Zechariah not only revealed the sobering truth about the final false shepherd; he also reiterated that God is sovereign over all things, including the rise and fall of Satan's counterfeit messiah. The Antichrist, like everything and everyone else, plays a part in God's predetermined plan for the future of this world.

THE CHARACTER OF THE FALSE SHEPHERD

Then Yahweh said to me, "Take again for yourself the equipment of a foolish shepherd. For behold, I am going to raise up a shepherd in the land who will not care for those who face annihilation, seek the young, heal the broken, or sustain the one standing, but will consume the flesh of the fat sheep and tear off their hoofs." (11:15–16)

The phrase **then Yahweh said to me** already occurred in 11:13 where the Lord revealed the first major consequence Israel would experience for rejecting the Messiah—namely, extended exile. This second occurrence introduced an even more terrible consequence of the nation's apostasy, the advent of the Antichrist.

Yahweh instructed Zechariah, **"Take again for yourself."** Thus far, Zechariah had taken on the role of a Good Shepherd, the Messiah, but now he needed to play a new role—that of the foolish shepherd. To that end, the prophet took up **the equipment of a foolish shepherd.** The term **foolish** denotes an "ignorant fool" (cf. Prov 1:7; 7:22), one who not only behaves in an utterly absurd fashion, but one who also acts as if God does not exist (Pss 10:4; 14:1). As Psalm 53:1 states, "The wicked fool says in his heart, 'There is no God,' they act corruptly, and commit abominable injustice; there is no one who does good." Such iniquity will certainly characterize the final false shepherd.

What are the implements of a foolish shepherd? They could be staffs like the ones Zechariah had just broken into pieces. Those would be tools only a foolish shepherd would use because they would be worthless. It could be a great club or a sharp spear instead of a gentle staff. Zechariah did not reveal what these tools were, but whatever Zechariah took up, it must have been obvious he was playing a threatening and sinister role. While appearing ridiculous, these implements also indicated that the person Zechariah depicted would be reckless and dangerous. He was equipped not to protect the sheep, but to harm them.

Having introduced the foolish shepherd, the Lord declared that the rise of the Antichrist is fully within the sovereign will of God: **"For behold, I am going to raise up a shepherd in the land."** God's sovereign power and plan will be on display as He ordains the events of history to **raise up** this false shepherd, allowing him to operate **in the land** of Israel and even make a pact with the nation (cf. Dan 9:27). Though terrible and powerful, the Antichrist will not operate outside of God's sovereign parameters. Just as the Lord controlled what Satan could and could not do in the life of Job (cf. Job 1:12), so He remains sovereign over the activity of evil people in this world, including the counterfeit messiah at the end of the age.

Having declared His sovereignty over the final false shepherd, Yahweh described him with a series of chilling details. This wicked leader will not intervene for those in the greatest danger; he **will not care for those who face annihilation.** The term **care** encompasses the idea of tending to those in distress. It could describe a caring shepherd seeking an animal in danger, to rescue it from cold temperatures, wild animals, or other serious injuries. However, the prophet states emphatically that the false shepherd will not intervene to save those **who face annihilation.** The word **annihilation** was used earlier (in vv. 8–9) and conveys complete destruction. When the people of Israel face such a threat in the end times, instead of delivering or defending them in their time of need, the Antichrist will turn to become Israel's deadliest enemy (cf. Matt 24:15–17; Rev 13:7–18).

The false shepherd will not even aid the most pitiable among the flock, since he will not **seek the young**. The **young** represent the most vulnerable, those on whom people would instinctively have compassion. A true shepherd would leave the ninety-nine to find the little one that is lost (Luke 15:4–6). But the Antichrist will be fiercely hostile to Israel; he will not **heal the broken**. One of the shepherd's responsibilities was to mend broken limbs. From time to time, a wandering sheep would break its leg, and a good shepherd would make a splint to preserve the life of the injured animal. But the Antichrist, by withholding lifesaving measures from those most desperate, will exploit the weak and helpless to their death.

The false shepherd not only oppresses the weak but also undermines and depletes the strong. Zechariah prophesied that the Antichrist will not **sustain the one standing**, referring to sheep that are healthy and strong. They require minimal special attention or assistance. But under the false shepherd, because the healthy sheep are not sustained, they will become malnourished and starve to death. After he breaks his treaty with Israel, the Antichrist will remove all provisions and protections from the people, using deprivation and starvation as weapons in his campaign of slaughter against the nation.

Zechariah continued by describing the false shepherd's violent and vicious actions toward the sheep. The prophet disclosed in graphic language that this wicked leader **will consume the flesh of the fat sheep**. Instead of feeding the sheep, he will feed on the flock as he **consumes** them. Rather than binding their wounds, he will tear their **flesh** apart and devour the **fat** sheep. Worse still, the false shepherd will **tear off their hoofs**. That vivid description conveys a sense of sheer and uncontrolled violence. This false shepherd will not merely devour the sheep, but mutilate them with senseless cruelty. Instead of protecting the Jews from danger, the Antichrist will pose a deadly danger to the nation. As Daniel prophesied, the Antichrist will "go forth with great wrath to destroy and devote many to destruction" (Dan 11:44). Zechariah later foretold that, "'It will be in all the land,' declares Yahweh, 'that two parts in it will be cut off *and* breathe their last'" (Zech 13:8). As a result of the Antichrist's campaign against Israel, two thirds of the people will die.

That is the reason the Lord Jesus forewarned those alive at that future time to "run for the mountains" (Matt 24:16). The prophet Jeremiah called that future era "the time of Jacob's distress" (Jer 30:7). During that time, the false shepherd will not tend the flock of Israel but tear it to pieces.

THE COLLAPSE OF THE FALSE SHEPHERD

"Woe to the worthless shepherd
Who forsakes the flock!
A sword will be on his arm
And on his right eye!
His arm will be totally dried up,
And his right eye will be utterly dimmed." (11:17)

In verse 16, Zechariah explained that God has sovereignly ordained the events that will give rise to the final false shepherd. But what about the Antichrist's demise? With the word **woe** in verse 17, the prophet explained that God will also cause the Antichrist to fall. The term **woe** is a strong cry of emotion (cf. Zech 2:6–7) expressing imminent ruin or alarming distress. Here it conveys the Antichrist's inevitable destruction, as divine wrath is unleashed against the **worthless shepherd. Worthless** describes one who has no redeeming quality but is as empty and despicable as false religion (cf. Lev 19:4; 26:1; Isa 2:8, 18). God loathes the false shepherd because he **forsakes the flock** of Israel, not only abandoning the sheep but also attacking them. Though Israel has had a long line of wicked rulers and corrupt shepherds throughout its history (cf. Zech 10:2–3), the Antichrist will exceed them all. The Lord will bring this vile individual to judgment for his atrocities.

God's wrath will fall on the Antichrist so that **a sword will be on his** [the Antichrist's] **arm and on his right eye**. The **sword** of divine vengeance will strike the false shepherd's **arm**, the symbol of one's full strength (cf. Deut 4:34) as well as **his right eye**, which allowed one to see and engage in battle. The Antichrist will be unable to deflect either attack, so that his **arm will be totally dried up, and his right eye will**

be utterly dimmed. This wicked ruler's **arm**, or power, will be **totally dried up**, evaporating his authority and strength. Moreover, his **right eye** will be **utterly dimmed**, meaning that his awareness and depth perception will be severely disabled (cf. Gen 27:1). In ancient times, a soldier often covered his left eye with his shield and used his **right eye** to see in combat. Without the right eye, one could not determine distance or fight effectively (cf. 1 Sam 11:2). By striking the Antichrist's arm and eye, God will incapacitate this counterfeit messiah, removing his power and impairing his vision. To do his job, a shepherd needed an arm to lift up his sheep (cf. Luke 15:5) and an eye to search for them (cf. Matt 18:12).[1] Without these essentials, the final false shepherd will be utterly debilitated. He will be defeated, dishonored, and subjected to divine judgment.

Other passages of Scripture also depict the Antichrist's demise. Daniel declared that the Antichrist and his empire will be subjected to utter and perpetual judgment as it will be "destroyed and given to the burning fire" (Dan 7:11). As Paul reminded believers, the Antichrist will be defeated by the breath of our Lord's mouth and brought to an end by the appearance of His coming (2 Thess 2:8). In Revelation 19, the Apostle John provided the fullest description of this judgment: "The beast was seized, and with him the false prophet who did the signs in his presence, by which he deceived those who had received the mark of the beast and those who worshiped his image. These two were thrown alive into the lake of fire which burns with brimstone" (Rev 19:20). In Revelation 20:10, John added, "The devil who deceived them was thrown into the lake of fire and brimstone, where the beast and the false prophet are also, and they will be tormented day and night forever and ever." The beast, referring to the Antichrist, will not merely be defeated at Christ's Second Coming but assigned to eternal punishment in the Lake of Fire. Though Zechariah warned that the Antichrist will one day come in all his terror, the God who permitted him to come to power will also crush him in everlasting defeat, in keeping with His sovereign plan for the end of history.

---

1 Eugene Merrill, *Haggai, Zechariah, Malachi: An Exegetical Commentary* (Dallas, TX: Biblical Studies Press, 2003), 278.

Israel's Final Deliverance: Physical Salvation

Zechariah 12:1–9

The oracle of the word of Yahweh concerning Israel. *Thus* declares Yahweh who stretches out the heavens, lays the foundation of the earth, and forms the spirit of man within him, "Behold, I am going to make Jerusalem a cup that causes reeling to all the peoples all around. Now *the one* in siege against Jerusalem will also *be* against Judah. But it will be in that day, *that* I will make Jerusalem a heavy stone for all the peoples; all who heave it up will be severely injured. And all the nations of the earth will be gathered against it. In that day," declares Yahweh, "I will strike every horse with bewilderment and his rider with madness. But I will open my eyes *to watch* over the house of Judah, while I strike every horse of the peoples with blindness. Then the clans of Judah will say in their hearts, 'A strong support for us are the inhabitants of Jerusalem through Yahweh of hosts, their God.' In that day I will make the clans of Judah like a fiery laver among pieces of wood and a fiery torch among sheaves, so they will consume on the right hand and on the left all the surrounding peoples, while Jerusalem will again be inhabited in its own place—in Jerusalem. Yahweh also will save the tents of Judah first so that the glory of the house of David and the glory of the inhabitants of Jerusalem will not be magnified above Judah. In that day Yahweh will defend the inhabitants of Jerusalem, and the one who stumbles among them in that day will be like David, and the house of

David *will be* like God, like the angel of Yahweh before them. And it will be in that day, *that* I will seek to destroy all the nations that come against Jerusalem."

Zechariah reverberates with messianic hope. The previous two chapters (Zech 10–11) placed considerable focus on the Messiah's first advent—including His humble entry on a donkey, His rejection by the nation, His betrayal for thirty pieces of silver, and the subsequent judgment of God on unbelieving Israel who rejected Him. Chapters 12 through 14 feature God's plan for Israel's future at Christ's second coming, when the Messiah will establish His earthly kingdom and fulfill His promises to the nation given through the patriarchs, David, and the prophets.

The final three chapters (Zech 12–14) parallel passages such as Ezekiel 38–39. Yet, they have no Old Testament equal in terms of the scope of their revelation regarding the return of Christ. Through Zechariah, the Lord unveiled remarkable truths about the end of the age, including the rise of a world confederacy against God's chosen nation, Israel's stunning victory over her enemies, the glorious appearing of the Messiah, and the spiritual transformation of the Jewish people through the Holy Spirit. The final chapters of Zechariah describe these remarkable events from multiple angles, providing vivid detail and magnifying the work of the Messiah. According to God's predetermined plan, Christ will return at the precise moment Israel needs Him most. He will rescue His people, regenerate them, punish the wicked, set up His kingdom, and celebrate His triumph with a great feast.

The phrase "in that day" appears seventeen times in Zechariah 12–14, emphasizing the eschatological focus of this prophetic content. All of it surrounds the Day of the LORD, or the Day of Yahweh, when God will judge the world and establish the Messiah's reign on earth. First, Zechariah 12:1–9 addresses Israel's physical deliverance in the Day of Yahweh. A massive siege will take place, in which the armies of the world amass against God's chosen nation. Despite the force, human and demonic, the conflict will not end the way the enemy expects. In these verses, the drama of that future battle unfolds under the following five headings: a sovereign declaration (v. 1), a stunning development (vv. 2–3), a severe debilitation (vv. 4–5), a smashing defeat (vv. 6–7), and a supernatural defense (vv. 8–9).

A SOVEREIGN DECLARATION

The oracle of the word of Yahweh concerning Israel. *Thus* **declares Yahweh who stretches out the heavens, lays the foundation of the earth, and forms the spirit of man within him.** (12:1)

Similar to Zechariah 9:1, the prophet began this section with the heading **the oracle of the word of Yahweh concerning Israel**. The word **oracle** fundamentally means "burden," conveying both the sobering heaviness of God's judgment and the weighty glory of Israel's salvation. This entire revelation came **by the word of Yahweh**, reminding the reader that Zechariah's proclamation did not consist of human speculation. It carried the full force of God's authority and certainty.

Though Zechariah's earlier oracle (9:1) concerned "the land of Hadrach," this oracle concerned **Israel**. The shift in subject traces the very flow of God's plan in history. Though God's focus is currently on the Gentile nations (Zech 9–11; cf. Luke 21:24; Rom 11:25), in the future His gaze will be fixed on Israel (Zech 12–14). Given the references to Jerusalem (12:2), Judah (12:2), the house of David (12:12), and the house of Nathan (12:12), the Lord was clearly not referring to believers generally, but specifically to ethnic and national Israel (cf. Rom 11:26). Here again, God revealed further features of His promises to His chosen nation.

The introductory phrase, **thus declares Yahweh**, emphasized the divine origin and absolute assurance of the promises made in this passage (cf. Obad 8). The Lord not only decreed His promises but also declared that He personally secures them. In verse 2, God said, "I am going to make..." In verse 3, He said, "I will make..." In verse 4a, He announced, "I will strike..." In verse 4b, He declared, "I will open..." In verse 6, He prophesied, "I will make..." In verse 9, He foretold, "I will seek..." In verse 10, He promised, "I will pour out..." Repeatedly, Yahweh added His personal guarantee to carry out His promises and plans for Israel. There can be no greater assurance, for He is the One who **stretches out the heavens, lays the foundation of the earth, and forms the spirit of man within him.** The sovereign Creator of and Ruler over the universe is He who **stretches out the heavens.** The image is one of spreading out the canvas of a tent from end to end. God created the entire infinite expanse of the sky (cf. Gen 1:1; Isa 42:5) and exercises complete control over it from one end of heaven to the other (cf. Ps 19:6), and over the entire realm of creation (Deut 4:32). God also **lays the foundation of the earth.** This does not only refer to the creation of the land (cf. Gen 1:1, 9) but to the establishment of the earth to its very core (cf. Job 38:4–6). Since God powerfully created and sovereignly sustains the created order, He has the power and wisdom to fulfill His Word for His people (cf. Isa 48:13). Nothing is too difficult for Him (cf. Gen 18:14; Zech 8:6).

In addition to the macro accomplishment of creating the external universe, the Lord also **forms the spirit of man within him.** God not only designed man's material body (cf. Gen 2:7–8; Ps 139:13–16) but also his immaterial soul. As the Creator and Sustainer of every human life (cf. Acts 17:25–27), Yahweh reigns over the universe and every person therein. Nothing and no one is outside of His sovereign control, and therefore nothing and no one can thwart His purposes or alter His plans. Based on God's nature, Israel's future is absolutely guaranteed.

A STUNNING DEVELOPMENT

"Behold, I am going to make Jerusalem a cup that causes reeling to all the peoples all around. Now *the one* in siege against Jerusalem will also *be* against Judah. But it will be in that day, *that* I will make Jerusalem a heavy stone for all the peoples; all who heave it up will be severely injured. And all the nations of the earth will be gathered against it." (12:2–3)

In verse 2, the prophet began to describe the final battle of the ages, the battle of Armageddon, when a global military force will come against the small, beleaguered nation of Israel (cf. Ezek 38:1–6, 14–16; Dan 11:40–44; Rev 9:13–16; 14:20; 16:12–16). Though this siege will be unlike any other conflagration in history, Zechariah first focused not upon the horrors of this battle but upon God's planned and ordained outcome. With the words **behold, I am going to make,** the Lord declared that His sovereign hand would be in control over this climactic conflict. The verb **make** denotes setting or establishing. It depicts how God will definitively orchestrate these circumstances to bring judgment to the nations and salvation to Israel.

At the apex of the battle, God will make **Jerusalem,** the main target of the enemy's assault, a **cup that causes reeling.** The word **cup** (*saph*) is not the usual word for cup but refers to a large basin from which many people could drink (2 Sam 17:27–29). Such vessels were prominent in the temple (1 Kgs 7:50; 2 Kgs 12:13; Jer 52:19; see discussion on Zech 12:6). In this future global assault, the nations will target Jerusalem, viewing it as a large and inviting cup, from which they could indulge their thirst for violence, death, and power. Instead, when they attack Jerusalem, they will drink deeply of God's wrath, resulting not in revelry but in **reeling.** They will stagger about, as if in a drunken stupor, unable to defend themselves against divine retribution (cf. Isa 51:17–23). This will happen **to all the peoples all around** who are attacking Israel (cf. Ezek 38–39; Joel 3:1–11; Zech 14:1–3). God will incapacitate every enemy **(all)** from every nation **(peoples)** no matter their strategy of attack **(all around).**

The Lord then elaborated that His intervention will not only be for Jerusalem but for all His people. In the final battle, the enemy's attack will not be limited to Jerusalem. The Lord explained that **the one in siege against Jerusalem will also be against Judah.** The war will rage across the nation with Jerusalem as its main objective. Accordingly, God's victory for Jerusalem will mean deliverance for the entire nation.

When the Lord intervenes, the turnaround for Jerusalem (and by extension all of Israel) will be stunning. Thus, God further declared, **"But it will be in that day, that I will make Jerusalem a heavy stone for all the peoples."** This is the first of many times the phrase **in that day** occurs in this chapter (cf. Zech 12:3, 4, 6, 8 [2x], 9, 11; 13:1, 2, 4; 14:4, 6, 8, 9, 13, 20, 21). In repeating this language, Zechariah joined his predecessors in painting a composite picture of the Day of the LORD—the time surrounding Christ's return, when Yahweh will reveal Himself to judge

His enemies and save His people. The phrase **in that day** served as a reminder that, despite the horrors of Armageddon, the Lord will appear in triumph and glory.

At that point, **God will make Jerusalem a heavy stone for all the peoples.** The text already mentioned that Jerusalem will be a "cup that causes reeling" (v. 2), and now Zechariah added that Jerusalem will be a **heavy stone.** This metaphor characterizes Jerusalem as a cumbersome and crushing weight, illustrating the devastating power of God that will destroy Israel's attacking enemies (cf. 1 Kgs 12:11; 2 Chr 10:11). In ancient times, heavy stones were used for physical conditioning. There were even weight-lifting contests involving large boulders. The weak could be crushed under the weight, resulting in serious injury or even death. Such heavy stones illustrate what Jerusalem will be like **for all the peoples** who attempt to destroy her. Thinking they are strong enough to gain victory, Israel's enemies will discover that the power of Israel's sovereign Defender will crush them.

In the next statement, the Lord reiterated that **all who heave it up will be severely injured.** The word **heave** shares the same Hebrew root as the word **heavy** used above. Israel's enemies will **heave** with all their might, but Israel's capital city will be too **heavy,** and they **will be severely injured** beneath its weight. The term **injured** was used in Leviticus 21:5 to describe cuts or lacerations in the flesh (cf. Lev 19:28), and its use here carries that idea. No nation will be able to overpower Israel, but rather all the enemies will be eviscerated under the crushing weight of divine judgment (cf. Zech 14:12). For the people of Israel, the strength to defeat their enemies will come not from the power of the city but from the Lord. As Yahweh said at the beginning of this verse, **"I will make."** He and He alone is responsible for the stunning triumph.

That the Lord is emphatic that His victory on that day will truly be comprehensive is stated clearly. **All the nations of the earth will be gathered against** Israel. The enemy will represent a global force, coming from every direction. From the west, there will be the revived Roman Empire (Dan 2; 7; cf. Rev 17:9–11) as well as nations as far as Tarshish, which is part of Spain (Ezek 38:10–23). There will also be countries from the remotest parts of the north (Ezek 38:6, 15) as well as the south (Dan

11:40) and cast (11:44). As described in the book of Revelation, there will be a global military, an army numbering in the hundreds of millions, that will assemble at the Plain of Megiddo, in the northern region of Israel. They will engage in a battle that rages across the entire length of Israel, spreading over a 200-mile range (cf. Rev 14:20; 16:16). The blood that is spilled will splatter as high as the horses' bridles. As this text states, these nations **will be gathered** by God Himself **against** Jerusalem and the surrounding regions. Though there is a sense in which Satan will gather this army (cf. Rev 16:13–16), God ultimately orchestrates it all. The Lord declared in Zechariah 14:2, "Indeed, I will gather all the nations against Jerusalem to battle." What appears to be a satanic plot against God and the chosen people, will in fact set the stage for God to secure Israel's ultimate triumph.

A SEVERE DEBILITATION

"In that day," declares Yahweh, "I will strike every horse with bewilderment and his rider with madness. But I will open my eyes *to watch* over the house of Judah, while I strike every horse of the peoples with blindness. Then the clans of Judah will say in their hearts, 'A strong support for us are the inhabitants of Jerusalem through Yahweh of hosts, their God.'" (12:4–5)

With the phrase **in that day**, the Lord revealed additional details about how He will achieve victory for Israel—a triumph that **Yahweh** Himself **declares** will take place. When Israel's enemies attack Jerusalem, the Lord will act decisively to disable them. As He said, "**I will strike every horse with bewilderment and his rider with madness.**" Once again, with the words **I will strike**, Yahweh reminded His people that He is the One driving this action forward. He will meet Israel's enemies with devastating power (cf. Exod 2:11–13) and strike **every horse with bewilderment**. The **horse** is symbolic of the strength of one's military resources. In ancient times, horses were a swift and lethal force in battle. In the future, the Lord will cause the technology and weaponry of Satan's forces to be **bewildered**, ineffective, immobilized, and useless.

God will not only damage every enemy weapon but also strike

the soldiers, represented by **his rider, with madness.** In addition to debilitating the enemy's military equipment, the Lord will disorient the soldiers, rendering them ineffective. Thus, He will deal with the totality of the enemy's forces (cf. Zech 10:5; and Exod 15:1 and 21; 2 Kgs 9:18–19; but cf. Esth 6:8–11). **Madness** describes fury or recklessness and was used of Jehu driving his chariot like a maniac (cf. 2 Kgs 9:20). Within a military unit, soldiers who act wildly or irrationally obviously create disorder and chaos. In the battle of Armageddon, the weapons of war will fail, and the soldiers who operate them will panic. In Deuteronomy 28:28, the Lord threatened to curse the Israelites with madness and bewilderment if they did not obey Him. At Armageddon, God will take that curse and put it on Israel's adversaries (cf. Gen 12:3). There were other times in Israel's history when God caused the enemy to be confused (Judg 7:22; 2 Chr 20:22–24; 2 Kgs 7:6–7). But this will be on a scale never seen before (cf. Zech 14:13), sending the enemy force into self-destructive chaos.

While enemy forces are reeling, Yahweh **will open** His eyes **to watch over the house of Judah.** God will not be swept away in the pandemonium of the battle; rather He will omnisciently engage with **open eyes,** vigilantly scrutinizing **the house of Judah** (cf. Ps 34:15; 2 Kgs 19:16; Isa 37:17; Dan 9:18). As noted before (cf. Zech 10:3), the **house of Judah** referred to the leadership of the nation. Though the enemy will be disabled, being consumed by confusion, Israel's leaders will be led by God and empowered to direct the nation to victory.

In further detail of His judgment, the Lord will **strike every horse of the peoples with blindness.** In biblical history, God used blindness to debilitate people (Gen 19:11) and to overcome militaries (cf. 2 Kgs 6:8–23). In this prophecy of the conflict called the battle of Armageddon, God declared that He will blind the **horses.** The first part of verse 4 indicated that the horses will be bewildered; now, Zechariah revealed the reason for their panic—they will not be able to see. While the eyes of the Lord will be open toward Judah, Yahweh will shut the eyes of the enemy. This contrast is amplified by the structure of the verse. The first and last parts of verse 4 concern Israel's enemies, while God's care for Judah is expressed in the middle. That layout depicts Judah surrounded by her enemies (cf. Ps 22:12; Jonah 2:5 for similar parallelism), and God in the midst of His people, protecting them.

When the Lord confounds Israel's enemies and protects His people, they will respond in praise. God continued, **"The clans of Judah will say in their hearts, 'A strong support for us are the inhabitants of Jerusalem through Yahweh of hosts, their God.'"** The designation **clans of Judah** refers to the major regiments of Israel's military (cf. Mic 5:2). The Lord's countermeasures (of blinding and bewildering the enemy) will embolden His people in battle. They will be encouraged **in their hearts** to know that there is **a strong support for** them, denoting both the courage to stand and the strength to overcome. The regiments of Judah will be greatly strengthened by the victory of **the inhabitants of Jerusalem**, recognizing that the triumph in the capital city will turn the tide of the entire battle (see discussion on Zech 12:2b). Importantly, they will rightly understand that Jerusalem's success comes entirely **through Yahweh of hosts, their God.** "Yahweh of hosts," Zechariah's favorite title for God, expresses that Yahweh deploys all His heavenly resources to defend His people. Upon seeing God fight for them, the people of Israel will confess boldly that Yahweh is **their God.**

As the clans of Judah declare these truths **in their hearts**, they will reflect the transforming work of God within them. While this will be discussed with greater detail later (cf. Zech 12:10–13:9), this expression demonstrates how transformative Yahweh's work for His people will be. God's deliverance will be so mighty that it will not only overcome the nation's enemies but even Israel's own unbelief and sinfulness. While God will blind Israel's foes, He will open the eyes of His people so they will call upon Him in saving faith.

A SMASHING DEFEAT

"In that day I will make the clans of Judah like a fiery laver among pieces of wood and a fiery torch among sheaves, so they will consume on the right hand and on the left all the surrounding peoples, while Jerusalem will again be inhabited in its own place—in Jerusalem. Yahweh also will save the tents of Judah first so that the glory of the house of David and the glory of the inhabitants of Jerusalem will not be magnified above Judah." (12:6–7)

With the next occurrence of the phrase **in that day**, the Lord declared what He **will make** happen during the next stage of the battle of Armageddon. The same verb **(will make)** is found in verses 2–3 to describe how the Lord established Jerusalem as a cup of reeling (cf. 12:2) and a heavy stone (cf. 12:3). Here God indicated that His work will spread beyond Jerusalem to the **clans of Judah**, the military regiments from all of Israel (cf. 12:5). Moving from defense to offense, the Lord promised to empower Judah to be **like a fiery laver among pieces of wood and a fiery torch among sheaves**. A **fiery laver**, or firepot, was a vessel filled with hot coals used as a fire starter. A **fiery torch** was also used to kindle a flame. In Judges 7:15–25, Gideon's warriors carried these kinds of torches with them into battle (cf. Judg 15). When placed among **pieces of wood** or **sheaves** of grain, a firepot or torch would immediately ignite the surrounding fuel, causing it to burst into flames. Such an ignition of flames describes what the warriors of Judah will do to their enemies on that eschatological day. They **will consume on the right hand and on the left all the surrounding peoples**. To **consume** is literally "to eat," but can depict a wildfire devouring everything in its path. A vivid example of this appeared in Numbers 16:35 when fire went out from heaven and incinerated, or "ate up," two hundred fifty men who opposed Moses. Only the censers they held remained (Num 16:39; cf. Lev 10:1–2). In a similar way, the devastation wrought on Israel's enemies on that day will be swift, fierce, and all-consuming. No one will escape Judah's divinely empowered counterattack, whether **on the right hand** or **on the left**. **All the surrounding peoples**—every enemy involved in the attack—will die (cf. Rev 19:21). The resulting death toll will be so massive that, according to Ezekiel, it will take seven months to bury the bodies of all those slain in this battle (Ezek 39:12).

It is noteworthy that Zechariah likened Judah to a **fiery laver**, since the word is distinctively used to identify the laver in the tabernacle (cf. Exod 30:18) and the temple (1 Kgs 7:38). The prophet also used temple imagery earlier in this chapter to depict Israel as a "cup" of reeling (cf. 1 Kgs 7:50). By utilizing such language, the Lord pointed to an aspect of His purpose in delivering Israel, namely, to accomplish His plan for the temple. One day, God's Son will return from heaven, vanquish every foe, take global domination, save Israel, and rebuild God's house (cf. Zech 6:11, 13–15). The hope of this future reality would have greatly encouraged those in Zechariah's day, who were themselves called to rebuild the temple.

In contrast to the desolation of the enemy, Zechariah revealed that **Jerusalem will again be inhabited in its own place—in Jerusalem.** Israel's adversaries will be slaughtered and their bodies scattered (cf. Ezek 39:12), but **Jerusalem will again be inhabited.** Rather than perishing in battle, the people of Israel will reassemble in their capital city, where they will dwell in safety and joy. The enemy will disappear, but Jerusalem will remain **in its own place.** The Lord stressed that Israel's capital will stay **in Jerusalem** as a monument to reflect the Lord's loyal love toward Israel, most powerfully demonstrated during the battle of Armageddon.

Beyond the city, God will also display His love for the rest of the Jews, as indicated by the statement: **Yahweh also will save the tents of Judah first.** The **tents of Judah** designate a different group than either the citizens of Jerusalem or the military regiments (clans) of Judah. Instead, **the tents of Judah** refer to families living throughout the land (cf. Gen 18:1; Judg 7:8; 20:8; 1 Sam 13:2; Isa 54:2). On that day, when **Yahweh will** intervene to **save** Israel, the **first** group He will start with will be the common people.

Consequently, **the glory of the house of David and the glory of the inhabitants of Jerusalem will not be magnified above Judah. The house of David** will have a form of **glory,** or beauty and honor, because it is royalty; and **the inhabitants of Jerusalem** will also enjoy honor because they reside in God's chosen city. Yet they will not win the battle through their own strength, nor will God rescue them first. For those reasons, they will not be **magnified above** the common people of **Judah.** The Lord's deliverance will cause every person in Israel—from the most common to the most elite—to recognize in humility that their only boast is in the Lord (cf. Jer 9:24).

A SUPERNATURAL DEFENSE

"In that day Yahweh will defend the inhabitants of Jerusalem, and the one who stumbles among them in that day will be like David, and the house of David *will be* like God, like the angel of Yahweh before them. And it will be in that day, *that* I will seek to destroy all the nations that come against Jerusalem." (12:8–9)

With another reference to **in that day**, Zechariah shifted from focusing on what God will do against Israel's enemies to how **Yahweh will defend the inhabitants of Jerusalem**. God will focus on **the inhabitants of Jerusalem** not because they are better than the rest of Israel or more deserving of His love (cf. Zech 12:7). Instead, Zechariah established that Jerusalem will be the epicenter of the battle; what will take place in that city will represent what happens for the entire nation. As **Yahweh will defend** this city, so will He defend all His people. The word **defend** carries the idea of being a shield. God used this very word in the days of Hezekiah to describe how He would defend Jerusalem from Assyria (2 Kgs 19:32–34; Isa 31:5; 37:35; 38:6). As part of that divine defense, the Angel of Yahweh slaughtered the Assyrian army in a single night, so that not one arrow was fired against Jerusalem (2 Kgs 19:35). At the end of the age, the Lord will engage in an even more miraculous defense and deliverance of Israel. Not only will Jerusalem be protected, but it will become a cup of reeling (Zech 12:2) and a heavy stone that crushes the enemy (12:3). Though her adversaries will be confused and consumed (12:4–6), Jerusalem will stand resilient and inhabited as Israel's capital city (12:6b).

God will also embolden the citizens of Jerusalem. As verse 8 explains, **"the one who stumbles among them in that day will be like David."** A soldier who **stumbles** was not merely one who lost his footing in battle, but one who proved to be inept, weak, or even cowardly (cf. Jer 46:6, 12; Lev 26:34–39). Zechariah prophesied that God would transform the weak warriors of Israel and make them like **David**, the epitome of military courage and strength. David was so renowned as a hero that the women sang in 1 Samuel 18:7: "Saul has struck his thousands, and David his ten thousands." In the last days, before the Lord sets up His earthly kingdom, there will be an entire population of redeemed Israelites with the boldness and bravery of David. The weakest inhabitant of Jerusalem will be heroic.

If that is what the weak will become, what about the strong? The prophet revealed that **the house of David will be like God**. On that day, the royal line that represents the leadership of Jerusalem will manifest the authority of God Himself. An analogous situation occurred in Exodus when God spoke to Moses about Aaron. The Lord explained that "he [Aaron] will become as a mouth for you [Moses], and you will become as God to him" (Exod 4:16). Later, God said to Moses, "See, I set you *as* God to Pharaoh, and your brother Aaron shall be your prophet" (7:1). In the days of the Exodus, because God so empowered Moses, when Israel's leader spoke, God spoke through him. In the future, God will similarly empower the royal house of David.

Along with this, the house of David will be **like the angel of Yahweh before them**. Since this phrase parallels the statement that the house of David will be like God, the **angel of Yahweh** must be understood to be divine—a truth already attested in earlier revelation (cf. Exod 13:21; 14:21; 23:20–23). The Angel of Yahweh often showcased God's power as the supreme warrior. For example, as noted above, He put to death 185,000 Assyrians in a single night to defend Jerusalem (2 Kgs 19:35). So, when the **house of David** becomes like the Angel of Yahweh, the prophet is declaring that the royal line will be equally fierce in defending the city. In addition, because the Angel of Yahweh is the Messiah (see discussion on Zech 1:12; 3:1, 5, 6), the house of David will reflect the glory of Christ. In fact, it will be Christ who will lead this spectacular host, for the Angel of Yahweh will go **before them**.

Verse 9 repeats the phrase **in that day**, reiterating the eschatological nature of the divine promises in this passage. Having promised to bless His people (v. 8), the Lord continued by pledging to judge their enemies (v. 9). Yahweh declared, **"I will seek to destroy."** In saying **I will seek**, God expressed that He will proactively pursue every foe (cf. Exod 2:15; 4:24; 1 Sam 25:26; Esth 9:2; Num 35:23) and eliminate every threat (cf. Zech 12:2, 3, 4, 6). In doing so, the Lord will complete a work He disclosed long ago. This word **destroy** was consistently used in God's promises to vanquish the nations in the days of Moses and Joshua. Speaking to Israel about the Canaanites, Moses said in Deuteronomy 9:3, "So you shall know today that it is Yahweh your God who is crossing over before you as a consuming fire. He will destroy them, and He will subdue them before you, so that you may dispossess them and make them perish quickly, just as Yahweh has spoken to you." Moses later added, "It is Yahweh your God who will cross ahead of you; He will destroy these nations before you, and you shall dispossess them" (Deut 31:3; cf. also 31:4; Josh 9:24; 2 Kgs 21:9; Amos 2:9). What God promised He would do in the books of Deuteronomy and Joshua, He will fulfill at the end of the age.

The Lord promised to destroy **all the nations that come against Jerusalem.** The phrase **all the nations** (cf. v. 3) was already used to indicate that God will gather the nations against Jerusalem in order to consume them. Here, Zechariah repeated the phrase to show that what God intended will indeed happen. No one will escape. Though in the days of Joshua various peoples and nations survived, in the future God will not allow His adversaries to escape. On that day, He will destroy every enemy. Those opposing Israel will not merely be repulsed but defeated and utterly destroyed. Thus, the conquest of the Promised Land and the ultimate deliverance of Israel will be accomplished.

As this passage reveals, one day a satanically inspired global army will surround Israel and attack Jerusalem. Israel's odds of victory, from a human perspective, will be zero. The nation will stand on the brink of annihilation. But the moment when all hope seems lost will be the moment of "the blessed hope and the appearing of the glory of our great God and Savior, Jesus Christ" (Titus 2:13). The Messiah will suddenly appear, accompanied by the host of heaven, and He will engage in the battle to deliver His people, defeat their enemies, and establish His earthly kingdom, centered in Jerusalem. Though the promises of Zechariah were given specifically to Israel, the saints of every age will be present with Christ during His millennial reign, serving Him and reigning with Him as He rules with righteousness and peace (cf. 1 Cor 6:2; Rev 20:4–6).

Israel's Final Deliverance: Spiritual Salvation

31

Zechariah 12:10–14

"And I will pour out on the house of David and on the inhabitants of Jerusalem the Spirit of grace and of supplication, so that they will look on Me whom they have pierced; and they will mourn for Him, as one mourns for an only son, and they will weep bitterly over Him like the bitter weeping over a firstborn. In that day there will be great mourning in Jerusalem, like the mourning of Hadadrimmon in the plain of Megiddo. And the land will mourn, each family alone; the family of the house of David alone and their wives alone; the family of the house of Nathan alone and their wives alone; the family of the house of Levi alone and their wives alone; the family of the Shimeites alone and their wives alone; all the families that remain, each family alone and their wives alone."

The deadly consequence of Adam's sin, both for him and his descendants, was not only physical but spiritual (Gen 2:17; Rom 5:12–14). As a result, sinners need far more than salvation from bodily harm. Though the Lord Jesus miraculously healed many sick and disabled people, He repeatedly emphasized the priority of spiritual life over temporal health. In Matthew 10:28, He reminded His listeners that the ultimate danger is not physical suffering in this life but God's eternal wrath in the next. He said, "Do not fear those who kill the body but are unable to kill the soul; but rather fear Him who is able to destroy both soul and body in hell." In Mark 8:36, He punctuated that point with a rhetorical question: "What does it profit a man to gain the whole world, and forfeit his soul?"

As Zechariah 12:1–9 revealed, at the end of the age God will provide physical deliverance for Israel. But He will not stop there. His plan for His people of that generation will culminate in their spiritual salvation. The Messiah will return not only to conquer Israel's enemies, but also to captivate their hearts. At the battle of Armageddon, Israel will face a massive assault from a global force, yet the Lord will shield and protect His people. In response, they will remember God's promises and look to Him in saving faith. They will realize that Yahweh alone is their defender.

The Lord will not only reveal Himself to be their Conqueror but also their Savior. As Zechariah prophesied, God will pour out His Spirit on His people (Zech 12:10a), causing them to respond with sorrowful repentance (12:10b) resulting in a national revival (12:11–14). He will open their eyes to look upon "Me whom they have pierced" (12:10), so that Israel will know that Jesus is the Messiah, the One crucified for the sins of His people (cf. John 19:37). These truths will sink deep into their hearts, and then the words of Romans 11:26 will be fulfilled, that "all Israel will be saved."

THE SOURCE OF ISRAEL'S SALVATION

"And I will pour out on the house of David and on the inhabitants of Jerusalem the Spirit of grace and of supplication..." (12:10a)

The Lord's opening words in this passage—**and I**—emphasized that Israel's future conversion will be a work of divine grace. Just as the Lord will fight to protect and preserve His people physically (cf. Zech 12:1–9), so He will both initiate and accomplish their spiritual deliverance. The salvation of a future generation of Israelites, like the salvation of sinners in any age, is entirely God's doing. He pursues the lost, draws them to Himself, and regenerates them by the power of His

Spirit (cf. Luke 19:10; John 3:3; 6:37). Paul emphasized God's initiative in salvation when he wrote that "God demonstrates His own love toward us, in that while we were yet sinners, Christ died for us" (Rom 5:8). In Ephesians 2, he further explained that sinners are hopelessly dead in their sins, "but God, being rich in mercy because of His great love with which He loved us" (v. 4) has made salvation available through His Son. Paul explicitly stated that salvation is not a result of good works on the part of the sinner but is a monergistic work of divine grace alone (vv. 8–9). The opening words of Zechariah 12:10 reiterate that truth—that salvation is entirely God's work.

Yahweh will save Israel by His Spirit regenerating the nation. The verb **pour out** paints a vivid image of God drenching the people with His Spirit as one douses an object with water. In other Old Testament contexts, it depicts flooding a place with blood (Lev 4:7, 18, 25, 30, 34), water (cf. Amos 5:8; 9:6), or even judgment (Ezek 20:8, 13, 21). Thus, when God pours out His Spirit on Israel, His people will be completely saturated with the Spirit's presence and ministry. As Yahweh announced through the prophet Ezekiel, "I will not hide My face from them any longer, for I will have poured out My Spirit on the house of Israel" (Ezek 39:29; cf. Joel 2:28). Centuries earlier, in Numbers 11:29, Moses exclaimed, "Would that all the people of Yahweh were prophets, that Yahweh would put His Spirit upon them!" Zechariah's prophecy reinforced that same expectation.

The future recipients of this divine outpouring, specifically identified in verse 10, will include **the house of David** and **the inhabitants of Jerusalem**. Because Jerusalem is the central city (Gen 14:18; Josh 10:3; 2 Sam 5:5; 2 Kgs 19:31; Isa 2:2), it is representative of God's eschatological activity throughout the nation. By highlighting both **the house of David** and **the inhabitants of Jerusalem**, the Lord emphasized that His saving work will affect both the royal line and the regular people of Jerusalem (see 12:7). When God saves Israel, there will be no distinction between upper and lower classes (Rom 2:11). The entire population will experience the regenerating work of His Spirit.

The **Spirit of grace and of supplication** denotes two primary aspects of the Spirit's ministry to Israel at that time. First, the Spirit will bestow the kindness and unmerited favor of divine **grace** on the people. He will regenerate their hearts (cf. John 3:1–15), so that they embrace the Lord in faith and repentance (cf. Deut 30:6). As a result, those in Jerusalem will respond with **supplication**, making requests to God in prayer. The Hebrew words for "grace" and "supplication" share the same root, indicating that the people of Israel will receive grace even as they ask for grace. Through the Holy Spirit, they will come to understand that salvation is entirely a gift of divine grace (cf. Luke 18:9–14). For the first time in history, the nation will wholly depend on the grace of God, rather than resting on their own wisdom or self-righteous works (cf. Rom 10:1–4).

THE SORROW FOR ISRAEL'S SIN

"...so that they will look on Me whom they have pierced; and they will mourn for Him, as one mourns for an only son, and they will weep bitterly over Him like the bitter weeping over a firstborn." (12:10b)

Because of the Spirit's work, Israel **will look** to Yahweh in faith (cf. Num 21:9) and hope (cf. Isa 51:1). They will also gaze upon Him under tremendous conviction, for they will realize that He is the One whom **they have pierced**. The term **pierced** vividly portrays a shameful and violent execution or death (cf. Deut 21:22–23; also see Num 25:8; Judg 9:54; 1 Sam 31:4; 1 Chr 10:4; Isa 13:15; Jer 37:10; 51:4; Lam 4:9; Zech 13:3). The Lord made it clear that Israel would pierce **Me**, a reference to Yahweh Himself. Though unthinkable, at some point in the nation's history, after Zechariah but before the end of the age, Israel would subject the Lord Himself to a shameful and violent death. Those living in Zechariah's day must have been stunned by this revelation. They undoubtedly wondered, "How could this be?"

The Apostle John answered that question directly. In recounting the crucifixion of the Lord Jesus, John cited Zechariah 12:10, noting its fulfillment at the cross (John 19:37). At Calvary, the Messiah was pierced for the sins of His people (cf. Isa 53:5). Because He is truly God and truly man, Christ alone can fulfill Zechariah's prophecy, making it one of the clearest attestations of Messiah's deity in the Old Testament. One day, Israel will come to realize the truth about Christ Jesus, the One whom they put to death in a violent and shameful way.

When that day comes, **they will mourn for Him**, meaning literally to strike the chest in heartfelt grief (cf. Isa 32:12). Such strong lament occurred at funerals and expressed how fervently a person loved the deceased (cf. Gen 23:2; 50:10; 1 Sam 25:1; 2 Sam 1:12). Israel will express overwhelming sorrow for Christ **as one mourns for an only son** (cf. Luke 7:12; 9:38; Rom 8:32). When Christ returns, the people of Israel will display that level of profound sorrow. They will realize their culpability in betraying the greatest son of Israel, God's only Son (cf. John 3:16–18). Their deep regret will convey their newly found love for Him, as they look on Him with eyes of faith.

In their sorrow, the people **will weep bitterly over Him**, expressing their anguish and self-loathing (cf. Exod 1:14; 1 Sam 30:6; Ruth 1:20). Their weeping will be **like the bitter weeping over a firstborn**. In Old Testament times, because the **firstborn** led his family and carried on its legacy (Gen 49:3; Exod 4:22; 13:1–16; 22:29–30; Num 18:15; Deut 21:17), his death represented a catastrophic loss for the family. Hence, for someone to kill the firstborn son of their own family would be unthinkable (cf. 2 Kgs 3:27). Yet, this is what the nation did to their Messiah (John 1:11). Israel put to death the firstborn of all creation (cf. Col 1:15). When Christ returns in triumph, the people will realize the atrocity of their blasphemous apostasy and express their devastation with bitter weeping. But as those regenerated by the Holy Spirit, their tears will flow from a godly sorrow indicative of repentance unto life (cf. 2 Cor 7:9–10).

THE SCOPE OF ISRAEL'S REPENTANCE

"In that day there will be great mourning in Jerusalem, like the mourning of Hadadrimmon in the plain of Megiddo. And the land will mourn, each family alone; the family of the house of David alone and their wives alone; the family of the house of Nathan alone and their wives alone; the family of the house of Levi alone and their wives alone; the family of the Shimeites alone and their wives alone; all the families that remain, each family alone and their wives alone." (12:11–14)

With the last occurrence of the phrase **in that day** in this chapter, Zechariah depicted the eschatological spiritual transformation that will pervade the entire nation. The revival will begin in Israel's capital as **there will be great mourning in Jerusalem.** The **mourning** described in the previous verse will build and become **great,** even **like the mourning of Hadadrimmon in the plain of Megiddo.** This referred to the death of the beloved King Josiah recorded in 2 Chronicles 35 (cf. 2 Kgs 23). Josiah was a righteous ruler who rediscovered the book of the law, carried out the necessary reforms for temple worship, restored the celebration of Passover, purged the land of idolatrous practices, and executed the false priests (2 Kgs 23). After he was killed in battle, the people mourned for him with intense grief. As 2 Chronicles 35 described, "All Judah and Jerusalem mourned for Josiah. Then Jeremiah chanted a *lament* for Josiah. And all the male and female singers speak about Josiah in their lamentations to this day. And they made them a statute in Israel; behold, they are also written in the lamentations" (vv. 24–25). Josiah's death prompted mourning throughout the entire country. When the Messiah returns, Israel's sorrow over His death will be far greater.

The mourning that begins in Jerusalem will take hold of the nation, so that the rest of the **land** of Israel **will mourn.** The entire population will express grief and repentance, from the nation corporately down to **each family** individually, showing that God will transform every part of Israelite society—starting with every family. The word **alone,** repeated eleven times in this passage, describes the personal, private, and sincere nature of this repentance. Each family in Israel will repent before the Lord, doing so from the heart, under the convicting power of the Spirit.

To illustrate that every family will mourn on this day, the Lord identified specific families that will repent. He started with **the family of the house of David alone and their wives alone.** Every person in Israel, including those from the royal house of David, will be convicted and transformed by God's Spirit. Both the men of the **family** and **their wives** will express godly sorrow. In fact, the word **wives** simply means "women," indicating that God's saving work will extend to all the members of the household, both male and female. Each of them **alone**, or individually, will respond to God in genuine repentance and saving faith.

The royal line will not be the only family to repent. The Lord also mentioned **the family of the house of Nathan alone and their wives alone**. While the crown passed through the line of Solomon, Nathan was the third eldest son of David (2 Sam 5:14; 1 Chr 3:5), and his house was part of David's broader family. Famous individuals such as Zerubbabel (cf. Luke 3:27, 31) and Mary, the mother of Jesus, descended from this line (Luke 3:23, 31).

God's saving work will also reach **the family of the house of Levi alone and their wives alone**. This refers to the priestly family through Aaron and his sons Nadab, Abihu, Eleazar, and Ithamar (Exod 28:1; Num 3; Deut 10:8–9). Like those in positions of political power, those in spiritual leadership will also repent. The entire **house** of Levi— including husbands and their **wives**—will embrace the Messiah with repentant faith.

Additionally, **the family of the Shimeites alone and their wives alone** will also join this national repentance. The **family of the Shimeites** was in the tribe of Levi, well-known at the time of Zechariah.[1] Because they descended through Gershom (Num 3:17–18), whereas the priestly line came through Kohath (Exod 6:8–26; 1 Chr 6:1–3), the Shimeites were not priests but those who assisted them. When the Messiah returns, He will not only save those with priestly privilege but also those who serve alongside them.

The Lord forcefully concluded His promise of future salvation by sweeping up **all the families that remain, each family alone and their wives alone**. This expansive statement encompasses the whole of Israel (**all the families**) that will survive the battle of Armageddon (**remain**). The men of **each family alone** along with **their wives** and children will join in Israel's national repentance. Having been regenerated by the Holy Spirit, they will each respond with godly sorrow and look to the Messiah in saving faith.

---

1 Eugene Merrill, *Haggai, Zechariah, Malachi: An Exegetical Commentary* (Dallas, TX: Biblical Studies Press, 2003), 297.

In describing Israel's future conversion, the Lord systematically identified each layer of Israelite society, including the royal line of David (through Solomon), the non-royal line of David (through Nathan), the priestly line (through Levi), the non-priestly line (the Shimeites), and every other Jewish family living when Christ returns (those that remain). The clear implication of the text is that every individual person, regardless of social status or rank, will respond in heartfelt sorrow, genuine repentance, and saving faith. The people will each embrace the Messiah on their own **(alone)** because their hearts will be transformed by the Spirit (cf. Zech 12:10). Corporately and individually, they will look with eyes of faith on the Lord Jesus Christ and confess the words Isaiah prophesied long ago, "He was pierced through for our transgressions, He was crushed for our iniquities" (Isa 53:5). As noted above, at that moment the promise of Romans 11:26 will be fulfilled. By God's grace, "All Israel will be saved."

The Cleansing of Israel

32

Zechariah 13:1–9

"In that day a fountain will be opened for the house of David and for the inhabitants of Jerusalem, for sin and for impurity. And it will be in that day," declares Yahweh of hosts, "*that* I will cut off the names of the idols from the land, and they will no longer be remembered; and I will also cause the prophets and the unclean spirit to pass away from the land. And it will be that if anyone still prophesies, then his father and mother who gave birth to him will say to him, 'You shall not live, for you have spoken falsely in the name of Yahweh'; and his father and mother who gave birth to him will pierce him through when he prophesies. And it will be in that day, *that* the prophets will each be ashamed of his vision when he prophesies, and they will not put on a hairy mantle in order to deceive; but he will say, 'I am not a prophet; I am a cultivator of the ground, for a man sold me as a slave in my youth.' And one will say to him, 'What are these wounds struck *here* between your arms?' Then he will say, '*Those* with which I was struck in the house of my friends.'"

"Awake, O sword, against My Shepherd
And against the man, My Associate,"
Declares Yahweh of hosts.
"Strike the Shepherd that the sheep may be scattered;

And I will turn My hand against the little ones.
And it will be in all the land,"
Declares Yahweh,
"That two parts in it will be cut off *and* breathe their last;
But the third will be left in it.
And I will bring the third part through the fire
And refine them as silver is refined
And test them as gold is tested.
They will call on My name,
And I will answer them;
I will say, 'They are My people,'
And they will say, 'Yahweh is my God.'"

As Zechariah 12 foretold, during the battle of Armageddon the Messiah will suddenly appear to rescue His people (cf. Rev 19:11–21). But His deliverance will be more than physical. It will be spiritual. In that moment, His people will look to Him in saving faith, responding with godly sorrow and genuine repentance (Zech 12:10). They will subsequently enter His kingdom in triumph, enjoying the blessings and glory of fellowship with their Savior. At that time, as God declared earlier in Zechariah, "They will be as though I had not rejected them" (10:6). The memory of the nation's disobedience throughout its history, along with the divine discipline that accompanied it, will be forgotten in the exhilaration and exuberance of millennial joy.

The promise of national repentance in chapter 12 is followed by the promise of spiritual cleansing in chapter 13. The Lord will purify His people (cf. Ezek 37:23), consecrating them in their love and devotion to Him. Centuries before Zechariah, at the beginning of the nation's history, "Yahweh spoke to Moses, saying: 'Speak to all the congregation of the sons of Israel and say to them, "You shall be holy, for I, Yahweh your God, am holy…. Do not turn to idols or make for yourselves molten gods; I am Yahweh your God"'" (Lev 19:1–4). Despite that divine mandate, the Israelites repeatedly defiled themselves with idols, provoking God's wrath and therefore enduring punishment (cf. Exod 32:1–10; 1 Kgs 11:4–5;

2 Kgs 17:7–18; Jer 3:7–10; Ezek 20:13–16; Amos 5:25–26).

Nonetheless, as Zechariah 13 reveals, the day is coming when God will purify His people, completely redeeming an entire generation of Israelites (cf. Rom 11:26). Having poured out His Spirit on them, causing them to repent in faith (Zech 12:10), He will cleanse them from their iniquity. The structure of this chapter can be organized under four headings related to Israel's future purification: the promise that it will happen (13:1–2), the picture of what it will produce (13:3–6), the prerequisite that makes it possible (13:7), and the process by which God will complete it (13:8–9). Though their sin was severe, and their judgment long throughout history, the Lord promised to purify Israel by cleansing them of their iniquity and consecrating them to Himself.

THE PROMISE OF PURIFICATION

"In that day a fountain will be opened for the house of David and for the inhabitants of Jerusalem, for sin and for impurity. And it will be in that day," declares Yahweh of hosts, "that I will cut off the names of the idols from the land, and they will no longer be remembered; and I will also cause the prophets and the unclean spirit to pass away from the land." (13:1–2)

The text begins with the expression **in that day**, referring to the eschatological Day of the LORD. Because that same expression is repeated in Zechariah 12, its use here links the content of Zechariah 13 to the previous chapter. On the day that God pours out His Spirit and all Israel repents (cf. 12:10), the Lord will also cleanse His people from their sin. The prophet likened God's cleansing work to a **fountain**. As opposed to a cistern (cf. Jer 2:13), fountains provide a steady source of fresh water. An **opened** fountain continuously pours forth water in great abundance. At the outset of the millennial kingdom, God will flood His people with the purifying work of His Son. From the royalty of **the house of David** to the commoners among **the inhabitants of Jerusalem**, all Israel will experience the Lord's purifying work.

Sin stresses the criminality of any infraction or violation of God's holiness (e.g., Gen 42:22; Exod 32:30–34; Lev 1:1–6; Deut 9:16–18; 1 Sam

15:24; Ps 51:4). The parallel term **impurity**, used to refer to a woman's menstruation (e.g., Lev 12:1–5) or to defilement with a corpse (e.g., Num 19:11–13), emphasizes the contaminating stain of sin that renders a person unsuitable to be in God's holy presence. By removing sin and impurity, God will not only make His people right with Him, but He will also make it possible for them to draw near to Him. As Ezekiel prophesied, Yahweh will "sprinkle clean water on you, and you will be clean," and so "you will be My people, and I will be your God" (Ezek 36:25, 28). One day, the Lord will purify His people and purge the land so thoroughly that it will be as if a fountain of cleansing gushed forth to wash the nation (cf. Hos 2:14–20).

With another occurrence of the phrase **in that day** (in v. 2), Zechariah revealed two outcomes from Israel's cleansing: first, the Lord will **cut off the names of the idols from the land, and they will no longer be remembered**; and second, He will **cause the** false **prophets and the unclean spirit to pass away from the land**. Throughout Israel's history, false prophets often led the people into idolatry and deadly error. During the reign of Ahab, for example, some 450 false prophets opposed the one true prophet Elijah (1 Kgs 18:20–46).

Nevertheless, **Yahweh of hosts** declared that one day He will eliminate the sin of idolatry and the false prophets who promote it. The Lord vowed to **cut off**, or completely eradicate, **the names of the idols from the land**. God will eliminate idolatry from the nation to the extent that even **the names of the idols** will be forgotten. In Scripture, a name is not merely a title but represents one's character, essence, and power (cf. Matt 28:19; Acts 4:12). People went to great lengths so that their name would be preserved (cf. Gen 11:4; 2 Sam 18:18; Isa 56:5). By cutting off **the names of the idols** from Israel, God will root out every trace of false religion. No evidence nor influence of pagan worship will remain in the entire **land**. Furthermore, Israel's past idols **will no longer be remembered**. The Lord will cleanse His people so thoroughly that even the memory of false gods will be erased (cf. Hos 2:17).

Yahweh will deal with false prophets in a similar fashion. He will **cause the prophets and the unclean spirit to pass away from the land**. The Lord will personally silence not only the false **prophets**, the messengers of damning error (cf. Isa 30:1; Ezek 13:1–2), but also the **unclean spirit** behind such blasphemous falsehood (1 Kgs 22:19–23; cf. Ps 106:34–39; Deut 32:17; Ezek 14:1–11; Jer 28). As the Apostle Paul explained, pagan religion is built on the doctrine of demons (1 Cor 10:20; 1 Tim 4:1). The Lord will not tolerate any satanic deception in His kingdom (Rev 20:3). False prophecy in all its forms will **pass away** from the **land** of Israel, so that not even a hint remains (cf. 1 Kgs 15:12; 2 Chr 15:8).

THE PICTURE OF PURIFICATION

"And it will be that if anyone still prophesies, then his father and mother who gave birth to him will say to him, 'You shall not live, for you have spoken falsely in the name of Yahweh'; and his father and mother who gave birth to him will pierce him through when he prophesies. And it will be in that day, *that* the prophets will each be ashamed of his vision when he prophesies, and they will not put on a hairy mantle in order to deceive; but he will say, 'I am not a prophet; I am a cultivator of the ground, for a man sold me as a slave in my youth.' And one will say to him, 'What are these wounds struck *here* between your arms?' Then he will say, '*Those* with which I was struck in the house of my friends.'" (13:3–6)

With the phrase **and it will be**, the Lord continued to describe Israel's future cleansing by painting a hypothetical picture to illustrate the zeal His people will subsequently have for righteousness and truth. As Yahweh explained, **if anyone** among the false prophets **still prophesies**, he will be silenced by those who hear him. This was not to suggest that there will still be false prophets in the millennial kingdom. The Lord had already revealed that He would cut them off completely from the land. Hypothetically, if such a situation were to arise, the false prophet would have no support. The very parents of a false prophet would intervene. Though they **gave birth to him** and gave him life, they would declare, "**You shall not live.**" Both parents—**his father and mother**—would be united in prosecuting their son. They would do so because he had **spoken falsely in the name of Yahweh**. In their zeal for **Yahweh** (cf. Zech 8:3, 19), they would neither tolerate **false** teaching nor bear to see the **name** of the Lord tarnished (cf. Ps 69:9). Such righteous zeal would fulfill what God commanded in Deuteronomy 18:20: "But the prophet who speaks a word presumptuously in My name which I have not commanded him to speak, or which he speaks in the name of other gods, that prophet shall die." This passion for truth would also fulfill Deuteronomy 13:6–9, in which Moses declared:

> If your brother, your mother's son, or your son or daughter, or the wife you cherish, or your friend who is as your own soul, entices you secretly, saying, "Let us go and serve other gods" (whom neither you nor your fathers have known, of the gods of the peoples who are around you, near you or far from you, from one end of the earth to the other end), you shall not be willing to accept him or listen to him; and your eye shall not pity him; and you shall not spare him or conceal him. But you shall surely kill him; your hand shall be first against him to put him to death, and afterwards the hand of all the people.

The Lord demanded His people's loyalty over their love for family and friends (cf. Matt 10:37). In the millennial kingdom, God's people will be characterized by that kind of wholehearted devotion to Yahweh.

The Lord continued by noting that, were such a situation to arise, the parents would not merely condemn their son's actions, they would execute capital punishment against him. As the text explains, **"his father and mother who gave birth to him will pierce him through when he prophesies."** To **pierce through** describes a violent execution, one driven by God's wrath and curse (cf. Deut 21:22–23; Zech 12:10). In Numbers, Phinehas pierced Zimri and Cozbi with a spear for their flagrant immorality (Num 25:8; cf. Judg 9:54; 1 Sam 31:4; 1 Chr 10:4; Ps 106:30). To pierce someone through with a sword or spear constituted the deadly punishment for the worst offenses, thereby underscoring the heinous nature of false prophecy. Though the scenario is only hypothetical, the **father and mother** serve as a vivid illustration of the zeal for God that will one day characterize the entire nation. With that kind of passion for holiness and truth, Israel will never again tolerate the sin of false prophecy.

The phrase **and it will be in that day** introduces a second hypothetical scenario, illustrating the extent of Israel's cleansing and the complete removal of false religion from the land. At that future time, not only will God's people be zealous against spiritual deception and error, but if there were false **prophets,** they would **each be ashamed of his vision when he prophesies.** The verb ashamed does not merely denote timidity, but self-loathing and the fear of being discovered (cf. Isa 42:17; Jer 22:18–23; Mic 3:7). Instead of boasting in a **vision,** as false prophets often did when they supposedly **prophesied, each** would be deeply embarrassed by his past association with idolatry. To avoid being found out, they would disguise their appearance. They **will not put on a hairy mantle,** a garment made of animal skin with the fur intact, a common form of clothing for prophets. True prophets like Elijah (1 Kgs 19:13; 2 Kgs 2:8), Elisha (2 Kgs 2:13–14), and John the Baptist (Matt 3:4) wore such garments. Because a hairy mantle was associated with the prophetic office, false prophets often wore them **to gain credibility for themselves and their lies** (1 Kgs 13:13–19; John 8:44; 2 Cor 11:14). Even in the modern day, false prophets often wear clerical garb in an effort to gain influence and prestige. However, in the Millennium no false prophet would even dare to dress like a prophet, much less engage in his former deception. If asked, he would deny it, saying, **"I am not a prophet."** Instead, he would insist, **"I am a cultivator of the ground,"** attempting to pass himself off as an upstanding Israelite farmer. This description **(cultivator of the ground)** appears frequently throughout Scripture and refers to a variety of people, beginning with Adam (Gen 3:23; cf. 2 Sam 9:10) and even including the true prophet Amos (Amos 7:14). In a further attempt to avoid culpability, a former false prophet might claim, **"A man sold me as a slave in my youth."** The implication would be that he could not have participated in false religion, having no freedom to do so because he was enslaved from the time of his **youth.** By making these claims, the prophet would seek to avoid responsibility and the corresponding repercussions.

Despite the false prophet's efforts, no one would believe his excuses and dubious claims. Rather, **one will** point to markings on his body and **say to him:** "**What are these wounds struck** *here* **between** your arms?" The term **wounds** denotes serious and visible injuries on the body, consistent with the self-flagellation in which false prophets often engaged (cf. 1 Kgs 22:35; 2 Kgs 8:29). In 1 Kings 18:28, the prophets of Baal "cried with a loud voice and gashed themselves according to their custom with swords and lances until the blood gushed out on them." Such practices were the reason God warned in Deuteronomy 14:1, "You are the sons of Yahweh your God; you shall not gash yourselves nor shave your forehead for the sake of the dead" (cf. Lev 19:28; Jer 16:6). Given the clear connection between paganism and violent self-asceticism, the false prophet's wounds would arouse suspicion. That is especially the case since the wounds will be **between your arms**, or literally, between your hands. This expression suggests that these wounds would be on the prophet's chest (cf. 2 Kgs 9:24), a part of the body tied to pagan rituals in the ancient near east. A false prophet would do anything to hide his true identity, but the evidence of his past religious activity would expose him.

When pressed about his scars, the false prophet would assert, "**I was struck in the house of my friends.**" The word for **friends** literally means "those who love me." Some have postulated that this is a reference to the man's parents, mentioned in verse 3. But that cannot be the case, since the parents did not merely injure their son but put him to death. Others have suggested that the **friends** refer to other false prophets in the context of immoral rituals and idolatrous worship (e.g., Hos 2:7; Ezek 16:33; Jer 22:20, 22). But that interpretation is also unlikely, since this prophet's goal is to distance himself from false worship, not to admit his association with it. The best interpretation is that this prophet is simply making a flimsy and far-fetched excuse for the scars on his chest. In that case, the **friends** would merely refer to his close associates and trusted companions. The thin veneer of his alibi will be immediately obvious to those inquiring, since no true friends would inflict such harm on someone they loved.

The preposterous excuses of this imaginary false prophet serve as a powerful illustration. In the Messiah's kingdom, false religion will be so taboo that no one will dare associate with it. Were a former false prophet to be there, he would go to great lengths and illogical extremes to avoid being found out. Though hypothetical, this scenario punctuated the Lord's point: one day He will thoroughly cleanse His people of their sin. They will subsequently be characterized by a holy zeal for the truth and a deep hatred for falsehood.

THE PREREQUISITE FOR PURIFICATION

"Awake, O sword, against My Shepherd
And against the man, My Associate,"
Declares Yahweh of hosts.
"Strike the Shepherd that the sheep may be scattered;
And I will turn My hand against the little ones." (13:7)

Having illustrated the folly and futility of the false prophets, the Lord turned His attention to the true Shepherd, the Messiah. In so doing, He highlighted the divine prerequisite for Israel's spiritual cleansing—the substitutionary atoning sacrifice of the Good Shepherd who would lay down His life for the sheep (cf. John 10:11; 1 Pet 2:24–25). Were it not for the work of Christ on the cross, spiritual cleansing would not be possible for any sinner, whether Jew or Gentile (cf. John 10:14–16). Yet, He gave Himself for His sheep so "that He might redeem [them] from all lawlessness, and purify for Himself a people for His own possession, zealous for good works" (Titus 2:14).

Yahweh depicted the Messiah's sacrifice by declaring, "**Awake, O sword.**" With these words, God summoned into action the instrument of divine battle (cf. Isa 51:9; Jer 50:35–38) and devastating judgment (Jer 47:6; Ezek 21:25–27). In a stunning twist, God commanded the sword of His wrath to be turned **against** the Messiah, so that He might bear the iniquity of His people (Isa 53:10–12). The Lord referred to the Messiah as **My Shepherd.** In contrast to the false shepherds (Zech 10:3; 11:3, 15–16), the true **Shepherd,** the Messiah, cares for His flock (cf. 11:7). Nonetheless, He would be betrayed by the nation (11:12–13). God revealed that His sword would turn against the Messiah so that, through His suffering, He might fulfill His role both as the rejected Shepherd and the redeeming Savior.

The Lord further described the Messiah as **the man, My Associate.** **Man** emphasized Christ's humanity (cf. Prov 24:5; Dan 8:15), while the description **My Associate** conveyed mutual fellowship and equality (cf. Lev 19:17; 25:17), in this case, with Yahweh Himself (cf. John 10:30; 14:9). This language presented the Messiah as being both human and divine. Because He is both God and man, Christ alone could fulfill the prophecy that God would be pierced for His people (cf. Zech 12:10) and be their true atoning sacrifice (Heb 9:25–26). That somber yet necessary truth was declared by none other than **Yahweh of hosts** Himself.

Having summoned His sword of judgment to action, God issued the order, **"Strike the Shepherd that the sheep may be scattered."** The word **strike** denoted a lethal blow, pointing specifically to the crucifixion. In contrast to the false prophets in the previous verse who merely claimed to be struck (cf. Zech 13:6), the Messiah would in fact be **struck** down to save His people.

The Lord also foretold that when the Messiah was killed, **the sheep** would **be scattered.** At times in the nation's history, the death of Israel's king or shepherd caused the people to flee (1 Kgs 22:17; 2 Chr 18:16; Ezek 34:5–6). The Lord prophesied that the flock of Israel would be scattered as a result of Christ's death. Furthermore, God declared that He would particularly **turn** His **hand against the little ones.** For God to **turn** His **hand** against an individual or nation meant that He was directing His might against them (cf. Ezek 38:12; Amos 1:8; Ps 81:15), or, as Isaiah 1:25 declared, against His own: "I will also turn My hand against you, and will smelt away your dross as with lye and will remove all your alloy." God would focus His discipline **against the little ones,** meaning His own remnant. His hand will be against them for their refinement and purification. Shortly before His arrest and crucifixion, the Lord Jesus cited these words from Zechariah to foreshadow the fearful response of the disciples on the night of His arrest (cf. Mark 14:27–30). Following Christ's death and resurrection, God dispersed the entire nation of Israel in judgment for their unbelief, which only caused the believing remnant to scatter further. They spread all over the world as sojourners and exiles to be purified in their trials and suffering (cf. Acts 8:1; Jas 1:1; 1 Pet 1:1).

One day, however, Israel will be regathered not only physically but spiritually (Rom 11:26). Together, they will recognize the truth about their Messiah and His sacrificial death, responding in sorrow, repentance, and faith (Zech 12:10). The death of Christ was both the reason they were scattered in judgment and discipline, as well as the reason they will be regathered in faith. Because of Christ's work of propitiation, a future generation of Israelites will be forgiven and welcomed with joy into His kingdom (Rom 11:26). When that day comes, the hand of the Lord will no longer be against Israel. He will be their God, and they will be His people.

THE PROCESS OF PURIFICATION

"And it will be in all the land,"
Declares Yahweh,
"That two parts in it will be cut off *and* breathe their last;
But the third will be left in it.

And I will bring the third part through the fire
And refine them as silver is refined
And test them as gold is tested.
They will call on My name,
And I will answer them;
I will say, 'They are My people,'
And they will say, 'Yahweh is my God.'" (13:8–9)

With the words **and it will be**, the Lord introduced a new and final thought in this chapter, explaining the refining process by which He will purify Israel. Though chapter 13 began by focusing on Jerusalem (v. 1), it concludes by speaking about **all the land** (v. 8). God's refining work will not be limited to the capital city but will encompass the entire nation.

What follows in verse 8 is a prophecy of the premillennial judgment, declared by **Yahweh** Himself, in keeping with the divine discipline and scattering predicted at the end of verse 7. The Lord revealed that **two parts in** the land **will be cut off and breathe their last; but the third will be left in it**. These sobering words predicted the widespread slaughter that will take place before the kingdom, specifically during the Great Tribulation (cf. Matt 24:21) and the battle of Armageddon. Here, the Lord revealed that two-thirds of Israel's population **(two parts)** will perish during those cataclysmic events. The expression **cut off** described a violent death, evidencing the catastrophic consequences of divine judgment (Gen 9:11; Lev 23:29; Obad 9). The phrase **breathe their last** reinforced the connection to God's wrath. It was used in Genesis 6 to describe the Lord's judgment of the earth in the global flood: "As for Me, behold I am bringing the flood of water upon the earth, to destroy all flesh in which is the breath of life, from under heaven; everything that is on the earth shall breathe its last" (Gen 6:17). In Zechariah 13, Yahweh revealed that in the future, two-thirds of Israel's population will perish in keeping with His sovereign purposes. Though sobering, this fiery judgment is part of the process by which God will purify the nation, removing the reprobate and rebellious from their midst.

Though two-thirds will perish, a **third** will remain alive. This is the indestructible third, the holy seed (cf. Deut 30:1–6; Isa 6:13; see discussion on Zech 6:10). The Antichrist and his forces will attempt to exterminate the entire nation. While the Lord will providentially use that to refine His people (cf. Gen 50:20), He will not allow all of Israel to perish. A **third** part **will be left in it** as the final remnant. God has always preserved a remnant throughout Israel's history, and He will do so to the end (cf. Ezra 9:13–15; Isa 6:10–13; 10:21–22; Jer 31:7; Ezek 6:8; Mic 2:12; Zeph 3:13; Rom 9:27; 11:5).

The Lord's purifying work will not only refine the nation in judgment by removing the rebellious, but will also cleanse those who remain. In verse 1, God described that He would open a fountain of water to cleanse His people. Here, in verse 9, He declared, **"I will bring the third part through the fire."** As God brings Israel through the fire of judgment, He will ensure the survival of His elect. Moreover, through this process, the Lord will **refine them as silver is refined**. The imagery depicts intense heat smelting away all contaminants and foreign elements, leaving pure silver behind (cf. Isa 1:21–26; Jer 6:28–30; Mal 3:2–3; Ps 66:10–12; cf. Lev 10:1–3; and see Num 31:21–24). The prophet Ezekiel provided a vivid description of how God would refine Israel in this way:

The word of Yahweh came to me, saying, "Son of man, the house of Israel has become dross to Me; all of them are bronze and tin and iron and lead in the furnace; they are the dross of silver. Therefore, thus says Lord Yahweh, 'Because all of you have become dross, therefore, behold, I am going to gather you into the midst of Jerusalem. As they gather silver and bronze and iron and lead and tin into the furnace to blow fire on it in order to melt *it*, so I will gather *you* in My anger and in My wrath, and I will lay you *there* and melt you. And I will collect you *together* and blow on you with the fire of My fury, and you will be melted in the midst of it. As silver is melted in the furnace, so you will be melted in the midst of it; and you will know that I, Yahweh, have poured out My wrath on you.'" (Ezek 22:17−22)

Using the heat and intensity of trials and tribulation, the Lord will melt away the dross from His people (cf. Prov 17:3). The future remnant of Israel will face the greatest, most fiery trial in the nation's history. The situation will be so intense that if God did not shorten those days, all would die (Matt 24:22). God will use those circumstances as a refining fire to bring His elect to saving faith (cf. Zech 12:10) and to sanctify them in holiness (cf. 1 Pet 1:6–9).

After the fiery ordeal is over, the remnant of Israel will be both purified and proven. The Lord said He would **test them as gold is tested**. To test gold is to verify its authenticity and purity (cf. Jas 1:12). Trials and tests are not only meant to refine but also to confirm that something is approved. Though the remnant will face great difficulty, they will emerge from the fire as a nation consecrated to God and approved by Him.

The Lord then declared that once Israel has been sanctified, **"They will call on My name, and I will answer them."** Throughout Old Testament history, the people of Israel often failed to **call on** the **name of** Yahweh or to depend fully on Him (cf. Pss 14:4; 53:4; Isa 65:1). One day, however, God will transform the hearts of the entire nation, and they will all turn to Him, calling on His name in saving faith (cf. Rom 10:13).

Not only will Israel cry out to God, but the Lord will also **answer them**. God is not obligated to respond to sinners. The Old Testament recounted times when Israel insincerely called on God's name, and He did not answer them. In Isaiah 1:15, Isaiah wrote: "So when you spread out your hands *in prayer*, I will hide My eyes from you; indeed, even though you multiply prayers, I will not listen. Your hands are full of blood" (cf. Prov 1:28; Mic 3:4). Similarly, in the time of Jeremiah, the Lord refused to listen to the cries of a rebellious people (cf. Jer 44:26). Zechariah had already revealed why the Lord rejected the calls of previous generations. He did not listen to them because they would not listen to Him (cf. Zech 7:13). But that will change in the future when Israel repents. Having been regenerated through the power of the Spirit (12:10), those who once hated God will call upon Him in love. In response, the One who previously refused to hear will **answer them**. The Lord's refining work will have its perfect effect, and Israel's broken relationship with Yahweh will be restored.

When that final restoration occurs and all Israel is saved (Rom 11:26), the Lord **will say, "They are My people," and they will say, "Yahweh is my God."** By declaring Israel to be **"My people,"** God reiterated His unique covenant relationship with His chosen nation (cf. Exod 3:10; 2 Sam 7:8–11; Jer 31:33; Ezek 36:25–28). Israel will respond by expressing their deep love for the Lord, exclaiming, **"Yahweh is my God."** They will worship **Yahweh** sincerely and exclusively. Even more, every Israelite will enjoy personal fellowship with the Lord, proclaiming personal allegiance to Him with the words, He is **my God**.

Those declarations of love, from God to His people and from His people back to Him, were always the goal of His covenant relationship with Israel (cf. Exod 6:7; Jer 7:23; 11:4; 30:22; Ezek 36:28). Throughout its history, the nation never experienced pure and perfect fellowship with the Lord (Hos 1:9). But, as Zechariah prophesied, the day will come when Israel experiences such a relationship with Yahweh. For the duration of the millennial kingdom and into the eternal state, the national conversion and spiritual cleansing of Israel will testify to the power and fidelity of God's promise and grace.

The Day of Yahweh's Return

33

Zechariah 14:1–8

Behold, a day is coming for Yahweh when the spoil *taken* from you will be divided among you. Indeed, I will gather all the nations against Jerusalem to battle, and the city will be captured, the houses plundered, the women ravished, and half of the city will go forth in exile, but those left of the people will not be cut off from the city. Then Yahweh will go forth and fight against those nations, as the day when He fights on a day of battle. And in that day His feet will stand on the Mount of Olives, which is in front of Jerusalem on the east; and the Mount of Olives will be split in its middle from east to west by a very large valley so that half of the mountain will move toward the north and the other half toward the south. And you will flee by the valley of My mountains, for the valley of the mountains will reach to Azel; indeed, you will flee just as you fled before the earthquake in the days of Uzziah king of Judah. Then Yahweh, my God, will come, *and* all the holy ones with Him! And it will be in that day, *that* there will be no light; the luminaries will dwindle. And it will be a unique day which is known to Yahweh, neither day nor night, but it will be that at evening time there will be light. And it will be in that day, *that* living waters will flow out of Jerusalem, half of them toward the eastern sea and the other half toward the western sea; it will be in summer as well as in winter.

Throughout Israel's history, the Lord repeatedly intervened to deliver His people. Many Old Testament examples illustrate this fact. When Abraham found himself in trouble, Yahweh rescued him and his family (cf. Gen 12:10–20; 20:1–18). The Lord also delivered Jacob from the schemes of his uncle (31:9–10) and providentially placed Joseph in Egypt to save his family from famine (37–50). When the Israelites were oppressed by Pharaoh, Yahweh liberated them with mighty signs and wonders (Exod 1–15; Deut 4:34). He subsequently protected Israel in the wilderness, despite the people's doubt and disobedience (Deut 1:45–2:3). When the Israelites entered the Promised Land, the Lord conquered the Canaanites (Josh 1–11) and later sent judges to rescue His people from their enemies (Judg 1–16). He raised up leaders like Samuel (1 Sam 7:3–17), Saul (11:1–15), and David (2 Sam 5:17–25) to repel Israel's enemies and strengthen her defenses. After the monarchy was divided, the Lord continued to deliver His people, whether through His prophets (1 Kgs 20:36–44), general providence (1 Kgs 22), or personal intervention (2 Kgs 18–19). Even during Israel's exile to Babylon, God was faithful to deliver. Daniel was saved from the king's schemes (Dan 1) and from the lion's den (Dan 6). Daniel's friends were also shielded from the flames of the fiery furnace (Dan 3). During the time of the Persian empire, when Haman sought the genocide of the Jewish people, the Lord used Esther and Mordecai to turn the tables on their enemies (Esth 9:1–10). To these accounts of divine deliverance, many more could be added. Israel's history is a continuous record of God's work to protect and preserve His people, a history which will culminate with the Lord's final deliverance described in Zechariah 14. Building on truths revealed in chapters 12 and 13, Zechariah revealed the full glory of that future salvation. Yahweh will return to conquer all enemies, renew the earth, establish His earthly kingdom, and fill the world with His glory.

Prior to Christ's triumphant return, Israel will face an unparalleled existential threat. In an effort to secure peace and protection, the nation's leaders will make a seven-year covenant with the false shepherd, the Antichrist (Dan 9:27; cf. Zech 11:16–17). They will initially experience a superficial peace, but in the middle of this seven-year period, the Antichrist will break his pact with Israel. He will desecrate the temple and demand to be worshiped. When the people refuse, he will gather a global military force against Israel. This will lead to a devastating siege of Jerusalem and the surrounding regions, culminating in the battle of Armageddon. According to Revelation 14, the battle will be so violent that the blood of those slain will reach the horses' bridles covering an area of 200 miles (the land stretches about 290 miles north-to-south, and 85 miles east-to-west at its widest point). The Antichrist and his hosts will appear victorious, with Jerusalem vanquished and the nation brought to the brink of extinction.

In Zechariah 14, the prophet addressed that future eschatological epoch, beginning with the final siege of Jerusalem. To those living in Zechariah's day, battling fear and discouragement as they worked to rebuild the temple, the prophet's message was one of ultimate hope. They would have been alarmed, undoubtedly, to learn that one day Israel would face a grave national threat. But, as Zechariah revealed, that would not be the end of the story. Just as the Lord faithfully delivered His people throughout their history, so He promises to rescue them again at the end of the age. The day of that future deliverance will begin as a day of devastating ruin (14:1–2). But when the Messiah returns to save His people, it will become a day of dramatic rescue (14:3–5) and divine restoration (14:6–8).

A DAY OF DEVASTATING RUIN

Behold, a day is coming for Yahweh when the spoil *taken* from you will be divided among you. Indeed, I will gather all the nations against Jerusalem to battle, and the city will be captured, the houses plundered, the women ravished, and half of the city will go forth in exile, but those left of the people will not be cut off from the city. (14:1–2)

With the call to **behold**, the prophet arrested the attention of his audience, directing their focus to **a day** that **is coming for Yahweh**. Throughout the previous chapters, the phrase "in that day" was used (cf. Zech 2:11; 3:10; 9:16; 11:11; 12:3, 4, 6, 8[2x], 9, 11; 13:1, 2, 4; 14:4, 6, 8, 9, 13, 20, 21). Though referring to the same future moment, the phrasing here, however, is distinct. It is not "in that day" or even "the day of Yahweh," but rather, **a day** designated **for Yahweh**. While the future will include many epic events and dramatic moments, the purpose of all history—from beginning to end—is to glorify God. His mighty works will be fully displayed on the eschatological day He has appointed **for** Himself. At that time, the Lord will not only deliver Israel, but by doing so will magnify His name by demonstrating His infinite power, righteous wrath, and transcendent majesty. The participle **coming** indicates ongoing action. Because history is perfectly ordained and providentially orchestrated by God, it is moving steadily toward the climactic day when the Messiah will return to conquer and reign (cf. Joel 2:1; Mal 4:1).

But before the brilliance of Yahweh's glory bursts onto the scene, the situation will be desperately dark and grim for Israel. In verse 1, the prophet explained that **the spoil taken from you** (Jerusalem) **will be divided among you**. The term **spoil** refers to goods pillaged by a conquering foe (cf. Josh 7:21; 2 Sam 3:22). Zechariah prophesied that the treasures of Jerusalem will not merely **be divided** by Israel's adversaries, but distributed **among you**, meaning within the city itself. Confident of their dominant victory, enemy soldiers will feel no danger from the residents, but will remain in the city to parcel out the treasures of their conquest (cf. Gen 49:27; Josh 22:8).

The Lord confirmed this by saying, "**Indeed, I will gather all the nations against Jerusalem to battle.**" In Revelation 16, the Apostle John explained that demonic forces will incite massive armies to engage in "the war of the great day of God" (Rev 16:14). There, the Apostle John referred to the gathering point of those armies as "Har-Magedon," or the Mount of Megiddo (16:16). The staging area for the Antichrist and his forces will be in the Jezreel Valley north of Jerusalem, where Megiddo is located. The ensuing battle is therefore known as Armageddon, even though the fighting will rage in Jerusalem. In that battle, **all the nations** will come against Israel's capital to besiege the city and **to battle** against it.

Yahweh declared that, by His sovereign power, He **will gather** these nations against Israel. The Lord has predetermined the events of this eschatological day, including the assembling of the enemy host **(I will gather)**, its number **(all the nations)**, its objective **(against Jerusalem)**, and its aggression **(to battle).** God will gather the armies of the nations together for three purposes. First, He will employ them as His agent to purge the rebellious and reprobate from among His people (cf. Zech 13:9). Second, He will assemble them to punish the nations for their wickedness (cf. 12:2–4, 6, 9). Third, He will use them to put Israel in an impossible situation, so that He might display the fullness of His saving power (cf. 12:10; 14:1–5). In these ways, the Lord will cause Jerusalem's future destruction to accomplish both His glory and the good of His people (cf. Rom 8:28). Even as Zechariah revealed the horrors the nation will face on that future day, he reminded his readers of God's sovereign power and plan for their deliverance.

The threat to God's people will be grave. **The city will be captured, the houses plundered, the women ravished, and half of the city will go forth in exile.** The situation in Jerusalem will be extremely desperate, since the entire **city will be captured.** As a result, **the houses** will be **plundered** by enemy forces eager to loot and vandalize. Beyond damage to property, the people will also suffer at the hands of their global adversaries. As Zechariah explained, **the women** will be **ravished,** and **half of the city will go forth in exile.** The residents of Jerusalem will be overpowered, assaulted, and humiliated; and half of them will be forced into exile. Israel had experienced exile before, a point Zechariah's audience would have vividly recalled from their own history. But the future day described in these verses will be worse than anything the nation had previously faced. It will indeed be "the time of Jacob's distress" (Jer 30:7).

Despite the violence and devastation, only **half of the city** of Jerusalem will go into exile. According to Zechariah 13:8, two thirds of the entire population will be killed during the battle. That includes the half of the city which will be exiled. Yet, as 14:2 explains, **those left of the people will not be cut off from the city.** Those **left** will be the righteous remnant (cf. 13:8) whom the Lord will protect. Zechariah prophesied that they **will not be cut off,** referring either to execution (Gen 9:11) or excommunication from Israel and from God's blessing (Gen 17:14; Lev 13:45–46). Neither will happen to the righteous remnant. In the darkest hour of Israel's history, the Lord will protect and preserve His remnant to bring them safely into His kingdom with all its blessings. This righteous remnant will be the sheep that come out of the judgment of the sheep and the goats when Christ comes in His glory and sits on His throne (Matt 25:31–46).

A DAY OF DRAMATIC RESCUE

Then Yahweh will go forth and fight against those nations, as the day when He fights on a day of battle. And in that day His feet will stand on the Mount of Olives, which is in front of Jerusalem on the east; and the Mount of Olives will be split in its middle from east to west by a very large valley so that half of the mountain will move toward the north and the other half toward the south. And you will flee by the valley of My mountains, for the valley of the mountains will reach to Azel; indeed, you will flee just as you fled before the earthquake in the days of Uzziah king of Judah. Then Yahweh, my God, will come, and all the holy ones with Him! (14:3–5)

In stark contrast to the darkness and defeat described in verses 1–2, the Lord will suddenly appear in glorious triumph. The reason the remnant will survive is that **Yahweh will go forth** and enter into battle to **fight against those nations** attacking Israel. The Lord will do so **as the day when He fights on a day of battle.** That phrase recalled occasions in Israel's history when God fought for His people. Yahweh will overwhelm the enemy in this future battle just as He did Egypt (cf. Exod 14:14), Jericho (Josh 6:16; cf. 5:13–6:27), Midian (Judg 6:16; cf. 6:13–7:25), Assyria (2 Kgs 24:16; 2 Chr 32:21), and all the rest.

In that day, the Day of Yahweh (cf. Zech 12:3, 4, 6) and the Day of His glory (cf. 14:1), the Lord will return and **His feet will stand on the Mount of Olives.** The reference here is to the Lord Jesus Christ, God incarnate. He will return in triumph to stand on the Mount of Olives, just as the angels promised to the disciples after the ascension (cf. Acts 1:11). The One who will go forth in battle, fight for His people, and stand in victory is the Lord Jesus Christ, the Messiah (John 1:18; Isa 6:5 and John 12:41; Col 1:15; 2:9).

At that time, He will stand on the **Mount of Olives**, the very place where earlier leaders fled in defeat. David fled over the Mount of Olives when challenged by Absalom (cf. 2 Sam 15:30). King Zedekiah fled this same way in an effort to escape the Babylonians (cf. 2 Kgs 25:4–6). On the night before His death, the Lord Jesus also came to the Mount of Olives, to the Garden of Gethsemane. But instead of fleeing the danger, He gave Himself up to His enemies to go to the cross, defeating sin and death, and securing salvation for His people. The Mount of Olives was a place of sorrow and agony at Christ's first coming (Matt 26:36–56; Mark 14:32–50; Luke 22:39–53; John 18:1–12). But when He returns to that place, it will be in judgment and triumph (cf. Rev 19:11–16). While Yahweh's glory had once departed "east of the city" (Ezek 11:23), the Lord will arrive to stand **on the east** of Jerusalem to show that Yahweh's glory has returned. Though prior kings turned their backs on the city and fled, the Messiah will be **in front of Jerusalem**, to defend and deliver the remnant of the nation.

Christ's return will be cataclysmic in the strongest sense of the word. Zechariah prophesied that **the Mount of Olives will be split in its middle from east to west by a very large valley so that half of the mountain will move toward the north and the other half toward the south**. The Messiah's return will trigger a divinely controlled seismic event of epic proportions. Indeed, the Lord prophesied that His coming would be accompanied by earthquakes. As Micah 1:3–4 foretold,

> For behold, Yahweh is going forth from His place.
> He will come down and tread on the high places of the earth.
> The mountains will melt under Him,
> And the valleys will be split,
> Like wax before the fire,
> Like water poured down a steep place.

Similarly, in Nahum 1:5 the prophet declared,

> Mountains quake because of Him,
> And the hills melt;
> Indeed the earth is upheaved by His presence,
> The world and all the inhabitants in it.

In Revelation 16:17–19, the Apostle John revealed the global impact of this seismic upheaval:

> Then the seventh *angel* poured out his bowl upon the air, and a loud voice came out of the sanctuary from the throne, saying, "It is done." And there were flashes of lightning and sounds and peals of thunder; and there was a great earthquake, such as there had not been since man came to be upon the earth, so great an earthquake *was it, and so* mighty. And the great city was split into three parts, and the cities of the nations fell. Babylon the great was remembered before God, to give her the cup of the wine of the wrath of His rage.

Christ's return will create an earthquake so powerful that the **Mount of Olives** will **split** down the **middle** and shift in opposite directions— **half of the mountain will move toward the north and the other half toward the south.** As a result, **a very large valley** will form between the two portions of the mountain, extending in two directions—toward the **west** and toward the **east.** This massive geological fracture will display the divine power of the Messiah, as He transforms the ground into a highway to deliver His people. He will turn the **Mount of Olives**, a place of defeat, into the place of victory.

Zechariah foretold that the righteous remnant **will flee by the valley of My mountains.** God will split the Mount of Olives to create two mountains for Himself and a valley between them (cf. Isa 14:25; 49:11; Ezek 38:21). This new valley will allow God's people in Jerusalem to flee through the open pass. Zechariah further revealed that **the valley of the mountains will reach to Azel.** This may be the same location as Beth-ezel, a fortified position in Jerusalem. Though **Azel** was historically viewed as a place of refuge and defense (cf. Mic 1:11), the remnant will run past it on this day to their true refuge, the Messiah. In fact, Israel **will flee just as you fled before the earthquake in the days of Uzziah king of Judah.** That **earthquake** was infamous in Israel's history, being mentioned in Amos 1:1 and recalled by Zechariah nearly three hundred years later. The future earthquake will be far greater in magnitude, and much more memorable. It will serve to deliver the people. With the greatest haste, they will **flee** through the valley that is created, running away from the enemy and toward their Savior, the Messiah.

At this time, as Israel runs to Christ, He will also come to them. Zechariah poignantly declared, **"Yahweh, my God, will come, *and* all the holy ones with Him."** The certainty of Zechariah's statement (that the Lord **will come**) was grounded in the truth that **Yahweh** always keeps His covenant promises. He is faithful to do so because of His personal commitment to His people; and He is able to do so because He is the omnipotent Sovereign of the universe **(God)**. When He comes, the Lord will be accompanied by **all the holy ones with Him. Holy ones** can refer to the saints, and it is true that New Testament saints will accompany Christ at His return (cf. 1 Thess 3:13). But Zechariah was primarily referring here to God's holy angels (cf. Ps 89:5, 8), as is confirmed by other parallel passages (cf. Matt 24:31; 25:31; Mark 8:38; 2 Thess 1:7). The presence of the angels will amplify the overwhelming magnificence and holiness of Christ Himself, since He is the Captain of heaven's hosts. The scene is so compelling that Zechariah cannot help but interject that **Yahweh** is **my God**. The prophet must express his adoration to God, for on that day when He returns, accompanied by an angelic army, the darkest night of Israel's history will turn into its brightest day.

A DAY OF DIVINE RESTORATION

And it will be in that day, *that* there will be no light; the luminaries will dwindle. And it will be a unique day which is known to Yahweh, neither day nor night, but it will be that at evening time there will be light. And it will be in that day, *that* living waters will flow out of Jerusalem, half of them toward the eastern sea and the other half toward the western sea; it will be in summer as well as in winter. (14:6–8)

God's future deliverance will apply not only to His people but also to His creation. Paul wrote in Romans 8:20–22: "For the creation was subjected to futility, not willingly, but because of Him who subjected it, in hope that the creation itself also will be set free from its slavery to corruption into the freedom of the glory of the children of God. For we know that the whole creation groans and suffers the pains of childbirth together until now." The Lord will first judge and devastate the world, but He will then renew the earth as part of His millennial reign.

At the end of the Tribulation, the sun will go dark, the moon will become blood red, and heavenly bodies such as asteroids will fall from the sky. The heavens will grow totally dark (cf. Isa 13:9; Joel 2:1–2, 10, 31; 3:16; Ezek 13:5–16; Zeph 1:15; Matt 24:29; Luke 21:11, 25–26; Rev 12:6–14), while on earth the mountains and seas will be displaced from their foundations (Rev 6:14). While this will not be the final destruction of planet earth, it will provide a glimpse of this world's ultimate annihilation, before it is replaced by a new heaven and a new earth in the eternal state (cf. 2 Pet 3:10; Rev 21–22).

Out of the pitch darkness, the blazing glory of Jesus Christ will appear, accompanied by His holy ones, to establish His kingdom on earth. In this kingdom, God will begin to make things new. Not only will the saints who come with Christ possess new and sinless bodies (Matt 22:30–31; Luke 14:14; 1 Cor 15:52; 1 Thess 4:16; Phil 3:20–21; Rom 8:20–23; Dan 12:2; Job 19:25–27), but God will also renovate the physical world. This divine restoration of earth will encompass at least three categories: new light (v. 6), new day (v. 7), and new waters (v. 8).

First, the millennial kingdom will bask in new light. The phrase **and it will be in that day** introduced yet another dramatic event in the Day of Yahweh (cf. Zech 12:1; 14:1). At the end of the Great Tribulation **there will be no light.** This darkness will represent an act of judgment. Isaiah 13:9–10 stated that during the Day of Yahweh, "the stars of heaven and their constellations will not flash forth their light; the sun will be dark when it rises and the moon will not shed its light" (cf. Isa 24; Joel 3; Matt 24). In Revelation 6:12–14, the Apostle John revealed further details:

> Then I looked when He opened the sixth seal, and there was a great earthquake; and the sun became black as sackcloth *made* of hair, and the whole moon became like blood; and the stars of the sky fell to the earth, as a fig tree casts its unripe figs when shaken by a great wind. And the sky was split apart like a scroll when it is rolled up, and every mountain and island were moved out of their places.

Like the plague of darkness against Egypt (cf. Exod 10:21–29), darkness will overtake the world as part of God's terrifying wrath.

The Lord's future judgment will not only be against light itself but against all that bears light. Zechariah described that the **luminaries will dwindle**. The **luminaries** refer to the sun, moon, and stars, which God created to mediate the light and to designate time and seasons (cf. Gen 1:14). Zechariah foretold that these heavenly bodies **will dwindle**. The word has the idea of coagulation. The sun, moon, and stars will harden, thicken, and darken.

Throughout history, people have worshiped the sun, moon, and stars. Even in Israel, God warned His people not to "lift up your eyes to heaven and see the sun and the moon and the stars, all the host of heaven, and be drawn away and worship them and serve them" (Deut 4:19; cf. Ezek 8:16). These celestial bodies will be diminished so that the One who is greater will receive all the glory. As Isaiah foretold, "Then the moon will be humiliated and the sun ashamed, for Yahweh of hosts will reign on Mount Zion and in Jerusalem, and *His* glory will be before His elders" (Isa 24:23). Isaiah also added that, "No longer will you have the sun for light by day, nor for brightness will the moon give you light; but you will have Yahweh for an everlasting light, and your God for your glory" (Isa 60:19). The Apostle John explained that this would continue into the eternal state: "There will no longer be *any* night, and they will not have need of the light of a lamp nor the light of the sun, because the Lord God will illumine them, and they will reign forever and ever" (Rev 22:5). God will cause the luminaries to fade away because His glory will fill the earth. He will be the new and only light of the world.

Second, because it will be characterized by new light, the Day of Yahweh **will be a unique day**. The events described by Zechariah will be unprecedented in human history, marking the beginning of the new era. The phrase **unique day** literally means "one day" and recalls what was said in Genesis 1:5, "There was evening and there was morning, one day." Genesis 1:5 was not merely referring to the first day at the beginning of creation. In speaking of "one day," it defined the nature of a single day, establishing the very way in which time would be measured. Zechariah also called this eschatological moment "one day" because it will not only mark the start of the millennial restored creation, but it will define the nature of a day in the new era.

Zechariah declared that this day is **known to Yahweh.** In His omniscience, God knows all days in detail. But that this future day, when He established His promised kingdom, is especially known to Him affirms His control over the end of history. Chronologically, God alone knows exactly when this day will arrive (cf. Matt 24:36). Eschatologically, He has designed it to showcase His glory in the culmination of His purposes for world history.

Unlike the creation days in Genesis 1, which were defined as evening to morning, in the millennial kingdom there will **be neither day nor night, but it will be that at evening time there will be light.** In this new "one day," there will be **neither day nor night.** Though people will still be aware of **evening time**, the darkness of night will be absent. Instead, **there will be light** all the time. God's glory, which will replace the sun, moon, and stars (see Zech 14:6; cf. Isa 60:19), will never stop shining. This change in how a day is measured reflects a profound shift of life within Christ's kingdom. In this sinful world, the days are evil (Eph 5:16), and life "under the sun" is characterized by futility (cf. Eccl 1:9; 2:11; 4:7; 9:9). But all of this will be done away with in the future. For a day will no longer be based upon light, darkness, or even the sun (cf. Eccl 12:2), but upon the brilliant light of God's Son.

Third, in addition to new light (v. 6) and a new day (v. 7), the Lord will create new waters (v. 8). Zechariah stated that **it will be in that day, that living waters will flow out of Jerusalem. Living waters** describe waters that continually flow. In arid regions like Israel, streams of flowing water were scarce. But in the millennial kingdom, such waters will be abundant.

These waters will flow from **Jerusalem**, marking not only a change of ecology but a change of topography. Israel's capital will become the new fountainhead, the point from which all water flows. The massive earthquake that will take place (cf. Zech 14:4, 10) will elevate this city above everything else in the region. As water flows out of Jerusalem, even out of the temple (cf. Ezek 47:12), the city will resemble the Garden of Eden. In Genesis 2:10, Moses wrote, "Now a river went out of Eden to water the garden; and from there it divided and became four rivers." At the beginning of earth's history, Eden was the capital of creation, the place from which water flowed, and where God placed man to have dominion over the earth (cf. Gen 1:26–28; 2:8). At the establishment of the kingdom, Jerusalem will be the center of the world. Streams of living water will flow from the city. And the last Adam will exercise dominion over all creation (cf. Ps 72:8–11; Isa 2:2–4; Mic 7:9–20).

In that day, when rivers flow from Jerusalem, **half of them** will flow **toward the eastern sea and the other half toward the western sea**. As the waters move to the **western sea**, the Mediterranean, the desert will blossom with life. This will fulfill what Isaiah prophesied: "The wilderness and the desert will be delighted, and the Arabah will rejoice and flourish" (Isa 35:1). At the same time, water will flow to the **eastern sea**, fulfilling Ezekiel's prophecy that the Dead Sea, one of the saltiest bodies of waters in the world, will become fresh water. What was once stagnant will teem with life so abundant that people will fish there (Ezek 47:10). Though the Dead Sea historically served as a reminder of God's judgment against Sodom and Gomorrah (Gen 19:1–29), one day that stigma will be washed away. Thus "a dry and weary land without water" (Ps 63:1) will be utterly transformed.

The flow of this life-giving water **will be constant since it will be in summer as well as in winter**. Throughout its history, the land of Israel depended on rainfall. Moses himself declared that the Promised Land "is not like the land of Egypt from which you came out, where you used to sow your seed and water it with your foot like a vegetable garden. But the land into which you are about to cross to possess it, a land of hills and valleys, drinks water from the rain of heaven" (Deut 11:10–11). In the **winter**, water was often plentiful during the rainy season, but in the **summer** the region became dry. However, in the future, Israel's water supply will not depend on rain at all. It will be like the beginning when "a river went out of Eden to water the garden" (Gen 2:10) even as "God had not caused it to rain upon the earth" (Gen 2:5). The paradise that was lost will be restored when Christ returns to Jerusalem. He will make all things—including light, day, and water—new (cf. Matt 19:28; Rom 8:21; 11:15).

For the original hearers of Zechariah's prophecy, and for every reader since, the message of chapter 14 moves from abject horror to incomprehensible hope. One day, the Messiah will return. He will vanquish His enemies, rescue the righteous remnant of His people, and establish His kingdom in Jerusalem, so that the world will be transformed from the dark apocalypse of Armageddon to the brilliant paradise of a new Eden. There, in the glory of the Millennium, the saints will worship the Messiah and reign with Him in righteousness (Rev 20:4–6).

Christ's Glory in His Kingdom

34

Zechariah 14:9–21

And Yahweh will be king over all the earth; in that day Yahweh will be *the only* one, and His name one. All the land will be changed into a plain from Geba to Rimmon south of Jerusalem; but Jerusalem will rise and inhabit its site from Benjamin's Gate as far as the place of the First Gate to the Corner Gate, and from the Tower of Hananel to the king's wine presses. And people will inhabit it, and there will no longer be *anything* devoted to destruction, for Jerusalem will be inhabited in security. Now this will be the plague with which Yahweh will plague all the peoples who have gone to war against Jerusalem; their flesh will rot while they stand on their feet, and their eyes will rot in their sockets, and their tongue will rot in their mouth. And it will be in that day, *that* abundant confusion from Yahweh will fall on them; and they will take hold of one another's hand, and the hand of one will go up against the hand of another. And Judah also will fight at Jerusalem; and the wealth of all the surrounding nations will be gathered, gold and silver and garments in great abundance. And in the same way, the plague on the horse, the mule, the camel, the donkey, and all the cattle that will be in those camps will be like this plague. Then it will be that any who are left of all the nations that went against Jerusalem will go up from year to year to worship the King, Yahweh of hosts, and to celebrate the Feast of Booths. And it will be that whichever of the families of the earth does

not go up to Jerusalem to worship the King, Yahweh of hosts, there will be
no rain on them. And if the family of Egypt does not go up or enter, then
no *rain will fall* on them; it will be the plague with which Yahweh plagues
the nations who do not go up to celebrate the Feast of Booths. This will be
the punishment of Egypt, and the punishment of all the nations who do not
go up to celebrate the Feast of Booths. In that day there will *be inscribed*
on the bells of the horses, "Holy to Yahweh." And the pots in the house of
Yahweh will be like the bowls before the altar. And every pot in Jerusalem
and in Judah will be holy to Yahweh of hosts; and all who sacrifice will
come and take of them and boil in them. And there will no longer be a
Canaanite in the house of Yahweh of hosts in that day.

  The hope and majesty of the Messiah's coming kingdom is one
of Scripture's most glorious themes. God's Word paints a magnificent
picture of that future golden age, which will commence when the Lord
Jesus returns to deliver His people, defeat His enemies, restore His
creation, and reign in Jerusalem for a thousand years. The Old Testament
prophets revealed key details about those future events. Zephaniah noted
that the Lord will establish His kingdom by pouring out His wrath on the
nations that assemble against Israel (Zeph 3:8; cf. Hab 3:13; Joel 3:2, 9–17).
Amos reminded the people that wicked Israelites will also be judged at
this time (Amos 9:10). Because God will crush every enemy, and remove
all the wicked, the millennial kingdom will be characterized by peace
among men. Christ, the Prince of Peace (Isa 9:6), will reign in perfect
righteousness (Isa 11:4; Jer 33:15; Hag 2:23). Nations will not lift up the
sword against other nations (Isa 2:4; Joel 3:10). Instead, the inhabitants of
every nation will stream to Jerusalem to learn God's law (Isa 2:2–4). They
will marvel at the glory of God (Isa 6:3) and rejoice in the knowledge of
Yahweh (Isa 11:9; cf. Joel 3:17). The curse on creation will be curtailed as
"the wolf will dwell with the lamb" (Isa 11:6) and "the nursing baby will
play by the hole of the cobra" (11:8). In this era, people will enjoy extended
lifespans, living well beyond one hundred years of age (65:20; cf. Zech 8:4).
  In the kingdom, there will not only be peace on earth but peace
with God. The Lord will fulfill His covenant with Israel so that the entire

nation will know Him (Jer 31:31–34). All idolatry will be removed (Mic 5:13–14). God's Spirit will be poured out upon His people (Zech 12:10). Israel's sins will be forgiven (Mic 7:18; Zech 13). As a result, Yahweh will truly "be their God, and they shall be My people" (Jer 31:33; cf. 32:37–42; Hos 14).

Israel's spiritual transformation will pave the way for the fulfillment of all of God's promises to His chosen people. Christ will fulfill the Davidic dynasty as the messianic King (Amos 9:11; cf. 14–15; Zeph 3:14–20; Obad 21). Jerusalem will be the dwelling place of God (Jer 33:16). His glory will return to the city and fill the rebuilt temple (Hag 2:7; Ezek 40–48). From there, the Lord's transcendent majesty will cover the entire earth (Isa 6:3; Ezek 43:1–3).

Scripture's anticipation of the Messiah's kingdom continues into the New Testament. Looking forward to Christ's earthly reign, the disciples asked, "Lord, is it at this time You are restoring the kingdom to Israel?" (Acts 1:6; cf. Matt 6:10). Earlier, the Lord had spoken of the time when the Son of Man will sit on His glorious throne and the world will be regenerated (Matt 19:28). Peter wrote of hastening the coming of the day of God (2 Pet 3:12). Paul noted that believers would one day judge the world (1 Cor 6:2). And to John it was revealed that in Christ's kingdom, Satan will be bound up, the dead in Christ shall rise, and the Lord shall reign with the saints for one thousand years (Rev 20:1–6). From Matthew to Revelation, the New Testament writers did not demur from the subject of the coming kingdom. Rather, they affirmed what the Old Testament prophets previously revealed.

Among the prophetic portraits of the Messiah's future kingdom found in Scripture, Zechariah 14 is one of the most stunning. With profound detail, the prophet described the command of the King (v. 9), the capital of the kingdom (vv. 10–11), the conquest of the enemy (vv. 12–15), the celebration of the people (vv. 16–19), and the consecration of Israel (vv. 20–21). In keeping with the rest of Zechariah's prophecy, this section provides a final testimony to the truth that Yahweh remembers His promises and will fulfill them completely.

THE COMMAND OF THE KING

And Yahweh will be king over all the earth; in that day Yahweh will be *the* **only one, and His name one.** (14:9)

Yahweh will be king marks the fulfillment of God's agenda for world history. It is the culmination of God's work through Israel (cf. Gen 12:1–3; 17:6), the Davidic dynasty (1 Kgs 8:16), the cross and resurrection (cf. Rev 5:9–16), and all that will take place on the Day of Yahweh. What creation has been waiting for (cf. Rom 8:19–21), what Israel has been anticipating, and what the world desperately needs will all be accomplished when the Messiah begins His millennial reign (cf. Rev 20:4–5).

Zechariah did not only say that **Yahweh will be king**, but that He will be King **over all the earth**. Christ's absolute sovereign authority will not be limited in any way; He will exercise all dominion—ruling over every nation (Rev 5:13; Hag 2:22) and every creature in both the natural and supernatural realms. Though Satan has currently been given authority as prince of the power of the air (Eph 2:2; cf. John 12:31; 14:30; 16:11; 2 Cor 4:4; 1 John 5:19), the Messiah will crush him (cf. Gen 3:15), casting him into the abyss (Rev 20:3) and ultimately into the lake of fire (20:10). As King, Christ will maintain absolute rule over the **earth** and all creation. The final Adam will possess the dominion lost by the first Adam.

Accordingly, **in that day Yahweh will be** *the only* **one**. Such language declares the very core of God's revelation to Israel as expressed in the *Shema*: "Hear, O Israel! Yahweh is our God, Yahweh is one!" (Deut 6:4). In the millennial kingdom, the world will display that the Lord is the only true God (cf. Deut 12:1–19; 13:1–18; cf. Isa 42:8; 48:11). All forms of idolatry and false religion, including all false prophecy, will be eradicated (cf. Zech 13:1–6). All worship will center in Jerusalem (Isa 2:2–4; Zech 14:17), focusing on Yahweh alone.

The *Shema* revealed the truth about God's oneness in a way consistent with His Triunity. This will also be displayed in the millennial kingdom. The Father will give the kingdom (1 Cor 15:27) to the Son who will rule as the messianic King over the earth (Zech 14:9) empowered by the seven-fold ministry of the Spirit (Isa 11:2; Zech 3:9; 4:10; Rev 1:4). The unity and exclusivity of God will be confessed by the nations, who will acknowledge that **His name** is **one**. The Lord will "cut off the names of the idols from the land" (Zech 13:2); only the name of Yahweh will be confessed and worshiped (cf. Phil 2:9-10). Such singular devotion and dominion will be the glory of the King as He reigns over all the earth.

THE CAPITAL OF THE KINGDOM

All the land will be changed into a plain from Geba to Rimmon south of Jerusalem; but Jerusalem will rise and inhabit its site from Benjamin's Gate as far as the place of the First Gate to the Corner Gate, and from the Tower of Hananel to the king's wine presses. And people will inhabit it, and there will no longer be *anything* devoted to destruction, for Jerusalem will be inhabited in security. (14:10-11)

When Christ returns, the topography of Israel will be transformed. Zechariah stated that **all the land will be changed into a plain from Geba to Rimmon south of Jerusalem**. The area described is expansive. **Geba**, the same location where Jonathan climbed a steep ravine to attack a Philistine garrison (1 Sam 14:5-14), is roughly five and a half miles northeast of Jerusalem. **Rimmon** is about 35 miles **south of Jerusalem** (Josh 15:32; 19:13), located near Israel's southern border, about 16 miles northeast of Beersheba (Judg 20:1; 1 Sam 3:20; 2 Sam 3:10; 1 Kgs 4:25). This entire area, about 41 miles in length, **will be changed into a plain**. Originally, the land was filled with valleys and ridges; however, one day it will be leveled.

God will flatten the region around Jerusalem for several reasons. First, the land will change to herald the coming of Christ. Isaiah prophesied, "A voice is calling 'Prepare the way for Yahweh in the wilderness; make smooth in the desert a highway for our God. Let every valley be lifted up, and every mountain and hill be made low; and let the rough ground become a plain, and the rugged terrain a broad valley'" (Isa 40:3-4). Second, the geographical changes will make it easier for the Jewish people to return to Jerusalem from around the world (cf. Zech 10:10–11). Third, this expanded plain will accommodate Jerusalem's millennial growth and prosperity (cf. Isa 54:1; Ezek 48:10, 13, 15; Zech 2:4).

Zechariah's final reason that God will level this vast area around Israel's capital city is that, in this way God will accentuate that **Jerusalem will rise.** In contrast to the level plain around it, the city proper will be elevated and exalted. It will be the highest point in the region, the envy of every mountain (cf. Ps 68:15–16), and the watershed of the entire area (cf. Zech 14:8). As Isaiah prophesied, Jerusalem will be a city that is "lifted up" (Isa 2:2) because of its association with the Lord who alone is "high and lifted up" (cf. Isa 6:1; 52:13).

Zechariah explained that the city will **inhabit its site from Benjamin's Gate as far as the place of the First Gate to the Corner Gate, and from the Tower of Hananel to the king's wine presses.** In Zechariah 12:6, the prophet noted that Jerusalem will **inhabit its site,** unmoved and resilient through the Tribulation and into the millennial kingdom. When Christ reigns, the city will retake all the land it was always supposed to occupy. The dimensions of **Benjamin's Gate as far as the place of the First Gate to the Corner Gate, and from the Tower of Hananel to the king's wine presses** described Jerusalem at its largest footprint in the eighth century BC. **Benjamin's Gate** was mentioned in Jeremiah's day as part of the city before it fell in 586 BC (Jer 20:2). The **First Gate** and **the Corner Gate** were restored in the days of Joash (2 Chr 25:23) and Uzziah (26:9), but they were later destroyed by Nebuchadnezzar. The prophet Jeremiah prophesied that the **Tower of Hananel to the king's wine presses** and even **the Corner Gate** would one day be rebuilt (cf. Jer 31:38). Their presence in millennial Jerusalem will be a restoration of what was lost and a fulfillment of biblical prophecy.

During the Messiah's reign, countless multitudes of **people will inhabit** Jerusalem, taking up permanent and secure residence there (cf. Zech 12:6). Though around the time of Zechariah the city was sparsely populated—one in ten Jews lived there (Neh 11:1)—the city in the millennial kingdom will burst with people (cf. Isa 54:1–3; Zech 2:4).

Israel's capital will also be a holy place since **there will no longer be anything devoted to destruction.** Such language referred to the practice of Israel, particularly during the conquest of the Promised Land, when Israel destroyed cities (Num 21:3; Deut 2:34; Josh 2:10) or objects (Josh 6:18, 21) to devote them to God's honor. But in the future kingdom, **there will no longer be** anything that warrants **destruction**, because everything will be purified and acceptable to Yahweh. Throughout its history, Jerusalem was constantly contaminated by paganism, impurity, and idolatry (Josh 15:63; 18:28; Judg 1:21; 3:5; 1 Kgs 12:32; 14:23; 2 Kgs 14:4). But in the Millennium, it will have no spot or stain as God's holy mountain (cf. Zech 8:3).

Finally, Zechariah noted that **Jerusalem will be inhabited in security**. The city will abide in peace without any threat. The repetition of **inhabit**, three times in two verses, emphasized the stability of everything described in this context. Jerusalem will inhabit its site (14:10), the people will inhabit the city (14:11a), and they will inhabit it securely (14:11b). Such a resplendent and resilient capital will reflect the glory of the millennial kingdom and the majesty of its King.

THE CONQUEST OF THE ENEMY

Now this will be the plague with which Yahweh will plague all the peoples who have gone to war against Jerusalem; their flesh will rot while they stand on their feet, and their eyes will rot in their sockets, and their tongue will rot in their mouth. And it will be in that day, *that* abundant confusion from Yahweh will fall on them; and they will take hold of one another's hand, and the hand of one will go up against the hand of another. And Judah also will fight at Jerusalem; and the wealth of all the surrounding nations will be gathered, gold and silver and garments in great abundance. And in the same way, the plague on the horse, the mule, the camel, the donkey, and all the cattle that will be in those camps will be like this plague. (14:12–15)

With the introductory **now**, Zechariah turned to a parenthetical thought regarding the battle of Armageddon, explaining why Jerusalem will be so secure after the battle is over. Though this battle was already discussed (cf. 12:1–9; 14:1–3), Zechariah added an important detail: **there will be the plague with which Yahweh will plague all the peoples who** have gone to war against Jerusalem. During the battle, Yahweh Himself will send a **plague** against Israel's enemies, like He did against Egypt during the Exodus (Exod 8:2; 9:14; 12:13, 23, 27; and cf. Num 25:8, 9, 18, 19; 31:16). The plague will be universal and inescapable, striking **all the peoples.** None of the nations **who have gone to war against Jerusalem** will be exempted.

The plague will also be devastatingly effective. Immediately afflicting its victims, it will cause **their flesh** to **rot while they stand on their feet, and their eyes** to **rot in their sockets, and their tongue** to **rot in their mouth. Rot** describes decomposition (cf. Lev 26:39) with all its distasteful features (cf. Ps 38:5). Specifically, the **flesh** of the enemy soldiers **will rot while they stand on their feet.** Their bodies will decay as their skin and muscles rapidly deteriorate and melt away. In this process, **their eyes will rot in their sockets,** and **their tongue will rot in their mouth.** As they meet their demise, they will be unable to see or to speak, making it impossible for them to look for help or call out a warning to others.

The Lord will send those who avoid the plague into complete panic. **It will be in that day**, during the battle of Armageddon (cf. Zech 12:1, 3, 6, 8, 9), **that abundant confusion from Yahweh will fall on them.** **Confusion** denotes chaos resulting in bewilderment and irrational behavior. In the past, God threatened to send the Israelites into such confusion if they rebelled against Him (cf. Deut 28:20). In the future, He will send Israel's enemies into confusion (cf. 7:23). This **abundant** disturbance of minds will come directly **from Yahweh** and will exceed other times in Israel's history when the Lord confused enemy forces (cf. 1 Sam 5:9–11; 14:20; Ezek 7:7).

The resulting pandemonium will force Israel's adversaries to **take hold of one another's hand, and the hand of one will go up against the hand of another.** This description was reminiscent of earlier times in Israel's history, when God secured the victory for His people by causing enemy soldiers to turn on one another (Judg 7:22; 1 Sam 14:20). Zechariah's prophecy was most similar to a battle in David's day when each enemy combatant grabbed the hand of another in order to kill him (2 Sam 2:16). The opposing army did not survive its self-inflicted defeat.

On a far greater scale, history will repeat itself when God confuses His enemies during the battle of Armageddon.

Whatever is left of the enemy, after plague and pandemonium, God will enable Israel to destroy in combat. Zechariah explained that **Judah also will fight at Jerusalem.** As Zechariah earlier foretold, God will empower those who are weak in Jerusalem to be as heroic as David, and He will make the strong to be as mighty as the Angel of Yahweh (cf. Zech 12:8). With supernatural strength, the armies of Israel will launch a valiant **fight** for their city, crushing the already beleaguered foe. Israel's counterattack will be so fierce **that the wealth of all the surrounding nations will be gathered, gold and silver and garments in great abundance.** Wealth refers to one's treasures and to any resource that provides strength, industry, or ability (cf. Judg 6:12; Zech 4:6). At the beginning of the battle, Israel will be pillaged (cf. Zech 14:1); but by the end, God's people will recapture all that they will have lost and far more. They will acquire the wealth of **all the surrounding nations.** The economic balance of the region will shift toward Israel as the nations will be defeated so soundly that all their wealth **will be gathered** by Israel. The mention of **gold and silver and garments** not only illustrated the breadth of wealth obtained, but also hearkened back to items obtained in Joshua's conquest (cf. Josh 7:21). Israel will possess these items **in great abundance,** demonstrating that the work of the Conquest will finally be fulfilled. The enemy will be completely destroyed, and all their **gold** and **silver** will be taken to adorn Israel's temple (cf. Hag 2:7) and to make a crown for Christ (cf. Zech 6:11).

Zechariah concluded this section by saying that **in the same way, the plague on the horse, the mule, the camel, the donkey, and all the cattle that will be in those camps will be like this plague.** The plague will kill not only the soldiers, but their animals as well. The **horse,** a key military resource, will die. Various beasts that carry people and supplies will perish, including **the mule** (2 Sam 13:29; 18:9; 2 Kgs 5:17; Ezek 27:14; Isa 66:20), **the camel** (cf. Gen 24:11; Job 1:17), and **the donkey** (cf. Gen 22:3; 1 Chr 12:41). The enemy's supply chain will be disrupted. Their food supply will also collapse, as **all the cattle** will perish. Because the devastation at the battle of Armageddon will be comprehensive, so that every enemy and even animal will die (cf. Rev 19:21), Christ's kingdom will begin in perfect peace.

THE CELEBRATION OF THE PEOPLE

Then it will be that any who are left of all the nations that went against Jerusalem will go up from year to year to worship the King, Yahweh of hosts, and to celebrate the Feast of Booths. And it will be that whichever of the families of the earth does not go up to Jerusalem to worship the King, Yahweh of hosts, there will be no rain on them. And if the family of Egypt does not go up or enter, then no *rain will fall* on them; it will be the plague with which Yahweh plagues the nations who do not go up to celebrate the Feast of Booths. This will be the punishment of Egypt, and the punishment of all the nations who do not go up to celebrate the Feast of Booths. (14:16–19)

In describing the celebration and worship that will characterize the Messiah's future kingdom, Zechariah began by identifying the worshipers as **those who are left**. This is the language of the righteous remnant whom God preserved and purified during the Day of Yahweh (cf. Zech 13:8). True worship can come only from those who genuinely love the Lord (cf. Deut 6:4–5) because the Father seeks those who worship Him in spirit and in truth (cf. John 4:23). This will characterize the worshipers of the millennial kingdom, who will not only be from Israel but from **all the nations**. Revelation 7:9 described this group as "a great multitude which no one could count, from every nation and all tribes and peoples and tongues." These redeemed peoples from the Tribulation, representing every nation on earth, will include even the nations **that went up against Jerusalem**. Those who should have suffered God's wrath will turn to God (Rev 1:7), corporately praise Him, and proclaim His supreme worthiness and sovereign dominion (cf. Ps 22:27–30; Phil 2:10–11).

This international assembly of worshipers **will go up** to Jerusalem **from year to year to worship** God. Such language was used to describe Israel's annual pilgrimages. In the past, the nation journeyed up to

Jerusalem three times a year to celebrate God's redemption and provision (cf. Lev 23; Deut 16). Because this was such a significant undertaking, their yearly calendar revolved around these major festivals. In like manner, worship in the millennial kingdom will not be a one-time event. Rather, the nations will unite with Israel, and worship will dominate the annual activities of Christ's thousand-year reign.

The world's worship will center on **the King, Yahweh of hosts**. With such titles, Zechariah impressed upon his readers the glory and worthiness of Christ. The title **"King"** is the ultimate title of honor. All authority, dominion, and might will belong to the Messiah (Dan 7:13–14). The people of every nation will acknowledge not only His reign on earth, but also that He is **Yahweh of hosts**, the divine Ruler of all of heaven (cf. Zech 1:7–17; 6:1–8; 14:5). Consistently throughout the millennial kingdom, the entire world will gather in recognition that Jesus is Lord over heaven and earth (cf. Phil 2:9–11).

Each year, the nations will also **celebrate the Feast of Booths**, one of Israel's three major festivals (Lev 23:34–43; Num 29:12–38; Deut 16:13–17). During this feast, Israel would go up to Jerusalem and live in booths, or tents, for seven days to commemorate how God brought them out of the wilderness into the Promised Land. This occasion also honored the Lord for His provision of the yearly harvest (cf. Deut 16:15). Because the Feast of Booths celebrated God's faithfulness to His people, those who returned from Babylon paid special heed to this festival (Ezra 3:4; Neh 8:14–17; Hag 2:1). They celebrated it in hope that just as God delivered Israel from the wilderness in the past, so He would one day deliver them from every oppressor. Zechariah's prophecy assured them that God would indeed accomplish the promised deliverance for which they longed.

In the future, all the nations will come to Jerusalem and live in booths to commemorate the way God brought His people out of the world (cf. 1 Pet 1:1) and into His kingdom. This explains why at the transfiguration, Peter requested to build booths (Matt 17:4). Beholding the glorious Christ, he wanted the millennial kingdom to come immediately. Though Peter had the timing wrong, the Lord Jesus made clear to him and the other disciples that the kingdom will surely come (cf. Matt

19:28; Acts 1:6–11). There will be a day when both Jew and Gentile come to Jerusalem to worship Christ for faithfully delivering His people, for bringing them to their true home (cf. Heb 11:13–16).

The prophet further revealed that anyone who ignores this celebration, thereby defying the priority of worship, will be punished. As Zechariah explained, **"And it will be that whichever of the families of the earth does not go up to Jerusalem to worship the King, Yahweh of hosts, there will be no rain on them."** The initial generation that will enter the millennial kingdom will consist of those who were redeemed in the Tribulation (cf. Isa 35:8–10; Zech 13:9; 14:16). But as they generate children and grandchildren, not everyone in the kingdom will truly embrace the Lord. Eventually, there will be many who dismiss God's call to worship, even if outright rebellion will not fully foment until the end of the thousand-year period (cf. Rev 20:7–10). Nevertheless, God's decree demonstrates the seriousness with which He will uphold the primacy of worship. Although the description of people as **families** emphasizes peace and unity, it underscores that God will act against anyone from anywhere on **earth** who disobeys, even just a small group. He will not tolerate any deviation from His decree to **go up to Jerusalem to worship the King, Yahweh of hosts.**

If there are those reluctant to worship the Messiah, God will ensure that **there will be no rain** on them. Only God can control the weather (cf. Job 36:24–33; 38:22–24; Ps 29:3–9), and without rain, people will not have the water or food they need to live. Such judgment will be inescapable. Zechariah explained that **if the family of Egypt does not go up or enter, then no rain will fall on them; it will be the plague with which Yahweh plagues the nations who do not go up to celebrate the Feast of Booths.** One might wonder why Zechariah singled out the **family of Egypt.** It was not because the Egyptians will be more wicked than the rest, since they will worship in Jerusalem like everyone else (cf. Isa 19:25). Instead, Zechariah singled out Egypt because the Egyptians obtained their water primarily from the Nile River (cf. Deut 11:10–12). Perhaps, someone there might think they could survive without rain since the river kept them well supplied. However, though Egypt might endure if **no rain** were to **fall on them**, Zechariah declared that there still **will be the plague** against them. The word **plague** appeared earlier in this chapter to describe how the nations will rot away even while they stand (cf. Zech 14:12). If Egypt does not suffer the consequences of the drought, they will be consumed by the plague for not going up to worship God. This plague will not only threaten Egypt but also other nations that refuse to worship God; it will be **the plague with which Yahweh plagues the nations who do not go up to celebrate the Feast of Booths.** Any who refuse to worship Christ will face God's immediate and unavoidable judgment.

Such severe consequences **will be the punishment of Egypt, and the punishment of all the nations who do not go up to celebrate the Feast of Booths.** Zechariah was emphatic that deadly drought and plague were acts of **punishment.** The word **punishment** is the Hebrew word for "sin." While at times, this term includes the consequence for one's sin, as it does here, the word still emphasizes one's rebellion against God. The Lord will punish **all the nations**, including **Egypt**, if they refuse to **celebrate the Feast of Booths**, because such a failure constitutes a blatant disregard for God. Worship is the ultimate priority, and during the Messiah's kingdom, any refusal to worship Christ will carry the severe penalty it deserves. God will ensure that the world engages in the worship it was created to express (cf. John 4:23), giving all glory and honor to His Son.

THE CONSECRATION OF ISRAEL

In that day there will *be inscribed* on the bells of the horses, "Holy to Yahweh." And the pots in the house of Yahweh will be like the bowls before the altar. And every pot in Jerusalem and in Judah will be holy to Yahweh of hosts; and all who sacrifice will come and take of them and boil in them. And there will no longer be a Canaanite in the house of Yahweh of hosts in that day. (14:20–21)

With the seventeenth appearance of the phrase **in that day** in Zechariah 12–14, the prophet added one final detail about the Day of Yahweh. It will launch an era of comprehensive holiness. Objects and places that were previously unholy or common will be consecrated and sanctified. Zechariah declared that **there will be inscribed on the bells of the horses, "Holy to Yahweh."** Throughout Israel's history, **horses** were far from holy. They were unclean to eat (Lev 11:1–8), a resource kings were not to multiply (Deut 17:16), an instrument used for violence (Josh 11:4; 1 Kgs 20:21; Mic 5:10), and a strength on which Israel was not to rely for deliverance (Ps 33:17). Earlier in Zechariah 14, the text identified horses as an instrument of war against God's people (cf. Zech 12:4; 14:15). But this will change in the millennial kingdom. Horses will no longer be harbingers of war. Rather, they will wear **bells** that ring in celebration as they carry Israelites to Jerusalem and others to the Feast of Booths (cf. Isa 66:20). Because of this new purpose, the bells on these horses will be inscribed with the words, **"Holy to Yahweh,"** a phrase previously found only on the turban of the High Priest (Exod 28:36–38; 39:30; cf. Zech 3:5). Animals which were unclean will one day be as consecrated as the priest who entered the Holy of Holies once each year (cf. Lev 16:15–16).

Zechariah further stated that **the pots in the house of Yahweh will be like the bowls before the altar.** Within **the house of Yahweh**, the **pots** had the lowliest purpose. They were used either to boil meat (Lev 7:15–16; 2 Chr 35:13) or to remove ash from the altar (Exod 27:3; 38:3). These implements were considered unworthy for offering sacrifices. In contrast, the **bowls before the altar** held the blood of the sacrifices (see Lev 1:1–5; 9:8–9, 12, 18; and cf. Exod 27:1–3; 38:1–3). These bowls were made out of precious materials like silver (cf. Num 7:31) or polished bronze (cf. 1 Kgs 7:45) to designate their holy and elevated purpose. In the millennial kingdom, the plain **pots** will be consecrated so that they **will be like the bowls before the altar.** Though these pots and bowls have different functions, they will all be equally sacred. Everything in the house of Yahweh will be characterized by His perfect purity.

In fact, **every pot in Jerusalem and in Judah will be holy to Yahweh of hosts; and all who sacrifice will come and take of them and boil in them.** Holiness will not only characterize the implements of the temple, but it will also pervade all **Jerusalem** and **Judah**. Zechariah spoke of the most common **pot** used for everyday tasks like cooking and cleaning. Such a pot was far less special than the lowliest pot used in the temple. Nevertheless, this mundane implement **will be holy to Yahweh of hosts**, being consecrated in a manner comparable to Israel's High Priest (Exod 28:36–38). Even the pots in Jerusalem will be so holy that **all who sacrifice will come and take of them and boil in them**. When the world comes to worship the Messiah, a vast host of people will offer their **sacrifice** of praise to God. These non-atoning, memorial sacrifices will be offered in worship to Christ for His work of redemption on the cross (Isa 56:7; Ezek 43–46; cf. Rom 12:1–2). Even with every item in the temple consecrated to the Lord, there will not be enough vessels for all the sacrifices that will be offered. Therefore, the worshipers **will come and take** the most common pot **and boil** their sacrifices **in them** (cf. Exod 29:31; 1 Sam 2:13). This will not be a problem, for the most mundane pot will have the same holy perfection as a bowl in the house of Yahweh. Indeed, everything will be consecrated to **Yahweh of hosts**, as the world gathers in Jerusalem to worship their King, and as Christ the King intimately communes with His holy people (cf. Lev 26:11–12; Ezek 48:35).

Zechariah concluded his prophecy by noting that **there will no longer be a Canaanite in the house of Yahweh of hosts in that day**. The term **Canaanite** was used to refer to those who are morally and spiritually unclean. Hosea 12:7 described a Canaanite as one "in whose hands are deceptive balances, he loves to oppress" (cf. Isa 23:8; Prov 31:24). To refer to someone as a Canaanite indicated that they were dishonest, and the word was often used with reference to untrustworthy merchants (cf. Job 41:6; Prov 31:24). Zechariah foretold that no such godless, deceitful person would set foot in **the house of Yahweh of hosts**. The Lord Jesus provided a preview of this when He overturned the merchant tables in the temple (cf. Matt 21:12; Mark 11:15–18), but the fullness of this will occur when He returns. Throughout Israel's history, the temple included the presence of the duplicitous and the degenerate (cf. 2 Kgs 16:10–18; Neh 13:4–13; Ezek 8:5–18; Mark 11:15–18). But the Lord will one day ensure that His temple is never defiled again. For those in Zechariah's day, laboring to rebuild the temple, the prophet's final words reminded them that their work was not in vain. It anticipated a day when the millennial temple would be characterized by the highest and holiest forms of worship, reflecting the beautiful holiness of Christ's entire kingdom.

All of this will happen **in that day**, the triumphant Day of Yahweh (cf. Zech 12–14). God has planned a climactic day when the history of the world will culminate in the judgment of the nations, the salvation of Israel, the restoration of creation, and the establishment of the Messiah's holy kingdom. All who love the Lord long for the day of His return (2 Tim 4:8; 1 Pet 1:7–8). That time is near (Rev 1:3; cf. Rom 13:11; Heb 10:24–25), and the saints await with eagerness (Titus 2:11–14). Maranatha! Come Lord Jesus (1 Cor 16:22; Rev 22:20)!

Bibliography

Baldwin, Joyce G. *Haggai, Zechariah, Malachi: An Introduction and Commentary*. Tyndale Old Testament Commentaries. Downers Grove, IL: InterVarsity, 1972.

Barker, Kenneth L. "Zechariah." In *The Expositor's Bible Commentary: Daniel–Minor Prophets*. Edited by F. E. Gaebelein, 7:593–697. Grand Rapids: Eerdmans, 1983.

Barker, Kenneth L. "Zechariah." In *The Expositor's Bible Commentary: Daniel to Malachi*. Edited by Tremper Longman III and David E. Garland, 8:721–833. Revised edition. Grand Rapids: Zondervan, 2008.

Baron, David. *The Visions and Prophecies of Zechariah*. Reprint edition. Grand Rapids: Kregel, 1972.

Boda, Mark J. *The Book of Zechariah*. New International Commentary on the Old Testament. Grand Rapids: Eerdmans, 2016.

Chou, Abner. "Zechariah 11:4–14: The Rejected Shepherd." In *The Moody Handbook of Messianic Prophecy: Studies and Expositions of the Messiah in the Old Testament*. Edited by Michael Rydelnik and Edwin Blum, 1271–84. Chicago: Moody, 2019.

Feinberg, Charles L. *God Remembers: A Study of the Book of Zechariah*. Portland, OR: Multnomah, 1965.

Feinberg, Charles L. *The Minor Prophets*. Chicago: Moody, 1976.

Hill, Andrew E. *Haggai, Zechariah and Malachi: An Introduction and Commentary*. Tyndale Old Testament Commentaries. Downers Grove, IL: InterVarsity Press, 2012.

Josephus, *The Jewish War: Books 1–7*. Edited by Jeffrey Henderson et al. Translated by H. St. J. Thackeray. Loeb Classical Library. Cambridge, MA: Harvard University Press, 1927–1928.

Keil, C. F. and F. Delitzsch. *Commentary on the Old Testament*. Peabody, MA: Hendrickson, 1996.

Klein, George L. *Zechariah*. New American Commentary. Nashville: B&H Publishers, 2008.

McComiskey, Thomas. "Zechariah." In *The Minor Prophets*. Edited by T. E. McComiskey, 3:1003–1244. Grand Rapids: Baker, 1992.

Merrill, Eugene H. *Haggai, Zechariah, Malachi: An Exegetical Commentary*. Dallas, TX: Biblical Studies Press, 2003.

Petterson, Anthony R. *Haggai, Zechariah & Malachi*. Apollos Old Testament Commentary. Downers Grove, IL: InterVarsity Press, 2015.

Smith, Ralph L. *Micah-Malachi*. Word Biblical Commentaries. Waco, TX: Word, 1984.

Stuart, Daniel E. "Zechariah 12:10–13:1: The Pierced Messiah." In *The Moody Handbook of Messianic Prophecy: Studies and Expositions of the Messiah in the Old Testament*. Edited by Michael Rydelnik and Edwin Blum, 1285–98. Chicago: Moody, 2019.

Index of Scripture

Index of Subjects